The Future of Cities

The editors would like to thank those members
of the Open University Course Team of DT201,
*Urban Development*, who suggested items for
inclusion. The major acknowledgement, however,
must go to Joan Murray and Sharon Stocker for
their labours with scissors and typewriter.

# The Future of Cities

edited by
*Andrew Blowers*
*Chris Hamnett*
*Philip Sarre*

at The Open
University

HUTCHINSON EDUCATIONAL
*in association with The Open University Press*

Hutchinson Educational Ltd
3 Fitzroy Square, London W1

London Melbourne Sydney Auckland
Wellington Johannesburg Cape Town
and agencies throughout the world

First published July 1974

Selection and editorial material
copyright © The Open University 1974

This book is filmset in Monophoto Times,
by BAS Printers Limited, Wallop, Hampshire,
printed in Great Britain by Anchor-Press, and
bound by Wm. Brendon & Son,
both of Tiptree, Essex

ISBN 0 09 119481 4

# Contents

Contents

# Illustrations

# Acknowledgements

For permission to reprint copyright material the course editors and publishers are indebted to the following: J. M. Dent & Sons Ltd. (Everyman's Library text) for Thomas More, *Utopia*; The Architectural Press Ltd. for Le Corbusier, *City of Tomorrow*; Faber and Faber Ltd. for Ebenezer Howard, *Garden Cities of Tomorrow*, P. Hall, *London 2000*; Longman Group Ltd. Journals (*Urban Studies*) for P. Willmott, 'Some Social Trends', P. A. Stone, 'Resources and the Economic Framework'; the Controller of Her Majesty's Stationery Office for C. Buchanan, *Traffic in Towns*; George Allen & Unwin Ltd. for R. Meier, *Mankind 2000*; Clark University, Massachusetts (*Economic Geography*) for J. Gottmann, 'Megalopolis'; Cambridge University Press for L. Martin and L. March, *Urban Space and Structures*; Massachusetts Institute of Technology Press for P. Davidoff, 'Normative Planning', *Planning for Diversity and Choice* (ed. S. Anderson); Milton Keynes Development Corporation for *The Plan for Milton Keynes, Volume 1* (published 1970); New Science Publications (*New Society*) for R. Banham, P. Hall, C. Price and P. Barker, '*Non Plan: An Experiment in Freedom*'; '*A Blueprint for Survival*' © 1972 by *The Ecologist*, published by Tom Stacey Ltd. and Penguin Books, reprinted by permission of Deborah Rogers Ltd. London; Japan Center for Area Development Research for C. Alexander, 'Major Changes in Environmental Form Required by Social and Psychological Demands', *Ekistics*; Secker & Warburg Ltd. for L. Mumford, *The City in History*; The Bodley Head for A. Toffler, *Future Shock*; A. P. Watt & Son and Hamish Hamilton for M. Davie, 'The End of the City', *In the Future Now: A Report from California*; Council for Educational Advance for C. Leicester 'Life in the Year AD 2000', *New Horizons for Education*; Mrs Laura Huxley and Chatto & Windus Ltd. for Aldous Huxley, *Brave New World*; King's College, Cambridge and The Society of Authors as the literary representatives of the E. M. Forster Estate for E. M. Forster, 'The Machine Stops', *The Eternal Moment and Other Stories*; *Daedalus*, Journal of the American Academy of Arts and Sciences, Boston, Mass., for M. Meyerson, 'Utopian Tradition and the Planning of Cities', K. Lynch,

## Acknowledgements

'The Pattern of Metropolis'; W. F. Payson for F. L. Wright, *Disappearing City*; Town and Country Planning Summer School, Swansea for J. S. Whyte, 'The Impact of Telecommunications on Town Planning'; *RIBA Journal* for L. March, 'Homes Beyond the Fringe'; Free Press, a Division of Macmillan Publishing Co., Inc., for S. Greer, *The Emerging City: Myth and Reality*; Penguin Books for B. Ward and R. Dubos, *Only One Earth, the Care and Maintenance of a Small Planet*; *Journal of American Institute of Planners* for J. Friedmann and J. Miller, 'The Urban Field'; *Town Planning Review* for M. Webber, 'Planning in an Environment of Change'; Weidenfeld and Nicolson (Science Fiction Book Club) for C. Simak, *City*.

# General Introduction *by Philip Sarre and Andrew Blowers*

The literature on the future city comes from a variety of sources, ancient and contemporary, artistic and technological. We have drawn on material from a wide range of these sources although we concentrate on the areas which seem most relevant to the planning of the future city. In this introduction we aim to set out a way of thinking about the future which integrates these disparate sources into a coherent conceptual approach. We hope that this Reader will help to encourage an active operational approach to the creation of the future city.

Until relatively recently, work on the future tended to be essentially visionary. Two styles may be distinguished. The first is associated in the public mind with names like that of Jules Verne: these authors used their intuition to make forecasts about life and technology at some point in the future. The second style was concerned not with what *might* be but what *should* be. This has a very long history from Plato and Aristotle, through Thomas More, who coined the word *utopia*; and it reached a climax in terms of volume in the late nineteenth century. In the twentieth century optimistic urban utopias have come from architects but literature has focussed upon the anti-utopia, with *Brave New World* and *Nineteen Eighty Four* enjoying outstanding prominence. The aim of utopian writers has been to influence real world policies toward the utopian ideal and away from the dystopian nightmare. Their efforts, with the exception of some of the architects, have always been indirect since they lacked control over the processes of change.

Since the industrial revolution most urban development has been accomplished by commercial enterprise. It has long been apparent that the private profit motive was liable to lead to great public costs. These involved a failure to provide an adequate urban infrastructure and a widening of the gap between rich and poor. There has thus been a trend toward more bureaucratic control over development. This takes two forms. The most obvious role is played by local authority and central government planners. In part this is active, building roads, new housing and even new cities, in part it is passive, giving and witholding planning permission in response to proposals from public and business. A less obvious but more powerful role is played by politicians through their

1

control over investment. They determine the funds available for different projects, manipulate the rules under which private enterprise and local planners operate and regulate the distribution of income and wealth through taxation. The activities of business managers, planners and politicians directly determine the shape of the future, unlike those of the utopians. Politicians, who have the greatest power also have the responsibility of controlling both planners and business for the public good.

At their best, these future determining activities are based on a coherent method of thinking about the future, at worst they reduce to a set of *ad hoc* efforts to tackle severe problems. There is considerable debate about the optimum balance of government, corporate and private initiative in designing the future, but little doubt that all of them need to improve the way they think out programmes of action. This is not to say that all-embracing plans for the future are possible or desirable: society is so complex that the future will produce surprises unless a repressive tyranny limits individual ingenuity. An improvement in future-thinking will, however, reduce the number of problems which have to be borne by the people of the future and remedied by future planners. The elements of such an improved approach are present in the range of literature we have surveyed and have been coordinated by some of the small but growing group of scholars who have been doing rigorous work on the future.

Even the most rigorous approach to the future differs in two ways from the scientific method as commonly conceived. First, since the future does not exist, it cannot be the object of observation but only of conjecture and, second, the main reason for studying the future is the desire to influence it rather than understand it. Both conjecture and influence have been improved beyond the stage reached by Jules Verne and the utopians by basing forecasts and policy on an understanding of past and present but a very large degree of indeterminacy persists: this should not necessarily be taken as a bad thing because it provides freedom for choice and originality.

The process of evolving a policy and programme for the future has come to be seen as an iterative process involving thought in two directions. The first is that of projection, the second involves setting goals and deriving programmes to reach them.

Projections of world population or car ownership must be familiar to most people in this society. Such projections look relatively simple when only single variables are taken into account, although the accuracy of forecasts falls off rapidly as time scales get longer. However, when interactions between phenomena are considered the problems become more severe: for instance the prospect of rising car ownership looks less convincing when projections are also made of rising congestion, fuel prices, insurance premiums and Press criticism of the car as a means of urban transport. The chances of accuracy are reduced by the occurrence of unpredictable events, for example technological changes (who in 1930 would have forecast that radio would be subject to serious competition from television?) or natural or man-made disasters (wars, floods and earthquakes spring readily to mind, but economic recessions may be as influential in the long term). For all these reasons, forecasting is an inexact art and perhaps the strongest single conclusion from studies of forecasts is that the future offers a ramifying set of possibilities, with the range of options increasing over time. In spite of the problems many people have attempted to assess the most probable future or futures, especially for the year 2000.

The second direction of thought, which complements the forecasting approach, is concerned with the establishment of goals toward which development should be guided. This work rests on two foundations: first, it attempts to derive from past and present societies ideas about what is desirable and, second, it makes value judgements about priorities for different desirable futures. The empirical base of goal-setting is slender because it is hard to compare satisfaction in different societies and because man is highly adaptable and can seem content in a wide range of circumstances. The ideologies are more rigorously thought out but the lack of evidence or agreed criteria of judgement makes it difficult to assess the ideal balance between individual and community, freedom and welfare, corporate or state enterprise, etc. In many cases existing ideologies are less appropriate to the future than they may have been in the past. They may be made more relevant by referring to the likely trends in society.

It is clear that projection and goal-formulation have important effects on one another. Consideration of possible futures may strengthen ideas about what we do and do not want in the future: the authors of anti-utopian novels clearly intend to motivate readers to take or support action which will lead to a preferable future. Similarly, consideration of likely trends may show that a future we desire is not likely to be achievable. It may be that a concerted effort to influence society toward some desired goal might lead to the achievement of a future which is *a priori* shown by primary forecasts to be unlikely, though not impossible. Iteration between goal-setting and forecasting, eliminating futures which are either undesirable or unachievable, may lead to the isolation of one or a few futures which appear close to an optimum. The process of demonstrating feasibility will shade into the production of a programme which lays out the measures which must be taken to guide development. The programme becomes a secondary or normative forecast, stating that if certain measures are taken a particular goal may be reached at some point in time.

3

The adoption of an iterative method such as this would not be a panacea. Many problems would remain, especially that of conflicting interests. There would be a need to up-date predictions, goals and programmes as time passed and more was learned and to take action retrospectively to eliminate unexpected problems. However, the effort to come to terms with the future would certainly be worthwhile; as the pace of change increases, the practicality of continuing the status quo or of judging change by trial and error diminishes and the need to improve our anticipations increases.

We have selected and organised the Readings in order to present our theme—the planning of the future city—from five viewpoints. The first is that of the visionary. Section 1 looks backward at some of the conceptions of the future made in the past. This is the utopian approach referred to earlier. The selection incorporates both the literary and design utopias that have influenced thinking on what the urban future *ought* to be. Literary utopias tend to be preoccupied with the evils or inadequacies of their own time and this concern is sometimes difficult to reconcile with our contemporary society and its problems. For instance, More's *Utopia* might well have been preferable to sixteenth century England but we might not welcome the conformity, lack of individual freedom, or strict moral code upon which it was founded. Literary utopias are usually static societies in which conflict and competition are absent. Little intimation is offered of whether such a state is possible, or how it may be attained. By contrast, design utopias are practicable, if costly, and they tend to neglect the social consequences of the changes proposed. Utopian writing is significant not so much for the specific solutions it proposes but for the alternative futures it enables us to recognise.

Section 2's viewpoint is that of the forecaster. It concentrates on the future that could emerge if present trends continue unchecked. We have already pointed out some of the problems inherent in primary (or trend) forecasting. The most commonly used method is extrapolation which, apart from inherent statistical problems, presupposes that future change will be consistent with past experience. The real difficulty with this method is that its predictions are often accepted as probabilities. On the other hand extrapolation may provoke the changes that are essential if an undesirable future is to be avoided. For example, a forecast of acute traffic congestion in city centres may encourage investment into alternative forms of transport to the car. In this way extrapolation serves as a background and a stimulant to the exercise of choice through the planning process.

Conventionally, planners have been primarily concerned with the spatial arrangements of the city. The future urban form is the viewpoint of Section 3. Continuing urban dispersal appears to be the outcome of

4

present trends, at least in the western world. There is, however, a range of possible future forms and specific ones are identified here. In particular certain planning proposals are advanced which offer a practical alternative to the extremes of high density and low density settlements by combining some of the advantages of both. This approach recognises the likely trends and constraints upon future urban forms and therefore differs from the utopian approach to urban design which allows imagination free rein.

Up to this point in the Reader the role of planning has been mainly confined to the physical aspects of urban development. The viewpoint of Section 4 is that planning is an all-embracing process in which all interests should be represented. Looked at in this way planning is no longer merely a physical process but a political one as well. Urban planning, whether it is something simple like resiting a bus stop or something complex like clearing and redeveloping a residential area, tends to advantage some individuals or groups relative to others. It is the politician's responsibility to define, in general, who is to be advantaged. It is the planner's task within his area of competence to give effect to the political will by ensuring that the desired degree of redistribution is achieved.

Section 5 of the Reader returns from the realm of abstraction to a consideration of future urban life. Its viewpoint is that of the individual inhabiting the city of the future. Each city described here manifests the progress of technology but the tone of the readings becomes increasingly pessimistic. They contrast sharply with the utopian vision presented in Section 1. Their purpose is different. The utopians were anxious to reform their own society, whereas these modern anti-utopians wish to evade a possible future one. These readings serve as a warning against the consequences of certain current trends and they provide an incentive for us to influence the process of urban development towards the achievement of a more humane future. They emphasise that the future can only be left to look after itself at our peril.

# 1. The future city as seen in the past

## Introduction *by Philip Sarre*

This section needs little in the way of introduction since the essay by Meyerson considers the relevance of utopian thinking to city planning. He, like us, is not primarily concerned to dwell on the details of the utopian *genre* but to derive from it ideas which may be useful to those concerned with the planning of the future city. There is an apparent paradox in looking to the past for a view of the future. We do so not to enquire who was the first author to forecast particular inventions but in recognition that many themes which are of vital relevance to the future, particularly those relating to social goals and the quality of life, originated in the utopian literature.

We were, of course, faced by an appalling problem of selection because the number of relevant works is astronomical. In fact, in a Reader with an emphasis on future orientation, there was no real possibility of being representative of the genre and we would refer any readers interested in it for its own sake to Armytage (1968), or the references of the Meyerson paper (1.1). We restricted ourselves to two early works. More's *Utopia* almost chose itself as the work which gave the genre its name and we decided to balance its optimistic assumption that human nature and society were perfectible by a more sceptical extract. We might have used Samuel Butler's *Erewhon* as a source but preferred part of *Gulliver's Travels* because it anticipated the theme of Section 4.

Most of the literary utopias concentrate on the state of society and give little attention to the city. As our primary interest is the city, we have given equal weight to extracts from works in the tradition of utopian *design*. Here the quantity of material is not so great and the selection problem simpler: the two authors we have chosen demand mention in any discussion of twentieth-century urban design. Finally, since any ideal future city must combine social and physical organization, we include an excerpt from a work which did much to synthesise the two utopian traditions and translate them into a practical programme.

The first extract from the literary tradition is from the work which gave the *genre* its name—More's *Utopia*. It consists of two books, the first of which lays bare the evils of sixteenth-century society. The second

6

book presents an alternative ideal community. It has been variously interpreted as a socialist manifesto or a blueprint for a reformed christianity. More's central concept is the community of property in which only necessities are produced and the welfare of all is ensured. In such a situation, competition for personal advancement is absent, money is irrelevant, and economic equality prevails. Although a system of direct democracy has been instituted, a paternalistic rule is exercised and individual freedom is constrained by communal surveillance and a strict moral code. The chief goal of Utopian society appears to be the pursuit of happiness which consists in 'every motion and state of the body or mind wherein man hath naturally delectation'.

In Book 2, the philosopher-traveller Raphael Hythloday describes Amaurote the capital city of Utopia which is designed to encourage individual families to participate in the communal life. He then explains the economic system of Utopia and some aspects of its social organization. He ends his discourse with the extract we have reproduced which compares the virtues of the Utopian commonwealth with the selfishness and exploitation that characterises contemporary (that is sixteenth-century) society and, one might add, that of our own day.

The second extract from the literary tradition is pessimistic where More was optimistic. Where More believed in man's ability to improve his society and environment, Jonathan Swift, in this excerpt from *Gulliver's Travels*, emphasises man's incompetence. Swifts 'projectors', armed with 'a smattering of mathematicks' and intending to improve every sphere of human activity, actually lack the technical ability to reach their goals and achieve only destruction. It is always worth asking whether city planners are really more successful than the projectors.

The first of our two extracts from the architectural school of utopian design is indeed based on mathematics and would involve a good deal of destruction before it could be built. Le Corbusier based his early thinking about cities on an almost metaphysical devotion to the straight line and right-angle. For him, rectilinear patterns were associated with purpose, order and efficiency and contrasted with the curved patterns originated by the pack-donkey. His design was also based on ideas about urban transport, a conviction that cities had to be rebuilt *in situ* and the belief that industrialised building would drastically reduce costs. Although there are numerous doubts about Le Corbusier's arguments, doubts which are reinforced by his ultimate shift to an anti-urban position, his *Contemporary City* was a major landmark in planning thought and remains strikingly fresh after half a century.

Whereas Le Corbusier emphasised the central area of his city, although most of the population lived in satellite Garden Cities, Frank Lloyd Wright, our second representative of the design-utopia school, emphasised the home. He foresaw the ability of technology, especially car and telephone, to allow decentralization of cities and a blending of urban and rural amenities. His insistence on low densities, with each family enjoying an acre of garden, is often seen as purely a desire to live near nature. Wright does indeed emphasise the organic, but he is willing to use advanced technology to give people access to it. Although he does not make the point explicit, provision of acre gardens would involve a substantial redistribution of wealth: many people even today cannot afford to buy a house at all, let alone a new house on such a large plot. If Broadacre City looks less original than the Contemporary City to the modern reader, it is because some of its features, for example low densities and 'wayside markets', are already commonplace in the newer and more affluent suburbs in the USA.

The final view of the future city as seen in the past is taken from Ebenezer Howard. His book *Garden Cities of Tomorrow* spans the two schools of utopian thought and has been the inspiration behind the building of the New Towns. The book concentrates on the economic and political arrangements which would allow ordinary people access to both urban and rural amenities but also includes sketch plans of layouts. The central idea was for a town of limited size, with a green belt. This was to be achieved by municipal ownership of land so that growth, usually inspired by private landlords seeking capital gains, could be controlled. In this way rents could be kept low and standards of living improved. Our extract explains how growth can be channelled into a 'constellation' of small cities linked by railways to permit access to facilities typical of large cities without losing access to the country. Howard envisaged such constellations drawing population out of the large cities and thus reducing rents and allowing improved amenities. The spatial form he chose introduces the argument of Section 3, but the fact that his ideas, though widely adopted, have not been as dramatically successful as he suggested reminds us that society contains more constraints and trends than he catered for.

## Reference

ARMYTAGE, W. H. G. (1968) *Yesterday's Tomorrows*, London, Routledge and Kegan Paul.

# 1.1 Utopian Traditions and the Planning of Cities
## Martin Meyerson

In 1516 Sir Thomas More published *Utopia*, thus kindling for the Renaissance as well as for our own times a literary tradition describing an ideal future society and by implication criticizing the society already in existence. A half-century earlier, two Italian architects, Leone Battista Alberti and Filareti (the pseudonym of Antonio Averlino), kindled a parallel utopian tradition of designing the ideal city. Alberti's proposals and Filareti's Sforzinda (a scheme for such a city, dedicated to Francesco Sforza), like More's Utopia, initiated other efforts to depict a desirable pattern for future living—but without saying how to achieve it. Curiously, these two traditions did not influence each other but developed apart. The literary utopias constructed a desirable future in terms of altered social organizations and institutions. The design utopias portrayed a desirable future in terms of altered artifacts and the organization of space.

C. P. Snow has censured the division of contemporary intellectual life into two separate cultures, that of the humanists and that of the natural scientists. Yet that division is no more marked than is the intellectual division between verbal and visual culture. The verbal or social utopias, if they have dealt at all with elements of physical environment, have done so but superficially: the forms and interrelations of housing, work-shops, facilities for education and recreation, and the distribution of open land, have followed, as afterthoughts, alterations in property, in family, in political and other institutions. Conversely, the utopias of visual design have ignored class structure, the economic base, and the process of government in the desirable future they present.

Despite their mutual isolation, these two traditions have some remarkable similarities. Most of the creators of social utopias believe that man will be happier, more productive, or more religious—or 'better,' according to some moral criterion, if the institutions of society are altered. Most of the creators of the physical utopias imply that men will be healthier, more orderly, more satisfied, more inspired by beauty —better in some other way, if the physical environment is appropriately

*Source:* Martin Meyerson, 'Utopian Tradition and the Planning of Cities' *Daedalus*, winter 1961, pages 180–193.

arranged. In both cases, utopia has a strong environmental and moralistic cast: if men are only placed within a proper setting (whether social or physical), they will behave as the creators of utopia believe they should behave.

More importantly, the two traditions have another trait in common—caricature. Man has neither the wisdom, nor the knowledge, nor the skills in communication to present a cosmic portrayal of a total future, let alone a total desirable future, even though some utopias, both social and cultural, presume to such a totality. Not only do the social utopias evade the physical environment, just as the physical kind of utopia evades social organization, but even in their own spheres the limitations of human understanding result in simplifications and therefore in exaggerations which often have a ludicrous aspect. The creator of utopia selects a few principles on which his desirable future society pivots; these may refer to certain social institutions or to certain conditions in the physical environment. Indeed, utopia can do no more than this. The anthropologist who tries to study a whole culture achieves insights only into segments of that culture; the psychologist does not comprehend the whole personality, but only facets of it. The utopian creator can only be selective and arbitrary in his constructs. While the analysis of the social scientist is also a partial one, his product, if he is capable, is not a caricature; he deals with the present, not the imagined future, and he describes rather than prescribes. The arbitrary, simplified view (or caricature) that has dominated utopias, on the other hand, has often left critics unsure as to whether their creators intended a parody or not.

Since utopias usually result in caricature, intellectuals have rarely been drawn to producing them. The large-scale, internally consistent panoramas of a desirable future often seem too constrained to attract them; or if they are activists, they dismiss utopias as impractical—the absence of any suggested means of achieving the ends makes the effort ridiculous. Moreover, since the Enlightenment, the intellectual's belief in rational progress has gradually eroded: the sophisticate is cynical rather than hopeful for man's prospects. Very rarely has a first-rate mind invented a utopia. When intellectuals, particularly those of the twentieth century, have chosen to caricature the world, they have constructed anti-utopias, panoramas their creators consider as undesirable and therefore as warnings. Perhaps the nature of caricature is best exploited when it is satiric rather than benign. As Margaret Mead (1957, page 958) says, Hell is always more vivid—and convincing—than Heaven.

Certainly, the sharpest intellectual contributions have been critical even when recommendatory, nor have they been attempts to portray the proposed future. Karl Marx tried systematically to demolish bourgeóis society and to demonstrate the inevitable downfall of capitalism, but he said almost nothing about the future conditions of society under his brand of socialism. He (and Engels), scorning other socialists as 'utopian,' dismissed their proposals for the good society as unrealistic but he offered no substitute. Socialism, it was thought, would develop its own logic, its own rules and dialectic of change. Apart from some vague predictions that the potentialities of man's creativity would be freed when socialism is achieved, Marx did not indicate what pattern of life would emerge. In a like sense, Freud systematically attacked the prevailing views of human personality and detailed a process by which man might rid himself of his psychic impediments, but he did not indicate what the successfully analyzed personality would be like, or what the form of a society of such personalities.

The greatest contributions of such minds came through their analyses rather than through the development of normative imagery. They were committed to change; their subtle and complicated minds rebutted the static in the human condition. They were not inclined (or were unable) to detail the end products of the changes they desired. Yet the power of their critical and analytical systems revolutionized men's ways of thinking and behaving. David Riesman (1947), in his brilliant essay on utopias, calls for a revival of utopian thinking as an intellectual challenge, precisely because it takes more courage to deal with what might be than with what is, and because it is more difficult to pose great alternatives than to choose among lesser evils. Without revolutionary changes in society, changes that demand substantial sacrifice, substantial gains in human well-being will not be made; to aim at lesser goals, he believes, may make for a real waste of human talents, since the goal least likely to be achieved is the maintenance of the *status quo*. It is not the motivational value of utopia, however, that I am affirming so much as its potential contribution to planning—specifically, to the planning of cities. The attributes of the utopian caricature, if they are recognized as caricature, can be extremely useful in posing potentially desirable ends and then in testing these ends with a logical model. Would such ends, if carried out consistently, result in a desirable state of affairs or not? Utopia specifies a desirable future state without detailing the means of achieving it. City planning is charged with specifying a desirable future state and also the means of attaining it.

City planning as a vocation has become widely accepted in the last few decades, particularly in English-speaking countries. The literature of city planning claims as one of its purposes and competencies the preparation of long-range, comprehensive plans for communities. In practice, however, city planning has either ignored the means (while still not proposing fundamental changes) or it has concentrated on the efficacy of means to the exclusion of ends.

11

As city planning clarifies its theory and sharpens its methodology, it will be faced with the choice of relinquishing the utopian elements now residual in its ideology or of capitalizing on them. I suggest that city planners ought to recognize the value of utopian formulations in the depicting of the community as it might be seen through alternative normative lenses.

City planning, in portraying a future state of affairs, tries to link economic and social policy with physical design to solve such urban problems as housing and transportation. The two separate traditions of utopia, that of artifact and that of institutions, can simultaneously be drawn upon for this objective. By developing alternative utopias of the community, both in physical or material terms and in social and economic terms, city planning would not remove the element of caricature. Instead, it would give that element meaning, since caricature would sharpen the scrutiny of the consequences of following alternative sets of ends and means.

It is the utopian process—the sketching out of the implications of altering certain fundamental features of society and environment—that should be emulated, rather than the utopian product. Indeed, since utopias are so diverse in their portrayals of the good life (or, in the case of the anti-utopia, the evil life), as Raymond Ruyer (1950) observes, the process of formulation is the main feature they have in common.

The social utopias of the past have sought many goals—political, social, religious freedom, sexual freedom, economic freedom, freedom of movement, and freedom from industrialization. They have suggested some fundamental changes in society to obtain these various goals. Freedom from want is a recurrent theme, especially in the utopias of early capitalism and industrialism. While the prototype utopias, such as Plato's *Republic*, were most of all concerned with moral values, the later ones often combined these with economic welfare. The utopias of the last few hundred years have often postulated material abundance as a major theme.

Each of the classic literary utopias became a caricature when it dealt with moral values and material abundance together. Almost all these caricatures were based on rationality, on the rational control of men's actions, on the participation of all in the work of the society, and on the manipulation of institutions.

Sir Thomas More, who coined the word 'utopia,' postulated an ascetic abundance, that is, an abundance of basic goods without luxury or ornament. Despite his Catholicism, his good society anticipated some of the features of the Protestant ethic, which later provided an ideology to reinforce the development of the civilization of industrial capitalism. This ideology emphasized work, thrift, self-restraint, and the voluntary fulfilment of one's duty. In More's Utopia the theme of material abundance was linked to the themes of work and participation. Each individual in Utopia had to participate actively in the affairs of the society and do his part of the work to achieve the benefits of the society. This triple achievement of abundance, participation, and work was to be brought about by elaborate sets of rigid social controls, social rewards, and punishments.

By rotating city and country living, men would acquire knowledge and working skills in both areas. Syphogrants, or magistrates, each elected to supervise thirty families, were responsible for seeing that all worked at their tasks. Deviations from work or from other requirements of the community were punished by sanctions, such as slavery.

Even in their leisure time, 'all men live in full view, so that all are obliged . . . to employ themselves well in their spare hours.' More's society simplified this obligation by forbiddding all alehouses, taverns, gambling, and other vices, and by frowning on such activities as hunting. Intellectual pleasures were encouraged by the example of Utopia's selected group of scholars and by the whole educational system, which taught that spare hours should be spent in reading or attending lectures. Thus the society achieved a level of abundance for which all worked and in which all participated. The level of abundance was maintained in part because the population was to be stationary. More, like Malthus after him, had but limited faith in the potentialities of increasing labor productivity and he feared overpopulation. If there should be an excess of people in Utopia, room for expansion would be found on an adjacent continent.

America, which became the outlet for Europe's expanding population, came to be regarded as a utopian setting. In a Rousseau-like fashion, some utopian thinkers subsequent to More conceived of colonial American society as resembling the simple, ascetic and 'happy' life of the Indians rather than the corrupt and sophisticated life of the Euro- peans. Books such as *The Kingdom of Paradise*\* assumed that the settlers in America became Indianized, and some writers even described the American Indian as the successor of the Greeks, and portrayed him wearing Greek dress.

Furthermore, there were two hundred or more utopias put into actual practice in America, but these communities (such as Owen's New Harmony, Oneida, the so-called Love Colony, and Brook Farm, the colony of the intellectuals) failed. Most of them failed, not through economic disaster, but through economic abundance. Almost all stressed group solidarity, rigidly defined social roles, hard work, participation— attitudes and functions which were indispensable to the battle against adversity but which dissipated when economic prosperity arrived.

\*For a discussion of this literature, see Kraus (1934).

New Harmony, Indiana, founded in 1824 by Robert Owen, the English industrialist, represented an applied effort to achieve a set of goals, some of which he described in his book, *A New View of Society*. In its rather cryptic last paragraph, he indicated that his scheme as written was only a compromise within the existing system of industrialization, against whose brutality he revolted. Owen believed that industry, if it were properly organized, would require but little labor and that it would at the same time provide abundance. He proposed, as did More, a simple physical structure of the community: most of its features would be collective—community dining halls, lecture halls, work places, and even sleeping quarters for the children. Owen, like More, stressed work, education, and participation. He expected that at New Harmony the ideas expressed in its constitution would be self-evident and therefore enforced by individuals and the group alike. These ideals included an equality of duties, community of property, and 'cooperative union in the business and amusements of life.'

These ideals were not realized at New Harmony. Within three years the community failed, but without having achieved the economic abundance that proved to be the nemesis of the other applied American utopias. There were ample facilities for employment for its eight hundred recruits, but there were no effective social controls to ensure conformity among the various kinds of personalities the community attracted. Owen had believed that the necessary behavioral responses would come spontaneously. He imported a 'Boat-load of Knowledge,' a group of scholars to lead the intellectual life of the community. He proclaimed equality, with an attack on private property, in 'A Declaration of Mental Independence,' which he believed would become as significant as the Declaration of Independence. Nevertheless, without built-in sanctions and rewards, the colonists lacked motives for performing as he anticipated. Lewis Mumford declares that a contributing cause of failure was the character of Owen himself, 'whose bumptiousness, arrogance, and conceit were bound to provoke reactions in other people which would have defeated the plans of Omnipotence itself' (1922, page 248).

More wrote at a time when capitalism was emerging, Owen, at a time when the early industrial revolution was showing both some of its promise and some of its brutalizing effects. In America, some of these effects became most apparent near the end of the nineteenth century, and probably as a result, in the 1890's more utopian books were published in America than at any other time anywhere. Edward Bellamy's novel, *Looking Backward* (1888) heralded this outburst. It sold over a million copies in America alone—the largest seller, and to John Dewey the most influential, since *Uncle Tom's Cabin*. It inspired many similar works and prompted the formation of a group of nationalist clubs organized to carry out Bellamy's vision.

Almost all the American literary utopias of the 'nineties conceived of the problems of society as economic. Almost all assumed that technicians could provide for society. Almost all assumed that human want could be eradicated through technological innovation and economic organization. The idea of conformity to the group pattern dominated this literature. One of Bellamy's protagonists described the compulsory labor service as being so natural and reasonable that it was no longer considered compulsory and commented, 'Our entire social order is so wholly based upon and deduced from it that if it were conceivable that a man could escape from it, he would be left with no possible way to provide for his existence. He would have excluded himself from the world, cut himself off from his kind, in a word, committed suicide.'

Bellamy's world was rational, orderly, friendly, technologically advanced (he foresaw the radio and other inventions), and offered material abundance not only to provide for basic needs but also for leisure. His world, too, was a static and rigid one. Bellamy, like Owen and More, saw in the utopian ideal a possibility for abundance that could be achieved only through a participation in the society and through work. To ensure participation in work, and thus abundance, strong social sanctions had to be established and conforming types of personality projected as suitable for the members of utopia. Only Charles Fourier, who recognized that work could be disagreeable and rewarded disagreeable work with the highest pay, conceived of a utopia in which minority tastes and behavior could be satisfied and a diversity of interests encouraged. Yet Fourier failed to envisage the potentialities of industrialization.

Utopias founded on a faith in mechanization and constructed at a time when the possibilities of industrialization were just unfolding did not encompass a pluralistic, permissive society. For achieving abundance through technology, they depended on the solidarity of a kind of folk society, a solidarity that may have been a realistic appraisal of the pressures necessary to shift nonindustrial workers into industrial occupations. The anti-utopians, such as William Graham Sumner in his 'Cooperative Commonwealth,' Aldous Huxley in *Brave New World*, and George Orwell in *1984*, satirize the rigidity, the totalitarian smugness and joyless security of utopia. Indeed, if utopias can be traced as far back as Plato's conception of the ideal state, then anti-utopias are at least as old as Aristophanes' *The Birds*, and their central theme is man's lack of freedom within a supposedly good society.

Certainly, the classical social utopias justify the charge that they present end products, not processes. They envisage no future change, they do not provide for it, they give no indication that society does evolve. Although in utopian literature man is supposed to choose the good life willingly when he is exposed to its advantages, his natural bent is not trusted, and therefore his behavior is proscribed. A person in More's Utopia, for example, was under constant observation by his neighbors and the magistrates, not only during his work hours but also in his leisure time, so that he should spend it correctly. Slavery was the punishment for two unauthorized journeys from one's city, and death, for any private political discussion. In Bellamy's new society, the inspectorate was alert in checking aberrations from the standards. In these utopias there is security—mainly the security of material well-being. What is sacrificed is the development of a wide spectrum of diversified personalities and the opportunity to express them. The complacency, the denial of change, and the imposition of a set of rigid sanctions and ideals cannot help but produce stereotyped personalities. The stereotyped citizen of utopia is as smug and complacent as the society that produces him.

W. S. Gilbert and Arthur Sullivan parody utopian complacency in their comic opera, *Utopia Limited, or the Flowers of Progress*, in which Utopia is converted by England, through a Utopian princess who had attended a British finishing school. When a Utopian citizen asks, 'Then in a few months, Utopia may . . . be completely Anglicized?' the reply is, 'Absolutely and without a doubt.' At this a Utopian maiden complains, 'We are very well as we are. Life without a care—every want supplied. . . . What have we to gain by the great change that is in store for us?' Her friend answers, 'What have we to gain? English institutions, English tastes, and oh, English fashions.' Near the end of the play, with the conversion accomplished, the chorus sings,

> In short, this happy country has been Anglicized completely!
> It really is surprising
> What a thorough Anglicizing
> We have brought about—Utopia's quite another land;
> In her enterprising movements,
> She is England—with improvements,
> Which we dutifully offer to our mother-land.
> *King:* Our city we have beautified—we've done it willy-nilly—
> And all that isn't Belgrave Square is Strand and Piccadilly.

The complacency, rigidity, and lack of opportunity for deviant behavior that characterized the utopias of the emerging industrial civilization persisted in those of the twentieth century. In its early years the literary and social utopia went into eclipse, but the physical or design utopia of the ideal city, through the work of Frank Lloyd Wright and Le Corbusier, achieved relative prominence. Each of these architects produced a twentieth-century utopia amid flourishing technical advances and an urbanized society. Half a century earlier, James Silk Buckingham, an English manufacturer, had called for a trust-like organization to construct a new town, to be called Victoria, as a physical utopia with the latest technical improvements. Wright and Le Corbusier, alarmed yet fascinated by industrial civilization, concluded that a new physical setting, such as they could create on the drawing board, was the right means of remaking industrial civilization.

One of the principles on which Le Corbusier based his ideal city was, 'A city made for speed is made for success.' The railroad station stood at the center of the city, like the hub of a wheel, linked to subways, buses, and other transportation facilities, and to the airfield by helicopter. His scheme for Paris (or any large city) was devised shortly after World War I. Near the center stood twenty-four skyscrapers, each sixty stories high; these great complexes served the commercial needs of the community; in the surrounding parks were luxurious restaurants, theatres, and shops. Most people lived in well-spaced, high, elevator apartment buildings with private hanging gardens for each unit, although a few lived in colonies of individual houses. The streets were on three levels so as to provide for different types of vehicles traveling at different speeds. The high degree of density concentrated people efficiently into small areas, thus freeing large areas for agriculture, recreation, and the contemplation of nature. Such a geometrically spaced urban development permitted many services, cultural and other, that require a concentrated consumer population and an adequate transportation system. Le Corbusier's conception of the city as a machine, or a complex of machines, for daily living also conferred on all men the right to light, greenery, spaciousness, silence, privacy, and beauty—rights otherwise enjoyed only by the peasantry and the privileged.

Whereas Le Corbusier postulated a concentrated urban society, Wright's idea was to disperse people and their activities. He built a large-scale model called Broadacre City and wrote several books setting forth his ideal society of Usonia (the term was borrowed from Butler's *Erewhon*). In Usonia the citizens were to live each on an acre or so of ground on which they could grow vegetables, and for occasional employment they were to commute to a factory some miles away. There were to be small institutions such as universities and museums proportionate in size to the small homesteads, all connected by automotive transportation. Wright believed that the fusion of town and country would be accomplished by the diffusion of city functions throughout the land. Whereas Marx and Engels wanted to eliminate what they called the 'idiocy of country life' by revising the differentiation between town and country, Wright aimed at eliminating what he regarded as the idiocy of city life.

Although neither Wright nor Le Corbusier dealt with the economic, social, or political aspects of their new societies, it is obvious that each made very different use of resources, and each had a different conception of the organization of social institutions, as well as of the behavioral and living patterns best suited to a people. They both assumed that if men are captivated by the prospect of a reorganized physical environment, they will create the institutions to obtain it. Their faith in the possibility of designing an urban utopia of the physical environment has spread to such mass media as the Sunday supplement, science fiction, and advertising copy.

Today any technological innovation appears feasible, even a reorganization of the total environment of the earth, and schemes for diverting the Gulf Stream so as to warm Greenland, melt the polar ice caps, and provide rich fish-farming areas are discussed in the responsible press. Any amount of consumption seems possible: an increase in comfort and esthetic satisfaction, as well as the abolition of drudgery, are promised. The folklore of modern utopia provides many a glimpse of effortless abundance and a life of ease. In popular culture confidence in the future as a bigger and better present is perceptible everywhere.* In his 1952 campaign, Adlai Stevenson stated, 'I do say to you soberly and sincerely that on the evidence of science, of technology, and of our own common sense, the United States at mid-century stands on the threshold of abundance for all, so great as to exceed the happiest dream of the pioneers who opened the vast Western country. Unless we allow ourselves to be held back by fear, we shall in God's good time realize the golden promise of our future.'†

When the automatic factory and office are commoner, the major problem will perhaps be, not motivation for work, but motivation for leisure pursuits. How are the former workers to be kept innocuously occupied? When productivity continues rising, it is not the satisfaction of wants but the creation of new wants that is challenging. Obviously, the old utopias are obsolete; the dream of material abundance is already a popular expectation and a component of the modern utopia.

When the great social utopias were created, at least two attitudes were prevalent: dissatisfaction with present conditions; and hope, even confidence, of change through man's mastery of his environment. If people feel complacent, they will not be motivated to change. If, on the other hand, they feel powerless and estranged, they will lack the courage and energy to venture into the unknown. Many contemporary observers have pointed to a combination of affluence and apathy that induces a complacency both in Americans and Western Europeans. On the one

---

*Science fiction has become an exception. In the days when H. G. Wells was proclaiming faith in the progress of technology and science, and even as late as the years immediately following World War II, science fiction seemed devoted to science, and scientists as often as not appeared critical, even fearful, of technology. In the 1950's, science fiction has shifted markedly into the anti-utopia camp, and is filled with satire instead of an enthusiastic endorsement of what is to come.

†Adlai E. Stevenson, quoted in Clarke A. Chambers (1958, page 219).

hand, high levels of employment and a rising standard of living inhibit any popular urge toward change. On the other hand, problems that are too complex and too removed from individual competence inhibit a sense of effective action. Thus the contemporary utopian folklore is in a sense reinforced by the complacency resulting from the material affluence that has spread throughout our middle class as well as through many groups of industrial workers and by the feeling of impotence deriving from the alienation of the citizen from the making of important decisions. By reinforcing the theme of automatic abundance, complacency and the sense of impotence sap the sources of motivation that in the past provided a clientele for social and literary utopias such as Bellamy's. Furthermore, when the imagery of the redesigned physical environment is taken over from the sophisticated high culture of a Wright or a Le Corbusier by the popular culture of the mass media, the prophetic element of such a utopia is lessened.

At the same time, a radical faith in man's ability to alter his society and his environment in any significant way by planning has increasingly been replaced by a Burkean belief in man's inability to do so. But even a utopian or radical faith does not produce utopias. Oscar Wilde once wrote, 'A map of the world that does not include Utopia is not worth even glancing at . . .' But he did not create a utopia—nor has David Riesman or Martin Buber or Karl Mannheim, other protagonists of utopia.

Since there appears to be little demand for utopia, since no one for a generation has produced social or physical-design utopias of importance, and since utopias are caricatures anyway, this essay amounts to an epitaph—but an epitaph only for the rigid, social and physical utopias of the past, for utopia as a product, and not for utopia as a process for clarifying policy, particularly in city planning.

Planning, like utopia, depicts a desirable future state of affairs, but unlike utopia, specifies the means of achieving it. In the Western world, planning, like utopia (and for many of the same reasons), has become suspect. Some of the intellectuals have seen society as too complex, and knowledge as too inadequate, to allow men purposefully to plan their world. But the planning of cities has been exempt from this view. Partly because it does not threaten the equilibrium of economic and political power, partly because cities appear to many to be a glaring failure of decision on the part of the market-place, partly because cities appear to some to be finite enough to comprehend and manage, the planning of cities has become institutionalized as the principal form of public planning in most Western countries.

In so far as city planning deals with the future, it must deal with both innovations in ends or values and innovations in means or courses of action. Utopian formulation is a method for testing innovation in city

19

and other kinds of planning. It is a method that could be used in two ways. First, as I envisage it, it could enable the city planner to set up a series of utopian models, each organized about a different set of principles. Each utopian model could then be logically examined in terms of both the direct and the indirect or side effects of following these principles. Second, after this kind of screening and modifying, the surviving alternative utopian models could be tested by the reactions of civic leaders and the citizenry at large. In 1949 I recommended to public officials in Chicago that a 'museum of the future' might highlight the civic possibilities; both leaders and citizens could be encouraged to participate in utopian thinking and thus help resolve policy as to long-term urban development.

This method would share certain characteristics with model-building in a field such as economics. However, most forms of model-building, if therapeutic at all, are adaptive, that is, they are concerned only with incremental changes, and with these changes only as means. Most changes, of course, can be only incremental and can take place only at that level, rather than as ends. But utopian model-building for city policy and planning may even suggest new incremental measures that otherwise would not have been conceived, as well as more drastic paths of desirable action.

Admittedly, these more drastic choices will be in the form of caricatures, but, unlike most utopias, they would be intended as such for the purpose of testing. Furthermore, I have presented a critical review of the utopian tradition largely in the hope that the course just recommended can transcend some of the limitations of past utopias, in particular, by uniting the verbal and the visual, the socio-economic and the physical-environmental traditions.* Even if the good social and economic life can be achieved apart from the good physical setting, the setting has a series of human consequences in benefits and costs which should be comprehended.

Another hope is that these models of utopian planning need not be restricted and rigid, as were those of the past. Having achieved a state of technology in which material abundance is no longer in doubt, we can delineate pluralistic urban utopias. We can be more permissive, without leaning on rigid social controls in order to motivate people to work, or on types of personality standardized so as to behave in a prescribed manner, or on the uniform physical patterns of a Wright or a Le Corbusier. This is the age W. W. Rostow characterizes as one of high mass consumption—admittedly, not available to all. Now we can not only permit deviation, we can also encourage it. Utopians now have the task of devising institutions and the material organization of society

*One example of such an enterprising blend is *Communitas: Means of Livelihood and Ways of Life*, by Percival and Paul Goodman, architect and philosopher, respectively.

to free men from the restrictions under which they have previously operated, instead of curtailing men's choices. This may be the time for the post-technological model, in which it is assumed that technical change and material production are so readily available that they cease to be important limiting conditions. If production and technology do wane, utopian formulations can more readily shift from the authoritarian to the permissive view of the human personality, from a kind of statistical concept of central tendency to one of dispersion, satisfying many minority aspirations. But the theme of production and technology itself is one that should undergo exploration in utopian models, for it is a theme that could radically alter the nature of cities, whether emphasized or diminished.

Earlier in this essay I have written that it was the utopian process rather than the utopian specific that should serve as present stimulus and inspiration. If we approach utopias experimentally, tentatively, consciously seeking alternatives, we should be able to avoid the static, complacent rigidity of past social and physical utopias, as the two traditions become blended into a single instrument for the planning of cities.

## References

BELLAMY, E. (1888) *Looking Backward 2000–1887*. Boston, Houghton Mifflin.

CHAMBERS, C. A. (1958) 'The belief in progress in twentieth century America', *Journal of the History of Ideas*, **19**, page 219.

GOODMAN, P. and P. (1947) *Communitas: means of livelihood and ways of life*, Chicago, University of Chicago Press.

KRAUS, M. (1934) 'America and the utopian ideal in the eighteenth century', *The Mississippi valley historical review*, **22**, pages 487–504.

MEAD, M. (1957) 'Towards more vivid utopias', *Science*, **126**, page 958.

MUMFORD, L. (1922) *The story of utopias*, New York, Boni and Liveright (Peter Smith reprint, 1941).

RIESMAN, D. (1947) 'Some observations on community plans and utopia', *Yale Law Journal*, December, pages 173–200.

RUYER, R. (1950) *L'Utopia et les utopies*, Paris, Presses Universitaires de France.

# 1.2 Utopia *Thomas More*

(Book 2 of *Utopia* takes the form of a discourse on the country of Utopia by one Raphael Hythloday a philosopher and traveller. In it he describes the economic system of the utopians, their political organiza-

*Utopia*

tion, their communal and family life, moral principles and religious observances. In the final section which is reproduced here Raphael Hythloday sums up the advantages which he considers the egalitarian society of Utopia has over all other nations. eds.)

Now I have declared and described unto you as truly as I could the form and order of that commonwealth, which verily in my judgment is not only the best, but also that which alone of good right may claim and take upon it the name of a commonwealth or public weal. For in other places they speak still of the commonwealth, but every man procureth his own private gain. Here, where nothing is private, the common affairs be earnestly looked upon. And truly on both parts they have good cause so to do as they do; for in other countries who knoweth not that he shall starve for hunger, unless he make some several provision for himself, though the commonwealth flourish never so much in riches? And therefore he is compelled even of very necessity to have regard to himself rather than to the people, that is to say, to other. Contrariwise, there where all things be common to every man, it is not to be doubted that any man shall lack any thing necessary for his private uses, so that the common store, houses and barns, be sufficiently stored. For there nothing is distributed after a niggish sort, neither there is any poor man or beggar; and though no man have anything, yet every man is rich. For what can be more rich than to live joyfully and merrily, without all grief and pensiveness, not caring for his own living, nor vexed or troubled with his wife's importunate complaints, nor dreading poverty to his son, nor sorrowing for his daughter's dowry? Yea, they take no care at all for the living and wealth of themselves and all theirs, of their wives, their children, their nephews, their children's children, and all the succession that ever shall follow in their posterity. And yet, besides this, there is no less provision for them that were once labourers and be now weak and impotent, than for them that do now labour and take pain.

Here now would I see if any man dare be so bold as to compare with this equity the justice of other nations, among whom I forsake God if I can find any sign or token of equity and justice. For what justice is this, that a rich goldsmith or an usurer or, to be short, any of them which either do nothing at all, or else that which they do is such that it is not very necessary to the commonwealth, should have a pleasant and a wealthy living, either by idleness or by unnecessary business, when in the meantime poor labourers, carters, ironsmiths, carpenters, and plowmen (by so great and continual toil, as drawing and bearing beasts be scant able to sustain, and again so necessary toil, that without it no commonwealth were able to continue and endure one year), should

*Source:* Thomas More's *Utopia*, Everyman's Library, Dent, First edition, 1910 (Revised 1951)

yet get so hard and poor a living and live so wretched and miserable a life, that the state and condition of the labouring beasts may seem much better and wealthier? For they be not put to so continual labour, nor their living is not much worse, yea, to them much pleasanter, taking no thought in the mean season for the time to come. But these silly poor wretches be presently tormented with barren and unfruitful labour, and the remembrance of their poor, indigent, and beggarly old age killeth them up. For their daily wages is so little that it will not suffice for the same day, much less it yieldeth any overplus that may daily be laid up for the relief of old age.

Is not this an unjust and an unkind public weal, which giveth great fees and rewards to gentlemen, as they call them, and to goldsmiths and to such other, which be either idle persons, or else only flatterers and devisers of vain pleasures, and of the contrary part maketh no gentle provision for poor plowmen, colliers, labourers, carters, ironsmiths, and carpenters, without whom no commonwealth can continue? But after it hath abused the labours of their lusty and flowering age, at the last, when they be oppressed with old age and sickness, being needy, poor, and indigent of all things, then, forgetting their so many painful watchings, not remembering their so many and so great benefits, recompenseth and acquiteth them most unkindly with miserable death. And yet besides this the rich men, not only by private fraud but also by common laws, do every day pluck and snatch away from the poor some part of their daily living. So whereas it seemed before unjust to recompense with unkindness their pains that have been beneficial to the public weal, now they have to this their wrong and unjust dealing (which is yet a much worse point) given the name of justice, yea, and that by force of a law.

Therefore, when I consider and weigh in my mind all these commonwealths which nowadays anywhere do flourish, so God help me, I can perceive nothing but a certain conspiracy of rich men procuring their own commodities under the name and title of the commonwealth. They invent and devise all means and crafts, first how to keep safely, without fear of losing, that they have unjustly gathered together, and next how to hire and abuse the work and labour of the poor for as little money as may be. These devices, when the rich men have decreed to be kept and observed under colour of the commonalty, that is to say, also of the poor people, then they be made laws. But these most wicked and vicious men, when they have by their unsatiable covetousness divided among themselves all those things which would have sufficed all men, yet how far be they from the wealth and felicity of the Utopian commonwealth! Out of the which, in that all the desire of money with the use thereof is utterly secluded and banished, how great a heap of cares is cut away! How great an occasion of wickedness and mischief is plucked up by the roots! For who knoweth not that fraud, theft, ravin, brawling, quarrelling, brabbling, strife, chiding, contention, murder, treason, poisoning, which by daily punishments are rather revenged than refrained, do die when money dieth? And also that fear, grief, care, labours, and watchings do perish even the very same moment that money perisheth? Yea, poverty itself, which only seemed to lack money if money were gone, it also would decrease and vanish away.

## 1.3 An academy of projectors *Jonathan Swift*

The continent, as far as it is subject to the monarch of the flying island, passeth under the general name of Balnibarbi; and the metropolis, as I said before, is called Lagado. I felt some little satisfaction in finding my self on firm ground. I walked to the city without any concern, being clad like one of the natives, and sufficiently instructed to converse with them. I soon found out the person's house to whom I was recommended; presented my letter, from his friend the grandee in the island; and was received with much kindness. This great lord, whose name was Munodi, ordered me an apartment in his own house; where I continued during my stay, and was entertained in a most hospitable manner.

The next morning after my arrival, he took me in his chariot to see the town, which is about half the bigness of London; but the houses very strangely built, and most of them out of repair. The people in the streets walked fast, looked wild, their eyes fixed, and were generally in rags. We passed through one of the town gates, and went about three miles into the country, where I saw many labourers working with several sorts of tools in the ground, but was not able to conjecture what they were about; neither did I observe any expectation either of corn or grass, although the soil appeared to be excellent. I could not forbear admiring at these odd appearances both in town and country; and, I made bold to desire my conductor, that he would be pleased to explain to me, what could be meant by so many busy heads, hands, and faces, both in the streets and the fields, because I did not discover any good effects they produced; but, on the contrary, I never knew a soil so unhappily cultivated, houses so ill contrived and so ruinous, or a people whose countenances and habit, expressed so much misery and want.

*Source:* Jonathan Swift (1726), *Gulliver's Travels*, Part 3, Chapter 4, Dent 1965 edition, pages 186–190

This Lord Munodi was a person of the first rank, and had been some years governor of Lagado; but by a cabal of ministers was discharged for insufficiency. However, the king treated him with tenderness, as a well-meaning man, but of a low contemptible understanding.

When I gave that free censure of the country and its inhabitants, he made no further answer than by telling me, that I had not been long enough among them to form a judgment; and that the different nations of the world had different customs; with other common topicks to the same purpose. But, when we returned to his palace, he asked me how I liked the building, what absurdities I observed, and what quarrel I had with the dress and looks of his domesticks. This he might safely do; because every thing about him, was magnificent, regular, and polite. I answered, that his excellency's prudence, quality, and fortune, had exempted him from those defects which folly and beggary had produced in others. He said, if I would go with him to his country house, about twenty miles distant, where his estate lay, there would be more leisure for this kind of conversation. I told his excellency, that I was entirely at his disposal; and accordingly we set out next morning.

During our journey, he made me observe the several methods used by farmers, in managing their lands; which to me, were wholly unaccountable: for, except in some very few places, I could not discover one ear of corn, or blade of grass. But, in three hours travelling, the scene was wholly altered; we came into a most beautiful country; farmers houses at small distances, neatly built, the fields enclosed, containing vine-yards, corn-grounds and meadows: neither do I remember to have seen a more delightful prospect. His excellency observed my countenance to clear up; he told me with a sigh, that there his estate began, and would continue the same until we should come to his house: that, his countrymen ridiculed and despised him for managing his affairs no better, and for setting so ill an example to the kingdom; which, however was followed by very few; such as were old and wilful, and weak like himself.

We came at length to the house, which was indeed a noble structure, built according to the best rules of ancient architecture. The fountains, gardens, walks, avenues, and groves, were all disposed with exact judgment and taste. I gave due praises to every thing I saw, whereof his excellency took not the least notice until after supper; when, there being no third companion, he told me with a very melancholy air, that he doubted he must throw down his houses in town and country, to rebuild them after the present mode; destroy all his plantations, and cast others into such a form, as modern usage required; and give the same directions to all his tenants, unless he would submit to incur the censure of pride, singularity, affectation, ignorance, caprice; and perhaps, increase his Majesty's displeasure.

That, the admiration I appeared to be under, would cease or diminish,

25

when he had informed me of some particulars, which probably I never heard of at court; the people there being too much taken up in their own speculations, to have regard to what passed here below.

The sum of his discourse was to this effect. That, about forty years ago, certain persons went up to Laputa, either upon business or diversion; and after five months continuance, came back with a very little smattering in mathematicks, but full of volatile spirits, acquired in that airy region. That, these persons upon their return, began to dislike the management of every thing below; and fell into schemes of putting all arts, sciences, languages, and mechanicks upon a new foot. To this end, they procured a royal patent, for erecting an academy of projectors in Lagado: and, the humour prevailed so strongly among the people, that there is not a town of any consequence in the kingdom, without such an academy. In these colleges, the professors contrive new rules and methods of agriculture and building, and new instruments and tools for all trades and manufactures; whereby, as they undertake, one man shall do the work of ten: a palace may be built in a week, of materials so durable, as to last for ever without repairing. All the fruits of the earth shall come to maturity, at whatever season we think fit to chuse, and encrease an hundred fold more than they do at present; with innumerable other happy proposals. The only inconvenience is, that none of these projects are yet brought to perfection; and, in the mean time, the whole country lies miserably waste; the houses in ruins, and the people without food or cloaths: by all which, instead of being discouraged, they are fifty times more violently bent upon prosecuting their schemes; driven equally on by hope and despair: that, as for himself, being not of an enterprizing spirit, he was content to go on in the old forms; to live in the houses his ancestors had built, and act as they did in every part of life without innovation: that, some few other persons of quality and gentry had done the same; but were looked on with an eye of contempt and ill-will; as enemies to art; ignorant, and ill commonwealthsmen; preferring their own ease and sloth before the general improvement of their country.

His lordship added, that he would not by any further particulars prevent the pleasure I should certainly take in viewing the grand academy, whither he was resolved I should go. He only desired me to observe a ruined building upon the side of a mountain about three miles distant, of which he gave me this account. That, he had a very convenient mill within half a mile of his house, turned by a current from a large river, and sufficient for his own family, as well as a great number of his tenants. That, about seven years ago, a club of those projectors came to him with proposals to destroy this mill, and build another on the side of that mountain, on the long ridge whereof, a long canal must be cut for a repositary of water, to be conveyed up by pipes and engines to supply the mill: because the wind and air upon a height agitated the water, and thereby, made it fitter for motion: and, because the water descending down a declivity, would turn the mill with half the current of a river, whose course is more upon a level. He said, that being then not very well with the court, and pressed by many of his friends, he complied with the proposal; and after employing an hundred men for two years, the work miscarried, the projectors went off, laying the blame entirely upon him; railing at him ever since, and putting others upon the same experiment, with equal assurance of success, as well as equal disappointment.

In a few days we came back to town; and his Excellency, considering the bad character he had in the academy, would not go with me himself; but recommended me to a friend of his, to bear me company thither. My lord was pleased to represent me as a great admirer of projects, and a person of much curiosity and easy belief; which, indeed was not without truth; for, I had my self, been a sort of projector in my younger days.

# 1.4  A Contemporary City *Le Corbusier*

The use of technical analysis and architectural synthesis enabled me to draw up my scheme for a contemporary city of three million inhabitants. The result of my work was shown in November 1922 at the Salon d'Automne in Paris. It was greeted with a sort of stupor; the shock of surprise caused rage in some quarters and enthusiasm in others. The solution I put forward was a rough one and completely uncompromising. There were no notes to accompany the plans, and, alas! not everybody can read a plan. I should have had to be constantly on the spot in order to reply to the fundamental questions which spring from the very depths of human feelings. Such questions are of profound interest and cannot remain unanswered. When at a later date it became necessary that this book should be written, a book in which I could formulate the new principles of Town Planning, I resolutely decided *first of all* to find answers to these fundamental questions. I have used two kinds of argument: first, those essentially human ones which start from the mind or the heart or the physiology of our sensations as a basis; secondly, historical and statistical arguments. Thus I could keep in touch with

*Source:* Le Corbusier, *The City of Tomorrow*, Architectural Press, 1971, Chapter 11 and diagrams from pages 182–183, 22 and 33

27

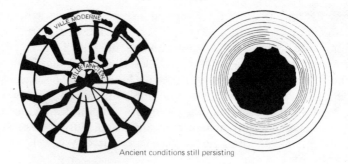

Ancient conditions still persisting

Present conditions leading to the crisis which is only just beginning

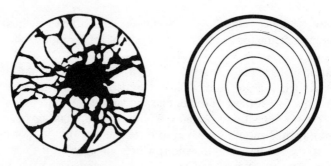

The existing congestion in the centre must be eliminated.

what is fundamental and at the same time be master of the environment in which all this takes place.

In this way I hope I shall have been able to help my reader to take a number of steps by means of which he can reach a sure and certain position. So that when I unroll my plans I can have the happy assurance that his astonishment will no longer be stupefaction nor his fears mere panic.

28

\*

## A CONTEMPORARY CITY OF THREE MILLION INHABITANTS

Proceeding in the manner of the investigator in his laboratory, I have avoided all special cases, and all that may be accidental, and I have assumed an ideal site to begin with. My object was not to overcome the existing state of things, but *by constructing a theoretically water-tight formula to arrive at the fundamental principles of modern town planning.* Such fundamental principles, if they are genuine, can serve as the skeleton of any system of modern town planning; being as it were the *rules* according to which development will take place. We shall then be in a position to take a special case, no matter what: whether it be Paris, London, Berlin, New York or some small town. Then, as a result of what we have learnt, we can take control and decide in what direction the forthcoming battle is to be waged. For the desire to rebuild any great city in a modern way is to engage in a formidable battle. Can you imagine people engaging in a battle without knowing their objectives? Yet that is exactly what is happening. The authorities are compelled to do something, so they give the police white sleeves or set them on horseback, they invent sound signals and light signals, they propose to put bridges over streets or moving pavements under the streets; more garden cities are suggested, or it is decided to suppress the tramways, and so on. And these decisions are reached in a sort of frantic haste in order, as it were, to hold a wild beast at bay. That BEAST is the great city. It is infinitely more powerful than all these devices. And it is just beginning to wake. What will to-morrow bring forth to cope with it?

We must have some rule of conduct.\*

We must have fundamental principles for modern town planning.

## *Site*

A level site is the ideal site. In all those places where traffic becomes over-intensified the level site gives a chance of a normal solution to the problem. Where there is less traffic, differences in level matter less.

The river flows far away from the city. The river is a kind of liquid

---

\*New suggestions shower on us. Their inventors and those who believe in them have their little thrill. It is so easy for them to believe in them. But what if they are based on grave errors? How are we to distinguish between what is reasonable and an over-poetical dream? The leading newspapers accept everything with enthusiasm. One of them said, 'The cities of to-morrow must be built on new virgin soil'. But no, this is not true! We must go to the old cities, all our inquiries confirm it. One of our leading papers supports the suggestion made by one of our greatest and most reasonable architects, who for once gives us bad counsel in proposing to erect round about Paris a ring of sky-scrapers. The idea is romantic enough, but it cannot be defended, The sky-scrapers must be built *in the centre* ◦ and not on the periphery.

railway, a goods station and a sorting house. In a decent house the servants' stairs do not go through the drawing-room—even if the maid is charming (or if the little boats delight the loiterer leaning on a bridge).

## Population

This consists of the citizens proper; of suburban dwellers; and of those of a mixed kind.

(*a*) Citizens are of the city: those who work and live in it.

(*b*) Suburban dwellers are those who work in the outer industrial zone and who do not come into the city: they live in garden cities.

(*c*) The mixed sort are those who work in the business parts of the city but bring up their families in garden cities.

To classify these divisions (and so make possible the transmutation of these recognized types) is to attack the most important problem in town planning, for such a classification would define the areas to be allotted to these three sections and the delimitation of their boundaries. This would enable us to formulate and resolve the following problems:

1. The *City*, as a business and residential centre.

2. The *Industrial City* in relation to the *Garden Cities* (*i.e.* the question of transport).

3. The *Garden Cities* and the *daily transport* of the workers.

Our first requirement will be an organ that is compact, rapid, lively and concentrated: this is the City with its well-organized centre. Our second requirement will be another organ, supple, extensive and elastic; this is *the Garden City* on the periphery.

Lying between these two organs, we must *require the legal establishment* of that absolute necessity, a protective zone which allows of extension, *a reserved zone* of woods and fields, a fresh-air reserve.

## Density of Population

The more dense the population of a city is the less are the distances that have to be covered. The moral, therefore, is that we must *increase the density of the centres of our cities, where business affairs are carried on.*

## Lungs

Work in our modern world becomes more intensified day by day, and its demands affect our nervous system in a way that grows more and more dangerous. Modern toil demands quiet and fresh air, not stale air.

The towns of to-day can only increase in density at the expense of the open spaces which are the lungs of a city.

We must *increase the open spaces and diminish the distances to be*

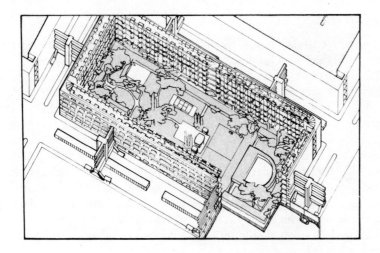

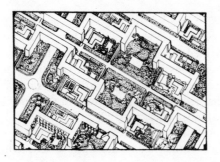

*Dwellings with 'set-backs'*

*covered.* Therefore the centre of the city must be constructed *vertically.*

The city's residential quarters must no longer be built along 'corridor-streets,' full of noise and dust and deprived of light.

It is a simple matter to build urban dwellings away from the streets, without small internal courtyards and with the windows looking on to large parks; and this whether our housing schemes are of the type with 'set-backs' or built on the 'cellular' principle.

## The Street

The street of to-day is still the old bare ground which has been paved over, and under which a few tube railways have been run.

The modern street in the true sense of the word is a new type of organism, a sort of stretched-out workshop, a home for many complicated and delicate organs, such as gas, water and electric mains. It is contrary to all economy, to all security, and to all sense to bury these important service mains. They ought to be accessible throughout their length. The various storeys of this stretched-out workshop will each have their own particular functions. If this type of street, which I have called a 'workshop,' is to be realized, it becomes as much a matter of *construction* as are the houses with which it is customary to flank it, and the bridges which carry it over valleys and across rivers.

The modern street should be a masterpiece of civil engineering and no longer a job for navvies.

The 'corridor-street' should be tolerated no longer, for it poisons the houses that border it and leads to the construction of small internal courts or 'wells.'

## Traffic

Traffic can be classified more easily than other things.

To-day traffic is not classified—it is like dynamite flung at hazard into the street, killing pedestrians. Even so, *traffic does not fulfill its function.* This sacrifice of the pedestrian leads nowhere.

If we classify traffic we get:

(*a*) Heavy goods traffic

(*b*) Lighter goods traffic, *i.e.* vans and so on, which make short journeys in all directions

(*c*) Fast traffic, which covers a large section of the town

Three kinds of roads are needed, and in superimposed storeys:

(*a*) Below-ground* there would be the street for heavy traffic. This

---

*I say 'below-ground', but it would be more exact to say at what we call *basement level,* for if my town, built on concrete piles, were realized (see *Towards a New Architecture,* Chapter IV), this 'basement' would no longer be buried under the earth. See also Chapter XII of this volume: 'Housing Schemes on the *Cellular* Principle.'

storey of the houses would consist merely of concrete piles, and between them large open spaces which would form a sort of clearing-house where heavy goods traffic could load and unload.

(*b*) At the ground floor level of the buildings there would be the complicated and delicate network of the ordinary streets taking traffic in every desired direction.

(*c*) Running north and south, and east and west, and forming the two great axes of the city, there would be great *arterial roads for fast one-way traffic* built on immense reinforced concrete bridges 120 to 180 yards in width and approached every half-mile or so by subsidiary roads from ground level. These arterial roads could therefore be joined at any given point, so that even at the highest speeds the town can be traversed and the suburbs reached without having to negotiate any cross-roads.

The number of existing streets *should be diminished by two-thirds*. The number of crossings depends directly on the number of streets; and *cross-roads are an enemy to traffic*. The number of existing streets was fixed at a remote epoch in history. The perpetuation of the boundaries of properties has, almost without exception, preserved even the faintest track and footpaths of the old village and made streets of them, and sometimes even an avenue. The result is that we have cross-roads every fifty yards, even every twenty yards or ten yards. And this leads to the ridiculous traffic congestion we all know so well. The distance between two 'bus stops or two tube stations gives us the necessary unit for the distance between streets, though this unit is conditional on the speed of vehicles and the walking capacity of pedestrians. So an average measure of about 400 yards would give the normal separation between streets, and make a standard for urban distances. My city is conceived on the gridiron system with streets every 400 yards, though occasionally these distances are subdivided to give streets every 200 yards.

This triple system of superimposed levels answers every need of motor traffic (lorries, private cars, taxis, 'buses) because it provides for rapid and *mobile* transit.

Traffic running on fixed rails is only justified if it is in the form of a convoy carrying an immense load; it then becomes a sort of extension of the underground system or of trains dealing with suburban traffic. *The tramway has no right to exist in the heart of the modern city.*

If the city thus consists of plots about 400 yards square, this will give us sections of about 40 acres in area, and the density of population will vary from 50,000 down to 6,000, according as the 'lots' are developed for business or for residential purposes. The natural thing, therefore, would be to continue to apply our unit of distance as it exists in the Paris tubes to-day (namely, 400 yards) and to put a station in the middle of each plot.

Following the two great axes of the city, two 'storeys' below the arterial roads for fast traffic, would run the tubes leading to the four furthest points of the garden city suburbs, and linking up with the metropolitan network (see the next chapter). At a still lower level, and again following these two main axes, would run the one-way loop systems for suburban traffic, and below these again the four great main lines serving the provinces and running north, south, east and west. These main lines would end at the Central Station, or better still might be connected up by a loop system.

## The Station

There is only one station. The only place for the station is in the centre of the city. It is the natural place for it, and there is no reason for putting it anywhere else. The railway station is the hub of the wheel.

The station would be an essentially subterranean building. Its roof, which would be two storeys above the natural ground level of the city, would form the aerodrome for aero-taxis. This aerodrome (linked up with the main aerodrome in the protected zone) must be in close contact with the tubes, the suburban lines, the main lines, the main arteries and the administrative services connected with all these.

### THE PLAN OF THE CITY

The basic principles we must follow are these:

1. We must de-congest the centres of our cities
2. We must augment their density
3. We must increase the means for getting about
4. We must increase parks and open spaces

At the very centre we have the STATION with its landing stage for aero-taxis.

Running north and south, and east and west, we have the *Main Arteries* for fast traffic, forming elevated roadways 120 feet wide.

At the base of the sky-scrapers and all round them we have a great open space 2400 yards by 1500 yards, giving an area of 3 600 000 square yards, and occupied by gardens, parks and avenues. In these parks, at the foot of and round the sky-scrapers, would be the restaurants and cafés, the luxury shops, housed in buildings with receding terraces: here too would be the theatres, halls and so on; and here the parking places or garage shelters.

The sky-scrapers are designed purely for business purposes.

On the left we have the great public buildings, the museums, the

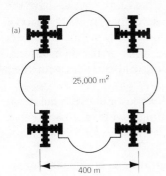

25,000 m²

400 m

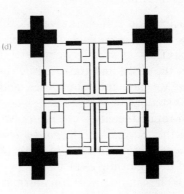

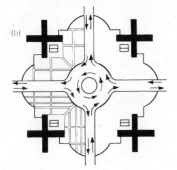

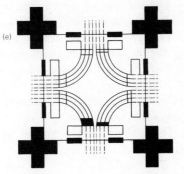

hall départ

reseau
SUD

(c)

reseau
EST

ascenseurs
grandes lingues

hall
arrivés

ascenseurs
banlieu

départ

réseau
OUEST

réseou
NORD   arrives

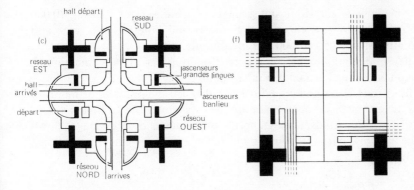

(a)  Upper level: The landing-stage for taxi-planes; 250,000 square yards.
(b)  Mezzanine level: The crossing for fast motor traffic.
(c)  Ground level: Showing the access to the various railway lines; the booking-halls and so on.
(d)  First level below ground: The Tubes (the main crossing).
(e)  Second level below ground: Local and suburban lines.
(f)  Third level below ground: The Main lines. ( Cf. in a later chapter the
     'Voisin' plan for Paris, where the main line system is designed for continuous or 'through' traffic by
     means of loops)
The entrance halls in connection with each system are exactly opposite the exits, in order to avoid crowding
or confusion, i.e. everything is on the 'one-way' system.
Given the immense spaces at our disposal, the technical staff for each system can be housed on the spot.
The four sky-scrapers abutting on the Central Station house the offices of the various lines.

35

municipal and administrative offices. Still further on the left we have the 'Park' (which is available for further logical development of the heart of the city).

On the right, and traversed by one of the arms of the main arterial roads, we have the warehouses, and the industrial quarters with their goods stations.

All round the city is the *protected zone* of woods and green fields.

Further beyond are the *garden cities*, forming a wide encircling band.

Then, right in the midst of all these, we have the *Central Station*, made up of the following elements:

(*a*) The landing-platform; forming an aerodrome of 200 000 square yards in area

(*b*) The entresol or mezzanine; at this level are the raised tracks for fast motor traffic: the only crossing being gyratory

(*c*) The ground floor where are the entrance halls and booking offices for the tubes, suburban, main line and air traffic.

(*d*) The 'basement': here are the tubes which serve the city and the main arteries

(*e*) The 'sub-basement': here are the suburban lines running on a one-way loop

(*f*) The 'sub-sub-basement': here are the main lines (going north, south, east and west)

## The City

Here we have twenty-four sky-scrapers capable each of housing 10 000 to 50 000 employees; this is the business and hotel section, etc., and accounts for 400 000 to 600 000 inhabitants.

The residential blocks, of the two main types already mentioned, account for a further 600 000 inhabitants.

The garden cities give us a further 2 000 000 inhabitants, or more.

In the great central open space are the cafés, restaurants, luxury shops, halls of various kinds, a magnificent forum descending by stages down to the immense parks surrounding it, the whole arrangement providing a spectacle of order and vitality.

## Density of Population

(*a*) The sky-scraper: 1200 inhabitants to the acre

(*b*) The residential blocks with set-backs: 120 inhabitants to the acre. These are the luxury dwellings

(*c*) The residential blocks on the 'cellular' system, with a similar number of inhabitants

This great density gives us our necessary shortening of distances and ensures rapid intercommunication.

*Note.*—The average density to the acre of Paris in the heart of the town is 146, and of London 63; and of the over-crowded quarters of Paris 213, and of London 169.

## Open Spaces

Of the area (*a*), 95 per cent of the ground is open (squares, restaurants, theatres)

Of the area (*b*), 85 per cent of the ground is open (gardens, sports grounds)

Of the area (*c*), 48 per cent of the ground is open (gardens, sports grounds)

## Educational and Civic Centres, Universities, Museums of Art and Industry, Public Services, County Hall

The 'Jardin anglais.' (The city can extend here, if necessary.)

Sports grounds: Motor racing track, Racecourse, Stadium, Swimming baths, etc.

## The Protected Zone (which will be the property of the city), with its Aerodrome

A zone in which all building would be prohibited; reserved for the growth of the city as laid down by the municipality: it would consist of woods, fields, and sports grounds. The forming of a 'protected zone' by continual purchase of small properties in the immediate vicinity of the city is one of the most essential and urgent tasks which a municipality can pursue. It would eventually represent a tenfold return on the capital invested.

## Industrial Quarters*

Types of Buildings Employed

For business: sky-scrapers sixty storeys high with no internal wells or courtyards (see the following chapter).

Residential buildings with 'set-backs,' of six double storeys; again with

---

*In this section I make new suggestions in regard to the industrial quarters: they have been content to exist too long in disorder, dirt and in a hand-to-mouth way. And this is absurd, for Industry, when it is on a properly ordered basis, should develop in an orderly fashion. A portion of the industrial district could be constructed of ready-made sections by using standard units for the various kinds of buildings needed. Fifty per cent. of the site would be reserved for this purpose. In the event of considerable growth, provision would thus be made for moving them into a different district where there was more space. Bring about '*standardization*' in the building of a works and you would have mobility instead of the crowding which results when factories become impossibly congested.

no internal wells: the flats looking on either side on to immense parks.

Residential buildings on the 'cellular' principle, with 'hanging gardens,' looking on to immense parks; again no internal wells. These are 'service-flats' of the most modern kind.

## GARDEN CITIES

### *Their Aesthetic, Economy, Perfection and Modern Outlook*

A simple phrase suffices to express the necessities of to-morrow: WE MUST BUILD IN THE OPEN. The lay-out must be of a purely geometrical kind, with all its many and delicate implications.

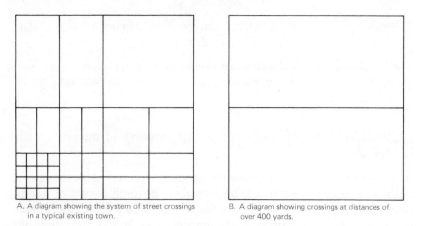

A. A diagram showing the system of street crossings in a typical existing town.

B. A diagram showing crossings at distances of over 400 yards.

A shows 46 crossings, and B only 6 crossings.

The city of to-day is a dying thing because it is not geometrical. To build in the open would be to replace our present haphazard arrangements, *which are all we have to-day*, by a *uniform* lay-out. Unless we do this *there is no salvation*.

The result of a true geometrical lay-out is *repetition*.

The result of repetition is a *standard*, the perfect form (*i.e.* the creation of standard types). A geometrical lay-out means that mathematics play their part. There is no first-rate human production but has geometry at its base. It is of the very essence of Architecture. To introduce uniformity into the building of the city we must *industrialize building*. Building is the one economic activity which has so far resisted industrialization. It has thus escaped the march of progress, with the result that the cost of building is still abnormally high.

The architect, from a professional point of view, has become a twisted sort of creature. He has grown to love irregular sites, claiming that they inspire him with original ideas for getting round them. Of course he is wrong. For nowadays the only building that can be under-taken must be either for the rich or built at a loss (as, for instance, in the case of municipal housing schemes), or else by jerry-building and so robbing the inhabitant of all amenities. A motor-car which is achieved by mass production is a masterpiece of comfort, precision, balance and good taste. A house built to order (on an 'interesting' site) is a master-piece of incongruity—a monstrous thing.

If the builder's yard were reorganized on the lines of standardization and mass production we might have gangs of workmen as keen and intelligent as mechanics.

The mechanic dates back only twenty years, yet already he forms the highest caste of the working world.

The mason dates . . . from time immemorial! He bangs away with feet and hammer. He smashes up everything round him, and the plant entrusted to him falls to pieces in a few months. The spirit of the mason must be disciplined by making him part of the severe and exact machinery of the industrialized builder's yard.

The cost of building would fall in the proportion of 10 to 2.

The wages of the labourers would fall into definite categories; to each according to his merits and service rendered.

The 'interesting' or erratic site absorbs every creative faculty of the architect and wears him out. What results is equally erratic: lopsided abortions; a specialist's solution which can only please other specialists.

We must build *in the open:* both within the city and around it.

Then having worked through every necessary technical stage and using absolute ECONOMY, we shall be in a position to experience the intense joys of a creative art which is based on geometry.

THE CITY AND ITS AESTHETIC

(The plan of a city which is here presented is a direct consequence of purely geometric considerations)

A new unit *on a large scale* (400 yards) inspires everything. Though the gridiron arrangement of the streets every 400 yards (sometimes only 200) is uniform (with a consequent ease in finding one's way about), no two streets are in any way alike. This is where, in a magnificent contrapuntal symphony, the forces of geometry come into play.

Suppose we are entering the city by way of the Great Park. Our fast car takes the special elevated motor track between the majestic sky-scrapers: as we approach nearer there is seen the repetition against the sky of the twenty-four sky-scrapers; to our left and right on the outskirts of each particular area are the municipal and administrative buildings; and enclosing the space are the museums and university buildings.

39

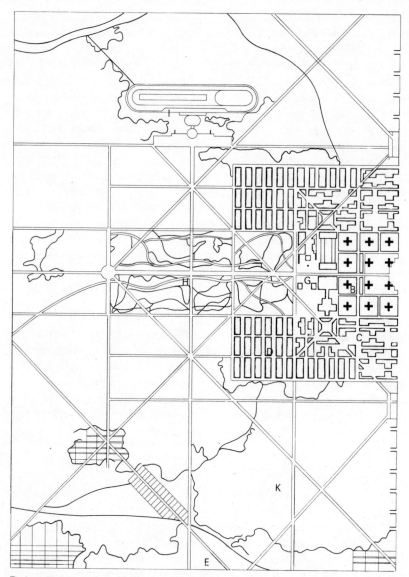

The heavy black lines represent the area built upon. Everything else is either streets or open space. Strictly speaking the city is an immense park. Its lay-out furnishes a multitude of architectural aspects of infinitely varying forms. If the reader, for instance, follows out a given route on this map he will be astonished by the variety he encounters. Yet distances are shorter than in the cities of to-day, for there is a greater density of population.

Then suddenly we find ourselves at the feet of the first sky-scrapers. But here we have, not the meagre shaft of sunlight which so faintly illumines the dismal streets of New York, but an immensity of space. The whole city is a Park. The terraces stretch out over lawns and into

40

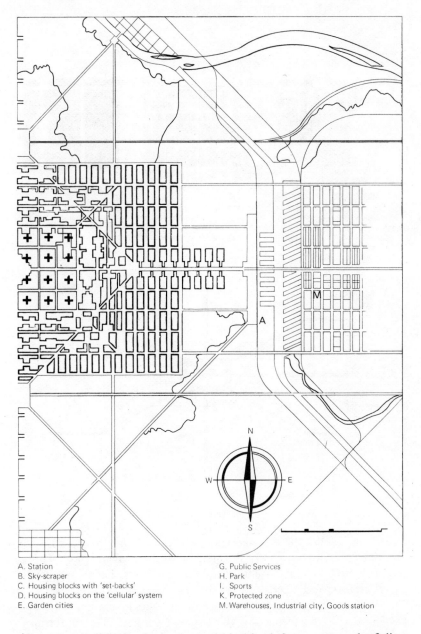

A. Station
B. Sky-scraper
C. Housing blocks with 'set-backs'
D. Housing blocks on the 'cellular' system
E. Garden cities

G. Public Services
H. Park
I. Sports
K. Protected zone
M. Warehouses, Industrial city, Goods station

groves. Low buildings of a horizontal kind lead the eye on to the foliage
of the trees. Where are now the trivial *Procuracies?* Here is the CITY
with its crowds living in peace and pure air, where noise is smothered
under the foliage of green trees. The chaos of New York is overcome.
Here, bathed in light, stands the modern city.

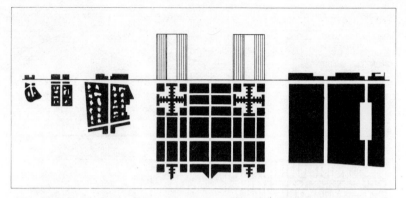

A diagram showing the increase in size of building sites from the fourteenth to the eighteenth and nineteenth centuries. In the nineteenth century the Boulevard Haussmann again offered the 'corridor-street' as a solution. But in this plan I allow for sky-scrappers at intervals of 400 yards and for blocks of dwellings with 'set-backs'. The magnification of the site unit is in proportion to the evolution that has taken place and to the means at our disposal.

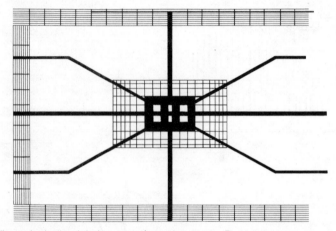

A diagram showing the relative importance of streets in a great city. The black lines give the width of the streets. This system, which indicates what is needed under the new conditions, is absolutely contrary to the present state of things (see the diagram at the beginning of this chapter).

Our car has left the elevated track and has dropped its speed of sixty miles an hour to run gently through the residential quarters. The 'set-backs' permit of vast architectural perspectives. There are gardens, games and sports grounds. And sky everywhere, as far as the eye can see. The square silhouettes of the terraced roofs stand clear against the sky, bordered with the verdure of the hanging gardens. The uniformity of the units that compose the picture throw into relief the firm lines on which the far-flung masses are constructed. Their outlines softened by distance, the sky-scrapers raise immense geometrical façades all of glass, and in them is reflected the blue glory of the sky. An overwhelming sensation. Immense but radiant prisms.

42

And in every direction we have a varying spectacle: our 'gridiron' is based on a unit of 400 yards, but it is strangely modified by architectural devices! (The 'set-backs' are in counterpoint, on a unit of 600 × 400.)

The traveller in his airplane, arriving from Constantinople or Pekin it may be, suddenly sees appearing through the wavering lines of rivers and patches of forests that clear imprint which marks a city which has grown in accordance with the spirit of man: the mark of the human brain at work.

As twilight falls the glass sky-scrapers seem to flame.

This is no dangerous futurism, a sort of literary dynamite flung violently at the spectator. It is a spectacle organized by an Architecture which uses plastic resources for the modulation of forms seen in light.

# 1.5 City of the Future *Frank Lloyd Wright*

In the City of Yesterday ground space was reckoned by the square foot. In the City of Tomorrow ground space will be reckoned by the acre: an acre to the family. This seems a modest minimum if we consider that if all the inhabitants of the world were to stand upright together they would scarcely occupy the island of Bermuda. And reflect that in these United States there are more than 57 acres of land, each, for every man, woman and child within its borders.

On this basis of an acre to the family architecture would come again into the service, not of the landlord, but of the man himself as an organic feature of his own ground. Architecture would no longer be merely adapted, commercialized space to be sold and resold by taximeter—no more standing room than competition demands.

Ground space is the essential basis of the new city of a new life.

\*

The present form of the motor car is crude and imitative compared with the varied forms of fleet and beautiful machines which manufacturers will soon be inclined, or compelled, to make.

The flying machine is still a more or less extravagant experimental form, unwieldy in scale; and with its exaggerated wings imitating a bird it is yet a hostage that gives itself to the mercy of the elements. No more than a primitive step in evolution.

*Source:* Frank Lloyd Wright, *Disappearing City*, 1932, W. F. Payson

Teletransmissions of sight and sound, too, are not only experimental but are in their infancy, as is the intelligence to which their operation is entrusted.

We are justly proud of the great network of highways, the hardroads systems of the country. But they too are in their infancy. We are only just beginning to build them.

Young as the highway system is, however, it requires but little imagination to see in the great highway, and in the power of all these new resources of machines and materials, a new physical release of human activity within reach of everyone . . . not only as adventure and romance with nature, but as a basis for safer, saner, less anxious life for a dignified and free people. A longer, happier life waits, naturally, upon this changed sense of a changed space relationship.

Any man once square with his own acre or so of ground is sure of a living for himself and his family, and sure of some invigorating association with beauty. Not only is the city itself a stricture, a handicap in production: the contributing railroad itself is too limited in movement, too expensively clumsy and too slow in operation. The end of the day of the long or short back and forth haul demanded by centralization is in sight. The end, too, of mass transport by iron rail.

Imagine spacious landscaped highways, grade crossings eliminated, 'by passing' living areas, devoid of the already archaic telegraph and telephone poles and wires, free of blaring bill boards and obsolete construction. Imagine these great highways, safe in width and grade, bright with wayside flowers, cool with shade trees, joined at intervals with fields from which the safe, noiseless transport planes take off and land. Giant roads, themselves great architecture, pass public service stations, no longer eyesores, expanded to include all kinds of service and comfort. They unite and separate—separate and unite the series of diversified units, the farm units, the factory units, the roadside markets, the garden schools, the dwelling places (each on its acre of individually adorned and cultivated ground), the places for pleasure and leisure. And all of these units arranged and integrated so that each citizen of the future will have all forms of production, distribution, self improvement, enjoyment, within a radius of a hundred and fifty miles of his home now easily and speedily available by means of his car or his plane. This integral whole composes the great city that I see embracing all of this country—the Broadacre City of tomorrow.

When every man shall own his own acre of ground then architecture shall become the servant of man. It will create appropriate new buildings in harmony not only with the ground but with the pattern of the personal life of the individual. No two homes, no two gardens, none of the three to ten acre farm units, no two factory buildings, need be alike. There need be no special 'styles,' but style everywhere.

Light, strong houses and workplaces will be solidly and sympathetic- ally built out of the nature of the ground into sunlight. Factory workers will live on acre home units within walking distance or a short ride away from the future factories. Factories beautiful, smokeless and noise- less. No longer will the farmer envy the urban dweller his mechanical improvements while the latter in turn covets the farmer's 'green pastures.'

Each factory and farm would be within a ten mile radius of a vast and variegated wayside market, so that each can serve the other simply and effectively and both can serve that other portion of the population which lives and works in the neighborhood of that market. No longer will any need exist for futile racing to a common center and racing back again, crucifying life just to keep things piled up and 'big.'

Without air, sunlight, and land, human life cannot go on. Recognizing this principle, as we are all beginning to do, the home life of tomorrow will conform. It will eliminate no modern comforts, yet it will keep the age-less healthgiving comforts too. Steel and glass will be called in to fulfill their own—steel for strength, durability and lightness; translucent glass, enclosing interior space would give privacy yet make of living in a house a delightful association with sun, with sky, with surrounding gardens. The home would be an indoor garden the garden an outdoor house.

Tall buildings are not barred, but having no interior courts, they must stand free in natural parks. A 'co-operative' apartment house might be eighteen stories, perhaps: tier on tier of immense glass screen-walls golden with sun, or shining steel or copper-sheathed frames, each tier with its flower and vine-festooned balcony terrace, an iridescence of vivid color, the whole standing in generously parked and blossoming grounds.

The principles of architecture are simply the principles of life. Just as a house built on makeshift foundations cannot stand, so life set on makeshift character in a makeshift country cannot endure. Good and lasting architecture gives or concedes the right to all of us to live abun- dantly in the exuberance that is beauty—in the sense that William Blake defined exuberance. He did not mean excess. He meant according to nature, without stint. A good and lasting life must yield that right to all of us. And the only secure foundation for such life is enlightened human character, which will understandingly accept and not merely ape the organic relation between the welfare of one and the welfare of the whole. Only that sort of character is fit for and able to create a permanent and universal well being.

And good architecture and the civilized architect of the future are necessarily modern, because life itself continually changes and new forms of building are needed to contain and express it sincerely without waste, and loving beauty.

To put it concretely again, architectural values are human values or they are not valuable. Human values are life giving, not life taking. When a man is content to build for himself alone taking the natural rights of life, breadth and light and space away from his neighbor, the result is a monstrosity like the pretentious skyscraper. It stands for a while in the business slum formed by its own greed, selfishly casting its shadow on its neighbors, only to find that it, too, is dependent upon their success and must fail with their failure.

What life has that toll-gatherer the big city to give to the worth while citizen now that the motor car stands at the door: the great, hard road systems of the country beckoning?

Voices and vision are everywhere penetrating solid walls to entertain and inform him wherever and as he goes; general and immediate distribution of everything he needs is becoming convenient to him wherever he may be. I see his buildings modern, sanitary, living conveniences, wherever he wants to be, produced as economically as his motor car— by a few hours' devotion to machinery. I see the factory too, divided and operated in humane proportions not far away from him in the country; and the time he spends now going to his office, the senseless and wasteful to and fro, he will usefully spend in his diversified modern Home. I see that home not so far away from the diversified farm units but that they may bring him, at the highway wayside markets, as he passes, food, fresh every hour.

I can see 'going places' a luxury and a pleasure to him and to his; and beautiful places to which he can go. I see his children going to small and smaller individual garden schools in parks that are playgrounds as their parents live individual lives that enrich the communal life by the very quality of its individuality in a beauty of life that is appropriate luxury and superior common sense.

Transport, buildings, all life spaciously intimate with the ground, all appropriate to each other and life to each and every man according to his nature or his need and love of life. Woods, streams, mountains, ranges of hills, the great plains—all are shrines, beauty to be preserved. Architecture and acreage seen as landscape.

*

Trained imagination and true thought are our human divinity. These alone may distinguish the human herd and save it from the fate that has overtaken all other herds, human or animal. All this leads to the realization of a new civilization with an architecture of its own, which will make the machine its slave and create nobler longings for mankind.

# 1.6 Social Cities *Ebenezer Howard*

'Human nature will not flourish, any more than a potato, if it be planted and replanted for too long a series of generations in the same worn-out soil. My children have had other birthplaces, and, so far as their fortunes may be within my control, shall strike their roots into unaccustomed earth.' NATHANIEL HAWTHORNE, *The Scarlet Letter*.

'The question which now interests people is, What are we going to do with democracy now that we have got it? What kind of society are we going to make by its aid? Are we to see nothing but an endless vista of Londons and Manchesters, New Yorks and Chicagos, with their noise and ugliness, their money-getting, their 'corners' and 'rings', their strikes, their contrasts of luxury and squalor? Or shall we be able to build up a society with art and culture for all, and with some great spiritual aim dominating men's lives?' *Daily Chronicle*, 4 March 1891.

The problem with which we have now to deal, shortly stated, is this: How to make our Garden City experiment the stepping stone to a higher and better form of industrial life generally throughout the country. Granted the success of the initial experiment, and there must inevitably arise a widespread demand for an extension of methods so healthy and so advantageous; and it will be well, therefore, to consider some of the chief problems which will have to be faced in the progress of such extension.

Let me here introduce a very rough diagram, representing, as I conceive, the true principle on which all towns should grow. Garden City has, we will suppose, grown until it has reached a population of 32 000. How shall it grow? How shall it provide for the needs of others who will be attracted by its numerous advantages? Shall it build on the zone of agricultural land which is around it, and thus for ever destroy its right to be called a 'Garden City'? Surely not. This disastrous result would indeed take place if the land around the town were, as is the land around our present cities, owned by private individuals anxious to make a profit out of it. For then, as the town filled up, the agricultural

*Source:* E. Howard, *Garden Cities of Tomorrow*, Faber, 1965, pages 138–147

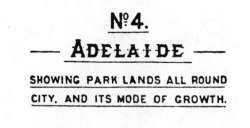

*Adelaide and its lands*

48

land would become 'ripe' for building purposes, and the beauty and healthfulness of the town would be quickly destroyed. But the land around Garden City is, fortunately, not in the hands of private individuals: it is in the hands of the people: and is to be administered, not in the supposed interests of the few, but in the real interests of the whole community. Now, there are few objects which the people so jealously guard as their parks and open spaces; and we may, I think, feel confident that the people of Garden City will not for a moment permit the beauty of their city to be destroyed by the process of growth. But it may be urged—if this be true, will not the inhabitants of Garden City in this way be selfishly preventing the growth of their city, and thus preclude many from enjoying its advantages? Certainly not. There is a bright, but overlooked, alternative. The town *will* grow; but it will grow in accordance with a principle which will result in this—that such growth shall not lessen or destroy, but ever add to its social opportunities, to its beauty, to its convenience. Consider for a moment the case of a city in Australia which in some measure illustrates the principle for which I am contending. The city of Adelaide, as the accompanying sketch map shows, is surrounded by its 'Park Lands'. The city is built up. How does it grow? It grows by leaping over the 'Park Lands' and establishing North Adelaide. And this is the principle which it is intended to follow, but improve upon, in Garden City.

Our diagram may now be understood. Garden City is built up. Its population has reached 32 000. How will it grow? It will grow by establishing—under Parliamentary powers probably—another city some little distance beyond its own zone of 'country', so that the new town may have a zone of country of its own. I have said 'by establishing another city', and, for administrative purposes there would be *two* cities; but the inhabitants of the one could reach the other in a very few minutes; for rapid transit would be specially provided for, and thus the people of the two towns would in reality represent one community.

And this principle of growth—this principle of always preserving a belt of country round our cities would be ever kept in mind till, in course of time, we should have a cluster of cities, not of course arranged in the precise geometrical form of my diagram, but so grouped around a Central City that each inhabitant of the whole group, though in one sense living in a town of small size, would be in reality living in, and would enjoy all the advantages of, a great and most beautiful city; and yet all the fresh delights of the country—field, hedgerow, and woodland—not prim parks and gardens merely—would be within a very few minutes' walk or ride. And *because the people in their collective capacity own the land* on which this beautiful group of cities is built, the public buildings, the churches, the schools and universities, the libraries, picture galleries, theatres, would be on a scale of magnificence which

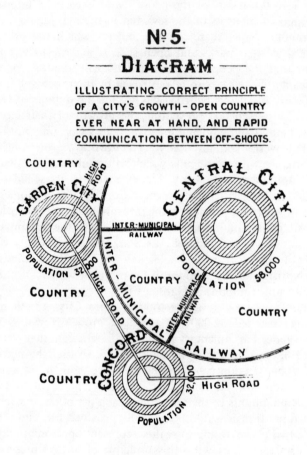

# Nº 5.

## — DIAGRAM —

ILLUSTRATING CORRECT PRINCIPLE
OF A CITY'S GROWTH – OPEN COUNTRY
EVER NEAR AT HAND, AND RAPID
COMMUNICATION BETWEEN OFF-SHOOTS.

*Correct principle of a city's growth*

50

no city in the world whose land is in pawn to private individuals can afford.

I have said that rapid railway transit would be realized by those who dwell in this beautiful city or group of cities. Reference to the diagram will show at a glance the main features of its railway system. There is, first, an inter-municipal railway, connecting all the towns of the outer ring—twenty miles in circumference—so that to get from any town to its most distant neighbour requires one to cover a distance of only ten miles, which could be accomplished in, say, twelve minutes. These trains would not stop between the towns—means of communication for this purpose being afforded by electric tramways which traverse the high roads, of which, it will be seen, there are a number—each town being connected with every other town in the group by a direct route.

There is also a system of railways by which each town is placed in direct communication with Central City. The distance from any town to the heart of Central City is only three and a quarter miles, and this could be readily covered in five minutes.

We should then be, for all purposes of quick communication, nearer to each other than we are in our crowded cities, while, at the same time, we should be surrounding ourselves with the most healthy and the most advantageous conditions.

Some of my friends have suggested that such a scheme of town clusters is well enough adapted to a new country, but that in an old-settled country, with its towns built, and its railway 'system' for the most part constructed, it is quite a different matter. But surely to raise such a point is to contend, in other words, that the existing wealth forms of the country are permanent, and are forever to serve as hindrances to the introduction of better forms: that crowded, ill-ventilated, unplanned, unwieldy, unhealthy cities—ulcers on the very face of our beautiful island—are to stand as barriers to the introduction of towns in which modern scientific methods and the aims of social reformers may have the fullest scope in which to express themselves. No, it cannot be; at least, it cannot be for long. What Is may hinder What Might Be for a while, but cannot stay the tide of progress. These crowded cities have done their work; they were the best which a society largely based on selfishness and rapacity could construct, but they are in the nature of things entirely unadapted for a society in which the social side of our nature is demanding a larger share of recognition—a society where even the very love of self leads us to insist upon a greater regard for the well-being of our fellows. The large cities of today are scarcely better adapted for the expression of the fraternal spirit than would a work on astronomy which taught that the earth was the centre of the universe be capable of adaptation for use in our schools. Each generation should build to suit its own needs; and it is no more in the nature of things that men should continue to live in old areas because their ancestors lived in them, than it is that they should cherish the old beliefs which a wider faith and a more enlarged understanding have outgrown. The reader is, therefore, earnestly asked not to take it for granted that the large cities in which he may perhaps take a pardonable pride are necessarily, in their present form, any more permanent than the stage-coach system which was the subject of so much admiration just at the very moment when it was about to be supplanted by the railways. The simple issue to be faced, and faced resolutely, is: Can better results be obtained by starting on a bold plan on comparatively virgin soil than by attempting to adapt our old cities to our newer and higher needs? Thus fairly faced, the question can only be answered in one way; and when that simple fact is well grasped, the social revolution will speedily commence.

That there is ample land in this country on which such a cluster as I have here depicted could be constructed with *comparatively* small disturbance of vested interests, and, therefore, with but little need for compensation, will be obvious to anyone; and, when our first experiment has been brought to a successful issue, there will be no great difficulty in acquiring the necessary Parliamentary powers to purchase the land and carry out the necessary works step by step. County Councils are now seeking larger powers, and an overburdened Parliament is becoming more and more anxious to devolve some of its duties upon them. Let such powers be given more and more freely. Let larger and yet larger measures of local self-government be granted, and then all that my diagram depicts—only on a far better plan, because the result of well-concerted and combined thought—will be easily attainable.

# 2. Trends and Constraints

## Introduction *by Chris Hamnett*

Cities are not isolated phenomena, distinct from and independent of the larger society. Instead, they are always embedded in specific societal contexts. These societal contexts determine, in large part, the nature of cities within any given society: their organization, functions, and form. This is as true of contemporary Los Angeles as it was of the cities of Renaissance Italy or those of the Tigris—Euphrates in 5000 B.C., despite the change in contexts. Just as we are unlikely to understand the nature of the future city without knowledge of its context, so too we are unlikely to be able to speculate on the nature of the future city if we have no knowledge of the changing trends and constraints occurring within society.

As the general introduction pointed out, however, the future has to be approached through an iterative procedure in which goals and forecasts are alternated. It is this process that led de Jouvenel to distinguish between primary and secondary forecasts. Forecasting, however, can never be wholly scientific. Indeed, in de Jouvenel's opinion, as hypotheses concerning the future are incapable of prior empirical verification, then *knowledge* of the future is a contradiction in terms. All we are left with is de Jouvenel's *Art of Conjecture*. This is not a mandate for lack of rigour, however, and all forecasters should endeavour to lay bare the intellectual and factual scaffolding upon which their forecasts are based.

The most basic and most important trends are social ones, and it is here that the problems of forecasting are most severe given the variability of human behaviour and attitudes. Willmott's paper meets these difficulties head on as the areas he deals with and the wealth of references indicate. It begins by examining the paradox of change within stability, especially where occupational structure, social class, education and standards of living are concerned, and then moves via an examination of changing patterns of family size and organization, to a consideration of the growing importance of leisure time and leisure activities.

One of the more obvious implications of increased leisure is a marked rise in personal mobility. Although the prediction of future car ownership in the extract on the 'Future of the Motor Vehicle' from *Traffic in*

*Towns* are based on the extrapolation of current trends, they rest upon a more sophisticated basis which de Jouvenel terms causality: that is, the isolation of a continuing cause and the specification of its necessary effect. The continuing causes in this case are the advantages conferred by private car ownership such as independence, door-to-door travel, and total route specification. The car opens up the possibilities of greater urban dispersal, and the destruction of many of the essential qualities of our towns and cities. The extract poses certain value judgements on the desirability of the predicted state of affairs if nothing were done to halt it.

Whyte's paper poses no such judgements, but instead sets out to specify a series of important questions concerning the relationship between developments in telecommunications, urban form and dispersal.

The extract from Greer's book both synthesises and develops upon some of the trends discussed in preceding extracts. Looking at both life styles and modes of social organization, he stresses the development of activity based rather on locality based groups. His main concern is to evaluate to what extent the traditional city—in terms of both organization and form—is breaking down in the face of a new emerging order.

It is inevitable that papers whose main focus is on trends will stress the rate of change. It is imperative, however, to examine the influence of constraints upon change, as it is the interplay between the two that, along with the goals we choose and the values we hold, will shape the urban future. The following three papers look at constraints and individual and social requirements at successively larger scales and with increasingly broad perspectives. Stone's paper focuses on the economic and resource constraints upon the built environment. From the starting point that the 'total requirements for the built environment depend basically upon the size and structure of the population and on its activities', Stone examines both population variables such as rates of household formation, and physical variables such as rates of output, demolition and decay. He is then able to examine, by relating these changes to the existing housing stock and to the costs and effects of different rates of maintenance and improvement, the implications for the built environment of changes in life styles, incomes and requirements.

In contrast to most of the papers in this volume which relate to advanced western capitalist societies, Meier's paper concentrates on the material resources required for the development of the less developed nations. The path he advocates of 'resource conserving urbanism' is based on the dual forecasts of a shortage of material resources in the less developed nations, and the steadily declining cost of communication, information and technological know-how. In Meier's view the latter must be substituted for the former, and this can only be done at present in urban environments.

Meier is not particularly concerned with the quality of the urban environment, and in this respect the extract by Ward and Dubos represents a concern peculiar to advanced countries at present. This is not to deny the importance of higher human needs and the extent to which they are met by the urban environment, however. Indeed the concerns both for environment and a just distribution of income and resources are likely to predominate in discussions on the future city for many years to come. Many of the problems we face stem, according to Ward and Dubos, from a lack of planning and the dominance of private economic motives. They conclude a brief empirical study of different planning approaches to urban problems with the words: 'None of the plans is perfect, almost any is better than no plan at all'.


# 2.1 Some Social Trends *Peter Willmott*


The purpose of this paper is to discuss some of the ways in which the social structure of Britain and the patterns of social life are likely to develop during the next two or three decades. What has been happening in the past is obviously one guide to what is likely to happen in the future and the paper, taking this as its starting-point, begins by discussing past and present trends in the occupational structure and in social class. It then examines in particular the suggestion that the social class structure is fundamentally changing—that 'we are all middle class now' and likely to become even more so in the future. This is followed by a discussion of some trends in social relationships and behaviour, first in family life and secondly in social life outside the family. Finally, some of the major questions are posed and some suggestions offered on research priorities.

If one looks to the past for guidance and asks how British society has changed since, say, 1900, one comes face to face with a paradox. Put simply, it is that the social structure seems both to have changed radically and not to have changed very much.* This is particularly true of the occupational structure and social class.

*Occupations and mobility*

The stereotype of what has happened to the British occupational

Source: *Urban Studies*, **6**, Number 3, 1969, pages 286–308
*Tom Harrisson (1961, pages 25–45) describes his impression, in comparing the Bolton of 1960 with that of 1936, of how much 'unchange' was mixed with 'change'.

structure since about 1900 is something like this: it has altered dramatically, particularly since 1945, the main changes being major shifts from unskilled to skilled occupations and from manual to clerical, with a large increase also in the professions and management.

In fact, as Routh (1965) shows in his *Occupation and Pay in Great Britain 1906–1960*, the trends are much less dramatic than they are commonly thought. The proportion of clerical workers among working men, for instance, was 5% in 1911 and 6% in 1951. The proportion of professional men was 3% in 1911, 6% in 1951. The comparable figures for unskilled male manual workers were 12% in 1911, 14% in 1951. In 1961 workers in 'manual' occupations, both men and women, still accounted for two-thirds of all the employed people in the United Kingdom.

Of course, there have been important changes in the economy. One is the entry of women into the labour force and the extent of the shift among them, much more marked than among men, from manual to clerical work. There have also been major changes, among men as well as women, between industries—notably the movement from agriculture, mining and textiles to new light industries, and the switch from manufacturing to services.

There is also some evidence that, despite the relatively slow rate of change until recently, the process may have speeded up quite sharply between 1951 and 1961. (*Manpower Studies*, Number 6, HMSO, 1967.) In particular, the proportion of scientists, engineers and technologists in the United Kingdom increased by 56% over that decade, and that of industrial technicians by 67%. Between them, however, they still amounted to less than 3% of the total labour force in 1961.

To the occupational changes already mentioned, others could be added. Manual work has, on the whole, become lighter, hours shorter, working conditions better and the structure of authority at work less oppressive. But in many respects the fundamental occupational structure seems relatively unchanged, especially for men. We may, as is sometimes suggested, be on the brink of major changes in technology that will radically transform that structure. All one can say is that the experience of the past 50 years or so should encourage caution.*

Another common assumption is that there is now much more movement across occupational strata from one generation to the next—that more sons of carpenters and dockers than in the past become managers and surgeons. The latest figures on this are not very up to date; they come from the study in 1949 by Glass (Glass, editor, 1954) and his colleagues at the London School of Economics, whose findings were

---

*The American experience so far seems to suggest that the likely effects of automation have been exaggerated. See Daniel Bell (Bell, 1967, page 676) particularly the reference to the President's Commission on Technology, Automation and Economic Progress.

published in 1954. This study showed virtually no change, as compared with the end of the last century, in the extent of inter-generational mobility in Britain. As Glass put it, the general picture was of 'rather high stability over time'. A review by Lipset and Bendix (1959, pages 33–38), drawing on historical data from a number of other industrial countries, also found little change over a period of about 40 years. A more recent study of American society, by Blau and Duncan (1967, page 424), came to the same general conclusion. With occupational mobility, as with the broad occupational structure, the main impression is therefore that society has changed less than is commonly supposed.

## Education and wealth

At first sight, education presents a different picture. For one thing, there is clearly more of it. The proportion of 14 year olds at school in England and Wales was 9% in 1902 and 30% in 1938. By 1954, 32% of 15 year olds were at school and ten years later 59%. The proportion aged 15 to 19 in grant-aided schools went up from 10% in 1956 to 19% in 1967 (Kaim-Caudle, 1969, pages 28–29). The numbers in full-time education in England and Wales have more than trebled in the past 20 years and nearly doubled in the last ten alone.

All this does not of course necessarily mean that working-class children are now getting a larger *share* of university places. What has apparently happened is that working and middle classes alike are benefiting from university expansion; their relative shares are, or at any rate were at the beginning of the 1960s, similar to what they used to be in earlier periods. The Robbins Report showed that, of 18 year olds from non-manual homes, 8·9% entered university in 1928 to 1947 and 16·8% in 1960; from manual homes, 1·4% of the 18 year olds entered in 1928 to 1947 and 2·6% in 1960 (*Higher Education*, HMSO, 1963, page 54). While later figures would show higher proportions for both, there is no reason to think that the relative shares have changed.

In other words, despite the changes, the divisions of social class are still formidable. It is, as far as one can judge, much the same with wealth and income. Meade has shown that there has been little change in the distribution of wealth in Britain: the proportion of total personal wealth owned by the richest 5% was 79% in 1936–38 and 75% in 1960 (Meade, 1964, page 27). On incomes, the changes are more difficult to trace. But Routh shows that there was little change between 1911–12 and 1958–59 in the share of incomes, both before and after tax, by the different occupational strata (Routh, 1965). Nicholson's study suggests little radical change in the distribution of income over recent years (Nicholson, 1964; Hughes, 1968). Furthermore, Titmuss has pointed out that 'fringe' benefits—firm's cars, housing, school fees, pensions, etc.—

ought to be taken into account, and that if they were the better off would undoubtedly be shown to benefit most from them (Titmuss, 1962, chapter 8).

These facts point to two general impressions about the last half century. The first is that, despite some changes, the social structure has in some of the essentials remained extraordinarily constant. The second is that this is particularly true in terms of social class.

## The other side

That is only part of the story. If one looks at it the other way round and asks how people's day-to-day lives have changed, the impression is utterly different. As is well known, living standards have risen. Mass production has put into the hands of the many what were formerly the privileges of the few. Social policy has plainly helped as well; the 'price' of primary and secondary education and that of health services have been fixed at zero, and social security has aided the poorest.

As a result of all this there has undoubtedly been some 'convergence' in tastes, consumption and behaviour within British society. There has also been an improvement in the social status of manual workers and their families.* And there is a ring of truth in Marshall's suggestion that social inequality has been reduced over the past three centuries by the spread of 'citizenship' among the social classes, characteristically through 'civil rights' in the eighteenth century, 'political rights' in the nineteenth and 'social rights' in the twentieth (Marshall, 1950, chapter 1).

This then is the paradox—the mixture of change and 'unchange' in the British social structure, particularly in terms of social class. How is one to reconcile these apparently contradictory trends and not only make sense of what has happened but, more relevant, make sound judgements about what may happen over the next two or three decades?

Clearly both sets of trends are likely to continue. First, despite the current economic setbacks, we are likely to get richer and, compound growth being what it is, at an accelerating rate. As Abrams (1968b, page 37) has put it, in stating the first of his 'assumptions' about consumption in the year 2000:

> . . . it is assumed that the average standard of living in Britain will be substantially higher in the year 2000 than it is in 1967; reasonably, it may be double; and, very optimistically it may have trebled. Within these limits the precise measure of growth, however, is not important; whatever the rate of increase, the broad mass of the population at the end of the century will have incomes that today are enjoyed by only a minority of richer households.

*W. G. Runciman (1966) reviewing changes in class, status and power in Britain from 1918 to 1962 concluded that 'inequality of status (i.e. prestige) was diminishing'.

That is an assumption that this paper makes also. Yet the relative shares of wealth and income by different sections of the population are unlikely to change fundamentally. In other words, though all will be richer, 'inequality' will not be reduced; indeed it may well increase. Meade demonstrates convincingly that there is a fundamental conflict between economic efficiency and what he calls 'distributional justice' (Meade, 1964; Hughs, 1968) the greater the emphasis on economic growth therefore—and it is likely to dominate national policy in the decades ahead as much as in the recent past—the greater the pressures towards economic inequality. For this reason, another of Abrams's 'assumptions' seems more questionable than the one already quoted. This second 'assumption' is that in the year 2000 'the distribution of net personal total incomes will be more equal than it is today' (Abrams, 1968b).

Enough has been said to show that it would be a mistake to assume this. The example brings into sharp focus the two contradictory elements—the trend towards some sort of social equality and cultural homogeneity, and the tendency for many of the essentials of the British social structure to stay as they are. With this theme in mind, the paper now looks in more detail at some emerging social patterns.

## Economic growth and standards of living

First, a closer look at what has happened to standards of living. As is well known, Britain's Gross National Product has been increasing, with some short-term ups and downs, since the 1880's. Real incomes have risen at the same time. Consumer spending has been increasing at least since 1900/05 and particularly since 1945; it rose by over a fifth between 1950 and 1960 (Rowe, 1965).

The biggest proportionate increases in consumer spending since 1900 have been in 'transport' and 'entertainment', Spending on most other things has increased too. More and more working-class families have bought, as well as cars, household equipment like washing machines, refrigerators and television sets. This is especially noticeable with housing. More working-class people live in modern homes; a quarter of our housing stock has been built since 1945. More own their homes: Donnison, using data from surveys in 1958 and 1962, has shown how much home-ownership increased over those four years alone. The proportion of skilled manual workers owning or buying their own houses went up from 33% to 39%, and of unskilled and semi-skilled from 20% to 26% (Donnison, 1967).

It seems reasonable to assume that this process will continue—that the Gross National Product will rise and, with it, household incomes and living standards. As a broad guide one can accept Abrams's suggestion, referred to earlier, that the average standard of living is likely to rise by the year 2000 to somewhere between double and treble what it is now.

Past experience seems a fairly good pointer to the main ways in which the extra consumers' income will be spent. The 130-year-old dictum described by Bell as 'Tocqueville's Law'—'What the few have today, the many will demand tomorrow'* seems to have been largely borne out by events. Though of course an over-simplification, it has proved not at all a bad general indication of likely future trends in consumption and patterns of life.

Thus many features of what is now middle-class life are likely to spread. More cars, more household equipment, more suburban-style homes and communities would not surprise anyone. Modern societies (perhaps to some extent all societies) seem to be characterised by a continuing process of 'diffusion', by which some values and patterns of behaviour percolate 'downwards' through the social strata.

It seems that diffusion is a cumulative process; that acquiring, for example, a car or a house of one's own can lead to changes in behaviour. Thus a working-class man living with his family in a 'semi' in the suburbs is more likely to live like his middle-class neighbour than like a man who is his neighbour only at work and still lives in an Islington slum. A Stevenage capstan operator with a Cortina is likely to use his car for shopping, for holidays, for family visits and Sunday 'drives into the country', and from the side of the road at any rate is indistinguishable from his white-collar counterpart in Hertford or Hitchin. As more manual workers own homes and cars, people's patterns of life will merge further.

The process is surely encouraged by TV and the other mass media which, whatever one's final judgement about their influence for good or evil, help to make for cultural homogeneity, by bringing the same models of behaviour into the homes of people in all strata. We increasingly share in a broad national, in some respects international, culture— the 'global village'. It is a matter for speculation how far regional, local and class sub-cultures can continue to survive in such a setting, and how far we can preserve 'pluralism', the 'diversity within unity' that seems so desirable. It is possible that the recent upsurge of Celtic nationalism represents some sort of reaction against the growth of cultural uniformity, and in that sense testifies to the extent to which cultural homogeneity has already taken hold. There are, of course, still important variations in behaviour, in values and in tastes, not only as between different occupational or economic strata and different kinds of people within them but also as between the different regions of Britain (some of them striking) (Allen, 1968). In some respects, too, contemporary

*Quoted from Alexis de Tocqueville, *Democracy in America*, by Daniel Bell (1967).

British society encompasses more 'deviance' and more variety than in the past. At the same time the general trend is clearly towards a broad homogeneity, over the great majority of the population, in consumption patterns and in social behaviour.

## Social class and life-styles

How can these suggestions be reconciled with the warning earlier— that in many fundamental ways the social structure remains unchanged? The key seems to lie in a distinction, first made by Weber, between people's situation in the economic structure and their 'style of life', reflecting their consumption standards and social patterns outside work (Gerth and Mills, 1948).

The difference between the work situations of manual workers and others is marked, and this difference affects values and behaviour. A study in Luton by Lockwood and his colleagues found, for instance, that most manual workers recognised that their prospects of personal advancement in their work (i.e. of promotion) were negligible (Goldthorpe *et al.*, 1969). Manual workers know that almost their only hope of economic advance is in the company of their fellows. Since they are paid by the week or hour, their security is limited. The middle-class man can with more justification see his job as a career-ladder up which, if all goes well, he will climb as he gets older, and he usually gets more 'satisfaction' from his work. The working-class man, may or may not like work; either way he sees it mainly as a means of earning a living. To the middle-class man work, or advancement in work, is more often the 'central life interest', to borrow Dubin's (1956) phrase.

There are a number of other related differences. Working-class people, for obvious reasons deriving from their work situation, are disposed to collective rather than individual action to achieve economic advance (Goldthorpe *et al.*, 1967, pages 19–20). Similarly, the attitude of most working-class men to politics seems relatively 'traditional', tied to class attitudes (Goldthorpe *et al.*, 1968).

There is some evidence, too, that the working-class view of leisure is rather different from the middle-class. Here it seems that the gap between the classes may in some respect be widening. Reisman has suggested that some members of the middle class, particularly professional people, increasingly see their leisure as 'instrumental'; for example, they use their social life to promote contacts with colleagues and professional clients, or they read the newspapers with an eye to their work interests. Manual workers, by contrast, are said increasingly to separate work and leisure (Reisman, 1958). Nevertheless, as is shown later, what people actually *do* in their leisure seems to vary less, and many middle-class patterns of leisure behaviour are likely to spread.

In some other aspects of social life there are still sharp class differences. In the old districts the familiar working-class attachments to kinship and neighbourhood die hard (Jennings, 1962; Rosser and Harris, 1965) and even in the new areas substantial elements of the old life survive or are re-established (Berger, 1960; Willmott, 1963; Gans, 1967). As the Luton Study shows working-class people also remain unlike middle-class for instance in belonging less often to formal organisations. In particular they certainly do not 'become middle-class' in the sense of mixing with white-collar workers (Goldthorpe *et al.*, 1967). Our own study in Woodford even suggested that in a suburb where there was a growing homogeneity of life-styles, the middle-class residents were increasingly inclined to lay emphasis on the small social differences that distinguished them from their working-class neighbours (Willmott and Young, 1960).

## Merging of social classes

To sum up so far, it is clear that in some respects the classes are 'merging' but also that there are limits to the process. In general, life outside work has changed more than life inside it. Diffusion, it seems, is more likely to occur with consumption patterns than with basic values linked to political attitudes or class loyalties.

The limits to the process of class 'merging' have been noted and are obviously substantial. It would clearly be wrong to talk as if the working class was near to extinction. Even more important, increasing affluence and 'bourgeoisification' will not in themselves eradicate poverty. First, there is the point made earlier that national emphasis on economic growth will if anything lead to a less equitable distribution of income and wealth. Secondly, even if the distribution of national income does not become less equitable, there will, as long as there are any variations in incomes, continue to be a distribution 'curve' and therefore a poorest 10% or 25%; in this sense, 'poverty' is obviously common to all industrial societies. Thirdly, even in the richest societies, some of the poorer strata remain so locked in a vicious circle of economic and social deprivation that they combine together in a 'culture' or, more correctly, 'sub-culture of poverty'; they thus remain in important senses excluded from the national society. It seems that in certain conditions economic expansion, far from reducing this sense of exclusion, may actually sharpen it and thus deepen social divisions.

We do not know whether the sense of 'relative deprivation' will grow. It certainly does not seem strong in British society at present. Reporting his 1962 survey, Runciman said: 'On the evidence of this question, relative deprivation is low in both magnitude and scope even among those who are close to the bottom of the hierarchy of economic class' (Runciman, 1966). But this may change with increasing cultural homogeneity and with increasing emphasis upon economic prosperity, national and personal, as the key index of achievement.

There are minorities of colour as well as of income. Again nobody can predict with any confidence whether the coloured minorities will, as they improve their lot, actually become more embittered about what they lack because of their skin colour—as has happened in the United States. Nor whether the same improvements may not sharpen the sense of 'relative deprivation' on the part of poor whites. What does seem likely is that the two linked problems of poverty and colour will continue and questions of income distribution and differential opportunity grow in importance at the same time as living standards rise generally.

## Family and Home

The paper now looks more closely at some particularly important changes in patterns of behaviour. First, the family. The kind of diffusion mentioned earlier affects the family as it does other social institutions. Despite the continuing role of kinship, there is increasing stress upon the immediate family and particularly the husband-wife relationship. The shift is from the 'consanguine' family, emphasising ties of kinship, to the 'conjugal', emphasising the husband-wife bond. It is clear that this pattern is becoming increasingly dominant, spreading 'downwards' from the middle class inside each country and from the richer to the poorer countries, as part of the growing 'Westernisation' of the world (Goode, 1963; Blisten, 1963).

One of the most striking trends in Britain, as in much of the rest of the world, is the growing popularity of family life. In the 1920's about 80% of women could expect eventually to marry (Cox, 1951); now the proportion is 95% (Registrar General, 1967, page 31). Marriages also now start at an earlier age: among women aged 20 to 24, in 1921 27% were married; in 1961 58%. Because of the longer expectation of life, marriages end later as well.

The change in the 'life-cycle' of marriage is shown in Table 1 (this is based upon assessments of the available demographic data, which are not all that one would like).*

These figures show a transformation in marriage. Marriages start earlier, as noted above, and last longer. The 'average' marriage, if wives outlived their husbands, lasted 28 years in 1911 and 42 years in 1967. If one assumes that children cease to be fully dependent at 15, then the period when the couple are largely alone has changed even more— from five years in 1911 to 23 years in 1967. The figures indicate that, in contrast with the earlier period, about as much of a couple's family

*These calculations were kindly made by P. R. Cox.

*Table 1*

Family Life-Cycle 'Profile' for Women
England and Wales, 1911, 1951 and 1967

|                                        | 1911 | 1951 | 1967 |
|----------------------------------------|------|------|------|
| Women's mean age at first marriage     | 26   | 25   | 23   |
| Women's mean age when last child born  | 34   | 28   | 27   |
| Women's mean age at husband's death    | 54   | 63   | 65   |
| Women's mean age at death as a widow   | 73   | 78   | 80   |

life is now spent without dependent children* as with.

Some years ago Titmuss, using rather different calculations, pointed out the implications of this change for the status of women (Titmuss, 1958), and the effect is shown in the change in the employment of married women, which has been touched on earlier. The proportions of wives working has gone up in Britain from 9% in 1921 (quoted in S. R. Parker *et al.*, 1967, page 50) to 27% in 1951 and again to 40% in 1966 (Stewart, 1969). The biggest increase has been among wives aged 35 to 44.

This means, for an increasing proportion, a different sort of marriage and a different sort of family life. Instead of the husband going away for long hours at work, leaving the wife at home with the children, more of marriage involves their both going out of the home (the wife for at least some of the time), working together in the home and sharing their leisure time together (Rapoport, 1967). The demographic change is an expression of the growth of partnership in marriage and has also helped to encourage it.

The partnership takes three main forms. First, it is a partnership in power, with major decisions being discussed and made jointly. Secondly, it is a partnership in the division of labour within the home, as the old distinctions between men's and women's jobs (though still made) become increasingly blurred. More wives go out to work and help paint the kitchen; more husbands take the children out in the pram and help wash the nappies. Thirdly, it is a partnership in social life, with couples spending more of their free time together and with their children. One could sum up by saying that, despite the inequalities that remain between the sexes, women now have higher status, and that there is greater equality in society and in the family. Children, too, have a higher status (Young and Willmott, 1957; Zweig, 1961; Newson, 1968).

Associated with the changes in family relationships is a trend towards what has been called the 'home-centred' society (Abrams, 1959; Klein, 1965). For most families, homes are more spacious and better equipped.

*This term itself could be criticised. Since, as noted earlier, more young people stay in education until a higher age, in one sense there is a contrary trend—children are economically dependent on their parents for longer than in the past. Even so, most are socially independent, or largely so, after about 15, and, as I argue later, this is likely to continue and extend to residential independence.

More time is spent in the home and a number of trends support and encourage this. Television, for instance, means that the family can be entertained—or bored—together in the home, instead of separately in the cinema.

One general question has to be posed about this process: will the changes to family and home in fact continue along the present lines, or will the next few decades see instead a reaction against the family, as Leach has suggested? (Leach, 1968) Certainly there are likely to be some modifications. The 'Dual-Career Family', described by the Rapoports, (1969) is likely to become more common, and at the same time the demand will grow for domestic arrangements that help it, including perhaps family 'service houses' like those appearing in Denmark and Sweden. Also, as living standards rise, children are likely to withdraw from the family circle at an earlier age and in particular more young people are going to demand the residential independence that their better-off fellows already enjoy. Even inside the home, there is likely to be greater emphasis on personal privacy and individuation, which involves more space, better internal sound-proofing, personal record players, television sets and telephones.

It is possible that the family may change more dramatically, that, as Leach suggests, some variant of the Israeli kibbutz or the Chinese commune may take the place of the present form of family (Leach, 1968).

However, the present trends seem so powerful, so world-wide, that it is hard to believe that Leach is right. What seems much more likely is that, with some modification, the shift to home centredness and family-centredness will continue. The two sets of changes reinforce each other; the changes in family relationships and the shift to home-centredness increase the demand for a suitable home, and the 'home-and-garden' life further encourages home and family-centredness. More and more people will choose to take part of their higher real incomes in the form of a home of their own. More and more families will have their own swimming pools and tennis courts, garages and workshops. All in all, the next 30 years or so are likely to see an ever-growing demand from an increasing number of families for separate spacious homes with gardens and for the lives that go with them.

Yet there may be a counter-trend to urban spread. The long period that couples now have and will have without children and the increase in wives working may between them somewhat check the rush to the suburbs. For one thing, since the average married couple are spending as much of their lifetime without dependent children as with them, many may be willing as they get older to exchange their three- or four-bedroomed house with garden for a smaller dwelling. Secondly, wives who work may prefer to give up suburban life for the greater accessibility to work they can find in inner areas.

*Family size and population size*

A question mark hangs over another aspect of family structure—family size. This is important for the future of urban life. The pressures on space, described earlier, will intensify even more, particularly in the most crowded regions, if the population grows rapidly. Of the population increase from 1961 to 1981 forecast in *The South East Study* (1964, page 24) more than two-thirds was due to the growth in the Region's existing population, less than one-third to migration from other parts of the country. But population projections for the end of the century (vital as they evidently are) could well be out by many millions either way—representing an immense variation in the demand for new housing, new road systems, new amenities.

This is because population size is so difficult to predict. Mortality and even migration are relatively easy to forecast; the big unknown is the birth-rate. The post-war 'Baby Boom', at first thought to be temporary, seemed to have ended in about 1952. But the birth-rate started to rise again in 1956 and through to the early 1960's. Time and again over those years, as the latest figures for births came in, the Government Actuary had to raise his sights. Over the past two or three years, however, the birth-rate has fallen; the estimates have been revised again, this time downwards.

What nobody knows is what lies behind these variations in birth-rate, yet this is just what we need to know to improve our guesses about the future. The increase in the marriage rate and the lower marriage age, referred to earlier, are apparently part of the explanation, but only part: the Registrar General has estimated that, of the increase in legitimate births between 1955 and 1962, the increase in the number of married women accounted for 12% and earlier marriage for 21%, leaving 67% due to more births per family (Registrar General, 1964, page 50). Thus the crucial two questions remain: why have couples had more children and what is likely to happen over the coming decades? To answer the first may go some way to answering the second.

One key to the answer lies in the change in the relationship between social class and family size. In the second half of the nineteenth century, the upper and middle classes led the way in controlling conception, and for about 70 or 80 years there was a clear-cut negative correlation between social class and family size. The lower the class, the larger the family. The correlation held throughout the century because family size fell more or less proportionately in all classes.

After 1940, as the birth-rate in general showed its first real rise, a new pattern began to emerge. In Britain and in the United States, the very sections of the population who had in earlier generations limited family size most effectively now started having more children. The 1951 Census confirmed the trend and the 1961 Census suggested that certain professional groups in particular were drawing still further ahead. Thus the larger-than-average families are now to be found among the professional classes and the unskilled, among some of the richest as well as some of the poorest sections of the population.

The central issue is whether family size will prove another example of class diffusion. As the unskilled follow the skilled manual workers in becoming skilled, at any rate about contraception, will a second and contrary wave spread 'downwards' through society? Will greater prosperity lead the clerks, then the skilled workers, and eventually the unskilled to turn back towards larger families as the professional people have already done? One would guess not, unless the occupational structure changes so radically that the lathe operator has as much security and can expect, as he gets older, as 'progressive' a climb in income as the architect or university teacher. In other words, it seems that family size is one aspect of life-style which depends more on work-situation and career prospects than on living-standards. But we cannot be sure. On this issue so central to future urbanisation, since we do not know the reasons for what is happening now, we cannot be at all confident in guessing what may happen in the future.

## Leisure time

From the general discussion of family and home, it might appear that people's interests are becoming narrowed down. More time is spent in the home; with television, telephones, deep freezers and the like, more activities can take place there—entertainment, education, even work. All this might seem to point to a future in which there is relatively little mobility. As is well known, however, there is also a contrary trend. As well as the concentration inside the home, there is also the tendency to go longer distances when outside it. This is likely to continue.

These changes are associated with the increase in leisure time. People have—and will have—more time to spend in the home, but also more to spend outside it. The 'standard working week' has fallen from the 60 hours that became general when the 'ten-hour' day was secured in the 1840's to 48 after the First World War, 44 after the Second, 42 in 1960 and 40 today. The fall in the actual hours worked has, because of overtime, been much less marked. Indeed, the average has remained fairly stable over the past 30 years (Roberts and Hirsch, 1966, page 111–113). There are some suggestions that professional people may work longer hours than in the past.*

*H. L. Wilensky, 1961, page 39; showed that half his (middle-class) sample worked 45 hours or more a week and one in five worked an average of eight hours or more at weekends.

Another *caveat* is about second jobs—'moonlighting'. It seems that some people, faced with the prospect of more leisure, prefer to fill this time with extra work (and earn extra money) instead. The rubber workers in the American town of Akron have enjoyed a six-hour day since the 1930's; Swados, studying them, found that the extra leisure was not always welcomed and that moonlighting was common (Swados, 1958). Wilensky, in another American study, found that one in ten of middle-class employees currently had a second job and one in three had been a 'moonlighter' at some time in the past (Wilensky, 1961).

Thus there are likely in the future to be some people who choose to fill their time with second jobs and others, mainly senior professionals and managers, who continue to find long hours essential to a successful career. These apart, the general long-term trend is unmistakable—for most people, the proportion of total time spent at work can be expected to continue to fall over the coming decades.

So far the discussion of free time has been solely in terms of hours worked per week. The balance of work and non-work time can be discussed in a number of other ways. One perspective is that of the life-cycle: if less time in total needs to be spent at work, then people could start work later in life and finish earlier—they might stay longer in full-time education or they might retire earlier. Both trends are already evident, and it is reasonable to predict that they will continue. In particular, more young people are likely to stay longer in further education. In addition, the expected changes in technology and in the occupational structure will mean that more and more adults will later in life need (and want) to re-enter the educational process in one way or another, often including some full-time study.

The division of work and non-work time can also be looked at on an annual basis. If less time is needed at work, there are broadly these choices:

(a) Shorter hours each day
(b) Less days at work each week
(c) Longer annual holidays

What seems to have happened in the last twenty years or so is that the emphasis has been on the last two rather than the first. In 1945 the five-day week was the exception; now it is almost universal. Annual paid holidays increased in most industries from one to two weeks in the 1950's; now nearly half of all manual workers have a paid holiday of more than two weeks (*Statistics on Incomes*, 1968).

It seems probable that leisure time will continue to extend in these forms. Thus for example the 30-hour week, when it comes, is more likely to take the form of a four-day week than a six-hour day. Annual holidays are in general already longer for non-manual workers, especially professional and managerial,* than manual, and the expected long-term changes in the occupational structure will encourage the existing trend to longer paid holidays.

It is worth noting that these trends in the division of leisure time fit in with the home-centred life described earlier. If the husband in particular has a lengthy journey to work, it is better for him and for the family if he can concentrate his work-life into a limited number of days each week and keep whole days free for home and family. It is at the weekend, above all, that family life comes into its own. And large slices of holiday, away from work and with the family instead, are also well suited to a society that values family life so highly.

## Second homes, holidays and travel

Much of the leisure outside the home is—and will continue to be—still in a family setting. With many activities the impression is that the strongest wish is to create another miniature 'home' elsewhere. The family car can be seen as a sort of home on wheels even without a caravan and, when the children are young, very much one for the whole family. Many recreational activities now increasing in popularity—for example, caravanning, cruising and sailing—are things that families usually do together. The impression is also that there is an increase in 'independent' family holidays—families renting chalets, country cottages, seaside flats, Mediterranean villas.

'Second homes' are an even more obvious means of combining family life with frequent 'holidays', and though firm evidence is sparse, these are surely on the increase. In a recent small survey in London in which 100 people were interviewed, we found a marked difference according to social class in the ownership of country cottages and other second homes. In a middle-class area of Kensington, a quarter of households had a second home, compared with none in a working-class area of Hackney. But among the latter, two-thirds expressed the desire for one as did over half the Kensington people without one. This and more substantial evidence† suggest that with rising living standards, a growing proportion of town-dwellers will acquire second homes, and a growing proportion of leisure time, mainly weekends and annual holidays, will be spent in them, either in Britain or abroad.

In addition, as more families get cars and higher real incomes, there will be an increase in travel and holidays generally. In 1967, according to the Family Expenditure Survey (quoted in Abrams, 1968a), households

*Many of the senior civil servants, top managers, architects and doctors who work a 50- or 60-hour week have a complete break of a month or more each summer.

†At present about 5% of households in Britain own second homes or caravans, according to the BTA/Keele survey of leisure (British Travel Association/(1967).

whose 'head' was middle-class in occupation, as compared with those whose 'head' was a manual worker, spent 76% more on 'private motoring' and nearly three times as much on 'holidays, hotels, etc.'. These are clear pointers to future growths in demand. So as well as the growing importance of home and family in leisure, there will also be an increase in mobility, including family mobility. More time and money will go into travel for social and recreational purposes, into holidays in hotels and the like, into rented holiday homes of various kinds, and into second family homes.

## Leisure and geographical dispersal

Increasingly people, as individuals this time rather than as family members, travel longer distances to engage in specialised interests. All this represents a greater variety and more choice. As was noted earlier, changes like these represent a qualification to the general picture of growing social homogeneity; it seems that we are moving both towards a greater homogeneity in certain areas of life and towards an increasing diversity in others. In any case, because of improved communications, the trend is indisputably away from the 'place community' and towards what Webber has called the 'interest community' (Webber, 1963, 1964).

Of course, it does not follow that the 'place community', i.e. the local community, is going to be rubbed out by the ease of communications. It continues to figure importantly in most people's lives. Its significance varies among other things by age, sex, social class, income and car ownership: on the whole women's social contacts, being more tied to the home, are less dispersed than men's; those of young children, of their parents and of old people are less dispersed than those of other people and those of unmarried adolescents and young adults most dispersed of all; those of car owners more than of people without cars; those of middle-class and richer people more than working-class and poorer.

This suggests a continuing rôle for local community, even among many for whom local relationships account for only a relatively small part of their social life as a whole. But it does also suggest that a whole series of pressures—higher living standards, more cars, more education—are likely once again to cause middle-class styles of life to spread, mobility to increase and dispersed 'interest communities' to flourish still more.

## Homes and suburbs

The shift towards home and family suggests that the spread of the city (if it can still be called that) will accelerate. The trends are already clearly evident—in what has happened around London and other large

British cities and in the experience of the United States—and it seems as if nothing can stop the process of further dispersal as living standards rise, even more so if at the same time the population increases substantially.

The issue is whether an acceptable environment could be provided for family life, something with the essential elements of the 'home-and-garden' but without a continuing geographical spread. The question is pointed up by the other demands for space in and around cities. The growth in car ownership means more space will be needed for parking and for roads. Higher standards mean larger school sites and playing fields. Changing tastes in recreation generate extra 'needs'. Golf courses and marinas may soon be 'essentials'.

These pressures mean that we must at least question whether suburbanisation is inevitable, or whether it would be possible to strike a balance that would more successfully meet people's needs. Two trends that have been noted earlier might encourage the alternative to Los Angeles: the changing family structure which might create a growing demand for smaller, gardenless dwellings, and the increase in wives working which might make more attractive the greater accessibility of inner urban areas.

There is also the predicted growth in second homes: it is possible that, particularly with a longer weekend, more and more families might choose high-density urban living close to their work, if this were combined with a second home in more rural surroundings (Grove, 1967, pages 93–94). These are all questions that deserve further research.

*Outstanding questions*

This paper suggested at the outset that what had happened in the past could help in looking ahead to the future. In trying to make some forecasts about changes in the social framework, this is the main approach that has been used—existing trends have been extrapolated, with modifiction where this seemed appropriate. The method has of course its' limitations and a good many questions remain obscure.

It is not just that technology may surprise us all, that some innovations may change social life much more radically than has been suggested here. It is also that, though in a general way 'Tocqueville's Law' has proved reasonably useful, we do not really understand much about it. We do not know how diffusion works, what aspects of the lives of the 'few' will in fact prove attractive to the 'many' or which 'few' (i.e. the 'top' minorities in income, education or occupation) will provide the models for which sorts of taste or behaviour. Nor do we know in what conditions diffusion may operate 'upwards' instead of 'downwards' or 'vertically' (e.g. in terms of age) instead of 'horizontally'. We can make guesses, as this paper has done, but they may prove wrong.

The bigger underlying question is the one raised in the first paragraphs of the paper. This is the paradox about the class structure—how far can the process of 'merging', of increasing cultural homogeneity, go while the fundamental differences remain apparently unchanging? Above all, to echo the questions posed earlier, what will happen to poverty, colour and 'relative deprivation' in the emerging society? Again, further research is needed.

In particular, the older and poorer urban areas certainly pose planning problems. The environment of the future must provide not only for the affluent car-owning suburbanites but also for the minorities of income and colour, who at present live mainly in the older areas. What happens in these older areas clearly affects the city as a whole. As the rush to the suburbs continues, a social 'polarisation' seems to be taking place inside the cities, though we do not have clear evidence about what is happening to the social composition of different types of residential areas. The inner urban areas seem to contain the poor and the very rich, while the rest live outside.* The process has gone even further in the United States, where divisions by colour and geography are all-important.† It could obviously happen in Britain too.

At present the impression is that some of the older central areas are deteriorating, physically and socially, much faster than they are being renewed. A co-ordinated attack, combining physical renewal and rehabilitation with the kind of 'positive discrimination' envisaged in the Plowden Report and in the Government's 'Urban Programme', is needed in the Brixtons and Notting Hills and in a different form in the Bethnal Greens and Bermondseys.

It would be tempting, in looking to the future, to concentrate resources upon new transport networks, better-planned new settlements, regional parks and the like. The older areas, particularly the poorest, plainly need attention as well. To strike the right balance between preparing for tomorrow and dealing with the inheritance from yesterday will not be easy, but it must be done. Thus, as well as social research on such topics as differences in the class structure, 'relative deprivation', life-styles, diffusion and suburbanisation, there needs to be detailed investigation of the poorer urban areas, so as to suggest the appropriate combination of social and planning policies.

*See Ruth Glass's (1964) discussion of the process of 'gentrification', by which middle-class owner-occupiers are displacing working-class residents.

†Ruth Glass (1964), the impression remains—and often it is the dominant one—that there is increasing segmentation' (page xxii).

# References

ABRAMS, M. (1959) 'The Home Centred Society', *The Listener*, 26 November.

ABRAMS, M. (1968a) 'Britain: The Next Fifteen Years', *New Society*, 7 November.

ABRAMS, M. (1968b) 'Consumption in the year 2000', in *Forecasting and the Social Sciences*, Edited by Michael Young, Heinemann.

ALLEN, D. E. (1968) *British Tastes*, Hutchinson.

BELL, D. (1967) Towards the Year 2000: Work in Progress, *Daedalus*, Summer.

BERGER, B. M. (1966) *Working Class Suburb*, University of California.

BLAU, P. M. and DUNCAN, O. D. (1967) *The American Occupational Structure*, John Wiley.

BLISTEN, D. R. (1963) *The World of the Family*, Random House.

BRITISH TRAVEL AGENTS/University of Keele (1967), *Pilot*, National Recreation Survey, Report Number 1.

COX, P. R. (1951) 'Marriage and Fertility Data of England and Wales', *Population Studies*, **5**, November.

DONNISON, D. (1967) *The Government of Housing*, Penguin.

DUBIN, R. (1956) 'Industrial Workers' Worlds', *Social Problems* **3**, Number 3, January.

GANS, H. (1967) *The Levittowners*, Allen Lane, The Penguin Press.

GERTH, H. H. and MILLS, C. W. (Editors) (1948) *From Max Weber: Essays in Sociology*, Routledge.

GLASS, D. V. (Editor) (1954) *Social Mobility in Britain*, Routledge.

GLASS, R. (1964) Introduction to *London: Aspects of Change*, Centre for Urban Studies, MacGibbon and Kee.

GOLDTHORPE, J. H., LOCKWOOD, D., BECHHAVER, F. and PLATT, J. (1967) 'The Affluent Worker and the Thesis of Embourgeisement: some preliminary research findings', *Sociology*, **1**, Number 1, January.

GOLDTHORPE, J. H. *et al.* (1968) *The Affluent Worker: Political Attitudes and Behaviour* and *The Affluent Worker: Industrial Attitudes and Behaviour*, Cambridge University Press.

GOODE, W. J. (1963) *World Revolution and Family Patterns*, The Free Press.

GROVE, D. (1968) 'Physical Planning and Social Change' in *Forecasting and the Social Sciences*, Edited by Michael Young, Heinemann.

HARRISSON, T. (1961) *Britain Revisited*, Gollancz.

*Higher Education* (1963) HMSO, Appendix I.

HUGHES, J. (1968) 'The Increase in Inequality', *New Statesman*, 8 November.

JENNINGS, H. (1962) *Societies in the Making*, Routledge.

KAIM-CAUDLE, P. R. (1967) Selectivity and the Social Services, *Lloyds Bank Review*, April.

KLEIN, J. (1965) *Samples of English Culture*, Volume One, Routledge.

LEACH, E. (1968) *A Runaway World*, BBC Publications.

LIPSET, S. M. and BENDIX, R. (1959) *Social Mobility in Industrial Society*, Heinemann.

*Manpower Studies*, Number 6 (1967) *Occupational Changes 1951–61*, HMSO.

MARSHALL, T. H. (1950) *Citizenship and Social Class*, Cambridge University Press.

MEADE, J. E. (1964) *Efficiency, Equality and Ownership of Property*, Allen and Unwin.

NEWSON, J. and NEWSON, E. (1968) *Four Years Old in an Urban Community*, Allen and Unwin.

NICHOLSON, J. L. (1964) *Redistribution of Income in the United Kingdom in 1949, 1957 and 1963*, Bowes and Bowes.

PARKER, S. R. *et al.* (1967) *The Sociology of Industry*, Allen and Unwin.

RAPAPORT, R. and RAPAPORT, R. N. (1969) The Dual Career Family: A Variant Pattern and Social Change, *Human Relations*, **22**.

REGISTRAR GENERALS' Statistical Review for 1962, Part III Commentary (1964) HMSO.

REGISTRAR GENERALS' Statistical Review for 1964, Part III, Commentary (1967) HMSO.

REISMAN, D. (1958) Leisure and Work in Post-Industrial Society in LARRABEE, E. and MEYERSOHN, R. (Editors) *Mass Leisure*, The Free Press.

ROBERTS, B. C. and HIRSCH, J. L. (1966) 'Factors Influencing Hours of Work' in ROBERTS, B. C. and SMITH, J. H. (Editors) *Manpower Policy and Employment Trends*, London School of Economics and Political Science.

ROSSER, C. and HARRIS, C. (1965) *The Family and Social Change*, Routledge.

ROUTH, G. (1965) *Occupation and Pay in Great Britain, 1906–1960*, Cambridge University Press.

ROWE, D. C. (1965) Private Consumption in W. BECKERMAN *et al.*, *The British Economy in 1975*, Cambridge University Press.

RUNCIMAN (1966) *Relative Deprivation and Social Justice*, Routledge.

*South-east Study* (1964) HMSO.

*Statistics on Incomes, Prices, Employment and Production* (1968) HMSO.

STEWART, C. M. (1969) The Employment of Married Women in Great Britain. Paper to International Union for the Scientific Study of Population, London.

SWADOS, H. (1958) 'Less-Work: Less Leisure' in LARRABEE, E. and MEYERSOHN, R. (Editors) *Mass Leisure*, The Free Press.

TITMUSS, R. M. (1958) 'The Position of Women', in *Essays on the 'Welfare State'*, Allen and Unwin.

TITMUSS, R. M. (1962) *Income Distribution and Social Change*, Allen and Unwin.

WEBBER, M. M. (1963) Order in Diversity: Community without Propinquity in L. WINGO Junior (Editor) *Cities and Space*, John Hopkins.

WEBBER, M. M. (1964) The Urban Place and the Non-Place Urban Realm in M. M. WEBBER *et al.*, *Explorations into Urban Structure*, University of Pennsylvania.

WILENSKY, H. L. (1961) The Uneven Distribution of Leisure, *Social Problems*, Summer.

WILLMOTT, P. (1963) *The Evolution of a Community*, Routledge.

WILLMOTT, P and YOUNG, M. (1957) *Family and Kinship in East London*, Routledge.

WILLMOTT, P. and YOUNG, M. (1960) *Family and Class in a London Suburb*, Routledge.

ZWEIG, F. (1961) *The Worker in an Affluent Society*, Heinemann.

## 2.2 The future of the motor vehicle
*Colin Buchanan*

The picture so far drawn shows a high degree of dependence upon the motor vehicle for transportation purposes, yet in many ways the arrangements for its use are grossly inefficient, self-defeating of the motor vehicle's own unique properties, and productive of side effects which add up to a major social problem. In the circumstances it is justifiable to examine the motor vehicle itself as a means of transport, and to inquire whether it really does seem to have a long-term future before it. This obviously involves some speculation, but it would be foolish to embark upon drastic and expensive alterations to towns to accommodate motor traffic if there were any serious doubt as to its continuance as a means of transport.

The motor vehicle of course cannot simply be 'disinvented'. Events have passed far beyond the point at which it would have been possible to revert to railways, though doubtless some loads could even now be transferred to them with advantage. A vast amount of development has been disposed around the country, including great suburban estates round the cities, on the basis of the motor vehicle as the form of transport, and life in these areas could not continue to thrive except with a substitute offering the same range of services as the motor.

### Possible substitutes for the motor vehicle

Perhaps some kind of individual jet-propulsion unit will eventually be developed, a rudimentary form of which has already been tried out in the USA for military use. This may well come about, but the problems of weather, navigation, air space, and traffic control appear so formidable that it may be questioned whether such a device would ever be practical for mass use, either for freight or for passengers, in the crowded conditions of the modern city. One only has to consider the rush-hour conditions in any large city to realize what would be involved. The preservation of privacy is another factor which, it may be hoped, will exercise a strong restrictive influence on a technical development of this

*Source:* The Buchanan Report *Traffic in Towns*, specially shortened Penguin edition (1964)

kind. The motor vehicle has been eroding many of the common amenities of life, but there is still some privacy left in back gardens, verandas, and bedrooms and on roof-tops. All these would be threatened if people could take off vertically at will, proceed in any direction, and hover about just as they pleased. Almost certainly strict canalization of movement would be demanded, and if this resolved itself into the equivalent of roads up in the air then the advantages of this kind of transport might not be as overwhelming as they appear at first glance. Vertical take-off aircraft may well be developed as freight cars and multi-passenger units, but in this case they would not be providing the individual, highly flexible, door-to-door service which, unquestionably, is the feature of the motor vehicle that gives it its greatest appeal. The competition would tend to be with existing methods of public transport, particularly long-distance transport, and the result might well be to leave motor transport in towns more or less unaffected.

The same argument would probably apply to the development of other means of transport such as monorails (which offer the great virtue of silence) and tracked hovercraft (which offer the possibility of very high speeds). In both cases the competition would tend to be with existing forms of longer-distance public passenger transport, particularly the railways, rather than with motor transport in towns. A development which may offer a more direct challenge to the motor car, assuming the problem of noise can be overcome, is the air-cushion craft. It seems to give scope for development as a small personal machine, usable perhaps eventually on ordinary pavements as a substitute for walking. Yet it may be questioned whether it would really take this form, whether the urge to put a perspex cover over it for weather protection, to use it at higher speeds, to add extra seats, and to affix luggage containers would not soon convert it into a motor car in all respects but the possession of wheels.

It is possible, of course, if serious technological studies were undertaken, that a whole range of new ideas for moving people and goods in cities would be produced. It is indeed to be hoped that we are not at the end of our ingenuity in the matter. The bus, for example, for all its convenience, does not appear to be the last word in comfort. The travalator seems to offer much scope for development. Continuously operating chair-lifts might be used in a highly attractive way between points of pedestrian concentration to augment existing means of travel. Conveyor belts, pneumatic tubes, and pipelines might well be developed for the conveyance of goods, perhaps even justifying rearrangement of commercial processes to make their use easier. Why, for example, should the streets have to carry large tankers delivering fuel oil to individual buildings, when it could be piped in the same manner as water or gas or (as in New York) steam?

Even so it is difficult to see any new method of movement coming along which will be seriously competitive on a big scale with the motor vehicle. There are so many advantages in a fairly small, independent, self-powered and highly manoeuvrable means of getting about at ground level, for both people and goods, that it is unlikely we shall ever wish to abandon it. It may have a different source of motive power so that it is no longer strictly a motor vehicle, it may be quieter and without fumes, it may be styled in some quite different way, it may be produced in smaller forms, it may be guided and controlled in certain streets by electronic means, it may have the ability to perform sideways movement, but for practical purposes it will present most of the problems that are presented by the motor vehicle of today.

Our conclusion, therefore, is that the future of the motor vehicle, or of some equivalent machine, is assured. It follows that a close, constructive examination must be made of towns and cities in order to see how the best use of the motor vehicle can be achieved in those places, and how the present difficulties can be overcome. This represents the basic standpoint of this study. We accept the motor vehicle as a potentially highly beneficial invention; and we reject, as an initial standpoint, a currently held view that the traffic problem in towns would take on an altogether different complexion—that it might indeed almost disappear—if motorists were obliged to pay the full economic costs of running their vehicles, including the rental of road space. The public can justifiably demand to be fully informed about the possibilities of adapting towns to motor traffic before there is any question of applying restrictive measures.

THE FUTURE GROWTH OF TRAFFIC

If the future of the motor vehicle is assured, and towns are to be examined in a constructive way to see how traffic can be accommodated, then three questions become very important in the assessment of the long-term problem. How many vehicles are there likely to be? At what rate will the numbers increase? And how much will the vehicles be used? Once again these are complex questions to which there are no straightforward answers.

*Increase in the number of vehicles*

The growth in the number of *private cars* would seem to depend primarily upon the growth of incomes, but it is also dependent upon the price of cars, insurance rates, taxation levels, and such factors as changes in shopping habits, the availability of garage space, the amount of frustra-

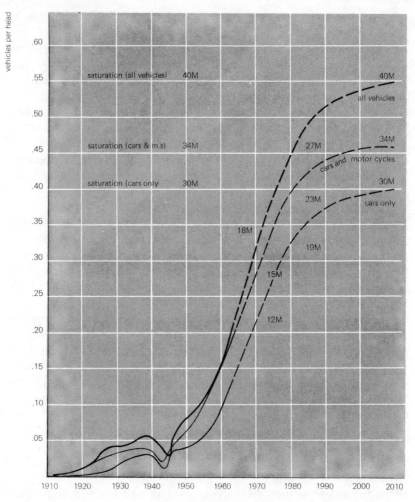

tion due to congestion, the existence of other cheap and convenient forms of transport, and the future patterns of recreation. It will also depend on the growing familiarity with and acceptance of the advantages of having a motor car. The increase in the number of *goods and commercial vehicles* will depend upon the usefulness of this form of transport to the firms involved, and to the coming into existence of new firms, new processes, and new or expanding markets. The future number of *public transport vehicles* depends largely upon the extent to which the public does or does not switch its travelling habits to private cars. Underlying both the growth in numbers and the usage of vehicles is a problem which has not previously been given any prominence but which yearly assumes greater importance, namely the sheer capacity of urban areas to accommodate motor traffic without serious deterioration of the environment.

78

With so many variables and imponderables, the assessment of the future number of vehicles can proceed only by the projection of past trends and consideration of the recent experience of the United States. On this basis, there is a prospect (in Great Britain) of 18 million vehicles (including 12 million cars) by 1970, of 27 million vehicles (including 19 million cars) by 1980, and 40 million (30 million cars) by 2010. There are at present (early 1963) some $10\frac{1}{2}$ million vehicles, so what is involved is a doubling of numbers within ten years, and nearly a trebling within twenty years. It is important to note that nearly half the total increase is expected *within the first ten years*.

These figures take account of the estimated increase of the national population to some 74 millions by the year 2010.* The significance of this particular date (or thereabouts) is that by then most of the people who want cars will have secured them. The total number of vehicles will still continue to increase if the population increases, but not at the rate that can be expected in the next twenty years.

Various ratios are in use to express the relationship between vehicle numbers and population. We are inclined to think that the *number of vehicles per 1000 population* is the most expressive, though in respect of cars another meaningful (even if somewhat imprecise) ratio is the *number of cars per family*. Expressed in these terms, the figures for the year 2010 would be 540 vehicles per 1000 population, 405 cars per 1000 population, and 1·3 cars per family.

## Increase in traffic

These are increases in the *numbers* of vehicles; the increase in the *usage* of vehicles (i.e. traffic) may well be in a greater proportion than this. Not only is usage held at an artificially low level at present by congested road conditions, but American experience shows that as vehicles increase in numbers the usage per vehicle also tends to increase at any rate up to the point at which there is an average of one car per family. On the basis of these figures, therefore, traffic may be more than trebled in a little over twenty years. This forecast, however, is for the country as a whole. It does not follow that *urban* traffic will be trebled everywhere; indeed there are likely to be important differences in the amount of increase as among urban, suburban, and country districts. On the other hand, with the great increase of car ownership peak period traffic flows associated with towns may be more than trebled. There are also likely to be considerable differences between various parts of the country.

*This estimate is based on the projection of a forty-year period contained in the December 1962 *Quarterly Return of the Registrar General for England and Wales*, and the twenty-year projection in the 1962 *Annual Report of the Registrar General for Scotland*. [Editor's note: this projection has now been revised downwards by several millions]

In particular, the rate of increase in south-east England looks like being much faster than the national average unless some far-reaching national policy for preventing it is adopted. What certainty is there that these very considerable and, in the circumstances of this small country, somewhat intimidating increases of vehicles and traffic will really come about? On the assumption that the population increases in accordance with the forecasts, an increase up to a total of 25 million vehicles (including $17\frac{1}{2}$ million cars, or an average of one car per family) must be regarded as certain. Beyond this, the increase is more speculative. On the other hand nothing would be more dangerous, at this critical stage in planning for the new mobility offered by the motor vehicle, than to underestimate its potential. Most previous studies have failed in this way. It does seem possible now to look ahead to the full development of the situation, and this is what we have endeavoured to do, preferring to risk slightly overestimating rather than to fail to foresee the trend, or to be guilty of deliberately glossing it over in order to make it seem less alarming or less demanding of expenditure on capital works.

Irrespective of the exact final total of vehicles, however, vehicle numbers are likely to double within ten years, and to treble in a little over twenty years. *The problems of traffic are crowding in upon us with desperate urgency.* It is sometimes maintained that these increases will not come about, that would-be owners of cars will be deterred by congestion and frustration. But we think this attitude would amount to a miscalculation of the mood of the country. The population appears as intent upon owning cars as the manufacturers are upon meeting the demand.

One matter of importance is obscured by global figures. It is the distinction between the future growth in numbers of business, commercial, and industrial vehicles (including many cars) on the one hand, and of private motor cars on the other. It only requires a glance at a map showing the land uses in a town to reveal what the future holds. The areas used for commerce and industry are limited in extent, they may be intensively developed and seething with activity, but the commercial and industrial traffic they generate is rational and calculable, for it is closely related to the activities going on. The residential areas on the other hand occupy by far the greater part of the town, and it is within these that there lies the huge potential for the future increase of traffic. It is here that personal mobility will increase, and people will seek to use their cars for journeys to work, for shopping, for visits to friends and theatres, and for a great range of other social activities and daily errands.

Outright ownership of a motor car might possibly soon cease to be a 'status symbol', and as a result there might for example be a much extended use of hire-cars, or more widespread taxi services. These would have their effect on traffic volumes, and the space required for parking and storage. This is clearly a line of development that needs to be kept under review, but the effects are likely to be marginal only; for whether or not a motor car is a status symbol, there is no doubt that to many people it is a fascinating possession, and to have one at one's immediate beck and call is an asset of the first order.

THE FORM OF URBAN AREAS

The motor vehicle appears to have a long-term future in its own right. There is also a very large potential demand for its services. But unless something is done the conflict between towns as they are arranged at present and motor vehicles as they are used at present is bound to get progressively worse. It can be stated categorically that the potential numbers of vehicles in towns are beyond anything that could be dealt with by one-way streets, waiting prohibitions, or other manipulative measures. This assumes, of course, that we desire both to exploit the door-to-door usefulness of the vehicle and to accommodate it decently.

## Urban dispersal

The conflict between towns and traffic obviously stems from the physical structure of towns. The manner in which the buildings and streets are put together is basically unsuitable for motor traffic. This became apparent soon after the invention of the motor vehicle because it soon exerted a strong influence towards changing the form of towns by encouraging the outward spread and sprawl of development. There have been two main reasons for this: first, the spatial demands of the vehicle itself for circulation and parking; and, second, the facility of movement which the motor vehicle provides, whereby (to take an extreme example) a factory can be set up in a rural area without any serious difficulties arising over the recruitment of labour or delivery of goods.

It can be argued that if this is indeed the 'natural' influence of the motor vehicle, and if we are to have motor vehicles in very large numbers, we might as well go the whole way with this dispersal of urban areas. It can be argued that with the added advantages of new telecommunication techniques there is no longer any need for concentrated towns in the traditional form. Offices and exchanges can keep in close touch even though separated by long distances. Shops, it is said, give better service in suburban areas than in crowded city centres. Theatres, restaurants, museums, clubs, zoos, and the other things previously thought fit to concentrate in centres could just as well be scattered about, provided they were intelligently sited in relation to a main highway network, and

81

in this way they might be even more accessible to more people than they are now. What does a thirty-mile drive to a theatre signify if it can be comfortably made in thirty minutes?

The future form of urban areas is complicated by two other factors. The first is the need to deploy a probable population increase of over 20 millions soon after the end of the century; and the second is the continuing need to redeploy population and activities from the large overcrowded cities. These two factors, in conjunction with the basic dispersive influence of the motor vehicle, make up a very powerful force towards a spread of development. There is no doubt that if it were left to itself it would rapidly result in a great part of the country, but particularly the south-east, being covered in vast irregularly shaped sprawls of building. So far, with our green belt and countryside conservation policies, the situation has been kept under control, but the pressures are present and are increasing all the time.

It would be beyond the scope of this study to discuss the actual manner in which the population might be deployed. To start on this would be to embark on the preparation of a national plan. However, certain general points which are relevant to the problems of motor traffic need to be mentioned. Meanwhile a word of caution is necessary regarding the more startling proposals which appear from time to time for various theoretical city plans based on transport systems—linear cities, annular cities, radial cities, and satellite systems. It is a healthy sign that such ideas should be put forward, and the day may come when, suddenly, there is a crystallization of views and it is clear that we should steer a new course. But this has not happened yet. For the period ahead into which we may reasonably peer—probably extending a little beyond the end of the century—it is reasonable to suppose that towns and cities will continue to exist broadly in their present form, for in spite of their acknowledged defects they contain great accumulations of material and cultural wealth. The enormous increase of population over the next decades may well require the urbanization of large new areas, where the capacity of existing towns to expand is quite inadequate. In such a case the new urban settlements could take on new forms based on transport systems. But this development would be complementary to existing towns and cities and would not alter the need for the methodical overhaul of the latter.

In all consideration of urban form, from the expansion of existing towns to the complexities of 'urban regions', the question of facility of movement of both persons and goods is of crucial importance. It deserves far more attention than has been bestowed on it in the past, for it must now become one of the prime factors in the determination of where population and activities are to be settled. Also a much greater understanding of the relationship between various kinds of development

and the demands for movement which they generate needs to be obtained. In this largely neglected field of research there is much to be
learned from current techniques in the United States. It is important
that movement demands be studied as a whole, not merely those that
involve the motor vehicle. All the indications (including those from the
United States) are that in a complex community no single system of
transport can provide for all the movements involved, and that coordination between systems is required.

It is important to recognize that, although persuasive arguments can
be adduced in favour of urban dispersal, this island is not big enough for
large-scale dispersal if a sensible relationship is to be maintained between
developed areas and open country. Opinions may vary as to the future
role of agriculture, but no one could question the special importance of
the countryside to the people of this crowded island, nor would anyone
be prepared, when really faced with the issue, to see a large part of it
sacrificed to a major dispersal of urban areas in order to accommodate
motor traffic. After all, to 'get out into the countryside' is one of the
main reasons why people buy cars.

It should be understood that dispersal, if taken beyond a certain
point, positively complicates transportation problems by increasing all
the distances that have to be traversed. Dispersal, in fact, can all too
easily become synonymous with 'sprawl', and if there are not already
sufficiently bitter lessons to be learned about sprawl in this country,
the United States demonstrates what happens when the motor vehicle
is given free licence to lead development where it will.

There are long-standing, well-tried advantages in the principle of
compactness for urban areas which are not to be lightly jettisoned in
favour of the supposed advantages of dispersal. In a compact area,
journey distances, including the all-important journeys to work and
school, are kept to the minimum. The concentration of people makes
it possible to provide a diversity of services, interests, and contacts.
There is a wider choice of housing, employment, schools, shops, and
recreational and cultural pursuits. It is easier in a compact society to
maintain the secondary activities, such as restaurants, specialist shops,
and service industries, which all too easily fail if there is not a large
clientele close at hand. The issue is not starkly between high density
flats and low density suburbs—towns should have both—but whether
to maintain or abandon the degree of compactness and proximity which
seems to contribute so much to the variety and richness of urban life.

## A problem of design

But whatever decisions may be reached about the deployment of the
population, if compactness is maintained there will still be towns

83

broadly in the form we know them today. Some will be old towns subjected to violent new stresses and strains as a result of the addition of population, some will be new towns, and others will be large cities, or groups of cities, exerting an influence over smaller settlements for miles around. In all these one common problem will arise: how can these agglomerations of houses, factories, shops, offices, markets, warehouses, schools, hospitals, depots, and yards be adapted to meet the wishes of people seeking to use motor vehicles of all kinds for every imaginable purpose of transport? Even where a completely *new* town is being built the question remains: how can the activities be arranged, and the buildings disposed on the ground, to enable motor vehicles to be used to the best advantage? These questions indicate a problem of design, of the actual layout and form of buildings and access ways, and the manner of distribution of traffic from one part of a town to another. It is a basic problem, as relevant to a small isolated town in East Anglia as to the constituent towns of the largest conurbation.

This, subject to two further questions, establishes the context of this study. The remaining questions are perhaps the most important of all. What sort of towns ought we to be thinking about in the latter half of the twentieth century? And what are we likely to be able to afford for change and renewal? We know by bitter experience that the motor vehicle is in conflict with the present structure of towns. By it, and because of it, grievous damage has been done to much we have previously cherished. Given its head the motor vehicle would wreck our towns within a decade. What should we expect of towns? Is it merely a matter of material convenience and accessibility for cars, or does it matter any longer what towns look like? It is an indication of the influence of the motor vehicle that it makes us ask what sort of lives we want to lead.

Nine tenths of the population of this country lives, and in all certainty is going to go on living, in towns large or small. Towns are the setting in which millions of people have to live. Only now is the influence of physical surroundings upon people's lives being learned. More subtly, many people are discovering unsuspected possibilities in the interior design of buildings—sheer convenience, colour, relationship of spaces and levels. Yet the possibility that our daily surroundings, outside our houses and offices, might be amenable to design in the same way for our delight and convenience is slow in being understood, though, judging by the numbers of visitors to famous cities—Venice, Paris, Oxford, Norwich, Cambridge—there must be something in the way some buildings have been designed and grouped that touches a chord of understanding in many people.

The overriding context in which the problems of urban traffic have to be considered is the need to create or re-create towns which are worth living in, and this means much more than the freedom to use motor vehicles. It is a mixture of all manner of things—convenience, variety of choice, contrast, architecture, history visible in the buildings—all more or less subtle qualities. Life in towns could no doubt be lived without any of them, but it would be poorer and emptier as a result.

## 2.3 The impact of telecommunications on town planning *J. S. Whyte*

### 1 Introduction

When I considered how to treat the subject on which I have been invited to address you this morning, it struck me that telecommunications administrators share one characteristic of their activity with town planners. Both are concerned with planning on a timescale that is measured in years, or decades. In the telecommunications business our investment in capital plant is planned on a rolling 5 year basis, and sites and buildings are usually planned on a 20 year basis. Much of the work at present in progress in our Research Laboratories is unlikely to enter public service for at least 10 years, and some of it may take nearer 20 years to reach this stage. Once installed, some types of telecommunications plant have a life approaching 40 years, so that equipment installed today may still be operating in the year 2012. Conversely, some equipment installed in 1930 is still in use. You will be well aware that such long timescales greatly enhance the difficulties of prediction. An eminent economist put it very succinctly when he remarked 'forecasting is difficult, especially about the future'. I therefore decided against attempting to make any firm forecast to you, and I do not propose to offer you a Delphic revelation of the impact of telecommunications on town planning by the year 2000. Rather, I intend to describe to you some of the new technological developments within my own discipline which are now in prospect, and which it seems reasonable to believe could enter service on a relatively large scale in the next few decades, and I hope that you will, during the course of the day, discuss in depth the extent to which such capabilities might be expected to influence the rôle, and the form, of the built environment.

### 2 The historical setting

The telephone was invented in 1876, and the first public telephone exchange in England was opened in London in August 1879. By Christmas

*Source:* Town and Country Planning Summer School Proceedings, Swansea, 1970, pages 27–30

of that year nine subscribers were connected to it. Early growth was slow, but in all the advanced countries of the world the picture today is the same: that of very rapidly expanding growth both of the system and its usage. Today, from the telephone in your home you can speak to anyone of more than 220 million other telephones throughout the world; speaking for 3 minutes to each of them would occupy more than 5,000 years. Our grandparents did not foresee the scale, the variety or the consequences of the invention of the telephone and the telegraph; yet they are accepted by our children as an integral part of the fabric of their lives. In Government, business and industry, telephone and telex services are an indispensable adjunct to the conduct of business; to attempt to operate in today's world without them would be inconceivable. And yet, despite the tremendous significance of the telephone and telex services, and the great impact they have had in shaping the course of the industrialised countries, they are relatively simple telecommunications media by comparison with those that are now in prospect. Society now stands on the threshold of a new era in which the scale and range of telecommunication services which are within our technical competence very greatly exceed those which have resulted from the whole previous history of the technology.

## 3 Things to come

In looking toward the future, it is important to resist the temptation to suppose that the future will merely be a somewhat bigger and slightly improved version of the present. The history of technology in the past 200 years has shown a progressively increasing rate of advance. The steady progress achieved between World War I and World War II has been superseded by a period of rapidly accelerating change. Those of us privileged to know what is happening in some of the most advanced laboratories of the world can see no sign that this acceleration is doing other than continuing.

The conventional forms of telecommunications will continue to grow until a penetration of at least one telephone per household has been achieved, and a large proportion of the telephone customers throughout the world will be able to call each other without operator assistance. Already 75% of trunk telephone calls are dialled by the customer in the UK and fully automatic service to many European countries is available to many UK subscribers. Intercontinental subscribers dialing from London started recently with the opening of automatic service to the United States, and this process will gather pace in the years ahead. The rate at which this international dialling service becomes available to UK customers will, after the first few years, be largely determined by the rate at which the less advanced countries throughout the world complete the automation of their internal telephone services. International telephone traffic is growing at the rate of 22% per annum.

## 4 Machine communications

Two particular features of the new era will be the emergence of rapidly growing requirements for man-machine and machine-machine telecommunications and an upsurge in demand for visual telecommunications. The communication facilities required for use by computers, which we usually call data communications, are already growing spectacularly in several countries. In the United Kingdom, data transmission services were first introduced in 1965 and have already grown so that more than 6000 terminals are in use and the rate of growth continuous at about 100% per annum. There are more data terminals in use in the UK today than in the *whole* of the rest of Europe. We expect the number of terminals in use to have reached 40 000 within 3 or 4 years and they may well reach over 1 000 000 by the end of the century. It is of particular significance that, at a time when computers are becoming more and more dependent on telecommunication facilities to expand the range of their application, certain parts of telecommunication networks are themselves beginning to look more and more like computers in the technologies they employ and in the manner in which they operate.

In the application of computers, the trend undoubtedly will be toward integrated systems in which the computers will draw the data on which they are to operate from widely dispersed sources, collecting the information automatically over the data transmission facilities, processing it and issuing commands to control other apparatus and processes in other locations. Increasingly this will involve not merely single computers but meshes of inter-connected computers, each contributing part of the data, part of the processing capability, and part of the algorithm that defines the entire system operation. The trend is likely to be toward capturing the data at the moment of its creation, whether this be on the cash register in the department store, on the machine tool or transfer machine in the manufacturing plant, or elsewhere. We may therefore see a vast requirement for low-cost data transmission at relatively low speed, to collect the data for the computers from large numbers of widely dispersed locations.

## 5 Business communications

The business man in the future will have many new aids to the more effective conduct of his business. Visual display units in his office will enable him to interrogate the computer remotely, calling up numeric and graphical data from the computer files. Being presented to him on demand, the information is more up-to-date than present hard copy methods permit and therefore more valuable. There is another less obvious advantage, however. Once he knows that he can call up the information instantly whenever he needs it, and his initial suspicion that the new system will not really work is found to be untrue, he will no longer need to call for, and hoard, voluminous reports and statistics. These are today held by many people as a precaution against not having them available quickly when they want them rather than because they are in constant use. Thus we may expect to see a trend away from paper-based business information systems.

The remote interrogation of computer-held data bases is only one of the many uses that can be foreseen for image transmission systems. These are really a whole class of services, which include information retrieval services, video conference facilities, audio-visual educational systems and Viewphone. In the British Post Office we have in operation an experimental Confravision system with which our business man of the year 2000 will certainly be familiar; we have recently announced plans to extend the experiment to several major centres of population in the UK.

In this system a specially equipped television studio is provided, looking rather like a company boardroom, which will accommodate up to five participants who can hold a business meeting with a similar number at a remote location.

The relatively high cost is likely to rule out the growth of Confravision as substitute for the telephone, so that it may be regarded as a complement, rather than a competitor, to Viewphone.

The latter is a telephone system incorporating a television-type display of the face of the distant party. The additional value that it confers, by comparison with voice only, is a subject of keen debate. The situation seems to have some similarity to that surrounding the application of automatic transmissions to motor cars. It is my observation that in both cases those people who have not experienced it are inclined to say that it has little value and that they don't particularly want it; whereas those who have once got used to using it do not wish to be without it. However, once the visual display facility is associated with the telephone instrument, the possibility of using it in association with all manner of other services arises. In combination with other devices, small static objects or diagrams may be displayed, with alphanumeric information retrieved from computer stores, and it can also be used as an output device for receiving images derived from remotely accessed microfilm libraries, and for the verification of signatures. There are, of course, limitations: economic considerations will constrain us for many years to use a relatively small picture size (for example, $5'' \times 6''$) and the definition available will be inadequate to permit ordinary typescript to be read. Nevertheless, the reproduction of straightforward output from a computer store can be entirely satisfactory.

## 6 *The organic business organisation*

These new capabilities will help to shape the environment of the future. In attempting to forecast the manner in which they will do so, it is, however, important to realise that the total environment is more than the sum of its parts. If we study the technological possibilities which will arise in many different disciplines and merely aggregate these, together with trend extrapolations of existing socio-economic systems, we are most unlikely to derive a reliable picture of the future. The point is simply that these new capabilities are interrelated and do not exist in isolation. Furthermore, and this is of paramount importance, existing societal structures are not necessarily well adapted to accepting, and exploiting, the new technology. In an iterative manner the new capabilities will modify society, and society itself will licence the allocation of resources in a manner that will be an important factor in determining the rate of advance in the different technological sectors.

For example, when computers were first introduced into the commercial environment, early system designers employed them to mechanise existing clerical processes. The resultant computer processes were a close reproduction of the stages that had formerly been carried out by the clerks and the results were not particularly impressive. The clerical processes used in the existing office procedures had been evolved over many decades and had been based on the physical movement of paper and suited to the means available for its manipulation. Thus work was broken down into units to form a convenient load for the individual clerk, and records were kept in a form suited to his mental processes and typical memory capacity. These human characteristics are not, in general, precisely duplicated by a computer, which has a much larger semi-permanent memory for structured detailed information, and works at a uniform (and known) rate virtually indefinitely without fatigue, but executes the command it receives with a moronic absence of initiative. The efficiency of utilisation of the computer in the elementary business environment leapt forward when these differences were recognised and the organisation of the work process was re-arranged to be more appropriate to the capabilities of the new tool. So too, with telecommunications, the organisations of business must evolve to adapt themselves to exploit the particular characteristics of the new capabilities if their full benefit is to be obtained.

## 7 Impact on town planning

We may distinguish two levels of impact on town planning by the new telecommunications. There will clearly be a direct impact of a kind that is already well known. This particularly affects the requirement that telecommunications undertakings have for sites, often in city centres. Because the location of a telephone exchange is of necessity intimately connected with the geographical distribution of the customers that it serves, it follows that there is little room for manoeuvre in its location. If it is moved away from the telephonic centre of gravity of the district it serves, all the incoming cables have to be extended to the new location and this may involve an extremely high cost penalty. Technical developments now in prospect will reduce the size of switching equipment, but this reduction is being more than offset by the extra equipment required to serve both the increased number of subscribers and the increased rate of calling.

The direct impacts that I have mentioned are, I suggest, of very much less importance to your deliberations in this conference than some of the indirect effects that may arise.

As planners we are, or should be, concerned with the interplay between the biosphere and the technosphere; a satisfactory relationship must be established if man is to survive. Professor Black has pointed out that ecosystems tend to be very fragile and that small disturbances can be very significant in their consequences. But I think that we should recognise that man himself is a part of the ecosystem, not a detached observer of it. Thus while modern ecologists are rightly concerned about the danger to the biosphere of ill-considered exploitation of our growing dominance over nature through technology, rather less attention has been paid to the impact on human relationships and social structures of other aspects of our technological prowess. I believe that we must devote a growing share of our attention to the study of these relationships in an endeavour to avoid degradation in the quality of life.

The steadily growing mobility of population over the past half century has diminished the rôle of the traditional local community. The self-help within closely knit family structures is increasingly replaced by the more impersonal support of the welfare services. This steady diffusion of formerly tight communities into the anonymity of the megalopolis is no sudden new event, but young people throughout the industrialized world have reminded us sharply within the past five years of our failure to understand, and to alleviate, the problems. This is a matter which particularly concerns town planners, and it will not be solved without inter-disciplinary studies involving not only technology in all its branches but also the human sciences and those concerned with human and ethical values. Telecommunications will be a factor in this debate and will appear on both sides of the balance sheet. For example, while on the one hand, by its potentiality for reducing travel, it may make some contribution to the diminution of pollution both of the atmosphere and by noise from various transport media, on the other hand, to the extent that it enables the individual to conduct virtually the whole of his work without leaving his home, and to receive both his education and his entertainment similarly in the home, it would be capable of creating a curious, and unnatural, form of isolation whose social consequences are difficult to foresee. I do not offer you solutions to these problems, nor do I suggest that in this extreme form they are problems that will arise in the near future. But the fundamental question of what cities are all about must be faced. It must be faced and answered within the relevant framework, otherwise any answers that we devise will be irrelevant. Le Corbusier described cities as 'machines for communicating'. But he did not go far enough—cities are about people and they must serve people. So the framework within which we must seek our answers is one which recognizes the human element as dominant and which relates our ideas to value systems and value judgements that are predicated by recognition of this, with all the implications that flow from it.

I hope, therefore, that you will devote a good deal of your time in discussion to a consideration of the much more intangible, and potentially far more important, impacts of telecommunications on planning. May I close, not by giving you all the answers, but by asking some questions to stimulate discussion:

(1) If cities have evolved because rural people discovered the necessity of living closely together in order to facilitate the provision of defence, services and communications, to what extent will the need for cities continue into the next century when defence is no longer a local matter and technology facilitates the widespread distribution of services and communications?

(2) Can telecommunications, enhanced by effective new forms including fast document transmission, remote library facilities, face-to-face visual communication, visual displays of information retrieved from computer data-banks and so on, diminish the need to concentrate large blocks of staff into office buildings and thereby contribute to an alleviation of the commuter problem?

(3) Is there a credible rôle for the 'office in the home' for a significant number of people?

(4) Should company office development proceed on the lines of relatively large numbers of small office blocks in close proximity to dwelling areas with the small office units integrated through advanced telecommunications facilities?

(5) To what extent would the large-scale development of Confravision

services reduce the need for business travel, thereby reducing pressure on the travel media?

(6) The telephone and the telegraph, in general, had insufficient decentralising influence to offset the more powerful centralising influence of direct physical communication. Will the addition of the new telecommunications media, such as face-to-face visual communication and fast document transmission, have sufficient power to offset the centralising forces and to initiate a significant decentralisation?

(7) Will the advantages of dispersal, such as lower office rentals, reduced travelling time for employees, and reduced pressure on national resources by alleviation of the commuter problem, be sufficient to offset the additional costs of decentralisation in the provision of the telecommunications facilities and some duplication of company overheads?

(8) Will these trends be frustrated by our present methods of accounting? For example, in present circumstances the costs of the additional telecommunications facilities required would fall upon the company, whereas the savings brought about by the reduction in travelling time benefit the employee, and the savings derived from reduced demand on commuter services benefit public funds. If overall cost-benefit analysis on a national scale demonstrates net advantage in dispersal, how should we persuade one organisation to accept higher costs in order that other organisations or individuals should make a more-than-proportional saving?

(9) Should economic cost benefit analysis be the sole criterion on which to judge the desirability of planning toward a particular life style? Are we in danger of forgetting that the built environment, with its technological embellishments, is merely the infrastructure and not an end in itself? Somewhere in all this there are people, real people, with hopes and fears, with views and aspirations, with inborn characteristics which make it essential for them to have personal contact with their fellow men and a need to feel wanted, to feel that they are making a contribution and that they are achieving self-fulfilment.

I will not go on—the questions that one could frame are endless. I hope that I have said sufficient to stimulate your interest and catalyze your debate.

# 2.4 The changing image of the city *Scott Greer*

Intellectual confusion and a problematic empirical ordering seem to be defining traits of the 'metropolitan problem.' The conceptual framework, already awry through the confusion of ideology, utopianism, and social science is doubly warped by indeterminacy in what we want of the city and the mixed metaphors of our theory. This state of affairs is common in the social sciences today, but it is accentuated by the rate of change in urban society, the unprecedented nature of our present situation, and the pluralistic normative order related to the community.

The contemporary world is one in which the traditional ordering of human behavior through group structures has changed radically. This change has proceeded, not through a weakening of group control, but through a shift in the relative importance of different kinds of group. The changing nature of exclusive membership groups, locality groups, and governmental structures, based upon the underlying transformation in the space-time ratio and the nature of production, present a multitude of facets necessitating study to the student of urban worlds. Some of these have been empirically interrelated through most of the history of urban settlement, but today they are empirically separating, and it is possible for us to make new dissociations—and new conceptual distinctions—that clarify the nature of the problem.

Urbanization has been conventionally used as a summary term for three different processes: (1) the growth of cities, (2) the increase in scale of a society, and (3) the culture of city dwellers, or urbanism. In the past the physical existence of the urban concentration was the most dramatic evidence of increase in scale, and was sometimes identified with it. (Thus Durkheim attempts to derive the division of labor from congestion.) In the same way, so isolated was the city from its hinterland that the 'urban' life style was as distinctive as an ethnic variation. 'Civilization' has its roots, as word and fact, in the enclave of traders, artisans, and rulers who existed within a sea of rustics.

It is clear today that increase in societal scale is the key process. The organizational transformation of the society, which binds in large net-

*Source:* Scott Greer, *The Emerging City: Myth and Reality*, Free Press, 1962

works of interdependence a region or a nation, makes possible and requires those concentrations of control centers and population we call cities. But at the same time, changes in the social organization resting upon interdependence result in drastic modifications of the urban settlement and its relation to the total society. The sheer size of the metropolitan population is impressive. More impressive are two trends: (1) increasing dispersion of population in space, and (2) increasing dispersion of the control centers formulating the dominant decisions that affect its order and shape.

The third process is also affected by increase in scale. There is in America today a consistent decline in the differentiation and social distance between countryman and urbanite. This rests also upon technological changes that have allowed a mastery of space never known before—one that makes possible rapid and precise communication and coordination of behavior across great differences. The culture of the large-scale society is urban in its essence; all ears are tuned to the nationwide communication networks, and behavior is ordered by the large-scale agencies of governmental bureau, corporation, and national market. In brief, the organizational necessities that once produced spatial density and a high degree of local autonomy are no longer coercive. The independent factory becomes the branch plant, while the nation-wide governmental agency pre-empts tasks once locally performed. Organizational space is a function of the shrinking space-time ratio.

It is clear that increase in scale is apt to continue. The web of interdependence continues to grow, with increasing specialization and differentiation of behavior and with increasingly complex mechanisms for integrating this behavior. The use of two-way telecommunication, supersonic aircraft, digital computers, and other innovations in communication and control make possible ever further increase in scale—and further conquest of geographical space. The growth and structure of cities becomes a dependent variable. Rather than the generator and limiting condition of increasing scale, the city is simply the convenient spatial location for centers of control, work, and residence. And convenience shifts with the demands of the national system. Thus the study of the city is the study of one temporary product of increasing scale—the changing nature of the human settlement.

## The City and the Metropolitan Region

The image of the city as a sovereign state, a military power, an integrated and powerful governmental unit, has eroded with the increasing scale of the carrying society. But what remains is not a vacuum to be neglected in our concern with the nation-state. It is a vast interconnected system of organizations operating in an inherited physical landscape and sharing in many respects a common fate. The metropolitan region is the local community of contemporary man. Though he uses it selectively, his selective use merely indicates the enormous complexity of the system— the differentiation of life patterns and the machinery of integration which keeps this human landscape stable and viable for his own path through social space.

Those who cry 'Danger!' at the disjunction between the official polity of the metropolis and its burgeoning problems of growth, planning, equity, and service have perhaps retained too great a loyalty to earlier images of the city. Emphasizing the lack of central authority, they have obscured the degree of order that prevails (Sayre and Kaufman, 1960). The metropolis, after all, is in no danger from invasion or collapse; it is supported by a national system. It works within broad tolerance limits and within these limits a minimal order maintains. When 'problems' are potentially lethal, the machinery for problem solving begins its creaky action—developing *ad hoc* solutions, expedients, special districts, or federal intervention. The metropolitan community is continuously improvised; its evolution is organic, not rational; change is crescive, not revolutionary; problems are solved by trial and error, not by fiat.

The specialized tasks within the metropolis change location as a result of changing modes of integration. As transport makes possible greater locational freedom, the older central city becomes a specialized area in which the newer migrants are acculturated, the poor are cared for, the working class has a home. Abandonment of the older residential neighborhoods by suburb-bound whites provides improved housing for the segregated ethnics. The changing complexion of the central city electorates gives the 'insulted and injured' a greater say in the polity here than anywhere else in America (Brotz, 1964). And within the working-class city the public monuments still stand symbolizing the center of the region. More important, as a result of urban geometry, within the central city lies the interchange of the area-wide transportation grid, the center of area-wide activities, and most of the great industrial concentrations. There is little danger that the central city will become a ghost town.

Nor is there much danger of its attracting its old-style residents back from the suburbs. The suburban areas will be the center of gravity for the masses of the metropolitan population for some time to come. Their choice of life style and their resulting household needs send them inevitably to the ranch houses on the peripheries. Here they develop the suburban neighborhoods and the communities of limited liability. Their differentiated portion of the metropolitan community remains an integral part of the whole, dependent upon the transportation grid and the interchange for its existence.

The over-all polity is, however, a sum of efforts ranging from those of neighborhood improvement associations to the negotiations between central city mayor and the plenipotentiaries of powerful organizations. In the absence of a central arena and polity, the public decisions are made in response to the politically potent demands of a fragmented electorate and the professional concerns of the political managerial elite. They suffice to accomplish a minimal ordering (Banfield, 1961).

Freeways are extended rapidly from each part of the periphery to the central interchange and the circumferential patterns multiply. The dozens of municipalities in the suburbs form a League of Municipalities and hire a professional manager; an organizational system is evolved which handles, adequately, some of the problems produced by contiguity and a common fate.

Such developments further reinforce the geographically defined dichotomy of the metropolis, solving the problems created by governmental split in the interdependent population. The resulting unit resembles, in its complexity and lack of symmetry, the government of a total large-scale society. The social scientist is dismayed and a little embittered by the lack of fit between the existing system and any simple, powerful, and elegant theory—much less his notion of a proper city government. His theoretical and normative yearning probably leads him to accentuate the deviation of the metropolis from such order. When, however, he continues empirical investigation of the polity, whether at the township, city, metropolitan, state, or federal level, he is forced to acknowledge again and again the looseness of the system through which our political fate is evolved.

Such may be the inseparable conditions of public decision-making in a society of increasing scale. The metropolitan community is without a moral and legal father, without a stable hierarchy, without obedient estates, without simple policy questions of right *or* wrong. It is, in this sense, the large-scale society in miniature.

## The Future of the City

As the organizational transformation of the society continues, new sources of energy allow further decentralization of work, new techniques of communication and transport allow further spread of organization. In the hinterland of any contemporary metropolis one encounters the industrial parks and planned residential developments that signify freedom from the locational determinants of other days. Still further away, along a 'country' highway far from any major city, one may see continuous development spreading for twenty or thirty miles—road-towns, for which the highway is Main Street.

The decentralization of residence, work, and play, around the metropolitan area, along with governmental fragmentation, are perhaps mere beginnings. Other functions, once considered native and proper only to the central city, may as easily be decentralized. Universities are experimenting with branch campuses and state-wide educational systems; there is no discernible reason that such cultural manifestations as ballet, symphony, and theatre should not rotate their performances through the giant subcenters that spring up where the freeways cross the circumferential highways. Perhaps only a lingering Puritanism persuades us that the person who is unwilling to devote two hours to transportation to and from the central business district has no right to 'culture.' The burgeoning little theatres and galleries throughout the Los Angeles metropolitan area may be some indication that the cultural dominance of the central business district is near an end. The patrons and customers of the arts are in the suburbs, notwithstanding the tropism of their creators for the center. Furthermore a great locational decentralization of entertainment has already taken place, through television, radio, and the movies. The locational requirements for a flourishing 'high culture' are now, to say the least, highly problematic, but the odds on maintaining the Downtown simply as a home for such performances would seem low.

Meanwhile, with the limited number of future migrants from the backwoods to the central city and the increasing spread of residences possible on the peripheries, it seems likely that the city will lose its monopoly of residential areas for colored persons. Though many may still choose the central city as a local area, many others only await the freedom from income and ethnic restrictions to move to newer and more convenient sites outside the congested center. As this occurs, the central city will require either an immensely expensive rebuilding or an orderly liquidation.

Whether the city can be rebuilt as a residential site is very problematical. For those who see the central city as 'hallowed ground,' no effort could be too great, and the polity as an economic force does not follow the rules of the market. It is possible that the ideologists of return, who envisage a central city organized in super-blocks and including headquarters, offices, apartments for those urbane in their life style, bohemias, public monuments, parks, and a limited number of single-family residences, will eventually prevail. Certainly the locational advantages of the central city can be greatly enhanced by developmental funds from the public treasury—and one could undoubtedly bribe middle-class persons to live in the center under some circumstances. However, without such efforts it seems doubtful that the locational demand of either industry or residential households will justify the enormous expense of razing much of the present structure and rebuilding. Thus a gradual shrinkage in the use-value of the central city as a whole seems inevitable in the short run.

Anthony Downs, a location economist, has indicated some pre-conditions for a 'recentralized city' (Downs, 1960). They are basic and major governmental programs that, in turn, will prime the pump for the use of private capital. They include clearance of many obsolete structures throughout the gray areas; a rigorous enforcement of housing and building codes to make owning slum property unprofitable; a massive improvement in policing to guarantee safety of person and property throughout the central city neighborhoods; the redevelopment of residential areas in very large blocks (at least as large as high school districts); redevelopment in *homogeneous* blocks that, similar in life style and social rank, would be competitive with suburban areas; maintenance and development of metropolis-wide cultural facilities in the central cities; and the creation of a transport grid that is meant to encourage and serve high-density residential areas.

Such a program would, in effect, suburbanize the central city's declining neighborhoods. It would require, however, very consistent and radical action by government—and we must recall the fragmented and immobilized state of local government in the metropolis. We must also remember Wood's remarks: New York City's redevelopment program, the largest and most vigorous in the nation, has completed, planned, or in progress, the renovation of one thousand acres (Wood, 1961). Five thousand acres need such renovation, and, so rapidly do neighborhoods change, the figure of five thousand acres may remain undiminished by the time present work is complete. One reason for the paucity of the response to blight is the enormously expensive practice of 'writing off' or subsidizing the difference between present market value and value as new land. (Vernon's estimate of the cost is approximately $160 000 000 per square mile of cleared land.) (Vernon, 1961). As Downs argues this would be much lower if the *legal* uses and restrictions of slum dwellings were regulated by government. But what central city political regime, dependent on the support of Negroes and the poor, has the determination to condemn thousands of dwellings and thus evict large and visible symbols of their supporting electorate? Central city governments are, in their way, as poor in political resources as the fragments of suburbia.

What is more likely, in the foreseeable future, is a continued dispersion of human activities and their sites within the metropolitan regions. Further, in a society of increasing scale in which wealth of all types multiplies, we may expect to see an increasing dispersion of metropolitan areas over the nation. And here it is worth remembering that such new areas have advantages over older ones comparable to those of suburbs over central cities: it is cheaper to build new plants from scratch if locational needs are comparable (Cotterell, 1955; Schmandt, 1960). In the larger system moreover, many functions can easily be allocated best in terms of such resources as climate—others can be practically location free. Such cities are typically continental assets, with a continental market—not mere centers for their hinterland and region. (Miami and Las Vegas, for example, are clearly without visible means of local support.) Los Angeles has grown from the beginning as part of the national market, for its hinterland includes chiefly desert and national parks. Phoenix, San Diego, Albuquerque, cities of phenomenal recent growth, continue the trend. The spread of metropolitan areas and the spread within each of them point to the possibility of loosely related complexes spreading over enormous distances—*regional cities*. In such cities no local subarea would have the density common to Chicago, Philadelphia, or New York, yet all would be easily accessible to other subareas through rapid transport and instantaneous communication.

Extrapolating from current trends, and utilizing Vernon's work on the New York Metropolitan Area, Downs sees the alternative to a recentralization of the city in these terms (Vernon, 1960).

'By the year 2000 the nation will find itself with several large "conurbations" of solid settlement, such as the Eastern Seaboard from Boston to Norfolk and west to Philadelphia, the West Coast from Santa Barbara south to Tiajuana and from Santa Rosa south to San Jose and west to Sacramento, and a vast weblike network in the Midwest uniting St. Louis, Chicago, Cleveland, Detroit, Indianapolis, Buffalo, and other cities along major freeways and railroads. According to this extrapolation model of future cities, more than 100 per cent of all metropolitan population growth will occur in suburbs, since central cities will actually lose population.'

Should this occur, the structure of the city as we know it would be at an end. The process of increase in scale, nurtured in cities and once thought of as unique to them, will have so transformed the society as to eliminate any need for urban centers. Such a society might be larger in scale than any we can conceive today, and its ways of life might well be described as 'urbane' if not urban, but settlement would be freed from spatial limitations, and the city would be no more.

Our options are not great. As C. Wright Mills (1956) has noted, there seems to be an 'organizational demiurge' central to contemporary social change. As it leads to efforts at predictability by the actors in one organization, these efforts tend to result in merger, accommodation, the rationalizing of the organizational environment. Thus, the networks of interdependence in the society continually expand, and from interdependence evolves an increasingly large organizational system. The more complex and mutually contingent the resulting social structure, the fewer its alternative courses of development. The way back to a simpler, smaller-scale society, is barred in the near future at least by the commitments necessary to insure the survival of the one that exists: only catastrophe can radically transform the evolution.

*The changing image of the city*

As organizational systems grow in scale the sacred values and esthetic themes of urban man are also changing. Today the ethos of an older city life leads us to feel the shock of disorientation when we consider that the central areas of St. Louis, Chicago, or Cleveland will never again be the symbol and hub of the entire urban community. Watching the decline of central city neighborhoods it is hard to resist a pious nostalgia and regret—and the suburban villas are no substitute for the communal life that is crumbling. Much of the culture, folklore, and ways of life that once stood for the city are casualties of change, for organizational transformation, like Shiva, destroys as it creates.

Among the casualties may also be the concept of local government as a democratic polity. We have noted that the small-scale nature of municipal government leads to its acquiescence in decisions made by large-scale organizations—corporations, unions, the federal government, the Port Authority, or the semiorganized markets. Such acquiescence means that significance evaporates: the local polity is largely irrelevant to the over-all position of the citizens. This, in turn, weakens the competence of local bodies. The entire process may be, however, circumscribed by one phrase—the increase in societal scale. Recalling the discussion of scale above, two aspects are crucial: it increases dependence upon large organization and distant centers of control specific to a limited membership—and it decreases dependence upon the near at hand, the locality group. Thus it strikes at the roots of the polity as a significant arena for the individual.

Indeed, it is likely that increase in scale is eventually inimical to the democratic local polity. Kitto's (1956) analysis of the decline and degradation of the Athenian polity rests, finally, upon the 'turning away of the citizens' from community affairs. Such withdrawal is common to both the Republican politics of the Midwestern country towns and the 'power elite' in large cities. It reflects the movement of significance, which follows organization, away from the locality group. Whether, and how, it might be recaptured is a subject for speculation—but not in this book.

So the older city appears to be dying—functionally, structurally, politically, and eventually, ideologically. Yet the compliance of the population with these changes we have noted has hardly been forced—indeed, as Wood points out, policy seems to follow the market. And, for the average man, the contemporary metropolis is a vast improvement over his share of the older city. Out of the row houses and tenements, the streetcar and the loft building, he has moved to the ranch house with its patio and two-car garage, the job in the pastel industrial park, the television, the children. . .

## References

BANFIELD, E. C. (1961) *Political Influence*, New York, The Free Press of Glencoe.

BROTZ, H. M. (1964) Social Stratification and the Political Order *American Journal of Sociology*, **69**, pages 571–578.

COTTERELL, F. (1955) *Energy and Society*, New York, McGraw-Hill.

DOWNS, A. (1960) *The Future Structure of American Cities*, paper presented at the Conference on Transportation held by the National Academy of Sciences at Woods Hole, Mass., 9 August.

KITTO, H. D. F. (1956) *The Greeks*, Chapter 9, Penguin.

MILLS, C. W. (1956) *The Power-Elite*, New York, Oxford University Press.

SAYRE, W. S. and KAUFMAN, H. (1960) *Governing New York*, New York, The Russell Sage Foundation.

SCHMANDT, J. (1960) 'The City and the Rings', *American Behavioural Scientist*, November, pages 17–19.

VERNON, R. (1960) *Metropolis, 1985*, Cambridge, Mass., Harvard University Press.

VERNON, R. (1961) The Economics and Finances of the large Metropolis *Daedalus*, Winter, pages 31–47.

WOOD, R. C. (1961) *1400 Governments: The Political Economy of the New York Metropolitan Region*, Cambridge, Mass., Harvard University Press.

# 2.5 Resources and the Economic Framework
# P. A. Stone

## Introduction

One of the more important restraints on the developing pattern of urbanisation is the availability of resources, both real and financial. The development, renewal and maintenance of the built environment requires a large proportion of national output, currently about an eighth. Increases in the output of construction work can be obtained through increases in the productivity of construction, by reductions in the resources available for the provision of other goods and services, or from increases in national output. The built environment is not alone in being inadequate in quantity and quality. There are many claims on the national output; more resources are required for improving industrial capital, for developing education, and the health and social services, and for increasing the availability of consumer goods and services. Urban development involves a large use of land, the supply of which is

*Source: Urban Studies* (1969) **3**, number 3

largely fixed. Moreover, the community is concerned not only with material standards but also with the quality of life and with leisure, the demand for which tends to compete with the demand for higher material standards. On the other hand, the built environment is not by any means just a form of consumption goods; part of it consists of productive goods which help in increasing national output and hence with the resources for improving the built environment. Thus, some aspects of urban development have greater priority than others.

Of course, not all aspects of urbanisation have a significant effect on the use of resources. Environmental quality depends on the way in which the resources are used as well as on the amount used. A change in the geographical patterns of location may not affect the national resources required, although it would require a change in their regional distribution. Again, new patterns of urbanisation resulting from changes in social patterns might have little effect on the use of resources, although it might result in changes in the directions of their use.

## Population, Human Activities and National Resources

The supply and demand for resources depends basically on population and human activities, and on their interactions with natural resources. Population increases result in more consumers as well as more producers. The movement in output and demand per head depends, other things being equal, on the demographic structure of the population.

The size and demographic structure of the population is the result of four separate types of change, births, deaths, and inward and outward migration. The difficulty in projecting future population for Great Britain tends to lie mainly in projecting the rate of birth. Birth rates have varied considerably in the past (Fig. 1). Live births per 1000 of population exhibit a cyclical pattern rather than a trend. The patterns of crude live birth rates depend partly on the age and sex structure of the population, partly on the age at which women marry and partly on their fertility, the probability of a married or unmarried woman of a given age having a child. Birth rates have been rising in the case of married women of all ages, a greater proportion of women have been marrying, they have been marrying younger and the proportion of births outside marriage have been increasing. While these factors explain the recent rise in birth rates they do not indicate whether the rise can be expected to continue in the long term. This depends on whether it is the timing of families which has changed or their ultimate size. The statistical data available only indicates what has happened in the case of cohorts of women who have completed their families and whose experience may not be relevant to women now of child-bearing age. In contrast changes in death rates, assuming no catastrophes, are reasonably predictable. In

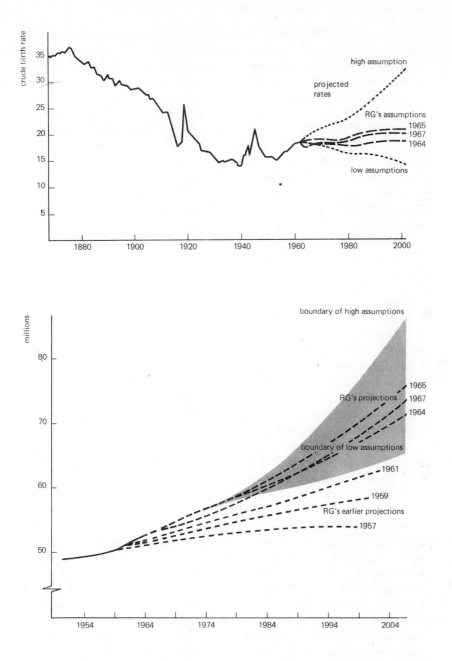

the past the scale of net migration has generally not been large enough to have much effect on population but changes in national policy for migration or changes in rates of emigration could result in their being more important in the future.

Thus the difficulty in projecting population is largely because of the volatile fertility and marriage rates and the unpredictability of the scale of migration. The official statisticians, the Registrars General, have made considerable modifications to their projections in the last few years (Fig. 2). The range of possible variation in future population could be very considerable. The shaded area (Fig. 2) indicates the limits of some projections made with 1964 data. While on the official basis of projection 53 million in 1964 would have increased to 72 million by 2004; boundary figures are 85 million and 56 million. The boundaries indicate what the levels would be, on the one hand, were marriage rates to continue to rise in accordance with the 1931–61 trend and if fertility rates were to rise by no more than two-thirds of the recent rate, and on the other hand, if marriage and fertility rates were to decline gradually to the levels of 1940. Both assumptions produced birth rates within the margin of experience of the last 80 years. Over a period of 40 years, projections on such assumptions would increase the official projections by 18% or reduce them by 9% (Stone, 1969).

However, not only could the total future population be very different from the total which appears probable today but its demographic structure could also be very different. While the number of persons over 40 at the end of the period cannot be affected by changes in births, the number of young people, under 15, could be 50% greater in the one case and 27% less in the other. The number of working age, 15–69, could be 9% greater against a population 18% greater, in the one case and 3% less as against a population 9% less in the other case. Thus the faster population increased as a result of natural increase, the more young people there would be to support and the smaller the proportion of population of working age to produce the national output. Of course, if the official projection is correct, the proportion of working age would still fall in the future; over a period of 40 years it would fall from about 70% to about 66% (Stone, 1969).

The working population, that is the total number of people actually available for work, is likely to increase more slowly than the number of people of working age. This is because it is expected that the increase in young people remaining longer in full-time education (Statistics of Education, 1964, 1965; Robbins Report, 1963) and a slight tendency to earlier retirement will more than offset expected gains from increases in the proportion of married women in employment (Ministry of Labour Gazette, 1963, 1965). Over the period of 40 years the reduction in the overall activity rate might be nearly 2%. The combined effect of a smaller proportion of people of working age with lower activity rates would reduce the proportion of workers by about 8%.

National output depends not only on the size of the population actually available for work but also on the rates of productivity, on the activities on which they are employed, on the number actually employed and on their hours of work. Clearly any projection of these factors over a long period must be very hazardous. The general expectation has been that it should be possible to achieve an annual growth rate in gross domestic product per person employed of 3% to 4%; the figure given in the National Plan (1965) was 3·4% a year over the period 1964–70 while Beckerman (1965) suggested a figure of 3·1% over the period 1960–1975. It has not been possible to achieve rates as high as these over the last few years because of balance of payment difficulties and other short-term problems.

Since the war national output per head in Great Britain has increased rapidly, though not as fast as in some other countries. Since 1951, the average rate of increase has been about 3%, although it was substantially higher in the earlier part of the period (National Income and Expenditure, 1968). Output per head has not risen as fast as this, or even risen at all. In the early part of the century, certainly the first 20 years, output per head was falling (Mitchell and Deanne, 1962). The level at the beginning of the century was probably not bettered for about 30 years. Over the first half of the century output per head probably only rose by just over 10%.

There can be no certainty that output per head will rise at current rates over the rest of the century. The higher the level of productivity reached, the more difficult it may be to sustain such rates of increase. The achievement of high rates of increase tends to require a high rate of capital formation and an adaptable and hard working labour force. The exchange of higher levels of goods and services for more leisure and a more comfortable industrial life might be preferred.

Despite the difficulties in projecting output, the projection of requirements is possibly even more difficult. This is because, basically, output depends on the size of the labour force, which, catastrophes apart, can be projected with more certainty than total population which is the base for projecting many of the requirements. While long-term projections of population are subject to possible errors of the order of 10%, the number and demographic structure of people of middle and old age can be estimated with reasonable precision. Up to 20 years ahead it is possible to produce reasonable accurate projections of the adult population. As a result, estimates of reasonable precision can be prepared of the number of households and for all the requirements which stem from households, of the size of the labour force, of the number of potential car owners and for other requirements which stem from adults. The further ahead projections are pushed the smaller the proportion of population for which reasonable precision can be obtained.

Thus it is reasonably certain that the greater the increase in the population, the greater the increase in requirements in relation to the size of the labour force and the more necessary it will be to follow a pattern of activities and life styles which tend to increase output per employed person.

## The Built Environment

Clearly the total requirements for the built environment depend basically on the size and structure of the population and on its activities. Since so many of the requirements for built environment depend more on the number of adults than on the total population, in the short run, up to about 20 years, there is a basic stability in the projections for the gross numbers of units of facility likely to be required. This element of stability is reduced to some extent by uncertainties about activities and life-styles. The net number of units to be provided depends, of course, on the size of the current stock and its expected rate of obsolescence. This in turn depends on the quality of the built environment which is required in the future.

It is perhaps easier to illustrate the inter-play of these forces in the case of housing than most types of built facility. In order to estimate the requirements for housing, it is necessary to consider rates of household formation, the occupation of dwellings, the standards likely to be required and the stock which is available.

Rates of household formation have been rising for some time and further rises in the future appear likely as real incomes rise. It appears reasonable to expect that in the future most married men and other adults who have been married, and about a half of older single people will form their own households. The proportion of young unmarried people forming their own households is currently very small, about 4% for unmarried men and women of 15 and under 40. Probably this rate will increase three or fourfold.

The sizes for each type of household can be obtained from the Census data, although the crude figures have to be modified to allow for the effect of changes in birth rates. Census data also provides the best guide to the number of rooms households will wish to occupy. Clearly, it would be incorrect to be guided by the occupation rates of households who are overcrowded or who have excess rooms. In 1961, the balance had on average one room for each 0·69 persons (Stone, 1969). This rate is, of course, far more generous of space than the minimum standards suggested by the Parker Morris Committee or at which people are initially housed in public authority dwellings. Even so, it appears doubtful whether this standard will be acceptable in future. If people become more home centred and have a greater variety of home recreations, they will probably need more rooms and hence larger dwellings (Willmott, 1969). Thus, while currently there is a need for additional

106

small dwellings, the average size required is likely to rise, especially if birth rates increase significantly.

At the current rate of output, about 400 000 dwellings a year\*(Housing Statistics), the number of dwellings available by the early nineteen seventies is likely to exceed the number of households. Of course, not all dwellings would necessarily be located in the areas in which they were most required. During the seventies and early eighties about 120 000 additional dwellings a year are likely to be needed, from the mid-eighties the number required each year appears likely to rise and to have reached 200 000 a year by the turn of the century. Of course, if birth rates were much higher than officially projected, the number required could be much greater.

Currently there are about 18 million dwellings in Great Britain. Of these over 4 million are about 90 or more years old, nearly 3 million are between 50 and 90 years old and another 4 million date from between the wars and are between 30 and 50 years old (Stone, 1969). The indications are that over 2 million of the dwellings are structurally unsound; these and a further 2 million need extensive repairs and redecoration. While most dwellings have a cold water supply, many lack other basic amenities. There are about 3 million dwellings without an internal water closet, about 2·5 million without a fixed bath and even more without a bathroom and an adequate hot water system. The environment of the housing is unsatisfactory for about 8 million dwellings and very poor for nearly 2 million of them. Only about a quarter of the stock of dwellings have garages and over a half have neither a garage nor a space for one. Generally, of course, it is the oldest housing which has the least amenities and which is in the poorest condition.

The rate at which the stock of dwellings has been improved in the past has been very slow. Currently 80 to 90 000 of the worst dwellings are being demolished each year (Housing Statistics). In addition about 30 000 a year are demolished to make way for road and town development; only a proportion of these are likely to be in a bad condition. Something over 100 000 unfit dwellings a year are known to have been made fit. Improvement grants are being provided for over 120 000 dwellings a year; some of these may have been for unfit dwellings. Since dwellings are deteriorating the whole time, it is doubtful whether the standard of the stock is even being maintained.

Clearly, even if extensive repair and improvement work were undertaken, many dwellings in the existing stock would become obsolete and need to be replaced before the end of the century. In the absence of information about the types of dwellings in the stock, age, which tends to be correlated with standard and condition, is perhaps the best indicator of the likely scale of obsolescence. Of course, the conveniently

\*The current figure is considerably lower [Editors]

planned good quality dwelling is likely to remain in use even though it is old. It will be seen from the figures given earlier, that the rate of replacement is likely to affect the number of dwellings to be built far more than differences in the need for additional dwellings. Between now and say the turn of the century the number of additional dwellings required is likely to be about 6 million (Stone, 1969). Even if the population was to reach the extreme projection (Fig. 2), less than 2 million more would be required. In contrast about 4 million dwellings would be required to clear and replace the equivalent* of the dwellings which would be over 120 years old by the turn of the century. About 7 million dwellings would be required if the target related to dwellings which would be over 80 years old by the turn of the century. Because of the scale of building between the wars about 11 million would be needed if this group of dwellings were included in the target for replacement.

If the current rate of constructing dwellings, about 400,000 a year, was maintained, it would take to about the end of the nineteen eighties to replace those at present structurally unsound and to end of the nineteen nineties to replace the equivalent of the pre-1880 dwellings. It would not be possible to replace the equivalent of the pre-1921 dwellings until the early years of the next century.

A comparison between expenditure on housing maintenance and the cost of maintenance at the standards adopted by local authorities, indicates that not much more than a third of the necessary work is carried out (Stone, 1969). That gap is likely to be only partially filled by the work of housing occupiers. Unless considerable additional resources can be found both to provide adequate current maintenance and to make good the backlog of maintenance and upgrading, the housing stock at the end of the century might be no better in quality than it is today.

## Resources for the Built Environment

The amount of resources likely to be required to develop, redevelop and maintain the built environment clearly depends more on the standards and forms of development than on the scale of population growth. While the level of error in predicting the needs for additional units of development can be estimated, the standards and forms depend on human choice in relation to the use of resources and it is possible only to examine the effect of choice.

Over the rest of the century additional housing to meet the needs of the officially projected population would appear to cost on average about £600 million a year (Stone, 1969). The cost would rise to about £1000 million if sufficient dwellings were also built to replace the equivalent of

*'equivalent' implies equal in number since clearly not all the older dwellings would be cleared first—some will be retained indefinitely.

pre-1881 dwellings. The replacement in addition of equivalent 1881–1921 dwellings would add about a further £250 million a year, while if replacement were extended to include the equivalent of pre-1941 dwellings about a further £425 million would be added. In contrast, the effect of the extreme population projection would only increase the costs by about £200 million.

These estimates are based on 1964 price levels and Parker Morris standards, with an addition of 10% to allow for the incidence of better quality housing. It has been assumed that the current form of development would be used with about 74% houses, 18% low flats, and 8% high flats. On this basis the average density would be about 59 habitable rooms per acre.

The costs of making good the arrears of maintenance and of upgrading dwellings in the existing stock, in so far as this would be economically worthwhile, would be about £8000 to £9000 million. While this work would have to be spread over a number of years, it is, of course, all urgent. The total would not be much affected by the proportion of dwellings in the stock which was replaced. In addition regular maintenance to local authority standards would appear likely to cost on average over the period nearly £1000 million a year (Stone, 1969).

In 1964, new housing work in Great Britain was costing something over £1000 million a year and maintenance on housing probably something about £500 million a year (Stone, 1969). While occupiers carry out some maintenance work themselves, this is likely to make only a small contribution to the maintenance work covered by these figures. Thus, while expenditure on new housing appears to have been at an adequate level to meet the needs for additional dwellings and to replace pre-1881 dwellings by the end of the century, the level of expenditure on maintenance has been quite inadequate.

The relative importance of building additional and replacement facilities naturally varies from one category to another. Replacement appears to be more important in the case of industrial and health buildings, while additional space appears to be more important for office, education and other categories of buildings except for buildings for distribution for which the importance of the two types of space are relatively evenly balanced. It would appear that on average the annual expenditure over the rest of the century for non-residential building construction would be about £850 million.

In addition to building and civil engineering resources the development of the built environment would require a considerable use of virgin land. The amount would depend on the densities of development as well as the scale of development and on the extent of redevelopment. In the past the densities of development were generally higher than today and generally fell from the nineteenth century to the nineteen thirties. Thus, the redevelopment of areas originally developed in the last century tends to result in a reduction of densities and in the need for more land elsewhere, whereas the redevelopment of inter-war development would tend to result in higher densities and would release land for additional development. On average, the scale of development visualised would require 40 000 to 50 000 additional areas of land for development each year.

## The Availability of Resources

The amount of land in Great Britain is more or less fixed. The amount can, of course, be marginally increased by draining and filling areas of shallow water around the coasts and estuaries but this process tends to be a heavy user of resources. Land for development can generally only be obtained by taking land currently used for some other purpose; this, in the long run, means taking land from agriculture.

The productivity of agricultural land varies considerably. A large proportion of it consists of rough grazing. Such land is of comparatively little value for agriculture or for development and is unlikely to be used for development purposes. Most development is likely to take place on land currently used for arable and permanent grass. About 5% of such land is likely to be required for development over the rest of the century. The output of agricultural land is increasing as husbandry improves, as better use is made of the land available, and as a higher proportion of land is used for the more valuable types of product. Although over the last decade, yields rose only by 1 or 2% per annum, the total value of net output rose over 3% per annum. It will seem that the output lost from farmland taken for development over the rest of the century could probably be replaced within three or four years. Even if the rate of improvement in productivity was only about 1·25% per annum, the remaining farmland would be able to produce enough food by the end of the century, assuming that the present proportion of food was imported, for a population larger than officially projected for that time. Changes in world conditions might, of course, result in it being expedient to import a lower proportion of food. It is, however, clear that the use of farmland for development is of minor importance compared with the size of the population and food import policy.

However, the best farmland produces about three times as much per acre as average land, and yields appear to be rising faster on the better land. It is therefore of some importance to steer development away from the better land as far as this is practical. The better land tends to be flat and well drained, and also the most suitable land for urban development. The costs of drainage and under-building tend to make the use of land unsuitable for development expensive to use. The value of the output from farmland is rarely sufficient to make it economic to save even the best farmland either by developing unsuitable land, or by saving land by using multi-storey or multi-level development. Since some regions are endowed with better land than others, it may be difficult in some areas to find sufficient low grade land suitable for development. Similarly there is a very uneven distribution of land suitable for recreational purposes. For these reasons difficulties are likely to be met in finding suitable land for all purposes in some parts of the country, for example, in the Midlands, where land is on average of a high quality.

## Scales, Standards and Forms of Development

Some estimate of the feasibility of achieving given scales, standards and forms of built environment can be obtained by relating estimates of the resources which would be required against estimates of probable output of the appropriate resources. It would appear that a moderate annual increase in the output of construction work, about 2%, the rate achieved over the last three years, would be sufficient in the long run to meet the resources required for the development, improvement and maintenance of the built environment at currently accepted good standards.

Clearly, present day standards are unlikely to continue to be acceptable over the rest of this century. The standard of living is likely to rise in step with increases in the productivity of the economy, and with it the standard of the built environment. It is thus likely that a large part of the expected increase in productivity in construction will be needed to meet the additional construction work associated with rising standards in the built environment, and will not be available for meeting the basic load. Over the last decade, the standard of living as measured by the consumption of goods and services per head, has increased by about 2·25% a year (National Income and Expenditure, 1968); the expenditure per head on housing has increased at about the same rate. At this rate standards would be doubled by the end of the century. This would suggest that most of the likely improvement in general productivity would be needed to meet a rise in standards. It would appear unlikely that productivity in such an old established industry such as construction, much of the work of which is maintenance work, would rise faster than that of the economy as a whole. Thus, the proportion of national resources devoted to construction work would probably need to be raised in order to meet the growth in demand. By the end of the century the proportion might need to be about two-thirds greater than it is today. The larger the population the greater the proportion of national output likely to be necessary.

Housing is the largest category of building. The development, improvement and maintenance of housing and housing areas could account for nearly a half of the total cost of the built environment. While the current expenditure on new housing, if continued over the rest of the century, would be about sufficient to meet the needs for additional housing and to replace the equivalent of pre-1881 dwellings, the level of current expenditure on maintenance is quite inadequate and is declining in real terms.

Even if the current rate of replacing dwellings was increased threefold it would take over a decade to replace the dwellings in the worst class, those with structural failures and serious physical deterioration. If, in the meantime, arrears of maintenance were not made good and regular maintenance was not carried out at an adequate standard, more dwellings would deteriorate beyond the point at which repair was worthwhile and it might be two or three decades before even the really unsatisfactory dwellings could be eliminated.

The resources required to carry out urgent housing improvement work and to raise the standards of regular maintenance to an acceptable level over the next decade would be equivalent to an immediate increase in the output of all construction of about an eighth and a continuation of increases in output as great as over the past decade. Clearly, even if increases on this scale could be obtained, they could not be devoted entirely to housing maintenance work. Moreover, if as suggested earlier, housing standards rose above those of today, meeting such rises in standard would absorb a substantial part of the annual increases in output.

In the absence of additional resources for housing, an alternative would be to reduce the rate of constructing new dwellings and to switch the resources released to maintenance work. For example, half the additional resources required could be obtained by reducing constructions to 300 000 dwellings a year. Further resources could be obtained by concentrating on the most economic forms of development. Since substantially less resources are required to improve a dwelling than to build a replacement, the rate at which additional satisfactory dwellings would be provided would be faster, even although the number of replacements was reduced. Moreover restored dwellings could be let much more cheaply than those newly built. If productivity continues to rise two or three times as fast in new work as in maintenance work, in the long run more output could be obtained from the same labour force by giving priority to maintenance work in the near future and postponing new work until later, when the comparative level of output in it would be relatively so much greater than today. By switching labour back to new work later in the century when the arrears of maintenance and improvement work had been completed, it would be possible to make good house construction sacrificed in the immediate future. In the long run the number of dwellings replaced need be no less; the stock would be younger and hence more likely to meet future needs.

The social categories of buildings have some features in common with housing. While the maintenance of such buildings has not generally been neglected to the extent of some housing, many of these buildings lack the equipment and amenities now considered essential. Often improvement would be more economic than replacement and lead to a more rapid build-up of adequate facilities. Such a policy would lead to more significant gains for the health buildings category than for the educational category for which the stock needs to be greatly expanded. Again for industrial buildings the major share of resources is likely to be needed for the improvement and rebuilding of the stock rather than for creating additional space. The sector of the economy with the greatest growth is likely to be services and it is there that a great deal of additional space will need to be created.

Thus, while in the absence of a large shift of national resources to construction, the annual output is only likely to increase slowly, there are needs for a considerable immediate expansion in the construction, improvement and maintenance of many categories of built facility. Unless there is a large scale shift of resources in the near future, many needs will inevitably remain unsatisfied and it will be necessary to decide where the priorities should lie. Probably priority will be given to facilities which are related to production since, in the long run, these will tend to result in a larger national output and in the availability of additional resources for the extension and improvement of the built environment. If priorities are decided in this way the scope for choice between better housing, social services and leisure facilities will tend to be limited.

Of course, the standards of the built environment can be raised in a number of ways; by raising the standards at which facilities are currently built; by a faster rate of replacing facilities in the existing stock; by improvements to existing facilities and by higher standards of maintenance. Generally, the rate at which new facilities are added to the stock is rather low. At any one time only 2% or 3% of the facilities in the stock are less than a year old. Raising the standards at which new facilities are built therefore tends to be a slow method of raising general standards. The estimates given earlier were based on the assumption that only 1% to 2% of the facilities in the stock would be replaced each year. Even on this basis it appeared likely that the proportion of national resources devoted to construction work would need to be substantially increased. Unless either a substantially greater share of national resources can be devoted to construction work or new techniques can be found which would allow structures to be built for substantially less than today without a reduction in their expected durability, it seems unlikely that the rates of replacement could be much increased above those assumed. Standards can generally be raised most economically by better maintenance and improvements to the existing stock of buildings.

113

The resources required for the built environment are also affected by urban form. Dwellings in four-storey flatted blocks outside London are nearly a quarter more expensive than equivalent dwellings in houses and bungalows; equivalent dwellings in twelve-storey blocks are two-thirds more expensive (Stone, 1969). The provision of garages with high blocks is also more expensive than with houses; while there are savings on development (roads and services) costs of these tend to be small. Maintenance and management costs also tend to rise with the number of storeys. Since densities tend to rise only moderately with increases in the number of storeys, the costs of saving land by building high tend to be considerable, between £40,000 and £50,000 an acre where high blocks are used (Stone, 1969). This is rarely worthwhile from a national point of view unless either the occupiers place a very high value on living in high flatted blocks, for which there is little evidence, or high density development reduces overspill sufficiently for travelling and other costs to offset the higher costs of development. It is difficult to find situations in which the balance of external economies would make this type of development viable. National housing costs would be raised 10% if average densities were raised from 59 to 80 habitable rooms per acre by using 50% houses and 30% high flats. Financially, this type of high density development is rarely worthwhile because land prices (outside Central London) do not generally reach high enough levels, because site prices per acre tend to rise with density, thus reducing the savings from high density development and because with land at high prices rents tend to be higher than most people can afford.

It has sometimes been suggested that large groups of people, even complete settlements, should be housed in a single large building. This would involve a large increase in circulation space, either vertical or horizontal, within the building. Such circulation areas would be more expensive to construct and operate than circulation space provided outside. A large proportion of the area of such a building would need to be artificially lit and ventilated. Unless energy became relatively much cheaper than it is today, the costs-in-use of such space would tend to be far greater than that of conventional buildings.

The multi-level use of space also adds to development and operation costs. Decked shopping and service cores are about five times as expensive as those developed on the ground. Land saved by the use of multi-storey car parks and decking over roads and car parking tends to cost £40,000 to £50,000 per acre. In fact, the amount of land which can be saved by multi-level development is rather small since such a small proportion of land is used for the base of buildings. For example, in a conventional new town only about an eighth of the land is covered with buildings, a sixth for roads and nearly three-fifths for gardens and open space (Stone, 1969).

114

It would appear that over the rest of the century, development on new land may be required for a population equal to about half the current population. About two-thirds of this number would be additional population and the balance would be people who, because of the lower densities obtained on redevelopment, could not be re-accommodated in the areas in which they formerly lived. This population could be accommodated partly by limited growth to existing settlements, partly by large scale forced growth to existing settlements and partly in new settlements. The new and expanded settlements could be organised in different ways and in different locations. While most existing areas of urban development would remain, the urban pattern of Britain could be radically changed.

## Life Styles, Values and Finance

So far, attention has been centred on the real resources that would appear necessary to achieve the various scales, standards and forms of urban development which have been considered. Real resources have been measured in terms of land and construction work. The scales of resources likely to be required have been compared with the availability of land and with the output of construction work which might be feasible given certain proportions of the national labour force and certain rates of improvement in productivity. These proportions and rates have in turn been compared with possible movements in the economy as a whole. However, the real resources are unlikely to be moved in the way required unless finance is available in the required amounts and at the right time. The availability of finance depends on peoples' willingness to use wealth in this way and on the existence of a mechanism to enable finance to have the required effects. If, for example, people preferred to spend their incomes on consumer goods and services, rather than on built facilities, labour and capital would be attracted to the industries catering for consumers' goods and services and the resources available for construction work would be inadequate. Such a situation might, of course, be modified by government action, for example, by increasing taxes on other goods and services, and using the revenue to subsidise the finance of construction work.

As pointed out earlier, nearly half the resources required for built facilities are required for housing. Housing dominates both the costs and the quality of the built environment. Inevitably, if the general standard of housing was improved, even only to broadly Parker Morris standards, housing costs would rise. Rebuilding and improving the existing stock of housing to the extent suggested earlier would raise housing costs on average by about two thirds. The poorer households would find it difficult, some impossible, to meet such costs without assistance. Thus, unless action is taken at government level to direct housing grants to those in greatest need, the improvements in the standards of housing would be unlikely to take place.

Moreover, while the ability to devote greater proportions of income to housing would increase as real incomes rose, many households might not value housing sufficiently to be prepared to pay comparatively more for it. It is notable that over the five years 1962–67 expenditure per head on housing only increased about the same as total consumers' expenditure (Ministry of Housing and Local Government). While expenditure per head on fuel and light increased slightly more than average, that on furnishing increased less that average. In contrast, the expenditure on motoring increased about five times as much as average.

The future patterns of urbanisation depend on the future population and life-styles, on technological innovations, on available resources and on the extent to which the community is able to communicate its sense of values and make effective its judgement on the use of resources. The effect of higher birth rates, the fall in activity rates, the greater demand for leisure and a more comfortable industrial life would be to reduce the volume of output resources. The more the resources were limited the more important it would be to improve rather than replace older facilities and the more the past patterns of urbanisation would restrict future patterns. Unless national productivity increases much faster than it has in the past, or a much larger proportion of resources are devoted to construction, the rate of redeveloping the existing urban environment will not be sufficiently rapid to enable either past neglect to be made good and standards substantially raised or sufficiently large to support radical changes in the patterns of urbanisation. Unless the more revolutionary changes in construction occur there would be little possibility of substantially shortening the life of facilities. However, built facilities tend to be very flexible and adaptable. Considerable changes in life-styles could take place without radical changes in the built form. Even if the scale of development was large enough to allow considerable changes in the locational patterns of urban development, the inertia of established communities might impose considerable restraints on such changes. Regionally and locally conflicting claims on land might impose some restraints. Since built form is and appears likely to continue to be relatively permanent and to act as a restraint on future patterns of urbanisation, it is all the more important that decisions in this field should be taken in the light of the best possible predictions about requirements for the future.

## References

BECKERMAN, W. and Associates (1965) *The British Economy in 1975*, Cambridge University Press.

HOUSING STATISTICS Great Britain (various dates), Ministry of Housing and Local Government, HMSO.

*Ministry of Labour Gazette* (July 1963, January 1965) HMSO.

MITCHELL, B. R. and DEANNE, P. (1962) *Abstract of British Historical Statistics.*

NATIONAL INCOME AND EXPENDITURE (1968) Central Statistical Office.

ROBBINS REPORT (1963) *Ministry of Education Committee in Higher Education*, Cmnd. 2154, HMSO 1963.

*Statistics of Education 1963 and 1964* (1964 and 1965) Department of Education and Science, HMSO.

STONE, P. A. (1963) Housing, Town Development, Land and Costs, *The Estates Gazette.*

STONE, P. A. (1969) *Urban Development in Britain: Standards, Costs and Resources 1964–2004, Population and Housing*, Cambridge University Press.

WILMOTT, P. (1969) Some Social Trends, *Urban Studies*, **6**, Number 3, November.

# 2.6 Material resources *Richard L. Meier*

## 1 Resource development and use

Although the amounts of land, energy, and other natural resource inputs required to maintain a man at adequate levels of living are declining,* indicating that technology is becoming more efficient over time, the overall demand for future consumption of resources exceeds still further the supplies available to countries endeavoring to develop. The principal reason for this paradoxical trend is that population growth has been accelerating in these areas.†

*Source:* R. Jungk and J. Galtung (Editors), *Mankind 2000*, George Allen and Unwin, 1969

*The amount of land required to support a man at constant caloric intake has been declining at a rate of 1–2% per year for the last two decades, and the amount of energy required to produce a standard amount of transport, cooking fuel, light, and home heat has been dropping almost as rapidly. *Cf.* H. H. Landsberg, L. L. Fischman, and J. J. Fisher (1963). If a 'One World' posture is accepted, as these authors do, the increasing efficiency argument should hold for some time to come.

†Latest reports in the newest *United Nations Demographic Yearbook* (1965) showed that 63% of the countries in Asia, Africa, and Oceania registered a rise in natural population growth rate as compared to the baby boom year of 1948. Countries with large populations, such as India, Pakistan, Nigeria, Egypt, and probably China and Indonesia, fall into this category.

Action is being taken on the population planning front, but the reversal of trend will take some time.* The conclusion could easily be reached that many countries are becoming so populous that the resources available per capita are too small to allow them to break out of the Malthusian trap (Table 1). However, such calculations are based upon output-resource use ratios for presently-recommended processes worked out in countries with plentiful resources. An assessment of possible resource-conserving technologies needs to be undertaken to discover whether a new path to economic development can be found which will cope with a greater population burden.

The best hope lies in the new knowledge acquired from the recent burst of scientific research and development. How will the additions to our stock of knowledge shift the projections? Does it suggest a more economic path to industrialization, urbanization, and modern institutions than the historic route pioneered by Western countries? External economies obtainable from the close integration of large systems offer the most opportunities for increased efficiency. Perhaps the scale of the industry may also yield some sizable improvements in performance.

The properties of the overall population-resources-knowledge system must be kept in mind while engaged in explorations of possible paths. Consider the normal history of a natural resource, whether a mineral deposit or a living population, as in a fishery. It can be identified as a natural resource only when the state of knowledge reaches a level where the potentials for human use are evident. Effort and skill are needed thereafter to wrest it from the site and convert it into an acceptable commodity. Firms and institutions are involved in determining what admixture, form, shape, quality standard, and image shall be imposed upon it. The ultimate fate of the resource is to be found in widely distributed deposits of ash, rust, scale, shavings, shards, bones, and similar debris along with carbon dioxide released to the atmosphere. New knowledge about resources eventually requires a bigger dust-bin!

Some lasting effects can be identified within the human population notwithstanding. Ecologists point out that added resources for any living population (human included) causes the members to become more robust, then to fatten, and shortly thereafter to expand in numbers. Thus extra access to resources yields increased bio-mass. The human race is presently responding in that manner to resources discovered one to two generations back. However, the leading resource-consuming societies have now advanced a bit further because the channel leading to

---

*The most comprehensive current review of progress throughout the world at the moment is a monthly publication of The Population Council (230 Park Avenue, New York 10017) entitled *Studies in Family Planning*. Taiwan seems to have reversed around 1960, South Korea around 1965, and Hong Kong some time in between. In each of these territories a steady downturn in births is recorded every year.

bio-mass formation has been throttled by more widely diffused knowledge about birth control; new channels have been opened up instead
which convert the utility of resources into enhanced social and cultural
activity that leaves a residuum in the form of enlarged institutions. In
popular cybernetic language, the negentropy of the natural resource is
transformed into the negentropy of social order and into the patterning
of symbols (recorded knowledge) at higher levels in the hierarchy of
organization (Meier, 1967). The exploitation of systems language
potentials requires the synthesis of a 'higher strategy' which overcomes
critical shortages experienced in subsystems.

The central arguments justifying the need for a fundamentally new
strategy can be outlined briefly as follows:

1. Resource levels per capita in most countries endeavoring to develop
are found to be a factor of ten to a hundred less than those of countries
which have already developed (Table 1).

2. Even a redistribution of the world's resources between the *have* and
*have-not* nations would leave grave deficiencies. Thus countries with
surpluses will not be in a position to meet critical shortages when they
arise.

3. A number of countries without a significant internal resource base
have recently stimulated economic growth at a rate equal to or greater
than those with very rich resources. The prime examples include Japan,
Greece, Italy, Malaysia, Formosa, Israel, South Korea, and Hong Kong.
They have found a means of developing human resources in such a way
they are enabled to seize opportunities in international trade.

4. The new path to economic development emphasized investments in
education, community building, entrepreneurial organization, borrowed
technology, and organized information acquisition, together with the
evolution of life styles that save energy, time, materials, and foreign
exchange (Meier, 1965).

5. The design of urban environments should reinforce resource-
conserving life styles, holding consumption close to the minimum
adequate standard, preventing waste, and taking advantage of economies
of scale. (Fig. 1 illustrates permissible levels of consumption as compared
with Western life styles.)

6. The building of wealth-creating institutions requires headquarters
areas (urban cores) in continous contact with each other, communication satellite relays, exchange of specialized persons, cultural borrowing,
and transfer of recorded knowledge.

Very briefly, that is the program. Any strategy for development
offering real hope for success forces us to consider wholly new and quite
strange alternatives, each of them placing unique demands upon applied
science and engineering. They seem to focus upon resource-conserving

## Table 1

Value of natural resources in less developed countries (*dollars per capita, current prices*)

| Country | Popula-tion 1967 estimate (millions) | Agric., forest and fisheries[1] | Coal reserves[2] | Iron ore[3] | Petrol-eum[4] | Non-fuel, non-ferrous reserves[5] | Hydro-electric power[6] | Totals[7] (round-ed) |
|---|---|---|---|---|---|---|---|---|
| China | 750 | 10 | 655 | 80 | 30 | 14 | 10 | 800 |
| India | 500 | 13 | 410 | 120 | 3 | 14 | 6 | 570 |
| Pakistan | 106 | 16 | 5 | — | 1 | — | 5 | 30 |
| Indonesia | 105 | — | 11 | 12 | 150 | 24 | 1 | 200 |
| Nigeria | 60 | 70 | 33 | — | 75 | 6 | — | 200 |
| Philippines | 34 | 121 | 5 | 300 | — | 32 | 13 | 500 |
| Turkey | 32 | 110 | 37 | 7 | — | 12 | 6 | 170 |
| Thailand | 31 | 116 | — | 1 | — | 40 | 1 | 160 |
| Egypt | 30 | 37 | — | 5 | 21 | 2 | 15 | 80 |
| S. Korea | 29 | 19 | 590 | 25 | — | 38 | — | 700 |
| Burma | 26 | 81 | — | — | 4 | 47 | 60 | 200 |
| Iran | 24 | 13 | — | — | 3000 | 4 | 3 | 3000 |

[1] Allows the value of the resource (mainly soils) to be assessed at ten times exports in the last reporting year.

[2] The value of presumably minable coal was set at $5 per ton.

[3] Technology is changing. Many ores losing value. Sets price at $5 for 55–6% Fe ore.

[4] Value at the pool is set at $1 per bbl. of probable reserves. Prices have been dropping.†

[5] Market values of extractable metals, sulfur, and phosphates were summed up, but where no reserve figures were indicated we took ten times export values in last year reported.

[6] Greatly reduced in value since 1965 due to improved economics of nuclear energy competitor. Now assessed at roughly the coal equivalent of ten years full operation.

[7] Comparable totals for the United States and the U.S.S.R. are close to $30,000 per capita, for Western Europe (except Italy) they fall into a range of $1000–5000.

*Sources:* United Nations documents, Mineral Yearbook, and miscellaneous national reports.

techniques that cannot be transferred routinely by consultants from the advanced countries but may only be elaborated in less developed countries around urban patterns of life adopted by the masses upon migrating to the city.

Curiously, none of the ideologies that divide the world today on issues of development policy seems to be pertinent. Both the socialist and the capitalist systems have demonstrated that they can generate economic growth. The Soviet Union requires somewhat more energy to produce a unit of gross national product* and it has greater difficulty

*An estimated 49 g of coal equivalent energy per ruble of GNP as compared to 28 g for the United States in 1963. *Source: U.N. Demographic Yearbook* (1965). The difference is attributed to weather and the costs of overcoming vast distances.

†Recent events such as the 1973 Arab-Israeli War and its aftermath have pushed prices up to $8–10 per bbl. and higher [Editors]

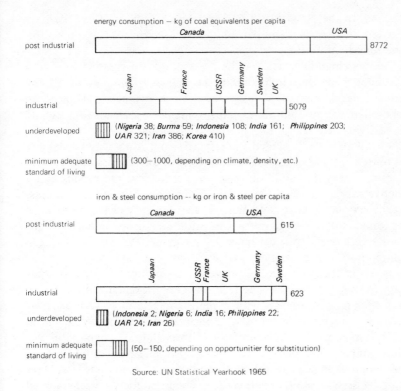

energy consumption — kg of coal equivalents per capita

post industrial — Canada | USA 8772

industrial — Japan, France, USSR, Germany, Sweden, UK 5079

underdeveloped — (*Nigeria* 38; *Burma* 59; *Indonesia* 108; *India* 161; *Philippines* 203; *UAR* 321; *Iran* 386; *Korea* 410)

minimum adequate standard of living — (300–1000, depending on climate, density, etc.)

iron & steel consumption -- kg or iron & steel per capita

post industrial — Canada | USA 615

industrial — Japan, USSR, France, UK, Germany, Sweden 623

underdeveloped — (*Indonesia* 2; *Nigeria* 6; *India* 16; *Philippines* 22; *UAR* 24; *Iran* 26)

minimum adequate standard of living — (50–150, depending on opportunitier for substitution)

Source: UN Statistical Yearbook 1965

*Fig. 1. Indicators of present resource use compared to requirements for developing* developing countries *1964* estimates.

organizing the use of soil resources, but it has also prevented at great deal of wasteful consumption. Their respective preferences for public and private ownership of production facilities and of land are similarly irrelevant, because what matters for any modernizing economy is the presence of a vigorous, effective management. It must be willing to adopt innovations that pay off to the consumer. Since innovation brings notable change in its wake, the management must be alert enough to shift its policies accordingly.

## Large-scale developmental urbanism

Since virtually all of the richest resources, and almost all the surplus commodities in the countryside, are consumed in cities, it is easy to understand why the higher strategy for development must be concerned with the organization of cities. They comprise also the only place that surplus people can go in the future. In the 19th century, large numbers

121

could come to the New World and seek out virgin land, but the only frontier left now for the extra pair of hands raised on the very poor farm is to be found within the city.

The most demanding task for the cities is that of creating jobs productive enough at least to maintain the masses of immigrants at the subsistence level. Simultaneously they must instigate advances in efficiency that permit continuous improvement, at least up to adequate levels of living. In the course of this transformation the masses will become differentiated, skilled, organized, and opportunity-seeking. Cities must continue in this fashion to absorb all the dissatisfied rural dwellers until a new equilibrium between the modern metropolis and a productive agriculture-based hinterland is reached. At that time we must expect, as is done in Japan and Europe, that 90–95% of the population will be found in the cities. Large urban regions, made up of constellations of cities, must come into existence to accommodate the influx, some containing hundreds of millions of people.

Industries in the new cities will have a very unfamiliar mix. We must expect strong pressures to economize on foreign exchange and to save natural resources, combined with a remarkable level of technological sophistication in the high priority, export-oriented industries. Such an emphasis is matched by a labor-intensive approach for the light industries (small machinery, microcircuitry, apparel, printing, plastics fabrication, etc.). As soon as the electrical grids have been set up, the power sources will employ predominantly nuclear fuels. The fossil fuels will be reserved as chemical reducing agents, as in steelmaking; or a source of carbon, as in plastics, rubbers, and fibers. Liquid fuels will still be needed for aircraft and water transport. Food technology must be a far more important component in the societies struggling to develop, and water processing will assume a large role because water supply will on some occasions become the crucial resource input.

The design of industries in such a way that the use of scarce resources is kept as low as possible is already quite familiar to engineers. They are less aware, however, of the system-wide consequences of this effort.

*The guiding principle in the design of resource-conserving industry and the urban utilities is to find ways of substituting information, computation, and communication for supplies of the scarce resource.* Because the marginal costs of production of basic commodities and services from resources are expected to rise over time, only a few managing to remain nearly constant, while the unit costs of computation and communication are expected to decline sharply for decades to come, this rule is quite rational. Communication, the most fundamental of these processes, appears to be dependent upon a resource also—best described as *channel capacity*—but the measurement of the extent and richness of the resource on a global basis is still very much in flux. We know, for example, that a mountain top in line of sight of a metropolis in the valley has become the most valuable property of the city when built up with antenna, but what its value will be when the standing satellite arrives is uncertain. Possibly cities may eventually have to install resource management for their channel capacity to the same degree that land is managed today and water will have to be managed soon. At present channel capacity is given away, like land to railroads and homesteaders in the lands century, with only a few fees to pay for the policing of rights. The limits are still not in sight so the substitution process can proceed for a long time to come.

The opportunities inherent in communications are so potent, each new and growing technology uses more information transmission per unit of output than its predecessor. The control centers of these communications networks are to be found in the headquarters buildings in city centers. Marketing information is generated almost entirely in the cities or imported from overseas, so the programming, management, and distribution of the output of these new technologies is also an urban task. Thus, cities of the future in developing countries must be designed to expedite a rapidly rising volume of communication.

Investments in human resources are as might be expected, more communications-intensive than investments in industry. They also seem to be more productive at the margin. The allocation of overall capital investment has been swinging strongly toward greater shares for education, and the countries accomplishing this transfer have prospered.* The bulk of the investments in human resources takes the form of time spent learning useful tasks so that the time of task completion is shortened and error frequency is very much reduced. Human capital, then, may be regarded as a repertory of useful routines and concepts possessed by members of a society. The greater the repertory, the more adaptive society [. . .].

Large corporations and complex social institutions, particularly universities, add even more to overall wealth-creating capability. 'Institution-building' is a common means of enhancing collective wealth. As with all social capital, an institution is created by negotiation, the building up of mutual obligation, and a set of internal rules for economizing that take advantage of economies of scale. Large organizations are able to assign specialized groups to research and planned innovation, making possible the support of individuals who are equipped to contribute to the body of knowledge. New knowledge should be thought of as an addition to cultural capital.

The process of capital accumulation, especially in these poorly under-

*Curiously enough, although the payout on investments in general education has been high, the return on vocational education as it has been organized to date seems to be very low. For a fine review of the theory and recent findings see M. J. Bowman, 1966.

stood information-intensive forms, occurs almost entirely in cities, but not all cities. Those cities that require net subsidies to keep going are almost certainly taking on obligations faster than they create assets.

## Planning for large wealth-producing cities

These shifts in viewpoint brought about by the potential productivity of human resources force us to rethink the plans for urban growth. The analysis must start from what can be done with the immigrants into the city.

A rural person, endeavoring to escape from grinding poverty in the village, should encounter an 'environment that instructs' upon entering the city. Most migrants will be literate, but teaching materials for the self-improvement of the illiterate must also be prepared. Each should be able to use his home dialect or language at the same time he learns the official language. He should be able to hold onto most of the customs and rules for behavior transmitted to him as a child, but add a number of others appropriate to the urban environment. Television, for example, can be an extraordinarily educational medium for people new to the city; the advertising can be most important of all because it describes how the substances on the inside of packages are actually used and what services are to be obtained at various addresses. Building a house of his own can also be programmed so that it teaches the whole family about construction, maintenance, property rights in cities, credit unions, and community organization at the very least. Making a living is the most difficult challenge of all, so a great deal of attention must be paid to on-the-job training.

As with advanced forms of educational organization, at least three paths into the urban milieu must be prepared, each of them gauged so that the learner is not overwhelmed and defeated, making him a drag upon the society. The fast track introduces the achieving migrants into part-time study, the libraries, and very soon into the most modern technology. They become the organizers and entrepreneurs as well as the technicians, often moving from the slum created by the settlement of urban migrants into the metropolis. The bulk will progress more slowly up the middle stream to the point where they establish a secure niche in the city, able to work at several kinds of jobs and produce quite a bit more on the average than their households consume. Some will be slow, bound to tradition, reluctant to venture out into the great city, suspicious of new foods and fashions, remaining either unskilled or highly specialized in a classical art. The developmental metropolis must find a way for them to live out their lives as productively as possible, without becoming an impediment to change.

The mechanism for accomplishing most of these ends is best described

124

as an *urban village*. Land at the growing edge of the metropolis is allocated for a community made up of a single ethnic group speaking the same dialect. Access to industry and the central city must be available. Provisions for allocating plots, providing essential services (water, health, public order, credit, schools, etc.), and promoting self-organization are now widely agreed upon (Turner, 1966). However, the features of an optimum design, aimed to overcome the scarcity of key resources and accelerate economic development, are still not put together systematically.

Operation of the water use sub-system makes up only a small share of the total cost of living at levels just above subsistence (perhaps 3–6%), therefore it does not pay to invest very heavily in equipment. However its involvement in food production, which would be partially dependent upon waste waters, allows for some refinement in design and construction.

*Food production and distribution sub-system.* Food will often become critical during the course of development, so high priority will be given in cities to the building up of several sources of supply. Enough insecurity is likely to remain so that an equitable rationing system must be established. The ration normally includes cereal products, pulses, cooking oil, and sugar, all of which must be imported from a distance by the city. Subsistence levels for a working population amount to about 500 g/cap/day.

Perishable foods—milk, meat, fish, vegetables, roots, fruits—pose a very serious problem, because their consumption increases very rapidly as people's incomes rise above subsistence levels. Transport costs and spoilage can be greatly reduced if very intensive food production can be carried out within the environs of an urban village. An integrated sequence can be proposed which extracts the nutrients from human and animal wastes, utilizes waste waters, and is able to produce a wide range of foods in exceedingly high yields. Each operation can be designed so it contributes significantly to the efficiency of one or more of the others but remains labor-intensive.

Aquaculture, an approach that is just now becoming technically feasible, can produce four to twelve crops a year of potatoes, yams, Chinese cabbage, tomatoes, peas, eggplant, melons, etc., using synthetic fertilizer and allowing none of it to become locked up or decomposed by the soil. Current licensed designs are relatively automatic,* but a labor intensive design will somewhat reduce capital costs without introducing risk, and estimated costs of production are 10–30% less than current bazaar prices.

*I was impressed with the design of the Hydroponic Gardens of California installation in the city of Fremont using the Auto-Gro process. Publicity has been surprisingly small. Reports on experiments leading in this direction have been made by J. R. Seagrave (1965).

Algae culture based on synthetic nutrients can produce protein suitable for direct human consumption, but a great deal of investment in its commercialization needs to be undertaken in various tropical and subtropical environments (Meier, 1966). The explorations in the underlying fundamental science are now relatively complete. Sewage-produced algae would be fed to chickens and fish (cattle do not need the protein) according to minor modifications of existing art in these forms of husbandry.

Altogether, about two thirds or more of the weight and at least a quarter of the caloric intake of the urban diet can very likely be produced economically inside the city itself using present knowledge. Communications investments could contribute to efficiency here as well, since persuasion through mass media should develop tastes for the high yield crops in greatest supply.*

*Transport modes.* Once cities begin to get larger than they are today, the greatest threat to their aspirations is that of congestion. It could cause a complete breakdown in the flows of people and goods. Urban transport is the most capital consuming utility, and its improvement requires the most careful planning. Any significant population of automobiles cannot be tolerated within resource-conserving urbanism. The wasteful uses of land and of capital are more important reasons than the effects upon the atmosphere for keeping automotive numbers at a minuscule level. Therefore, although the urban villages may be connected to the central city and industrial estate initially by bus and truck, plans should be made for displacing these vehicles by economical forms of mass transit. The locations of urban villages should be chosen so as to minimize the costs of moving passengers and freight.

The central city may quickly become fully electrified, with cabs and buses depending upon nuclear-derived electric power. Bicycle scale vehicles will provide the best mode for short trips off the mainstream movements. Some of these will be propelled by light engines, as in a number of Asiatic cities today. The motorized cycle will be quite popular around the urban fringes.

Airlines will be many times more important than at present. Many of the exports from developing cities to the rest of the world will find the airlines offer economical means of exit. Indeed, almost everything valued in excess of $5 per kg. is likely to move by this mode. However, as a megalopolis comes into being, the air space may well become saturated.

---

*Advertising is best suited to selling surplus commodities or processed foods with a relatively bland taste. Among the latter the most likely to be accepted are breads, baby foods, frozen custard, dehydrated soup, fine-grained sausages, *to-fu* (jellied bean curd), soy sauce, additives to curry, etc. The Japanese marketed two varieties of algae-based yogurt, using the Chlorella species popular in laboratory work as a key ingredient, during the year 1966.

Then a high speed 'New Tokaido line' or tunnel transport mode will have to be installed for intramegalopolis trips of 25–300 miles.*

Water transport modes have an important future also. Heavy freight would be barged as much as possible. Intense shoreline use for recreation will give priority to passenger ferries and resorts on floating marine structures (spar buoys and platforms) of a kind that are just now being considered and promoted in developed countries but will be still more important to large new cities due to the shortage of open spaces the latter anticipate. This capability for movement, combined with those introduced earlier, suggests a continuous urbanization at the shoreline whereever the topography and the floodplains permit. Long beaded strands of coastal urbanism have not come into being earlier mainly because the expense of the control of congestion has been so great.

Similar sub-systems for the developmental metropolis can be constructed for communication, power production, several kinds of manufacturing, construction, health, religion, recreation, and other sectors. The close links between them and those already described are already evident. The designs of these also must of necessity be vastly different from the prototypes found in countries well along in the path to development. A large number of possible technological improvements in the various sub-systems deserve investigation. [. . .].

## Expediting the transfer of technology

In urban areas, the process of accepting new technique or a new design that promises to be resource-conserving is very different from the village. Instead of individual cultivators and artisans being persuaded to change their ways and then assisting in the spread of the innovation among their counterparts in neighboring communities by means of the 'demonstration effect', the decision must be carried up to the responsible executive in a centralized organization. Once the innovation is accepted, there the change is transmitted down through the hierarchy as instructions to the men on the job. Each stage, moving up and down, requires adjustments in relation with other groups, both inside and outside the hierarchy. If the chain of communications breaks down, for whatever reason, it causes general frustration. Thus the construction of the city itself and the operation of its utilities and services will make a considerable difference in expediting the central decision-making and the rate at which new technology can be accepted and digested. [. . .].

*A review of recent thinking on megalopolitan transport was formulated as a total system for the United States Northeast Corridor. If applied to India most costs would increase, resulting in fares of 3–10 c/mile, by our estimate, which is tolerable only as a last resort, Massachusetts Institute of Technology (1965).

The structure of the central city that propagates growth today hardly conforms to the recommendations of contemporary city planners. Certainly those cities that are most effective—Tokyo, Hong Kong, Sao Paulo, Osaka, San Juan—are never cited as examples to be imitated. However city planners, at least up to the present, have been seeking what may best be summed up as 'serenity' rather than the capacity to accomplish a transformation. The kind of city that will be able to compete successfully in the future is one that generates wealth, therefore the planning will need to take a different tack.

The greatest challenge henceforth is presented by the construction of an urban core that promotes the rapid completion of a balanced set of transactions—economic, social, cultural, and political. Necessarily embracing the headquarters offices of manufacturing firms, retailing chains, banks, and transport services, it will also possess the securities exchanges, commodities markets, and insurance houses. National, regional, and city governments will be forced to maintain major bureaucratic establishments immediately adjacent or lose control over business. International firms will want a precinct of their own nearby, and the consulates of the main trading nations will choose to be on hand. The consulting professions—law, accounting, advertising, medicine, engineering—ordinarily fit into the odd nooks and crannies in this general vicinity. Somewhere in the heart of this complex a communications nexus must be founded that will link channels from the Comsat satellite to microwave relays, television, and the telephone exchanges. Intercity transport must come into this core either underground, as in Manhattan, or high overhead, as in Tokyo. Hotels, department stores, and leading shops cluster as closely as they can to sites on top of the terminus, or along main channels carrying passengers away from it.

Any experienced traveler would feel immediately at home in such a central city. The urban ecology is exceedingly familiar. It represents the outcome of competitive forces that prevail in all metropolises and are modified somewhat only in the capitals of nations. Some things should be noticeably different in a resource-conserving future, however. Most striking, perhaps, is the earlier point that automobiles would be very scarce. Also, the spacious, residential suburbs reserved for top administrators and professionals would be replaced by more closely packed neighborhoods not far from work. This reduces the heavy investment in commuter lines. Similarly, the economy should extend to a parsimony of monuments and expensive landmarks equivalent to cathedrals. Conspicuous production needs to be avoided as much as conspicuous worship or conspicuous consumption, because the central city needs to be in flux, fitting land to new purposes when opportunities arise.

Cosmopolitan types of people, with their universities, libraries, cinemas, restaurants, coffee houses, and parks will accumulate in central cities. The gross densities of settlement are expected to be about 100,000 persons per square mile. This concentration can be very inconvenient if not comprehensively planned so that virtually all the space is available for human use at all times of the day and night. Thus areas given over to emergency reservoirs, waste treatment, water processing, and fish feeding may also become parks. The most economical housing proposed thus far is a set of very light prefabricated units that can be stacked on top of each other, much as in the Habitat group in Montreal's Expo 67, but can be disassembled easily and put up elsewhere in another frame (Paraskevopoulos, *et al.*, 1966). (Although far from economical in Montreal, it remains promising in a tropical climate and in a city where water consumption is kept at an absolute minimum.) The face of the city —the structural form and the images on the structures—should be replaceable within a matter of months rather than years. The object is to conserve scarce materials and space, but otherwise remain relatively labor-intensive.

The greatest challenge of all is the programming of movements and some of the other activities so as to allow such a central city to operate almost continuously close to peak levels. The transition to a multiple shift society should extract enough extra use out of public facilities to reduce the capital costs per capita for urban infra-structure by at least half. Thus far the attempts to stagger shift changes and spread out peaks have failed, even in wartime when coercion could be used. The programming is expected to be feasible in the future only because huge amounts of routine data can be collected, processed, and digested by the enormous computing capacities expected to exist within a decade or two. If people don't know how to obtain desired services from the city they can take up short term instruction (equivalent in complexity to driver training for automobiles) in order to discover how to exploit the routines to their own advantage. Such a program maintains what amounts to a continuous census and an up-to-the-minute map of all facilities tied closely into the central city; it would predict demand, and then schedule the movements of transport equipment according to pre-set criteria for optimization.

Approaches to optimization are likely to be undertaken in stages, sector by sector and level by level. The limitation is most likely to be imposed by the difficulties in the transfer of the social technology required to measure values and estimate behavior. Social technology includes the techniques of management science, attitude survey, motivational analysis personnel testing and evaluation, accident prevention, community development, etc. The urban systems designer will have to utilize a good deal of it before he comes close to the optimum.

## Conclusion

The key to the conservation of resources for the predominant share of the poor populations which are poorly endowed with resources lies in the control of consumption. The person engaged in technology transfer will find that many Western techniques already being adopted are much too wasteful. New findings reported in the past few years suggest that sub-systems for water, food, transport, housing, and central city organization can be proposed which promise to be far more economical in resource use than anything in existence today. The basic principle to be used in their design is to seek out means of substituting human resources for natural resources. This strategy puts much stronger emphasis upon the transfer of social technology and urban planning than has been evident until now.

## References

BOWMAN, M. J. (1966) 'The Human Investment Revolution in Economic Thought' *Sociology of Education*, **39**, Spring, pages 111–137.

LANSBERG, H. H., FISCHMAN, L. L. and FISHER, J. L. (1963) *Resources in America's Future*, Baltimore, John Hopkins.

MASSACHUSETTS INSTITUTE OF TECHNOLOGY (1965) *Survey of Technology for High Speed Ground Transport*, prepared for the US Department of Commerce, Cambridge, Mass.

MEIER, R. L. (1965) *Development Planning*, New York, McGraw-Hill.

MEIER, R. L. (1966) *Science and Economic Development*, Second Edition, Cambridge, M.I.T. Press.

MEIER, R. L. (1967) Resource Planning in *International Encyclopedia of the Social Sciences*.

PARASKEVOPOULOS, S. C. A. *et al.* (1966) *Structural Potential of Foam Plastics for Housing in Under-developed Areas*, Architectural Research Laboratory, University of Michigan, Ann Arbor, Michigan, Second Edition.

SEAGRAVE, J. R. (1965) Aquaculture-*Agriculture*, *Pakistan* **XVI**, 3, pages 257–72.

TURNER, J. F. C. (1966) Uncontrolled Urban Settlement; Problems and Policies, Working Paper 11, United Nations Inter-regional Seminar on Development Policies and Planning in Response to Urbanization, Pittsburgh, U.S.A. 1966.

## 2.7 Human needs *Barbara Ward and Rene Dubos*

How do man's built-up and natural environments and their interactions meet or frustrate his human needs? This may seem a straightforward question. But there are difficulties in arriving at satisfactory definitions of what human needs really are once we leave behind a basic biological minimum. We know that people need to eat, to be housed, to be healthy and to grow up in some sort of family or clan. But beyond this basic minimum, we enter areas of great cultural difference and also of a considerable ignorance of the facts. We can guess that few human beings are born to be happy in complete idleness. But we do not know much about optimum and minimum amounts of work. Tribal families in subsistence economies work hard for not more than three to four months a year. There is evidence—from the number of saints' days and festivals —that medieval man may not have clocked up much more than 190 days a year. With the onslaught of the industrial revolution, when for a century men worked for seventy to eighty hours a week in inhuman noise, dirt and stench, some deeply ingrained habits of self-entertainment must have been profoundly disturbed. And the cities built to accommodate this pitiably exploited work force were not designed for anything but sleeping and sweating it out.

Yet now that the formal work week is steadily falling, recent surveys in a number of industrial cities do not give any very clear picture of the degree of leisure people seek. In the sixties in Britain, for instance, one man in ten had a second job and one in three did overtime. Income was clearly more inviting than more hours of leisure.

How much of the time used for leisure is spent outside the home is also difficult to judge. Some surveys suggest that not more than one citizen in ten takes part in any kind of organized sport. Television keeps people indoors. But the motor car takes them out and clearly becomes the prime instrument of leisure when young families are formed and weekend visits to picnic sites and seashores produce the endless traffic blocks on all major roads leading back to big urban settlements on Sunday evenings.

*Source:* Barbara Ward and Rene Dubos, '*Only One Earth' The Care and Maintenance of a Small Planet*, Penguin, 1972

That urban man obviously likes to get away to non-urban surroundings is confirmed by the phenomenal growth in international tourism. Since the last war, there has been a remarkably large increase in the number of long-distance journeys during the period of what is now a fairly general two-to-three-week holiday. The United Nations reports that between the mid-fifties and the mid-sixties, the number of tourists arriving in some 60 to 70 countries rose from 51 million to over 157 million. These figures also tell us something more about modern man's less basic needs. He wants sunshine. He seeks the sea and the mountains. He is drawn by old and beautiful cities. He positively swamps areas where—as in the Mediterranean or the Alps—he can get a combination of some or all of these things. Tourists in Greece have trebled in the last ten years. So have visitors to America's National Parks. People do not cross the oceans and the continents to look at industrial plants or inspect uniform suburbia. The hunger lives on for beauty and for natural things.

Can we say how strong this hunger is? Will an annual escape to the isles of Greece—or, more likely, the towering hotels and crowded beaches of the Costa Brava—be enough to keep a citizen's aesthetic budget in balance?

Besides, we do not fully understand the longer-term results of extreme cultural, ethical and emotional starvation. When we remember under what continuous stimulus of natural variety—of colour, of scent, of sound and light and touch—the first men began to develop their imaginative grasp upon living reality and feel their way towards fully conscious and creative humanity, we may wonder what will be the result of a continuous adaptation of human existence, over centuries, to towering buildings, concrete walls, personal isolation, darkened skies, roaring traffic, raucous noise, polluted water and dirty streets. Such an urban environment might begin to produce human beings whose very ability to survive in such conditions could mark the beginning of a retreat from realizing their full human potential. The remarkable, the resilient thing about man is his ability to adapt and survive. But some adaptations become deformations.

These are new questions because it is new for man to live in unrelieved urban or suburban man-made surroundings and because most city dwellers in developed countries have, so far, found avenues of escape— to the sea, to the lakes, to the mountains. The issue will become more critical as the developing world undergoes its urban revolution and, by 1980, adds to its city populations the equivalent of the entire present population—roughly a billion people—of the developed world.

However we define the basic needs of urban man, he is unlikely to find any city designed in such a way as to satisfy them. Integrated urban planning for all the varieties of human needs and uses has been the exception. The land has been dragged along in the wake of industrial and technological change and rapid population growth. Economic decisions have tended, until recently, to influence a very large part of the shape and texture of the settlements. This fact is due to the role of private decision-making in market economies and to the overwhelming need for economic expansion in the centrally planned systems. The result is an arrangement of space which only partially satisfies man's basic needs.

Beginning with the centre city, we will take for granted the cleaning up of air and water, the better disposal of wastes and the role of the automobile, since they have already been discussed in some detail. But the point can be made here that a form of pollution we have not discussed—that of noise—is intimately bound up with the scale of machine-use and motorized traffic, private and commercial, operating in a city. All the arguments for underground garbage disposal, for emissionless electrical motors, for pedestrian precincts, for belts and oases of parkland within cities are enormously reinforced by man's limited tolerance for noise above a certain decibel level.

Of all forms of pollution, noise is perhaps the most inescapable for the urban dweller. It pursues him into the privacy of his home, tails him on the street and quite often is an accompaniment of his labour. We do not begin to know the price we pay in impaired hearing, in enervation, in aggravated hostilities and nervous tension. But scientists report that, when animals are made to listen to noise, 'they grow sullen, unresponsive, erratic or violent.' May not the same be true of us?

Noise is one element in the wider issue of beauty and amenity in central cities. Here we must distinguish between ancient cities with beauty to preserve and modern cities which have yet to create it. In beautiful cities, the chief problem is to care sufficiently and efficiently for the urban heritage. On balance, this seems to be better done when public authorities have the necessary control over land use. One of the most remarkable achievements of this kind, against the worst of all possible odds—the nearly total destruction of war—was the post-war reconstruction of Warsaw with a respect for the past, with a loving attention to detail that restored to the citizens not only their familiar townscape but their sense of historical continuity and heroic resistance. Another remarkable achievement of restoration in a great urban work of art is the renewal and, indeed, the enhancement of Peter the Great's magnificent centre of Leningrad. Where, however, city authorities and planners have less control over the disposal of urban land, some tragic collisions of interest can destroy a city's heritage.

There can in fact be a fateful connection here between the private land market and the destruction of urban values. We have already noticed the nineteenth-century treadmill effect of low rents requiring overcrowding to create a profit and the resulting profit forcing up the value of land in urban areas. These values, created very largely by the pressures and needs of the community, can, when netted by private developers, create a new kind of treadmill—the need to secure very large returns on the limited amounts of land available in central areas and hence the development of the huge skyscraper with all its destructive influences on the urban landscape.

It is destructive first because it can put every other traditional building out of scale. As late as 1945, London's skyline was one of its glories. The tall spires of Wren's churches, the balanced and monumental dome of St Paul's, above the wide flowing arc of the Thames, the great parks, the green rise of Hampstead and the hazy outlines of the North Downs gave London well into the middle of this century the proportion and splendour Canaletto had painted two hundred years before. This beauty has faded in only twenty-five years. Commercial and public buildings of monumental size and ugliness have risen haphazardly in all parts of the city, like a scattering of tall pepper pots on a carelessly laid table.

We need not say that all buildings of thirty floors and upwards are visually outrageous. Carefully grouped, in balanced relation to different planes and levels, they can have a stimulating effect, particularly in new cities. But, in new cities or old, skyscrapers built by the chances of zoning controls or land purchase are virtually certain to be haphazard intrusions on the city's human scale. Built all together in long lines along canyon-like streets as in Manhattan, they make an environment for ants, not men.

Their defects are more than visual. High-rise towers have proved a disastrous experiment in urban dwelling. They give many of their occupants acute uneasiness. Some people arrange their furniture so as to avoid any view of the vertigous plunge from their thirtieth-floor window. For mothers with small children, they present insoluble problems of play and supervision. The elevators become places of dirt and danger. The wholesale bulldozing of little streets and houses to make way for them destroys delicate networks of service and friendship which are simply not recreated between different floors in new apartment houses. The ground areas between the towers, which were supposed to provide needed air and space and greenness, can become windy deserts below vast buildings which tunnel the weather down their vertical sides as do mountain ranges.

Some town planners even maintain that the claim made for high-rise dwellings—that otherwise even more little houses would be scattered over the countryside—is not borne out by economic or spatial necessity. In a number of cities, areas of similar size, with alternations of four to eight floor blocks round enclosed gardens and courtyards, can house virtually the same number of people and provide the intimacy and security which parents in particular look for in an urban home.

It is surely significant that two of the most densely populated countries in the developed world, Britain and Holland, are reconsidering high-rise living. In the chief towns going up on land reclaimed from the Zuyder Zee, the bulk of the housing is in single houses with gardens. Recently, the Greater London Council removed all future high-rise dwellings from its drawing boards—a not irrational response to the discovery that 80 per cent of their tenants were miserable in them.

But perhaps the worst urban evil represented by high-rise commercial buildings in a number of developed cities is the evidence they give of resources diverted from the most fundamental of all environmental urban evils—festering slums and hopeless ghettoes. This is particularly flagrant in any city where no taxes are paid on large office blocks and they stand empty earning capital appreciation while the slums survive or where tax concessions and even tax havens are available in relation to commercial building while public and private construction of homes for the poor lag behind.

Many of the new constructions—high-rise buildings, apartment blocks, even handsome new streets and layouts—represent a further degradation of living conditions for the poorest citizens. In the name of slum clearance, their streets are knocked down. And what is rebuilt is far beyond their modest incomes. They move on, doubling up in older houses and spreading urban blight still further. As early as the mid nineteenth century, a rueful London verse ran thus:

> Who builds? Who builds? Alas, ye poor
> If London day by day 'improves',
> Where shall ye find a friendly door
> When every day a home removes?

A decade later, the ruthless Baron Haussmann, carving out his celebrated boulevards in Paris, scattered the dispossessed poor to garrets in nearby slums, greatly increasing the density of population and with it the ravages of tuberculosis. Yet in the next century, the first large-scale experiments in slum clearance or 'urban renewal' in the United States had some of the same effects, increasing the land available for developers to produce apartments at higher rents and squeezing the urban poor into other run-down neighbourhoods which then deteriorated still further.

The high value of urban land is not only responsible for the anti-social aspects of high-rise buildings. It also accounts for the fact that too many modern cities are wildernesses of stone. Again and again, we find that the great parks, vistas and open spaces that make London or Rome or Paris such targets for tourism are the legacy of earlier royal or aristocratic initiatives. The treeless city among everlasting concrete trenches and barrack-like agglomerations of brick and stone reflects in market economies the over-valuation of every inch of urban land.

In some of the centrally planned economies, comparable conditions reflect the extreme pressures of forced draft industrialization and, more recently, an expensive rebuilding after war. In wealthy lands, these city deserts are made more unviable by the alienation bred of spectacular poverty of some city quarters and relative affluence everywhere else. The effect is particularly brutal if the poor citizen is cut off not only by poverty but by a different ethnic or cultural background.

Usually, in developed countries, the cause of these pockets of dilapidated housing, poor services, ugly surroundings, dirt and disease is basically the same. In a relatively short time, a wave of rural migrants has poured into the city, with few skills, little money and no urban experience. They have taken over the rundown buildings of earlier dwellers who have now improved their incomes and, as often as not, moved to a suburb. In nineteenth-century America for instance the migrants came from Europe. As they imposed their standards, the form of American assistance to housing—mortgage guarantees—both before and after the Second World War enormously increased the movement outwards to suburban single-family homes. Since 1950, four million houses have been built for people whose average income in 1968 was over $10,000 a year. But into the vacated areas there came—in all the Northern cities—a massive black migration from the rural South.

A similar movement away from rural poverty brought Jamaicans and Asians to England and Algerians to Paris. Some of the same problems occur even when the rural migrants are of the same culture and stock. Sicilians have moved massively to Milan, country dwellers have streamed into the great Soviet cities—Leningrad and Moscow grew from 2 million to 7 million between 1932 and 1962—in spite of administrative attempts to stabilize the size of the cities. The consequences have tended to be the same—a pile up of the least skilled in the worst quarters, and a desperate need for new and heavy expenditure in urban infra-structure, schooling and housing, These were major Soviet pre-occupations once the immediate damage of war had been made good. In Britain too, although urban housing compares well with that of any other country, in some recent surveys it has been suggested that at least a million families are ill-housed and below the poverty line. Poor housing and lack of home-ownership have continued to be a source of unrest and dissatisfaction in Italy's industrial towns. In the United States, so far, the funds needed for a full-scale and radical elimination of ghetto dwellings have not been made available. In fact, only about two-thirds of the estimated annual need for subsidized housing for the poor is being met, and meanwhile the housing stock deteriorates further.

There can be no doubt about the centre city's chief environmental priority and it is not one that the unaided market will supply. It is the rebuilding and rehabilitation of all remaining slums—by public investment, private inducements, rent subsidies, tax rebates and all other appropriate policies. But this priority only indirectly deals with the problem of restoring the city's role and dignity in the wider metropolitan context.

There needs to be a dual approach to the problem. The first can be accomplished in the city itself. The second depends upon its relations with surrounding suburbs and upon the planners' ability to reduce the pressures which arise when a centre city has to serve too large an urban region. Within the city, the aim must be to try to build up among and around the modern high-rise citadels new neighbourhoods built to a human scale, where people of different occupations and classes can live together in distinguishable communities—like New York's Greenwich Village or Rome's Trastevere—walk to work and keep the city alive when the offices close. The Barbican area in London is being planned to fulfil this function.

The offices themselves can, as it were, rejoin city life particularly after office hours if, as in parts of Manhattan, they are built only on condition that their street floors contain theatres, restaurants, arcades and generally agreeable access for the city dwellers. Parks—like those in Amsterdam—can be introduced to give the variety and freshness of greenery throughout the central area, small square parks, long thin parks, winding through the big blocks, 'hanging' gardens between tall buildings, fountains in city squares, flowers tumbling out of window boxes and hanging from lamp posts. Traffic free areas—or days—can be introduced so that, say, during summer lunch hours people can come out and picnic on the streets and wrest back to social purpose the dehumanized concrete and asphalt realm of the motor car.

It was said of the capital city of the Sungs that no street was without 'the sound of water and the scent of flowers'. Those who have visited Hankow recently speak with wonder of the sense of greenness and spaciousness in what is now an industrial city of nearly a million people. The transformations are thus possible but they demand in market economies a far greater public commitment to the ideal of urban excellence.

But the restoration of life and dignity to the centre city also depends upon its links with the suburban regions which surround every major city and are the fastest growing areas of human settlement. Yet for all their obvious drawing-power, they cannot be said, any more than the city centres, really to be satisfying the needs and hopes of urban man.

*Suburbia*

Nobody intended suburbia. It began and has in part continued as an escape from the dirt and pressure of the modern industrial city or simply from the city as such. It is therefore not wholly surprising that what has been basically a random but self-reinforcing process has not, whether for work or leisure or community or even contact with nature, provided wholly satisfactory answers.

Take work first of all. As the suburbs spin outwards and one city's spread is only stopped by the next city's sprawl, work tends to involve a longer and longer journey. It is true that light industry and services follow the commuters outwards—with the incidental effect of filling up all the green spaces they had hoped to enjoy. But this has not simplified the commuting pattern. Many workers in the suburb continue to rely on the centre city for employment. Yet a number of workers living in the city are quite as likely to be travelling outwards for the new opportunities of suburban work. Either way, enormous amounts of commuting time have to be absorbed. If workers drive themselves to work, the sheer loss of time, the fatigue and strain are far indeed from the leisure and variety of which the car is supposedly the symbol. Yet public passenger services have tended to run into financial difficulties which reduce maintenance and comfort and increase fares.

In any case, by car or train, there is a certain disamenity, not to say insanity, in spending two to three hours every day in crowded trains or on crowded roadways. If, in addition, the workers are putting in over-time, they can end a work week not noticeably different from the seventy-hour grind of the mid nineteenth century.

At higher managerial levels, it seems a general rule. In the case, family enjoyments can shrink to a briefly shared weekend, and when children are young there is a considerable risk of marooning the be-leaguered wife. Clearly, one can become acclimatized to the routine—although the costs to lungs, nerves and family harmony may be cumulative. Once again, may we not confront here an adaptation which is in essence an injury and a loss?

Yet the centre city is not necessarily better off. Sometimes it is a question of funds. If suburban communities cash out of the costs of maintaining a city centre upon which they depend for work and for important cultural stimulus, they, in fact, cash in on the benefits and out on the price. This is particularly serious in cities where some sectors are run-down and present particularly heavy costs of rehabilitation. At the same time, a large suburban belt, particularly if it sets up ethnic or social barriers to the outward movement of poor people, can condemn the inner-city family to a life that is wholly divorced not only from beauty and natural surroundings but in some cities from desperately needed opportunities for work.

In any case, as the suburban belt grows, the inner city tends to spread, absorbing nearer suburbs into a solid built-up mass. On the outer fringes, open country and useful farm land recede. At last the wilderness itself may be under threat. A sense of 'boxed-in-ness' can even overcome the wealthy suburbanite on a seven-acre lot, so he buys a villa in Antigua or Majorca as well. For the slum child, the trap closes on what is one of the most inadequate ecologies ever designed for living things.

Can anything be done about a process which appears to follow in the wake of every movement towards urbanization and is accentuated sharply by the coming of the motor car? Are we dealing here with irresistible technological forces which condemn us to a poor and under-nourished urban existence—between commuting suburbs and deteriorat-·ing city cores? The answers can be given not so much in terms of theory but from the experience of countries which are making the attempt to canalize and direct the urban flood.

Britain, like Holland, has experimented with new towns to take the strain off the big cities. They are linked by good if traditional rapid transit systems with the centre city but in theory they are supposed to be self-sufficient enough to take the load off the centre's facilities. However, in neither scale nor variety have they developed much beyond dependent communities and they are still, in essence, part of the com-muter belt. The same kind of problem has incidentally emerged round Stockholm, where a new town like Vällingby, built at thirty minutes' commuting distance from the city and intended as a separate entity, still has over half of its wage-earners working in Stockholm.

These shortcomings have led to new thinking. In the last decade city planners have begun to wonder whether their earlier concepts, although innovatory, may not have been insufficiently comprehensive and radical. They ask whether they may not have been aiming at better versions of the same thing, at improvements on the old, fixed urban structure of concentric circles, a central core surrounded by subordinate districts. Now should they not think about cities in new terms—of growth rather than size, of mobility, or alternatives and choices rather than a rooted environment?

A radically new pattern begins to emerge. The basic principle is that if the megalopolis acts as a giant magnet, drawing greater numbers of people and square miles into itself, then it must be met with an effective counter-force, diverting the pressure of more population and the crush of their artefacts away from the original centre.

Since the urbanization of man is a reality, the counter-magnet can only be one or more cities (either brand new or existing ones developed in accordance with careful planning) that lie close to but outside the existing urban 'magnetic field'. And the counter-city must be of sufficient size, with sufficient industry and amenities, to act as a counterbalance;

otherwise more varied employment, education, entertainment will still pull the commuter into the 'great wen'. This is the thinking underlying the construction of a new urban centre at Milton Keynes in Britain and the development of a regional authority for the whole basin of the Seine in France.

What can we learn from these various experiments? Man has long been a city-builder, a creator, and he has not stopped being so in our era. The difference is that where in the past he learned to achieve this with order, he does it now in all too many countries in a disorderly way. It is therefore important to understand in which directions the new sense of need for urban order is leading the modern state. Some governments are now experimenting with metropolitan control over the whole conurbation, to allow pressures to be relieved, costs to be shared and the optimum arrangements to be made over limited space for all urban man's variety of activities. In another range of experiments, particularly in new cities, public ownership of the land gives the city planners a much greater range of choice simply because they are not battering their way against very high land costs in centre areas. The Dutch are extending the practice in existing cities. Two-thirds of Amsterdam, for instance, is owned by the City Council. Those who feel such extensions of public ownership simply add to the cost citizens have to carry need to remember that one way or another urban costs have to be met. The people are there. They cannot be dumped all over the landscape. If there is no planning, a few developers may make great fortunes, the mass of middle-income consumers will get good homes together with commuting and inconvenience, the poorest will be left out. If totally free market systems produced good cities, we should have them now. It is because the market is a limited tool for dealing with *collective* needs and systems that city planning and a measure of public financing are indispensable parts of a decent human environment.

Yet urban planning should be simply part of a much wider approach to the national territory as a whole. It attempts, on the basis of the present distribution of the people, on industry, on history, on climate, rivers, hills and soils, to make the best, most efficient but also most beautiful use of a land area which is seen ever more clearly to be limited, to impose choices, to need solutions, to be profoundly destructible unless the twin needs of overall standards and local variety are kept in some kind of balance. In a sense, a national plan is ecology practised at the country level, a sorting-out of habitats and environments, an understanding of special niches, a creative reaction to forces of dynamic change, a rejection of single-thrust development based upon a purely economic consideration, a search for patterns which satisfy a wider variety of human needs. None of the plans is perfect. Almost any is better than no plan at all.

# 3. Future Urban Forms

## Introduction *by Chris Hamnett*

The greatly increased size and scale of urban settlements is one of the major distinguishing characteristics of the contemporary era. Paralleling the demise of the distinct, separate and clearly bounded towns and cities of the relatively recent past, conventional distinctions between urban and rural have become blurred. Just as individual urban dwellers have had to come to terms with these changes, so too academics and planners have attempted to conceptualize them. One of the first was Jean Gottman with his Megalopolis. Although he has suggested that it has application in Europe it was formulated specifically to describe the 600 mile length of highly urbanized American eastern seaboard stretching from Boston in the north, via New York and Philadelphia, to Washington in the south. The American context of the concept is important, for on several of Gottman's criteria, the whole of England and Wales could be described as megalopolitan. The second important point which needs to be made in relation to the concept, is that it was advanced partially to differentiate the far larger, more discontinuous and inter-related urban systems of today from those of the past.

Megalopolis is far from being a continuously built up area like Greater London. It was in order to try and convey the far greater inter-relationship between major urban centres and the area within about two hours drive (100 miles) of them, that Friedmann and Miller advanced their concept of the urban field. The bulk of these urban fields are, of course, not built up but although they may be physically rural they are tied into the social and economic sphere of the metropolis via greatly increased commuting flows and recreational trips. The concept of the 'urban field' has the advantage that it is broadly defined; no rigid or predetermined formulations being laid down. It is also a social as well as a physical concept embracing both activities as well as form and thus corresponds better to complex present day realities. Finally, it is applicable to any city of over 300,000 people which lends it a general quality the concept of megalopolis lacks.

The two papers considered so far described project and conceptualize certain trends relating to the new scale of urban life and form. The next three are, in contrast, concerned more with the analysis of certain spatial properties with a view to developing 'better' urban form and layout. Thus in *Homes beyond the fringe*, March indicates how dispersal into the countryside might be achieved whilst avoiding the consumption of land entailed by current modes of development. March's solution is basically planned linear development, which, he feels, offers better access to the countryside than either nucleation or dispersal, as well as the *subjective impression* of being less built up. With linear development March believes it would be possible to have semi-detached rural living at 200 people to the acre, as well as having the entire population of England and Wales in the year 2000 on the same urbanized land acres as existed at the turn of the nineteenth century!

The new possibilities March's ideas would seem to offer stem from different geometrical layouts to the ones currently employed. It is from exactly the same basis that Sir Leslie Martin's innovatory ideas expressed in the 'Grid as generator' are derived. They differ only as they are related more specifically to the internal layout of the city, and as they are based on court form developments, rather than linear ones. As March and Martin have shown elsewhere, however, both the linear and the court— forms of development are inherently more efficient types of layout than the 'pavilion' or tower which is extremely wasteful of space.* Martin demonstrates that the grid of streets defines the general plot pattern, and that for any grid there exists an optimum balance between it, the plot pattern and amount of building that can reasonably be supported. He further shows that whilst the pressure for floor space has generally increased in cities, the forces of inertia have militated against the logical solution—an increase in the scale of the grid, the balance between the various elements disappearing in the process.

Martin emphasises that what is important is that we are aware of the range of choices and possibilities open to us. This is exactly the same point made by Lynch though this focus is more on the different urban patterns open to us, rather than on their internal layout though the two are clearly inter-related. As well as outlining the basic elements of urban form and their significant features, Lynch advances a set of *criteria* on the basis of which he evaluates five different urban forms—the dispersed sheet, the core city, the galaxy, the ring and the urban star. Lynch concludes on the important point that cities are dynamic entities, whose forms are basically responses to human needs and demands, however disturbed those responses may be. Therefore any urban plan must be open ended, enabling adaption and change to fresh circumstances and requirements, on the basis of pre-determined goals.

*See MARCH and MARTIN (1972) *Urban Space and Structures*, pages 35–38.

# 3.1 Megalopolis or the urbanization of the northeastern seaboard *Jean Gottmann*

The frequency of large urban units scattered along the Atlantic sea-board in the northeastern United States was a striking realization to the foreigner who first visited the area, even 15 years ago. In February, 1942, after a first trip from New York to Washington, the writer, being asked by Isaiah Bowman in Baltimore what was the most striking impression he had had as a geographer in his first months in this country, answered: 'The density of great cities along this coast, from Boston to Washington.'

In 1950, on the basis of the new census, the Bureau of the Census prepared a map, later published as an illustration to a booklet of statistics on *State Economic Areas*, which showed clearly the continuity of an area of 'metropolitan' economy from a little north of Boston to a little south of Washington, more precisely from Hillsborough County in New Hampshire to Fairfax County in Virginia. This seemed to be a first statistical demonstration on the map of the existence of a continuous stretch of urban and suburban areas, the main NE-SW axis of which was about 600 miles long, and within the frame of which dwelt even in 1950 some 30 million people.

In the geography of the distribution of habitat this was a phenomenon unique by its size not only in America but in the world. It resulted obviously from the coalescence, recently achieved, of a chain of metro-politan areas, each of which grew around a substantial urban nucleus. The super-metropolitan character of this vast area, the greatest such growth ever observed, called for a special name. We chose the word *Megalopolis*, of Greek origin, and listed in Webster's dictionary as meaning 'a very large city.'

*What is the Meaning of a Study of Megalopolis?*

Although unique today, *Megalopolis* obviously has been and still is an extraordinarily interesting laboratory *in vivo* where much of what may well be accepted as the 'normalcies' of the advanced civilization of the latter part of the twentieth century is slowly shaping.

*Source:* Economic Geography (1957), **33**, number 3, pages 189–200

By its size and mass, Megalopolis is both an exceptional growth and a pioneer area; exceptional, for nowhere else could one find another concentration of population, of industrial and commercial facilities, of financial wealth and cultural activities, comparable to it. However, in several other points in America and on other continents growth of continuously urbanized spaces may be observed. More of such enormous 'metropolitan' bodies can be expected to arise as the evolution, already well advanced in and around New York, Philadelphia, Boston, Washington, reaches other cities and their environs. In this sense Megalopolis is a pioneer area: the processes which develop therein will help toward an understanding of, and will forecast ways and obstacles to, urban growth in various other parts.

In fact Megalopolis has already been pioneering in the organization of urban life for quite some time. Such features as skyscrapers, building elevators, city and suburban networks of trains, traffic lights, and one-way streets started here on a large scale to gain later world-wide adoption. Megalopolis grew up from the network provided by the early mushrooming of sea-trading towns along the coast from Boston to New

*Fig. 1.*

York and then along the Fall line, from New York to Washington. The size of its principal urban nuclei, especially New York and Philadelphia, caused the subsequent mushrooming of suburbs filling in the spaces between the larger cities. James Madison defined New Jersey as a 'barrel tapped at both ends'; that this state's function was essentially to link the area of New York and Philadelphia was apparently understood by such a clever observer at the end of the eighteenth century. But the polynuclear origin of Megalopolis is beginning to be repeated in other regions. A vast urban and suburban area is rapidly expanding around Los Angeles, for instance; inland it has already reached, in fact, San Bernardino; it may unite with San Diego on the coast. Around Chicago, on the shore of Lake Michigan, another impressive urban continuity is shaping. The metropolitan areas stretching in Ohio between Cleveland and Pittsburgh are close to coalescence; and the St. Lawrence Seaway, once opened, may accelerate and expand these trends in the area south of Lakes Erie and Ontario. And as more metropolitan areas are pushing forth suburban tentacles one towards another throughout the nation, additional but smaller Megalopolis-like clusters will be formed. This is a process involving considerable changes in the American modes of living. The trends may become better understood once the case of the largest and most advanced of these areas, the present Megalopolis, is thoroughly analyzed.

## What are the Problems of Megalopolis?

Two categories of problems, particularly pressing in all downtown sections of modern cities, have attracted attention and have been given much study: the traffic difficulties and the slums. Two other problems are nowadays receiving increasing attention in competent quarters: water supply and local government. Both appear inadequately set to answer the present needs of the huge cities and their quickly expanding suburbs. The rapidly mushrooming metropolitan commissions and committees seem to herald already deep changes forthcoming in the traditional concepts and practices of local government. Interstate compacts may arise to help solve transportation problems (such as the Port of New York Authority); experiments in metropolitan government may be more difficult to start in parts of Megalopolis because of the mass and variety of interests at stake—but the very difficulties make every attempt more significant.

Megalopolis as a unit has taken shape only within the last few years. Its laws and customs will take much longer to evòlve into new forms better adapted to the needs and resources of such an enormous urban territory. A survey of the new problems, in their variety, should nevertheless be of some help even at this time. While legislation and institu-

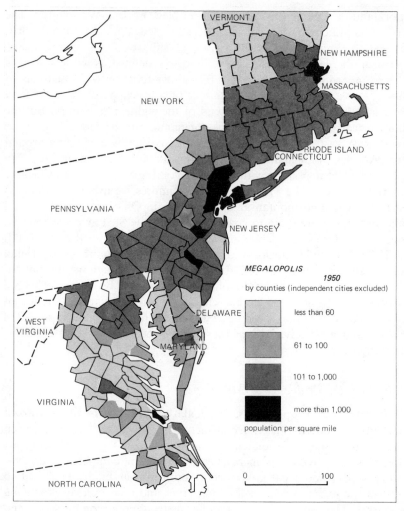

MEGALOPOLIS
*1950*
by counties (independent cities excluded)

less than 60

61 to 100

101 to 1,000

more than 1,000

population per square mile

0                    100

*Fig. 2.*

tions change slowly, modes of living evolve far more rapidly. Novelists have satirized certain aspects of megalopolitan life: a quarter century after the 'cliff-dwellers' were strongly established on Fifth and Park Avenues, we hear about the 'exurbanites.' The basic fact is the double trend of the large cities: part of the population moves out and commutes from an 'outer suburbia' which often extends 50 miles beyond; and parts of the cities are converted into immense apartment house groupings (paradoxically sometimes called 'villages'). These two trends are particularly clear in Manhattan and in Washington, but they are gaining other big nuclei of Megalopolis as well. The threat of the recent spread of juvenile delinquency seems to increase the migration of families to the

146

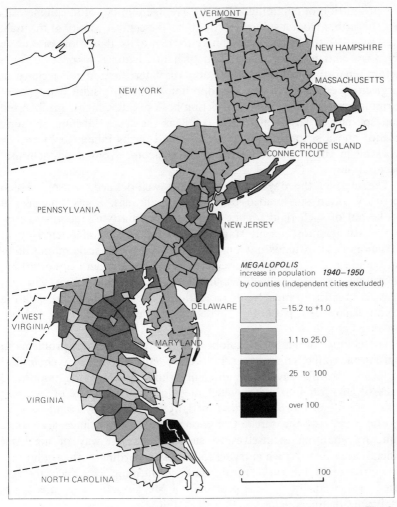

*Fig. 3.*

periphery of metropolitan areas. The new mode of life involves more
daily traveling, more traffic jams, and more highways outside the downtown areas; a redistribution of marketing channels (illustrated by
proliferating suburban shopping centers and department store branches);
some changes in the type of goods needed; an increasing interest in
zoning, gardening, and nature conservation.

Because more megalopolitan, the way of life of an increasing proportion of the population becomes more country-like although not really
rural. The Bureau of the Census has had to revise several times its
standards for the definition of metropolitan areas; the criteria of
integration with the central urban district include such measurements as

the proportion of commuters and the average number of telephone calls per subscriber from a suburban county to the central county of the area, etc. In 1950 the Bureau even had to revise its definition of 'urban territory' and introduced the term 'urbanized areas' to provide for a better separation between urban and rural territory in the vicinity of large cities, especially within metropolitan areas. New suburban types of farming are also developing, consisting both of a few highly mechanized and specialized large enterprises (such as the truck farming on Long Island) and a scattering of numerous small farms inhabited by people working in the cities and deriving their income from nonagricultural occupations.

The city, in the days of yore, was a well-defined, densely settled territory, often surrounded by walls or palisades. Some time ago it broke out of such rigid frames and developed outlying sections, *extramuros*. In its most recent stage of growth, already characteristic of Megalopolis, it extends out on a rapidly expanding scale, along highways and rural roads, mixing uses of land that look either rural or urban, encircling vast areas which remain 'green' (and which some wise endeavors attempt to preserve as recreation space for the future), creating a completely new pattern of living and of regional interdependence between communities.

The coming of age of Megalopolis thus creates, besides problems in legislation, traffic, engineering, marketing, etc., also new psychological problems: people have more difficulty thinking along the traditional lines of division into states when megalopolitan sections of different states are much more integrated in daily life than they could be with up-state areas of the same 'Commonwealth'; people have also some difficulty adapting themselves to such a scattered way of life; and officials are often lost when trying to classify according to the traditional categories of urban, rural, rural non-farm, farming, etc. Such are, too briefly reviewed, the various problems of Megalopolis. They are worth analyzing for the conclusions that may follow.

## Lessons from an Analysis of the Megalopolitan Process

A detailed analysis of Megalopolis, as it appears today, seems a worthwhile enterprise despite the present unique character of this region. Its trends acquire immediate national, and sometimes international, significance by the sheer size and weight of Megalopolis in economic and social matters. But it is also, as has been shown, a pioneering area in terms of urbanization. What is observed and experimented with here may serve, though on a smaller scale and in many cases only after some time, to avoid delays and errors in other growing urban areas. It may help improve our management of the intricate process of urbanization.

This process is an old one and has greatly contributed, as many authors have shown, to the growth of western civilization. Far from having reached its optimum, in the middle of the twentieth century, the process of urbanization accelerated its pace. The United States has demonstrated that enough agricultural commodities of all kinds can be produced for a populous nation, enjoying a high standard of living, by the work of only one-eighth of the total population. This proportion of the farmers within the nation may and probably will be further reduced. Thus 90 per cent of a prosperous nation must live from nonagricultural pursuits, but not in congested slums. This momentous evolution, one of the major American contributions to this century, leading to semi-urbanized status, is most advanced in Megalopolis.

The new forms thus attained, the intensity of the problems, the solutions attempted, must be compared to what happens in all these respects in other principal metropolitan areas in the United States and perhaps in Canada. A clearer mode of classification for both problems and possible solutions may thus be worked out, based on factual observation rather than generalized theory. The whole survey may help to evaluate this new expanding frontier of the American economy: the urbanization of the land.

Outside the North American continent many other countries are already faced with a similar acceleration of the process of urbanization. Their policies could greatly benefit from a full analysis of Megalopolis today and its comparison with other urban growths in America. None of the continuous chains of metropolitan areas or conurbations shaping now in other parts of the world is indeed comparable in size or shape as yet to the American Megalopolis. The one most nearly approaching it, which may perhaps coalesce sometime within the next 20 years, would be in our opinion in northwestern Europe, from Amsterdam to Paris, including perhaps a bulge eastwards as far as the Ruhr and Cologne along the Rhine and Meuse rivers.

Another possible super-metropolitan system of this kind could well be forming in England. A giant U-shaped urban chain surrounds the southern Pennines, extending from Liverpool and Manchester to Leeds and Bradford, via Birmingham and Sheffield. This U may some day unite southwards with the expanding suburbs of Greater London. Then the whole system may enter the megalopolitan family. It would remain, nevertheless, quite different from Megalopolis on the north-eastern seaboard. Each large area of such kind will long keep its originality, resulting from its own past and its relation to a given zone of civilization. Large urbanized areas do not need, however, to grow up to megalopolitan size to be able to profit by the lessons in metropolitan organization obtained in Megalopolis.

## How Far Could Megalopolis Grow?

Several important studies of the metropolitan areas around New York City, Philadelphia, etc., are now in progress. These surveys will attempt to forecast future growth, by projecting curves for the next 10 to 25 years. Urban and suburban territory is expanding at a fast pace in the United States, and this pace has been notably accelerated in recent years. A vast area like Megalopolis would not have arisen without it. The time has perhaps come to ask once more the question: How far could Megalopolis grow? And in which directions?

In 1955, a group of city planners at Yale University began to speak about a citylike, well-knit system extending from Portland, Maine, to Norfolk, Virginia. Such may be the impression provided by road transportation maps. This writer's observations on completion of a study of Virginia by January, 1955, did not seem to warrant as yet the absorption into Megalopolis of more than a few counties in northern Virginia. Richmond and the Hampton Roads area had not yet been consolidated with the Washington-to-Boston more intensely urbanized system. Beyond eastern Massachusetts northwards, urbanization was felt mainly in the summer as a seasonal migration of vacationing or semi-vacationing people from Megalopolis. However, there could be no doubt that Megalopolis is daily expanding its territorial scope. Our definition (see Fig. 1) based on the census of 1950 is certainly an under-estimation in area for 1957.

Expansion proceeds in many directions, of course, all around the outer fringes. Consolidation of the urban land use within the 1950 limits goes on at the same time. The existing densities of population (see Fig. 2) and the trends of increase of this density by counties in the recent past (see Fig. 3) concur in stressing a relative saturation of most of the areas within Megalopolis between Philadelphia and Boston. Although a great deal of new construction still goes on even in those parts, the more striking increases appear in the southern section of Megalopolis and an expansion in the Virginian Tidewater and northern Piedmont seems unavoidable.

Thus Megalopolis is pushing southwards and southwestwards. It may indeed reach Richmond and Norfolk some day in the foreseeable future. Another set of directions, this time inland, and breaking away from the fateful axis of U.S. 1, may be inferred from an attentive examination of the distribution already in 1950 of the metropolitan areas in the north-eastern section of the United States, between the Atlantic seaboard, the Great Lakes and the Ohio Valley (see Fig. 4). A rather impressive density of such metropolitan areas is found inland along the route of the New York Central Railroad up the Hudson-Mohawk route and the southern shores of Lakes Erie and Ontario. Then from Cleveland south-

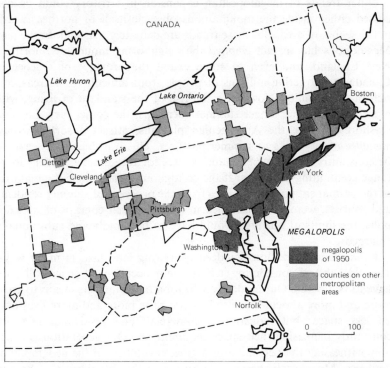

Fig. 4.

wards a little interrupted chain extends towards Pittsburgh, Pennsylvania. Between Megalopolis on one hand and the trans-Appalachian urbanized and industrialized areas, the valleys and ridges of the Appalachian Mountains cause a clearcut break. But if the Pittsburgh-Cleveland-Syracuse-Albany chain would come to be consolidated, even mountain ranges could be overcome and an enormous sort of annular megalopolitan system could arise; the St. Lawrence Seaway, if it developed into a major artery of navigation, could precipitate such a trend.

A much smaller but curiously 'annular' urban system is already shaping in the Netherlands, as after the coalescence of the cities along the main seaboard axis of Holland, from Amsterdam to Rotterdam, urbanization is gaining inland, along the Rhine from Rotterdam to Arnhem, and along roads and canals from Amsterdam to Utrecht. The coalescence between Arnhem and Utrecht is on its way. In England the U-shaped chain of the metropolitan type outlined above from Manchester to Leeds has not been filled up in between these two cities along the shortest line into another annular formation because of the topographical obstacle of the Pennine range, still an empty area. This obstacle is comparable, though it is on a much smaller scale, to the Appalachian ridges back of Megalopolis.

151

Other trends of megalopolitan expansion in territory could be discussed either inside the mountainous obstacle itself or northeastwards in the seaboard area. But these trends are definitely seasonal. In the past Megalopolis has in fact *emptied* the neighboring mountains, northern New England, and even to some extent the province of Quebec in Canada by attracting millions of people from difficult rural areas, less rich in opportunity. Now, with the rise of the standard of living, with more people taking longer summer vacations, the cooler New England seashore or hills, the Appalachian plateaus, attract a sort of *transhumance* of city folks to summer pastures. This transhumance seems to be constantly on the increase and creates for the summer months long-range commuting problems. If the contiguous areas, where the majority of the permanent population lives from the proceeds of summer residents and tourists, were to be included in the territorial concept of Megalopolis, the limits of our area would have to be rapidly and substantially enlarged.

Urban land utilization is indeed devouring land fast, in many ways. The old habit of considering it as a minor occupant of space will soon have to be revised. Our modern civilization has found the means to grow more and more agricultural products, to raise more and more livestock, on less space; but industrial, commercial, and residential uses are constantly increasing their space requirements. Our generation is probably witnessing the beginning of a great revolution in the geography of land use. Megalopolis heralds a new era in the distribution of habitat and economic activities.

# 3.2 The urban field
## John Friedmann and John Miller

*The inherited form of the city no longer corresponds to reality. The spatial structure of contemporary American civilization consists of metropolitan core regions and the intermetropolitan peripheries. The former have achieved very high levels of economic and cultural development at the expense of the latter, leaving the periphery in a decadent state. Current and projected trends in technology and tastes suggest that a new element of spatial order is coming into being—the urban field—which will unify both core and periphery within a single matrix. The implications of the urban field for living patterns and for planning are discussed.*

Source: *Journal of the American Institute of Planners*, **31**, November 1965

## In Search of a New Image

There has been a growing dissatisfaction with the historical concept of the city. Don Martindale, in his brilliant introduction to Max Weber's (1958, page 62) essay, *The City*, has composed a fitting epitaph:

The modern city is losing its external and formal structure. Internally it is in a state of decay while the new community represented by the nation everywhere grows at its expense. The age of the city seems to be at an end.

If this is so from a sociological standpoint, it is equally true from the perspective of a physical planner. Various concepts have been put forward in the endeavor to capture the expanding scale of urban life. Metropolitan region, spread city, megalopolis, ecumenopolis ... each attempt to redefine the new reality has led to a broader spatial conception. Behind these efforts lies an awareness of the constantly widening patterns of interaction in an urbanizing world.

Modern utopian constructs have been equally intent on fitting city concepts to the possibilities created by our communications-based society. Clarence Stein's (1964) *Regional City* is a constellation of moderately sized communities separated by great open spaces and bound closely together by highways. Frank Lloyd Wright's (1958) *Broadacre City* represents a complete melding of the urban and rural worlds that, without pronounced centers, would uniformly dissolve throughout a region. Both these constructs see the city as an essentially unlimited form of human settlement, capable of infinite expansion.

None of the new concepts, however, has been completely successful. The Bureau of the Census has had to shift the meaning of metropolitan region from 'metropolitan district' to 'standard metropolitan area' to 'standard metropolitan statistical area' in order to keep pace with our improved understanding of what constitutes the fundamental ecological area of urban life, and it is once more reexamining the question.

The much looser conception of *spread-city* has been applied only to the New York region, and no attempt has been made to generalize from it to other urban areas. Jean Gottmann's (1961) *megalopolis* appears as a geographic place name for the chain of metropolitan giants along the Boston-Washington axis. Although later writers have taken it as a generic term for contiguous metropolitan regions, the concept, lacking precision as well as generality, has frequently been misapplied. One writer has gone so far as to extend its meaning to the entire region from Phoenix to Minneapolis (Berkman, 1964, pages 4–5). His Midwest Central Megalopolis is a geographic and conceptual absurdity. Finally, C. A. Doxiadis' *ecumenopolis* is no concept at all but a poetic vision (Doxiadis, 1965).

Planners therefore, are left in a quandary. 'Modern metropolitan

153

trends,' wrote the late Catherine Bauer Wurster, 'have destroyed the traditional concept of urban structure, and there is no new image to take its place' (Wurster, 1963). Yet none would question the need for such an image, if only to serve as the conceptual basis for organizing our strategies for urban development. Our hope in this paper is to meet this great need, suggesting an image of the new *polis* that will be adequate to the tasks that face the nation in the decades ahead.

## The Enlarged Scale of Urban Life

It has become increasingly possible to interpret the spatial structure of the United States in ways that will emphasize a pattern consisting of *one*, metropolitan areas and *two*, the inter-metropolitan periphery. Except for thinly populated parts of the American interior, the inter-metropolitan periphery includes all areas that intervene among metropolitan regions that are, as it were, the reverse image of the trend towards large scale concentrated settlement that has persisted in this country for over half a century. Like a devil's mirror, much of it has developed a socio-economic profile that perversely reflects the very opposite of metropolitan virility.

Economically, the inter-metropolitan periphery includes most of the areas that have been declared eligible for federal area redevelopment assistance. This is illustrated in Map I, which shows the geographic extent of substandard income and high unemployment areas relative to the urbanized regions of the United States. Situated almost entirely outise the normal reach of the larger cities, these areas are shown to be clearly peripheral. They have a disproportionately large share of low-growth and declining industries and a correspondingly antiquated economic structure. Nevertheless, one-fifth of the American people are living in these regions of economic distress.

Demographically, the inter-metropolitan periphery has been subject to a long-term, continuous decline (Map II). This trend reflects the movement of people to cities, especially to the large metropolitan concentrations. Although the smaller cities on the periphery have to some extent benefitted from migration, their gains have been less, on the average, than for all urban areas (Northam, 1963). In addition, migration from economically depressed regions has been highly selective, so that the age distribution of the remaining population has become polarized around the very young and very old. In Appalachia, for example, the two million people who left the region during the 1950's were, for the most part, drawn from the productive age groups from 18 to 64. At the same time, the population over 65 years old increased by nearly one-third. In some areas, recorded death rates now actually exceed birth rates.

The emergence in large sections of the country of the inter-metro-politan periphery as a major problem area has been the direct result of the concentration of people and activities around closely contiguous metropolitan cores. Growth in and around these cores has drawn off the productive population, economic activities, and investment capital of the periphery, but the forces of urbanization are now in the process of reversing this trend.*

Looking ahead to the next generation, we foresee a new scale of urban living that will extend far beyond existing metropolitan cores and penetrate deeply into the periphery. Relations of dominance and de-pendency will be transcended. The older established centers, together with the intermetropolitan peripheries that envelop them, will constitute the new ecological unit of America's post-industrial society that will replace traditional concepts of the city and metropolis. This basic element of the emerging spatial order we shall call the *urban field*.

The urban field may be viewed as an enlargement of the space for urban living that extends far beyond the boundaries of existing metro-politan areas—defined primarily in terms of commuting to a central city of 'metropolitan' size—into the open landscape of the periphery. This change to a larger scale of urban life is already underway, encouraged by changes in technology, economics, and preferred social behavior. Eventually the urban field may even come to be acknowledged as a community of *shared* interests, although these interests may be more strongly oriented to specific functions than to area. They will be shared because to a large extent they will overlap and complement each other within a specific locational matrix. Because urban fields will be large, with populations of upwards of one million, their social and cultural life will form a rich and varied pattern capable of satisfying most human aspirations within a local setting.

It is no longer possible to regard the city as purely an artifact, or a political entity, or a configuration of population densities. All of these are outmoded constructs that recall a time when one could trace a sharp dividing line between town and countryside, rural and urban man. From a sociological and, indeed, an economic standpoint, what is properly urban and properly rural can no longer be distinguished. The United States is becoming a thoroughly urbanized society, perhaps the

*The Economic Research Service of the U.S. Department of Agriculture in a study of the effects of metropolitan growth trends on rural counties asserts that 'the existence of a large, dense, and growing urban population in a region tends to create conditions of population growth in rural counties of the same region. This is true not only because an ever-larger number of the rural counties are within commuting range of urban centers, but also because more distant counties are affected by the accession of businesses or residents who do not need frequent commutation to the city but whose work or choice of residence is related to the city—especially the large metropolitan city. These are counties beyond "exurbia" which the geographer Wilbur Zelinsky has referred to as the "urban penumbra".'

155

first such society in history. The corresponding view of the city is no longer of a physical entity, but of a pattern of point locations and connecting flows of people, information, money, and commodities. This new understanding of the city has been incorporated into the census concept of a Standard Metropolitan Statistical Area and has since been widely accepted as a basis for public and private decisions.

The idea of an urban field is similarly based on the criterion of inter-dependency. It represents a fusion of metropolitan spaces and non-metropolitan peripheral spaces centered upon core areas (SMSA's) of at least 300 000 people and extending outwards from these core areas for a distance equivalent to two hours' driving over modern throughway systems (approximately 100 miles with present technology). This represents not only an approximate geographic limit for commuting to a job, but also the limit of intensive weekend and seasonal use (by ground transportation) of the present periphery for recreation. A system of urban fields delineated by this criterion without attempting to draw a dividing line between metropolitan cores that are less than 200 miles apart, is presented in Map III. Between 85 and 90 per cent of the total United States population falls within the boundaries of this system while less than 35 per cent of the total land area of the country is included. These are facts of signal importance, for as the area of metropolitan influence is substantially enlarged nearly all of us will soon be living within one or another of the 70-odd urban fields of the United States.*

The urban field of the future, however, will be a far less focussed region than today's metropolitan area. The present dominance of the metropolitan core will become attenuated as economic activities are decentralized to smaller cities within the field or into the open country, but because proximity will continue to account for a good deal of local interaction, the urban field will be a coherent region.

To define this region on a map, the main criterion should be that exchange relations *within* each field are more intensive than among them, during the course of an entire year. The calculation of this measure on an annual basis instead of at a single point in time is important because some of the functional relationships among subareas may be subject to seasonal variations. The enjoyment of summer and winter recreation areas is the outstanding example of this phenomenon. These areas should be allocated to that realm whose population makes the most intensive use of them.

It is important to recollect what this projected geographic expansion

*It is significant to note that if all present SMSA's of between 200 000 and 300 000 people were to reach the critical threshold size of 300 000 during the next generation, only a small expansion of the area now included in urban realms would occur. Most of these centers are located within or close to the edge of an existing urban realm and are thus encompassed by the boundaries we have provisionally defined.

156

**ARA — Designated 1950 -- 60 by County Eligible Areas**

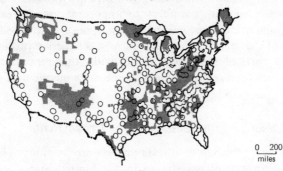

O 25 mile radius from cities of 25,000　■ area designated redevelopment counties
population of more - 1960　　　　　　　June 15, 1963

**Population Change 1950 — 60 by County**

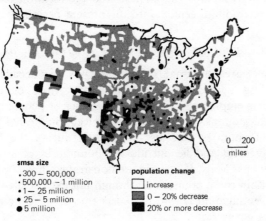

smsa size
· 300 — 500,000
· 500,000 – 1 million
● 1— 25 million
● 25 – 5 million
● 5 million

population change
□ increase
▨ 0 — 20% decrease
■ 20% or more decrease

**The Urban Field**

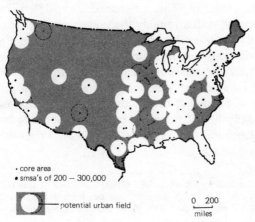

· core area
● smsa's of 200 – 300,000

—potential urban field

0　200
miles

of urban living space will accomplish. First, it will turn the resources of the inter-metropolitan periphery to important uses by existing metropolitan populations; second, as the periphery becomes absorbed into the urban field, it will be eliminated as a distinctive problem area. The remaining parts of the United States will either remain in low density agrarian uses or revert to wilderness for the enjoyment of distant populations.

## Forces Underlying the Emergence of Urban Realms

Our case for the urban field rests on two propositions. The first is that the future growth of population in the United States will take place almost exclusively within the areas we have defined as urban fields. The second is that within each urban field substantial centrifugal forces will propel the settlement of population and the location of activities from existing metropolitan centers into the present periphery.

## Continued Population Concentration in Urban Fields

One of the clearest national trends of the past few decades has been that of increasing demographic concentration. Most of the discussion, however, has emphasized the pulling together of people in metropolitan and coastal regions. It has been less well publicized that the great majority of counties that lost population during the 1950's are predominantly rural and lie outside the boundaries of any urban realm. The gains, as Map II clearly demonstrates, have occurred almost entirely within these boundaries, though not exclusively in metropolitan counties. We have no reason to expect this trend to be reversed during the coming generation.

In 1960, an estimated 150 million Americans lived in potential urban fields. We have projected their number to more than double the present number by the year 2000. This increase of 150 to 180 million will have to be accommodated within roughly the same area that we have provisionally delimited. The question arises as to where, within a given field, this population will be living. In approaching this question, we are mindful of the New York Metropolitan Region Study which for 1985 foresees as many people living in the 'outer ring' as in the central core. This 'outer ring' extends as far as 100 miles from New York City and is not today part of the daily life of the metropolis.* Elaborating on this startling projection, Raymond Vernon (1960, page 224) writes that employment and population trends

*The Core (New York City's four major boroughs and Hudson County) total population in 1985 is estimated by Vernon to be 7 810 000, a decline of almost half a million from the 1955 population. The Outer Ring (90 minutes from Manhattan to up to 30 miles beyond that) total is given to be 7 809 000, an increase of over 300 per cent.

cast doubt on any image of the Region as a giant cluster of human activity held together by a great nub of jobs at the center. Instead . . . [they afford] a picture of a Region in which the centripetal pull is weakening. This, in turn, means a further modification of the oversimplified picture of the Region as a ring of bedroom communities in the suburbs emptying out their inhabitants every morning to the central city. Incomplete and misleading as this picture is today, it promises to be even more misleading in the decades ahead . . . And the chronic complaint of the outlying areas that they lack an 'economic base' may continue to lose some of its realism and force.

Vernon has foreshadowed the appearance of an urban field that would have New York City as its core. What are the forces, then, which suggest this occupancy of the periphery by people and activities, not only for New York, but for all other core regions in the United States? And what specific forms will it assume?

## Centrifugal Forces: Resources of the Periphery

The main pull, we submit, is the increasing attractiveness of the periphery to metropolitan populations. It has space, it has scenery, and it contains communities that remain from earlier periods of settlement and preserve a measure of historical integrity and interest.

Demand for these resources will be generated by three main trends: increasing real income, increasing leisure, and increasing mobility. Although these trends are familiar, brief discussion of them will help to suggest their cumulative impact.

The President's Council of Economic Advisors estimates that output per man-hour may undergo a three-fold expansion by the year 2000. Holding constant both working hours and labor force participation rates, this would raise average family income (in today's prices) to approximately $18,000. Although there is every reason to expect that part of the potential gains in income will be taken in the form of greater leisure through a combination of shorter working hours, longer vacations, later entry into the labor force, and earlier retirement, the prospective rise in wealth is still very substantial. If present patterns of consumption are any guide, we can expect a good share of this new wealth to be devoted to the purchase of space, privacy, travel, education, culture, and various forms of recreative leisure.

The present allocation of leisure time is distributed among numerous activities. The Stanford Research Institute reports that already 50 million Americans are actively participating in amateur art activity; that 32 million are musicians, and 15 million are painters, sculptors, and sketchers. There are more piano players than fishermen, as many painters as hunters, and more theater goers than boaters, skiers, golfers, and skin-divers combined.

159

The United States Department of Health, Education and Welfare has published statistics showing that new museums, including aquariums and zoos, are being established at the rate of one every three days, and that one-third of all existing museums in the country have been opened since 1950. Other cultural activities have shown equally phenomenal gains. For instance, there are now 1400 symphony orchestras in the United States, compared to only 100 in 1920.

These new cultural facilities are more mobile, more intimate, and more dispersed than their predecessors. They are different from the grand centers of high culture left in our central cores by the nineteenth century cultural ideology.

Participation in outdoor sports is likewise on an impressive scale. In 1964, there were an estimated 38 million boaters, 20 million campers, 7 million skiers, and an equal number of golfers. Skiing enthusiasts alone have jumped by 600 per cent during the past ten years. And attendance in official park and forest areas has been rising at a cumulative annual rate of about ten percent.

With increasing leisure time available, the prospects for the future show no abatement in these activities. For the mass of the people, nearly two-thirds of their waking hours will be essentially in free, unstructured time.* It is therefore not surprising that the Outdoor Recreation Resources Review Commission has predicted a tripling in the overall demand for recreation by the year 2000 (ORRRC, 1964, page 8). For the hedonistic leisure society we are becoming, this estimate may indeed be a conservative one.

The combined trends in income and leisure are bound to arouse great popular interest in the periphery, but their full effect will be transmitted through the increased mobility which our technology affords.

The gradual lifting of constraints which during the industrial era packed jobs and people into tightly confined urban spaces will encourage what Jean Gottman has called the 'quasi-colloidal dispersion' of activities throughout the urban field. Impending communications technologies suggest the possibility of relaxing the need for physical proximity in distribution, marketing, information services, and decision-making.

The combined effects of greater income, leisure, and mobility will be felt, by virtue of these arguments, primarily on the present periphery of metropolitan regions, as demand for the use of its resources are vastly intensified. Some of these uses are shown in Table 1. They are distinctly urban in character. And they remind us of Lewis Mumford's prophetic vision of the 'Invisible City.'

Gone is primitive local monopoly through isolation: gone is the metropolitan

---

*The National Planning Association has projected an average work week of only 30 hours for the year 2000.

monopoly through seizure and exploitation. . . . The ideal mission of the city is to further [a] process of cultural circulation and diffusion; and this will restore to many now sub-ordinate urban centers a variety of activities that were once drained away for the exclusive benefit of the great city.

## Table 3
Uses of the Intermetropolitan Periphery

*Recreation*

camps
parks
forests
wilderness areas
nature sanctuaries
resorts
outdoor sport areas
quietist retreats

*Institutions*

boarding schools
junior colleges
universities
museums
cultural centers
scientific research stations
conference centers
hospitals
sanatoria
government administrative offices

*Communities*

holiday communities
retirement communities
vacation villages
art colonies
diversified 'new towns'
historical communities
second home areas

*Economic Activities*

agro-business
space-extensive manufacturing plants
research and communications-based industries
mail order houses
warehouses
insurance companies
jet airports

## Emerging Life Styles of the Urban Field

The projected incorporation of the periphery into the urban realm will be accompanied by significant changes in American patterns of living. On the whole, we expect that these changes will be evaluated favorably. Derogatory slogans, such as 'sprawl' and 'scatteration,' bandied about in ideological campaigns, will have to be discarded in any serious search for what it means to live on the new scale. Although not all the consequences can be foreseen now, a few merit closer attention. We shall restrict our comment to only three of them: a wider life space on the average, a wider choice of living environments, and a wider community of interests.

1. *A wider life space.* The effective life space of an individual includes all the geographic areas within which his life unfolds. It includes his home and its immediate vicinity; his place of work or schooling; the places in which he does his shopping and engages in leisure activities; the more distant places to which he travels for business, recreation, or learning; the residence areas of the friends and relatives he visits; and the connecting paths over which he travels to reach his destination.

The higher speeds, greater versatility, and lower costs expected in transportation and communication during the next few decades will encourage a dispersion of people and activities throughout the urban field and a further thinning out of metropolitan core areas on an unsurpassed scale. Technological innovations will make it possible to substitute mobility for location. The strong likelihood that this will occur is suggested by foreseeable changes in patterns which underlie the location decisions of families and firms.

For individual families, locational decisions will be increasingly influenced by larger incomes that will permit the purchase of more space, more privacy, and more transportation; by a growing concern with the qualitative aspects of life, especially with the quality of the physical environment; by the gradual relaxation of the puritanical distinction between work and play, especially among professional and business elite groups; and by the desire for an environment that will permit a richer family life. All of these forces will tend to render the intermetropolitan periphery more attractive as a place to live, and help to tie it more closely into the urban field.

The locations of business firms will encounter fewer economic constraints within the urban field than at present. This is especially true for the new kinds of service activities—professional, managerial, research- and communications-based—which are the leading edge of a post-industrial society. Urban infrastructure and services will be nearly ubiquitous throughout the urban field; the pressing need for physical propinquity among firms is declining; and the expansion and improvement of transport and communication services will tend to make regional as well as national markets equally accessible. If only those economic factors that operate generally throughout a given field are taken into account, thereby excluding local subsidies or differences in local tax structure, which provide only small and temporary advantages, it is possible to assert that firms may locate nearly at random throughout the field, subject only to the constraint of labor force distribution. Location of the labor force will then become a primary determinant in business location decisions, with the result that firms will be attracted in increasing numbers into what is now the inter-metropolitan periphery. Firms as well as families will substitute mobility and machine-interposed communications for location.

2. *A wider choice of living environments both for resident and nonresident use and more frequent interchange among environments.* The urban field offers a heterogeneous landscape, consisting of metropolitan cores, small towns, and varied open spaces.* Within it, a wide variety of living environments may be sought and created. There is nothing rigid or predetermined about the physical form of the field: rather, it may be viewed as a mosaic of different forms and micro-environments which coexist within a common communications framework without intruding spatially on each other.

For the family, the urban field offers a far greater choice of living environments than do the old metropolitan areas. Alternatives include country and in-town living, perhaps combined, through a steep increase in the frequency of second homes for year-round use; single family dwellings and apartment towers; dense metropolitan clusters and open countryside; new towns and towns with an historical tradition; and functionally specialized communities.

No part within the urban field is isolated from another. There is rather an easy-going interchange among all the parts, encouraged not only by the wider distribution of population but also by the larger amounts of time available for the pursuit of leisure. All areas are located no further than two hours driving distance from old metropolitan cores. And although these cores will lose much of their present importance to the people of the field as functions are decentralized, they will continue for at least a few more decades to attract many people to the activities that are traditionally carried out within them, such as major educational and governmental institutions, famous museums, outstanding music, artistic, and sport events. Many cultural facilities,

---

*It will be recalled that the definition of an urban field is based on a metropolitan center of at least 300 000 inhabitants. From this it follows that an urban field may include within its perimeter smaller metropolitan areas as well as 'satellite' cities of varying size up to the size of the metropolitan core area.

however, will be dispersed throughout the realm and many metro-politan services will become available at any point within it through extended distribution systems. At the same time, easy access to other urban fields can be provided through a regional system of airports capable of handling short-distance jets and vertical take-off craft. High-speed rail transport may be a significant means for inter-realm travel in some parts of the country, such as the 'Northeast Corridor.'

3. *A wider community of interests.* The already noted increase in the effective life space of the population suggests that each person will have interests in happenings over a larger segment of the field than at present. In the course of a year, he may actively participate in the life of a number of spatially defined local communities. As a result, he is likely to be less concerned with the fate of the community where he resides and more with activities that may be scattered throughout the field but are closest to his interests, leading to a stronger identification on his part with the realm as a whole at the cost of a declining interest in purely local affairs. (In some places, this loss may be offset by the smaller size of his resident community which would encourage more active participation in problem-solving.)

## Bibliography

*Post-industrial urbanization is discussed also in these publications.*

THE AMERICAN ASSEMBLY. Columbia University. *Automation and Technological Change* (Englewood Cliffs, N. J.: Prentice-Hall, Inc., 1962).

BARLOWE, Raleigh, 'Our Future Needs for Nonfarm Lands,' *Land:* The Yearbook of Agriculture 1958 (Washington, DC: The United States Department of Agriculture, 1958), pages 474–479.

BLESSING, Charles A. 'A Comprehensive Role for Urban Design,' *Journal of American Institute of Architects,* **XLIII** (November, 1964), 73–96.

BLUMENFELD, Hans 'The Urban Pattern,' *The Annals of the American Academy of Political and Social Science,* **CCCLII** (March, 1964), 74–83.

BOULDING, Kenneth E. 'The Death of the City: A Frightened Look at Post-civilization,' *The Historian and the City,* edited by Oscar Handlin and John Burchard (Cambridge, Mass.: The M.I.T. Press and Harvard University Press, 1963), pages 133–145.

CHURCHILL, Henry S. 'Trends,' *The City is the People* (New York: Harcourt, Brace & World, Inc., 1945), pages 147–186.

CLAWSON, Marion and R. BURNELL HELD, 'Demand for Rural Resources in the Context of Long-Range National Needs,' *Journal of Farm Economics,* **VL** (December, 1963).

CLAWSON, Marion 'How Much Leisure: Now and in the Future,' *The Annals of the American Academy of Political and Social Science* (Monograph No. 4, 1964).

DICKINSON, Robert E. 'The City Region,' *City Region and Regionalism* (London: Routledge and Kegan Paul, 1947), pages 165–171.

DYCKMAN, John 'The Changing Uses of the City,' *Daedalus*, XC (Winter, 1961), 111–131.

FLEISHER, Aaron 'The Influence of Technology on Urban Forms,' *Daedalus*, XC (Winter, 1961), 48–60.

GAFFNEY, M. Mason 'Urban Expansion—Will It Ever Stop?' *Land:* The Yearbook of Agriculture 1958 (Washington, DC: The United States Department of Agriculture, 1958), pages 503–522.

GOTTMAN, Jean, *Economics, Esthetics, and Ethics in Modern Urbanization* (New York: The Twentieth Century Fund, 1962).

GREEN, Howard L., 'Hinterland Boundaries of New York City and Boston in Southern New England,' *Economic Geography*, XXXI (October, 1955), 283–300.

GULICK, Luther, 'Metropolitan Organization,' *The Annals of the American Academy of Political and Social Science*, CCCXIV (November, 1957), 57–65.

GUTHEIM, Frederick, 'Designing Inter-City Growth,' *Progressive Architecture*, XLIII (August, 1962), 98–108.

HIGBEE, Edward, *Farms and Farmers in an Urban Age* (New York: The Twentieth Century Fund, 1963).

HOOVER, Edgar M., and Raymond VERNON, *Anatomy of a Metropolis* (Cambridge, Mass.: Harvard University Press, 1959).

JOHNSON, Hugh A. 'Planning for the New Land Frontier,' *Land:* The Yearbook of Agriculture 1958 (Washington, DC: The United States Department of Agriculture, 1958) pages 568–583.

LYNCH, Kevin, 'The Pattern of the Metropolis,' *Daedalus*, XC (Winter, 1961), 79–98.

MAYER, Albert, 'The Challenge Ahead: New Towns: And Fresh In-City Communities,' *Architectural Record*, CXXXVI (August, 1964), 129–138.

MAYER, Albert, 'The Challenge Ahead: The Role of Regional Policy,' *Architectural Record*, CXXXVI (September, 1964), 197–206.

MEIER, Richard L., 'The Evolving Metropolis and New Technology,' *Planning and the Urban Community*, edited by Harvey S. Perloff (Pittsburgh: University of Pittsburgh Press, 1961), pages 28–42.

MUMFORD, Lewis, 'The Future of the City: The Disappearing City,' *Architectural Record*, CXXXII (October, 1962), 121–128.

MUMFORD, Lewis, 'Planning for Urban Growth,' *The City in History* (New York: Harcourt, Brace and World, Inc., 1961), pages 514–524.

New York State. Office of Regional Development, *Change, Challenge, Response: A Development Policy for New York State* (Albany: The Office, 1964).

WINGO, Lowdon, Jr., 'Recreation and Urban Development: A Policy Perspective,' *The Annals of the American Academy of Political and Social Science*, CCCLII (March, 1964), 129–140.

WOOD, Samuel E. and Alfred E. HELLER, *California Going, Going . . .* (Sacramento, California: California Tomorrow, 1962).

WOOD, Samuel E. and Alfred E. HELLER, *The Phantom Cities of California* (Sacramento, California: California Tomorrow, 1963).

WURSTER, Catherine Bauer, 'Can Cities Compete with Suburbia for Family Living?' *Architectural Record*, CXXXVI (December, 1964), 149–156.

## References

BERKMAN, H. C. (1964) *Our Urban Plant:* Essays in Urban Affairs (Madison, Wisconsin: The University of Wisconsin Extension).

DOXIADIS, C. A. (1965) 'The Ekistic Grid,' *Ekistics*, **XIX**, March.

GOTTMAN, J. (1961) *Megalopolis* (New York, The Twentieth Century Fund).

MUMFORD, L. (1961) *The City in History*. New York, Harcourt, Brace and World.

NORTHAN, R. M. (1963) Declining Urban Centres in the United States: 1950–1960 *Annals of the Association of American Geographers*, **LIII**, March, pages 50–59.

OUTDOOR RECREATION RESOURCES REVIEW COMMISSION (1964), *Action for Outdoor Recreation for America* Washington, Citizens Committee for the ORRRC Report.

STEIN, C. S. (1964) A Regional Plan for Dispersal *Architectural Record*, **CXXXVI**, September, pages 205–206.

WEBER, M. (1958) *The City*, Glencoe, Illinois, The Free Press.

WRIGHT, F. L. (1958) *The Living City* New York, Horizon Press.

WURSTER, Catherine, B. (1963) 'The Form and Structure of the Future Urban Complex' in Lowdon Wingo Jr, (Editor) *Cities and Space*, Baltimore, John Hopkins Press.

# 3.3 Homes beyond the fringe *Lionel March*

*Lionel March, Cambridge University School of Architecture, challenges conventional wisdom on urban structure: the housing yardstick is based on 'dangerous conventions about density'; high densities 'make the greatest sense in the countryside'; wasteful segregation of land uses must be abandoned; skyscrapers are 'extravagant irrational gestures'. He argues that the most reasonable form for the city is linear, not nuclear, a free, loose development along a network of routes beyond the urban fringe.*

Just 70 years ago Ebenezer Howard was putting the finishing touches to a little book called *Tomorrow: a peaceful path to real reform*, later to become known as *Garden Cities of Tomorrow*. He addressed himself to Robert Blatchford's question at the beginning of *Merrie England*: 'The problem we have to consider is: Given a country and a people, find how the people may make the best of the country and themselves.' For good reasons he decided that this question was too big and he

*Source:* from The Proceedings of the Town and Country Planning Summer School, Swansea, 1969

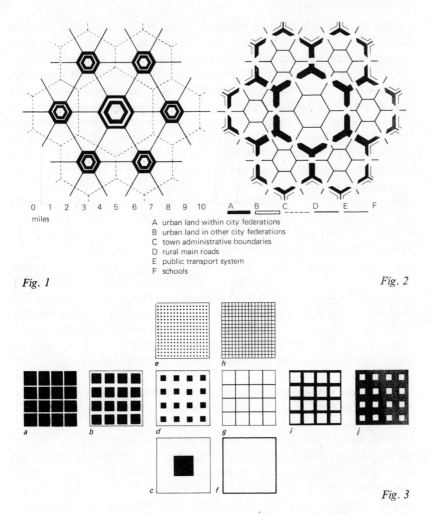

0 1 2 3 4 5 6 7 8 9 10
miles

A urban land within city federations
B urban land in other city federations
C town administrative boundaries
D rural main roads
E public transport system
F schools

*Fig. 1*

*Fig. 2*

*Fig. 3*

suggested it would be better to study a smaller problem first, namely: 'Given, say, 6,000 acres of land, let us endeavour to make the best use of it. For then, having dealt with this, we shall have educated ourselves to deal with the larger area.'

Diagram 1a is a version of Howard's cluster of towns forming a city federation of 250 000 persons. By the year 2000 we would need 250 of these clusters to accommodate the whole expected population of England and Wales. Suppose for a moment we built these clusters and demolished everything else. 250 000 people would live in easy reach of one another and all social facilities. Schools would be within walking distance of all homes. Shopping would take place indoors. Everyone who wanted to would have a house and garden. The minimum plot size is 20 ft by 100 ft. The roads would easily accommodate the motor car. The towns have

167

hollow centres and the road system is more like a simple grid wrapped round upon itself than a radial and circumferential system. The minimum road width is 60 ft, whilst the six principal boulevards are 120 ft, as are the two principal avenues. We would be living in towns then, which could accommodate the motor car yet be small enough to permit easy pedestrian access to many different functions. All of us would be able to own a house and garden. Yet the really remarkable thing about the proposition is this: 4 000 000 acres of land that we expect to be built on by the year 2000 would not be required. In fact, although the population would be twice the size of that of Howard's day it would have been accommodated on the same land as was urbanized in 1898. Since then the urban land stock has doubled, and it is expected to have trebled by the year 2000. We cannot blame Howard for any waste of land.

A simple question that can be asked is this: if every household in the year 2000 could have a house, a garden and a car on 2 000 000 acres of urban land, why will they not have a house, a garden and a car on three times as much? The answer almost certainly has nothing to do with land use *per se*, but with the pattern of land ownership. A more equitable distribution of land would ensure a house and a garden for all who want one. Yet, even if land were not distributed evenly, this simple desire could be answered to some extent by more rational land use planning in relation to the built forms required for the house and garden.

This paper will look at some of the questions that we are asking ourselves in the land use and built form studies we are now starting in Cambridge.

First, let us look at how 10 per cent of a land area might be covered by urban uses. This 10 per cent is the present proportion of urban land to all land in England and Wales and it includes urban open spaces like parks, but not agricultural land within urban administrative boundaries. Diagram 3c shows the 10 per cent coverage distributed in a concentrated nuclear form (one single blob) and 3e in a dispersed nuclear pattern (in this case 256 blobs). Diagrams 3f-h, however, show the same amount of urban land distributed in a linear matter. I shall describe pattern 3f as concentrated linear (a coarse mesh) and 3h as dispersed linear (a fine mesh). Diagram 3a shows 90 per cent nuclear coverage, and 3b 50 per cent coverage, while diagrams 3i and 3j show the inverted scheme of linear coverage.

There are three properties of the distribution. The topological property of being nuclear or linear corresponds to thinking blobs, *or* thinking of the spaces between. I shall refer to these two distinct ways of seeing the pattern as think-blob and think-line. The second property is concerned with scale. The property of being concentrated or dispersed is dependent on the scale chosen to observe the pattern. If for instance I were to isolate and look at 1/256 of the dispersed blob pattern (3e) it would look exactly like the concentrated blob pattern (3c). The only difference would be scale. The third property I have illustrated is the amount of coverage. This can be high (90 per cent) or low (10 per cent). So far I have not assumed any population. Let us assume that it is fixed and is independent of land coverage. It will be clear that if the land coverage is high (90 per cent) the gross residential density will be relatively low and proportional to $\frac{100}{90} = 1\cdot1$. If, on the other hand, the land coverage is low (10 per cent) the gross residential density will be high and proportional to $\frac{100}{10} = 10$. Thus low coverage is associated with high density, and high coverage with low density. But the important point I want to make is that the notions of concentrated or dispersed developments have no relationship to population density. It is as possible to have a high density dispersed pattern as a low density concentrated pattern.

Next, I should point out that if the pattern is assumed to be continuous and isotropic there are just three geometric arrangements—triangular, rectangular or rhombic, and hexagonal. For the sake of simplicity I shall use the rectangular pattern throughout this paper with the sole exception of my next example. This shows (1b) the think-line version of Howard's city federation. Exactly the same proportion of land is urban here as in the think-blob arrangement, and I should remark that approximately one-quarter of this urban land is open space. It is not solidly built-up.

It can be shown mathematically that the schools are likely to be more accessible in the linear form. The same is true of any other social function that is distributed evenly with the population. But perhaps the most significant difference between the two arrangements is that in the nuclear pattern driving across country requires movement across the town (or alternatively the construction of a special ring road), whilst the linear pattern is interrupted only briefly by urban development and, if the urban parks are placed at these points, cross-country routes need not pass through built-up areas at all.

We have done some preliminary studies of what it means to say that a country feels built-up or not. Clearly in this example the linear form makes it possible to drive without passing through a built-up area and yet these roads pass through, and join, urban areas. The feeling of driving through such a country would be of it being less built up than in the nuclear pattern. Special routes, by-passing urban areas, would need to be constructed in the nuclear pattern to provide an impression of undeveloped countryside. If that were done it is interesting to note that the linear arrangement actually requires fewer roads to achieve the same results.

Let me be more specific. If we go back to diagrams 3c–h we may ask how open or built-up each arrangement of the 10 per cent urban coverage might feel. One way of measuring this might be to consider being in an urban area where extent is defined by some measure, for example, a five-minute drive. We can then measure built-upness by asking what the probability is of the next area we move to being built-up or not built-up. The first thing that is clear is that the area chosen is vital to the answer. To take an extreme situation: if the area is the full square then all six arrangements would have a probability of 1 assuming the contiguous areas were developed similarly. We would then say that everywhere we went the place seems built-up. On the other hand if small squares are taken, the size of the cells in 3h, then the probabilities of built-upness for the six schemes are shown below.

|         | concentrated | medium | dispersed |
|---------|--------------|--------|-----------|
| nuclear | ·76          | ·375   | 1         |
| linear  | ·265         | ·285   | 1         |

This means that too much dispersal will prevent our escape from a built-up area. This we might have expected. Too much concentration means that the probability of not getting away from a built-up area is high with the nuclear development and low with the linear pattern. The best arrangement for the nuclear form is with a medium distribution, but again the linear pattern gives more opportunity of leaving the built-up area than the nuclear.

It is possible then that the linear pattern will give an overall impression of being less built-up than the nuclear pattern. I think in this country that that could be important. I mean, how built-up or not development *seems* to be.

I now want to look at some properties of networks. Diagram 4 shows three road layouts: (a) fine mesh of two-lane roads, (b) mesh of three-lane roads and (c) coarse mesh of four-lane roads (dual carriageway). Each scheme uses exactly the same amount of road surface. Let us suppose that the cost of the road is proportional to its surface area. Then all three schemes will cost the same. But their traffic capacities are very different as this table shows:

|              | Ratio of traffic capacity (2 lane = 100) | Ratio of No. of routes (2 lane = 100) |
|--------------|-------------------------------------------|----------------------------------------|
| 2 lane       | 100                                       | 100                                    |
| 3 lane       | 122                                       | 67                                     |
| 2 × 2 lane   | 208                                       | 50                                     |

Thus by decreasing the number of routes by half, the capacity of the system can be increased just over twofold. It should also be noticed that a greater number of junctions have also been eliminated in the concentrated distribution. Diagram 5 shows a system with a capacity about 1·50 times that of the fine mesh. It is the classic ribbon development arrangement of a dual carriageway with paired service roads.

Because of a law called after its formulator, Poiseuille, a similar argument applies in the case of a pipe system only more dramatically so. It can be shown, assuming cost is proportional to the run of pipe times diameter, that the three equal-cost schemes with pipe widths proportional to 2:3:4 have flow capacities proportional approximately to 1:4:32. That is, a reduction of pipe runs by one-half could lead to increase in capacity of 32 times the original situation. It looks as if concentrated linear development might pay. Incidentally, the fine-mesh dispersed-linear road and sewer system is typical of concentrated nuclear developments. That is to say, where an area has to be developed all over, roads need to penetrate it evenly. The small mesh is wasteful in other ways. Each corner site is served by two routes. Consider an area arranged as a block with a road all round, and the same area as an elongated block with a route on one side (i.e. ribbon development). The road length is more than halved in the second case, and four junctions are eliminated. At this point I could argue that the forces behind the most spontaneous and energetic form of urban growth to have occurred this century in this country, namely ribbon development, are seen to be not only rational but economical in respect of road and services. And that, paradoxically, if these forces had been directed to create planned ribbons the feeling of built-upness in the country as a whole could have been less, not more, than today's emphasis on urban envelopes will produce.

But let us now turn to the problem of accessibility and social meeting places. In turning Howard's nuclear cities inside out I suggested that schools remained as accessible, if not more so. Consider now this example. In a concentrated nuclear development suppose there are 30 institutions within one mile of a centre, and at quarter-mile intervals from each other. Now although some institutions will be twice as far from the centre in the linear version, the mean accessibility distance to any one institution is marginally less in this case than in the nuclear arrangement. But on a time basis it is much more likely that the travel speed will be higher in the linear (no junction) system, so that even the most distant institutions could be brought within the same time limits as in the nuclear form whilst reducing the mean travel time by perhaps half. A good example of this principle is to be seen in Boston's limited access Route 128 development. The route is some ten miles or more out from the centre, and along its length have grown up new industries and suburbs. Clearly these are highly accessible to one another.

171

Next I want to look at the unfortunate correlation of residential building forms and density. The present housing yardsticks, for example, implicitly assume that as densities increase houses decrease in favour of flats, and low buildings give way to high. This is only true because of the professional separation of land-use planning from its architectural implications. With favourable land-use planning, semi-detached houses can be built at 200 persons to the acre. Three-storey terraces under more normal circumstances can be built up to 265 persons per acre. These are facts. And when we come down to it we shall discover that all this density business is dangerous convention. Thus, instead of permitting the highest densities in the countryside where they can make the greatest sense, we insist on putting the highest density towards the centres of our cities.

This tendency may be represented by considering a city marked out from its centre in equal width bands (6a). If each of these bands accommodates an equal amount of built space it will be clear that, since the least amount of space per unit distance from the centre is to be found near the centre, the built space will have to be achieved in the sky whilst on the perimeter this same quantity of space will be found on the ground. In conventional terms, if the plot ratio is 4:1 in the centre it will be, at the nineth ring, only ·055:1, or if a building on the outskirts is one storey high it will require to be 72 storeys high, assuming the same land coverage, in the centre. Now if we abandon the density cone concept the whole built form could be disposed at an average plot ratio of ·11:1, or just twice that of the outermost ring before and marginally higher than the mean of the four outermost rings, but a great deal lower than the mean of the five inner rings (6b). I simply draw attention to the similarity between this built form land-use diagram and a typical land-value model. Diagram 6c shows the same built space distributed in a linear form. I have already indicated that closeness and accessibility of similar functions is likely to be improved in a linear route development and since skyscrapers do not use central land very efficiently, the only sense that high buildings make in nucleated centres is in terms of real estate speculation. In terms of accommodating built space on urban land they are extravagant and irrational gestures.

To return to housing densities. I must warn that there would not be much point in thinking of densities as great as 200 persons per acre (when the mean density is likely to be not more than 25 persons per acre in the year 2000), if it were not that by taking extreme situations it is often possible to see principles more clearly.

In the study of Hook New Town, 16 acres of open space (including recreational areas) were allowed for every 1000 persons. At this rate 1280 persons would require about 20 acres, or a space 900 ft square (7a). These persons could be housed in a ribbon of three-storey housing

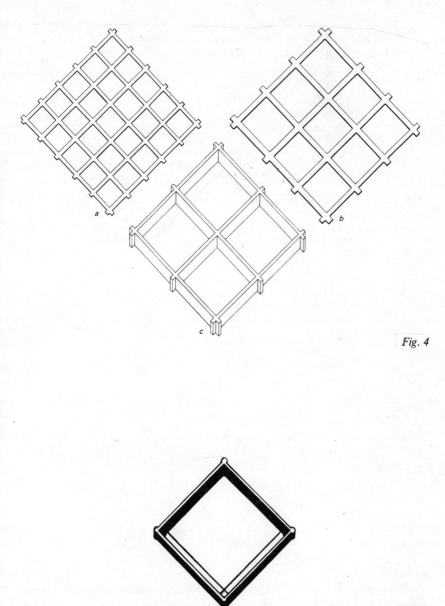

*Fig. 4*

*Fig. 5*

with a small garden at 200 persons to the acre around their own public
open space. The spatial effect would be like Parker's Piece in Cambridge,
and the housing could be like Bill Howell's terrace overlooking Hamp-

173

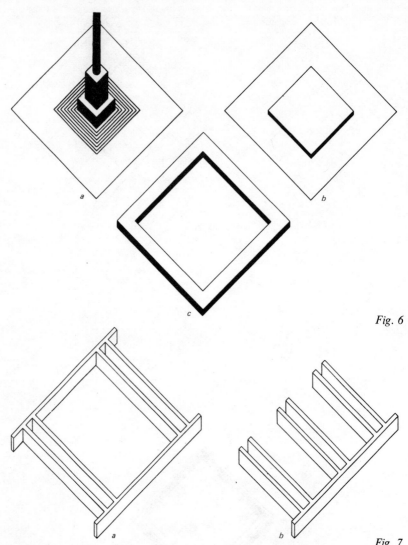

Fig. 6

Fig. 7

stead Heath. The access road would be like any simple terrace development. When one considers just how complex housing at this kind of density has become, it is timely to ask whether we might not achieve more by a return to relaxed simplicity. A further modification is shown in 7b where all the houses might have a view of the countryside.

The matter of density is essentially a matter of how much or how little private open space a household is to have. The confusion of road, open space and house plot areas in the general term 'residential area' disguises the fact that less and less residential land is owned and maintained by

174

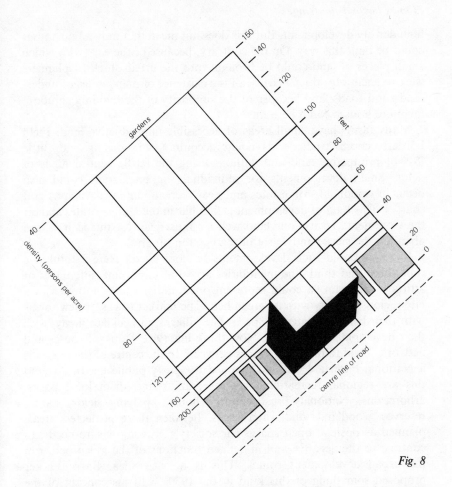

Fig. 8

the occupiers, and a growing amount of land is becoming public open space although not accounted for as such.

Diagram 8 shows a group of semi-detached houses along a small farm road. The house stands with its back to a paddock and has a small flower border in front. The arrangement is typical of many pleasant cottage developments in the country. There is room for a car alongside the house. This is semi-detached living at 200 persons to the acre. At 100 persons to the acre there is an ample garden area. The cost of this development is likely to be at least £3000 less for construction and land costs than city centre development at 200 persons per acre. It seems possible that it would be far less expensive to subsidize private transport than public housing.

There is a difficulty here that arises because of our customary think-blob attitude. Only a few houses could be built like this in any one place. That is to say, this type of development is an example of dispersed

175

high density development. But this does not mean that only a few houses could be built this way. On the contrary, because of the ease with which small pieces of land could be brought into the urban stock (if planners were to encourage this), because of the existence of many miles of under-used rural roads, and because of the simplicity of the building solution, far more houses could be built.

Many farms have small areas of accessible unproductive land. Field borders, copses and woods could accommodate housing with little loss of productive land and without using the fertile central areas of fields. Small developments for individuals or association could also occur in woodlands, on estates and near recreational areas such as golf courses. This kind of development is familiar in the United States and on the Continent. To use our land well we must plan for mixed uses and abandon the sterile and wasteful segregation of land uses.

But how could such developments be controlled? Here I think the think-blob and think-line mentalities arrive at important differences of attitude. Diagram 9a could represent our familiar think-blob idea of a city region. The city with its green belt. The market towns or new towns with their belts of protected space. The villages, in necklace array, with their development envelopes. Now think-line (9b). Think of routes and networks. And think of the spaces between. In the centre of the region is a National Park laid out and planned to satisfy public needs. Around this are regional recreational centres and around them local parks, arboretums, National Trust country houses, playing fields, nature reserves, woodlands and water areas. Between these protected areas, planned as positive open spaces for society's growing leisure needs, in contrast to the negative and ill-defined functions of the green belt, run the urban development routes. This is no new idea. Barry Parker proposed something of this kind in the 1930s with his concept of the parkway in parkland (10), whilst Le Corbusier's linear industrial city with its loose, informal growth around the four routes is a more deve-loped proposal.

Nor is it just an idea: it is also fact. Here is one example. Route 1 city stretches from Jacksonville, Florida, to Miami. These are the two radio-concentric cities of exchange in Le Corbusier's terms. Between them, and alongside Route 1, lies one of the most powerful industrial areas in the United States, 350 miles long and barely three miles wide. Much of the coastline is protected and along it runs route A1A, a scenic highway, narrow, twisting and intermittently developed. Two or three miles in-land is Route 1. This is virtually one continuous commercial, industrial and residential strip that could be cut anywhere and, like the common earthworm, would be found to have enough of everything in each seg-ment to regenerate itself. Then a further two or three miles inland is Sunshine State Parkway, Federal Route 95. This is a limited-access high-

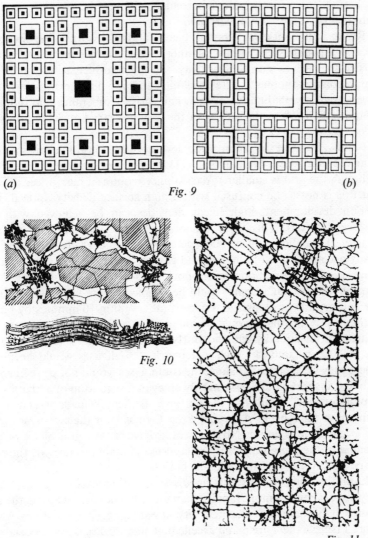

(a)

(b)

Fig. 9

Fig. 10

Fig. 11

speed route with no development frontage. It rolls, cuts and bounds across the landscape.

You can drive from Jacksonville to Miami as you please. Time-saving is achieved on the parkway. Cross to Route 1. Within a mile or two you will find almost any urban activity you want along this congested and bustling route. Cross again to route A1A and enjoy the lazy coastline, the view across the Atlantic or across Indian River Lagoon to the shimmering beaches. In true Le Corbusier manner the city has four routes: there is the Intercoastal Waterway, the railway, the airway

177

with frequent airports, and the roads including the parkway and the commercial route, *la rue marchande*.

Route 1 city works. It is not all beautiful, but it works. The developed area is a people's city, not a planner's. The planner have largely concerned themselves with the parkway, the splendid recreational areas and the national monuments. The developed area is a direct expression of the diversity of its inhabitants, of their enterprise, exuberance and industry: from honky-tonk to the arcady of the new industrial parks (Corbusier's *usines vertes*).

Finally, imagine the countryside developed by a grid five miles square. (Bucks County near Philadelphia (11) has emerged as a city of this form although the grid is smaller.) Accessibility requires a high linear density, but this is not to be confused with a high surface density. Indeed, with ribbon development, high linear densities can be achieved with low surface densities. This is its unique property. Now suppose a linear density along the route of 5000 persons per mile—a high density, but easily accommodated in houses and gardens—then at one-mile intervals there would be functions to support 5000 persons and one of these, nearest the resident's home, could be reached by a $\frac{1}{2}$-mile walk through the countryside or along the service routes. Within 10 minutes by bus or 5 minutes by car there would be facilities to serve 100 000 persons. In a quarter of an hour by car and thirty minutes by bus a regional centre for 500 000 persons. In such a network city all uses would be placed where they were best sited along the route. Uses would not be segregated. Public transport would serve evenly an even distribution of activities and populations. All could live in the town at their front door and in the country at their back. All could keep their car on their own property. All could have a house. No one would have to live in a block of flats because of the present inability of land-use planning to provide the right shape of plot for the right type of building.

In all this the rural districts have a tremendous part to play. Already they are developing more rapidly than the urban areas, excepting the new towns. It is there that the new city is emerging. What pattern will it take? I believe there are many excellent geometrical reasons, especially of a probabilistic nature, to suppose that a free, loose development along a network of routes has advantages of capacity, accessibility, density and use distribution not possible in nuclear development and that, with a positive policy towards open spaces, it is likely to prove the most reasonable form for the emergent city.

## 3.4 The grid as generator *Sir Leslie Martin*

THE grid of streets and plots from which a city is composed, is like a net placed or thrown upon the ground. This might be called the framework of urbanisation. That framework remains the controlling factor of the way we build whether it is artificial, regular and preconceived, or organic and distorted by historical accident or accretion. And the way we build may either limit or open up new possibilities in the way in which we choose to live.

How does the framework of a city work? In what way does the grid act as a generator and controlling influence on city form? How can it tolerate growth and change?

The answer to these questions is best given by historical examples, and in order to give the argument some point we can deliberately choose the most artificial framework for a city that exists: the grid as it has been used in the United States, and so well illustrated by Reps (1965).

In order to trace the influence of the grid, we can examine the building arrangement that developed within it in New York. We can identify at once what might be called the streets and the system that is established by the grid. If we now use the language of the urban geographers, we know that this defines the general plot pattern. The building arrangement develops within this (Conzen, 1962).

The stages of this latter process can be traced in the early plans of Manhattan produced in 1850. The grid of roads is already built. Within this general plot pattern the separate building plots are being established. To the north, on the building frontier, there is a line of huts and shacks. Further south more permanent but separate buildings are being built. And in the most developed area further towards the tip of Manhattan the full building arrangement has solidified into connected terraces of four to six-storey houses arranged around the perimeter of the site and enclosing private gardens. Views of Manhattan in the 1850s show a city developed in this way: and this pattern of building arrangement can still be seen in many areas. At this point the building land is replete. A balance is maintained between the plot, the amount of building that it can reasonably support and the street system that serves this.

*Source:* March, L. and Martin, L. (1972), *Urban Space and Structures*, Cambridge University Press, pages 13–22

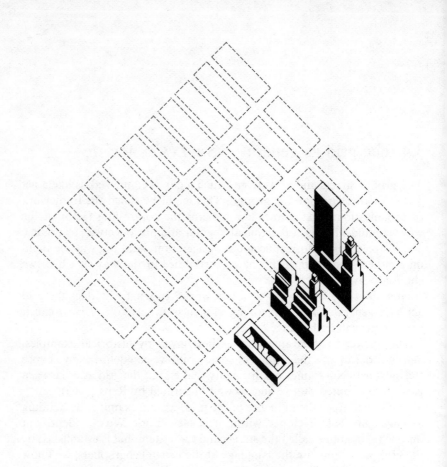

*Fig. 1. The basic plot layout of Manhattan is shown again in the dotted lines. The building forms show three stages of development including the original 4–6 storey perimeter form with a garden at the centre which was characteristic of the city in the 1850s, and two examples of the more intensive development during the present century.*

But as the pressure for floor space increases, the building form changes intensively at certain nodal points (Fig. 1). Deeper and higher perimeter buildings first of all submerge the internal garden space. A process of colonisation of the individual building plots begins, so that larger areas of the general plot are covered by higher buildings. In 1916 the first single building to occupy an entire city block rose a sheer 600 ft; its roof space almost exactly equalled the area of its ground plan. It was this building that most clearly illustrated the need for the comprehensive zoning ordinances adopted that year, after arduous study and political compromise, to safeguard daylight in streets and adjoining buildings. But the grid now exerts a powerful influence: the limited size of the grid suggests the notion that increased floor space in an area can only be gained by tall buildings on each separate plot. The notion suggests the form; the regulations shape it into ziggurats and towers. Under the regulations that prevailed until recent years, if all the general building plots in central Manhattan had been fully developed, there would have been one single and universal tall building shape. And, to use an old argument by Raymond Unwin (1912), if the population of those buildings had been let out at a given moment, there would have been no room for them in the streets. The balance between area of plot, area of floor space and area of street has disappeared.

Now these descriptions of the grid, which have been used as a basis for the argument, have exposed the points at which it can be, and has been, extensively attacked for more than a century. A grid of any kind appears to be a rigid imposition on the natural landscape. It is this reaction against the grid that is voiced by Olmstead and Vaux writing in support of their design for Central Park in 1863: 'The time will come when New York will be built up, when all the grading and the filling will be done and the picturesquely varied rocky formation of the island will have been converted into formations for rows of monotonous straight streets and piles of erect buildings' (Reps, 1965).

In their opposition to the grid, the relief from its monotony became a specific aim. Central Park itself is an attempt to imitate nature and to recreate wild scenery within the grid.* The garden suburb with its curving streets is one form of attack on the grid system, and an attempt to replace it. And at the end of the century, the Chicago Fair (1893), Cass Gilbert's schemes in Washington (1900), and the plans for San Francisco (1905) and Chicago (1909) by Burnham are another attempt to transform the urban desert by means of vistas and focal points, into the 'city beautiful'. However, we recognise at once a contrast. The various types of grid that have been described opened up some possible patterns for the structure of a city but left the building form free to develop and change within this. The plans of the garden city designers or those concerned with making the 'city beautiful' are an attempt to impose a form: and that form cannot change.

It is not possible to deny the force behind the criticisms of the grid. It can result in monotony: so can a curvilinear suburbia. It can fail to

---

*This movement which began with gardens, was less appropriately applied to city layout. In Olmstead's words, 'lines of roads were not to press forwards'. Their curving forms suggest leisure and tranquility. Compare this with the almost contemporary (1859) statements by Cerda in his plan for Barcelona in which there is 'a reciprocal arrangement between that which is contained' (building plot and arrangement) and 'that which contains' (grid and street system). 'Urbanisation is an appendix to universal movement: streets are for movement but they serve areas permanently reserved and isolated from that movement which agitates life' (the environmental area).

work: so can the organic city. What has been described is a process. It is now possible to extract some principles. Artificial grids of various kinds have been laid down. The choice of the grid allows different patterns of living to develop and different choices to be elaborated. The grid, unlike the fixed visual image, can accept and respond to growth and change. It can be developed unimaginatively and monotonously or with great freedom. There can be a point at which the original grid fails to respond to new demands (Fig. 2). As in Manhattan, it congeals. And it is at this point that we must try to discover from the old framework a new ordering principle that will open up new opportunities for elaboration by use.

It is precisely this that Le Corbusier underlined when he paid his first visit to New York in 1935 and made the comment: 'What about the road?' (Le Corbusier, 1939, 1947.) The diagrams by which he illustrates this remark show the regenerative process that is necessary (Fig. 3). By increasing the size of the street net in Manhattan, Le Corbusier shows that the grid ceases to restrict. New building arrangements become

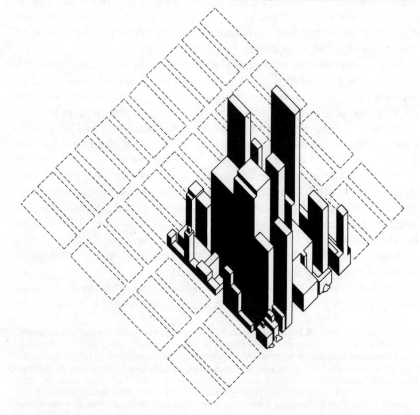

*Fig. 2. The illustration shows building plot development in its most intensive form.*

possible and the balance between plot, building and street can be restored.

In the larger and more open mile square network of Chicago Frank Lloyd Wright had given a similar and vivid illustration of the capacity of the grid to respond to diversity and freedom. In 1913 a competition was held in order to 'awaken interest in methods of dividing land in the interests of a community' (Yeomans, 1916). The site was the standard section of the mile square grid. The standard subdivision of the grid, if rigidly applied, could divide it into 32 rectangles each 600 ft long by 250 ft deep. Mr Wright accepts the established gridiron of the city 'as a basis' for subdivision. He accepts the 'characteristic aggregation of buildings . . . common to every semi-urban area of Chicago'. The same number of people are housed. The business buildings, the factories, the heating plant, the utilities of the area are all there. But to use his words 'they cling naturally to the main arteries of traffic. By thus draw-

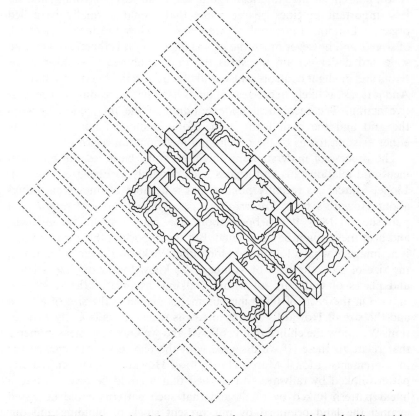

*Fig. 3 Change in the scale of the grid. Le Corbusier's proposals for dwellings with setbacks (from his proposals for a city for 3 million people) are superimposed on the Manhattan grid and open up new possibilities in the building form.*

ing . . . all buildings of this nature into the location that they would prefer the great mass of the subdivision is left clear for residence purposes'. Within this area parks (with their exhibition galleries and theatres), tree-lined avenues and stretches of water diversify the layout. The range and choice of housing is wide. It is all natural, relaxed, capable of infinite variation and change as it develops within the framework of the grid. Mr Wright's descriptive text includes these words: 'in skilled hands the various treatments could rise to great beauty'. It is prefaced by a quotation from Carlyle: 'Fool! the ideal is within thyself. Thy condition is the stuff thou shalt shape that same ideal out of.'

In the case of these American cities the grid or framework can be regarded as an ordering principle. It sets out the rules of the environmental game. It allows the player the freedom to play with individual skill. The argument can now be extended by saying that the grid, which is so apparent in the American examples, is no less controlling and no less important in cities nearer home that would normally be called organic: London, Liverpool or Manchester. They too have a network of streets and however much the grid is distorted, it is there. At a certain scale and under certain pressures the grid combined with floor space limits and daylight controls is just as likely to force tall building solutions. And it is just as likely to congeal. It lends itself just as readily to regenerative action. The theoretical understanding of the interaction between the grid and the built form is therefore fundamental in considering either existing towns or the developing metropolitan regions.

The process of understanding this theoretical basis rests in measurement and relationships and it goes back certainly to Ebenezer Howard. Lionel March has recently pointed out a number of interesting things about Howard's book *Tomorrow: a peaceful path to real reform* first published in 1898. It is a book about how people might live in towns and how these might be distributed. But the important thing is that there is no image of what a town might look like. We know the type of housing, the size of plot, the sizes of avenues. We know that shopping, schools and places of work are all within walking distance of the residential areas. On the basis of these measurements we know the size of a town and the size of Howard's cluster of towns which he calls a city Federation. We know the choice that is offered and we know the measurements that relate to these. If we disagree with the choice we can change the measurements. Lionel March (1967) took Howard's open centred city pattern linked by railways and showed that it could be reversed into a linear pattern linked by roads and that such patterns could be tested against the land occupied by our present stock of building and our future needs.

Now that is theory. It contains a body of ideas which are set down in measurable terms. It is open to rational argument. And as we challenge it successfully we develop its power. The results are frequently surprising and sometimes astonishingly simple. Ebenezer Howard's direct successor in this field was Raymond Unwin. The strength of his argument always rests in a simple demonstration of a mathematical fact. In an essay 'Nothing gained by overcrowding' (Unwin, 1912), he presents two diagrams of development on ten acres of land. One is typical development of parallel rows of dwellings: the other places dwellings round the perimeter. The second places fewer houses on the land but when all the variables are taken into account (including the savings on road costs) total development costs can be cut. From the point of view of theory, the important aspect of this study is the recognition of related factors: the land available, the built form placed on this, and the roads necessary to serve these. He demonstrated this in a simple diagram.

Unwin began a lecture on tall building by a reference to a controversy that had profoundly moved the theological world of his day, namely, how many angels could land on a needle point. His method of confounding the urban theologians by whom he was surrounded was to measure out the space required in the streets and sidewalks by the people and cars generated by 5, 10 and 20-storey buildings on an identical site. The interrelationship of measurable factors is again clearly demonstrated. But one of Unwin's most forceful contributions to theory is his recognition of the fact that 'the area of a circle is increased not in the direct proportion to the distance to be travelled from the centre to the circumference, but in proportion to the square of that distance'. Unwin used this geometrical principle to make a neat point about commuting time: as the population increases round the perimeter of a town, the commuting time is not increased in direct proportion to this.

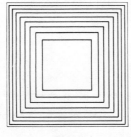

*Fig. 4*

The importance of this geometrical principle is profound. Unwin did not pursue its implications. He was too concerned to make his limited point about low density. But suppose this proposition is subjected to close examination. The principle is demonstrated again in Fresnel's diagram (Fig. 4) in which each successive annular ring diminishes in width but has exactly the same area as its predecessor. The outer band in the square form of this diagram has exactly the same area as the central square. And this lies at the root of our understanding of an important principle in relation to the way in which buildings are placed on the land.

Suppose now that the central square and the outer annulus of the Fresnel diagram are considered as two possible ways of placing the same amount of floor space on the same site area: at once it is clear that the two buildings so arranged would pose totally different questions of access, of how the free space is distributed around them and what natural lighting and view the rooms within them might have. By this process a number of parameters have been defined which need to be considered in any theoretical attempt to understand land use by buildings.

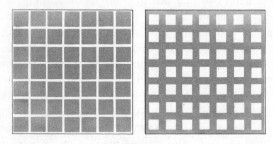

*Fig. 5*

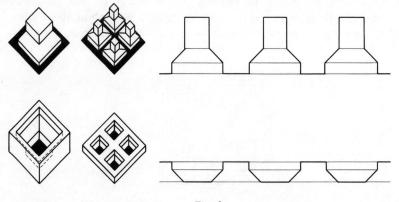

*Fig. 6*

This central square (which can be called the pavilion) and the outer annulus (which can be called the court) are two ways of placing building on the land. Let us now extend this. On any large site a development covering 50% of the site could be plotted as forty-nine pavilions, as shown in Fig. 5, and exactly the same site cover can be plotted in court form. A contrast in the ground space available and the use that can be

186

made of it is at once apparent. But this contrast can be extended further: the forty-nine pavilions can be plotted in a form which is closer to that which they would assume as buildings (that is low slab with a tower form over this). This can now be compared with its antiform: the same floor space planned as courts (Fig. 6). The comparison must be exact; the same site area, the same volume of building, the same internal depth of room. And when this is done we find that the antiform places the same amount of floor space into buildings which are exactly one third the total height of those in pavilion form (Martin and March, 1966).

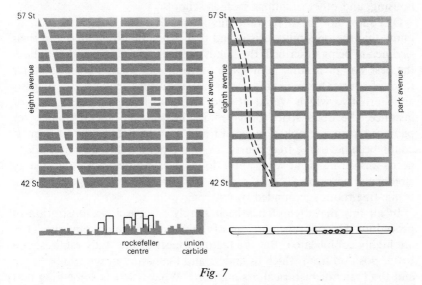

*Fig. 7*

This brings the argument directly back to the question of the grid and its influence on the building form. Let us think of New York. The grid is developing a certain form: the tall building. The land may appear to be thoroughly used. Consider an area of the city. Seen on plan there is an absolutely even pattern of rectangular sites. Now assume that every one of those sites is completely occupied by a building: and that all these buildings have the same tower form and are twenty-one storeys in height. That would undoubtedly look like a pretty full occupation of the land. But if the size of the road net were to be enlarged by omitting some of the cross streets, a new building form is possible. Exactly the same amount of floor space that was contained in the towers can be arranged in another form. If this floor space is placed in buildings around the edges of our enlarged grid then the same quantity of floor space that was contained in the 21-storey towers now needs only 7-storey buildings. And large open spaces are left at the centre.

187

Let us be more specific. If the area bounded by Park Avenue and Eighth Avenue and between 42nd and 57th Street is used as a base and the whole area were developed in the form of Seagram buildings 36 storeys high, this would certainly open up some ground space along the streets. If, however, the Seagram buildings were replaced by court forms (Fig. 7) then this type of development while using the same built volume would produce buildings only 8 storeys high. But the courts thus provided would be roughly equivalent in area to Washington Square, and there could be 28 Washington Squares in this total area. Within squares of this size there could be large trees, perhaps some housing, and other buildings such as schools.

Of course no one may want this alternative. But it is important to know that the possibility exists, and that, when high buildings and their skyline are being described, the talk is precisely about this and not about the best way of putting built space on to ground space. The alternative form of courts, taken in this test, is not a universal panacea. It suggests an alternative which would at once raise far-reaching questions. For instance, the open space provided in the present block-by-block (or pavilion) form is simply a series of traffic corridors. In the court form, it could become traffic-free courts. In this situation the question which needs answering is: at what point do we cease to define a built area by streets and corridors? At what point could we regard a larger area as a traffic-free room surrounded by external traffic routes?

In all this the attempt has been simply to give a demonstration of procedure. The full repercussions of the questions are not obvious. They are highly complicated. But the factual aspect of the study establishes a better position from which to understand the nature of the complication and the limits of historical assumptions. What is left is something that can be built upon and needed decisions are brought back to the problem of the built form of an urban area not merely of a building. Here, the choice of the built form is critical in a number of ways, not least as a means of securing a new unity of conception.

We can choose. We can accept the grid of streets as it is. In that case we can never avoid the constant pressure on the land. Housing will be increasingly in tall flats. Hospitals will have no adequate space for expansion. Historic areas will be eaten into by new building. A total area once unified by use will be increasingly subdivided by traffic. We can leave things as they are and call development organic growth, or we can accept a new theoretical framework as an outline of the general rules of the game and work towards this. We shall know that the land we need is there if we use it effectively. We can modify the theoretical frame to respect historic areas and elaborate it as we build. And we shall also know that the overlapping needs of living in an area have been seen as a whole and that there will be new possibilities and choices for the future.

## References

DE CERDA, ILDEFONSO (1867) *Teoria General de la Urbanization* (Madrid).

CONZEN, M. R. G. (1962) The Plan Analysis of an English City Centre, in *Proceedings of the I.G.U. Symposium in Urban Geography*, Royal University of Lund (Lund, Sweden).

GOODMAN, P. and GOODMAN, P. (1960) *Communitas*, Vintage Books, New York.

LE CORBUSIER (1934) *Oeuvres Completes 1934–1938*, Girsberger Zurich.

LE CORBUSIER (1947) *When the Cathedrals were White*, Routledge, London.

MARCH, L. (1967) 'Homes Beyond the Fringe', *R.I.B.A. Journal*, August (reprinted in this volume).

MARCH, L. and MARTIN, L. (1966) 'Land Use and Built Forms', *Cambridge Research*, April.

REPS, J. W. (1965) *The Making of Urban America*, Princetown University Press.

UNWIN, R. (1912) 'Nothing to be Gained by Overcrowding', in Creese, W. L. (Editor) 1967, *The Legacy of Raymond Unwin: A Human Pattern for Planning*, M.I.T. Press, Cambridge, Mass.

YEOMANS, A. B. (1916 *City Residential Land Development*, University of Chicago Press.

# 3.5 The Pattern of the Metropolis *Kevin Lynch*

The pattern of urban development critically affects a surprising number of problems, by reason of the spacing of buildings, the location of activities, the disposition of the lines of circulation. Some of these problems might be eliminated if only we would begin to coordinate metropolitan development so as to balance services and growth, prevent premature abandonment or inefficient use, and see that decisions do not negate one another. In such cases, the form of the urban area, whether concentrated or dispersed,[7] becomes of relatively minor importance.

There are other problems, however, that are subtler and go deeper. Their degree of seriousness seems to be related to the particular pattern of development which has arisen. To cope with such difficulties, one must begin by evaluating the range of possible alternatives of form, on the arbitrary assumption that the metropolis can be molded as desired. For it is as necessary to learn what is desirable as to study what is possible; realistic action without purpose can be as useless as idealism without power. Even the range of what is possible may sometimes be extended by fresh knowledge of what is desirable.

*Source:* Kevin Lynch (1961), 'The Pattern of Metropolis' in *Daedalus*, Winter, pages 79–98

Let us, therefore, consider the form of the metropolis as if it existed in a world free of pressures or special interests and on the assumption that massive forces can be harnessed for reshaping the metropolis for the common good—provided this good can be discovered. The question then is, how should such power be applied? We must begin by deciding which aspects of the metropolitan pattern are crucial. We can then review the commonly recognized alternative patterns, as well as the criteria that might persuade us to choose one over another. Finally, we may hope to see the question as a whole. Then we will be ready to suggest new alternatives and will have the means of choosing the best one for any particular purpose.

There are at least three vital factors in our judging the adequacy of the form of the metropolis, once its total size is known. The first of all is the magnitude and pattern of both the structural density (the ratio of floor space in buildings to the area of the site) and the structural condition (the state of obsolescence or repair). These aspects can be illustrated on a map by plotting the locations of the various classes of density ranging from high concentration to wide dispersion, and the various classes of structural condition ranging from poor to excellent. Density and condition provide a fundamental index of the physical resources an urban region possesses.

A second factor is the capacity, type, and pattern of the facilities for the circulation of persons, roads, railways, airlines, transit systems, and pathways of all sorts. Circulation and intercommunication perhaps constitute the most essential function of a city, and the free movement of persons happens to be the most difficult kind of circulation to achieve, the service most susceptible to malfunction in large urban areas.

The third fact that makes up the spatial pattern of a city is the location of fixed activities that draw on or serve large portions of the population, such as large department stores, factories, office and government buildings, warehouses, colleges, hospitals, theatres, parks, and museums. The spatial pattern of a city is made up of the location of fixed activities as well as the patterns of circulation and physical structure. However, the distribution of locally based activities, such as residence, local shopping, neighborhood services, elementary and high schools, is for our purpose sufficiently indicated by mapping the density of people or of buildings. Hence, if we have already specified structural density and the circulation system, the remaining critical fact at the metropolitan scale is the location of the city-wide activities which interact with large portions of the whole.

When we come to analyze any one of these three elements of spatial pattern, we find that the most significant features of such patterns are the grain (the degree of intimacy with which the various elements such as stores and residences are related), the focal organization (the interrelation of the nodes of concentration and interchange as contrasted with the general background), and the accessibility (the general proximity in terms of time of all points in the region to a given kind of activity or facility). In this sense, one might judge that from every point the accessibility to drugstores was low, uneven, or uniformly high, or that it varied in some regular way, for example, high at the center and low at the periphery of the region. All three aspects of pattern (focal organization, grain, and accessibility) can be mapped, and the latter two can be treated quantitatively if desired.

It is often said that the metropolis today is deficient as a living en-

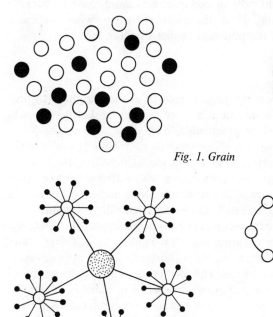

*Fig. 1. Grain*

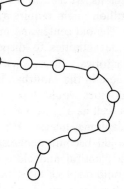

*Fig. 2. Focal organization*

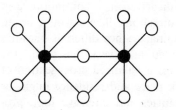

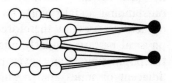

*Fig. 3. Accessibility*

vironment. It has suffered from uncontrolled development, from too rapid growth and change, from obsolescence and instability. Circulation is congested, requiring substantial time and a major effort. Accessibility is uneven, particularly to open rural land. The use of facilities is unbalanced, and they become increasingly obsolete. Residential segregation according to social groups seems to be growing, while the choice of residence for the individual remains restricted and unsatisfactory. The pattern of activities is unstable, and running costs are high. Visually, the city is characterless and confused, as well as noisy and uncomfortable.

Yet the metropolis has tremendous economic and social advantages that override its problems and induce millions to bear with the discomforts. Rather than dwindle or collapse, it is more likely to become the normal human habitat. If so, the question then is, what particular patterns can best realize the potential of metropolitan life?

## The Dispersed Sheet

One alternative is to allow the present growth at the periphery to proceed to its logical conclusion but at a more rapid pace. Let new growth occur at the lowest densities practicable, with substantial interstices of open land kept in reserve. Let older sections be rebuilt at much lower densities, so that the metropolitan region would rapidly spread over a vast continuous tract, perhaps coextensive with adjacent metropolitan regions. At the low densities of the outer suburbs, a metropolis of twenty million might require a circle of land one hundred miles in diameter.

The old center and most subcenters could be dissolved, allowing city-wide activities to disperse throughout the region, with a fine grain. Factories, offices, museums, universities, hospitals would appear everywhere in the suburban landscape. The low density and the dispersion of activities would depend on and allow circulation in individual vehicles, as well as a substantial use of distant symbolic communication such as telephone, television, mail, coded messages. Accessibility to rural land would become unnecessary, since outdoor recreational facilities would be plentiful and close at hand. The permanent low-density residence would displace the summer cottage.

The system of flow, concerned solely with individual land (and perhaps air) vehicles, should be highly dispersed in a continuous grid designed for an even movement in all directions. There would be no outstanding nodal points, no major terminals. Since different densities or activities would therefore be associated in a very fine grain, the physical pattern similarly might encourage a balanced cross-section of the population at any given point. Work place and residence might be adjacent or miles apart. Automatic factories and intensive food production might be dispersed throughout the region.

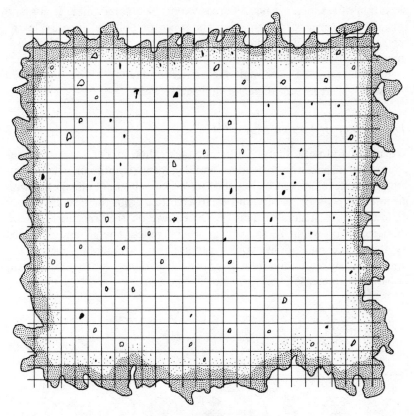

Fig. 4. The dispersed sheet

Frank Lloyd Wright (1940) dreamed of such a world in his Broadacre City. It is this pattern toward which cities like Los Angeles appear to be moving, although they are hampered and corrupted by the vestiges of older city forms. Such a pattern might not only raise flexibility, local participation, personal comfort, and independence to a maximum, but also go far toward solving traffic congestion through the total dispersion and balancing of loads. Its cost would be high, however, and distances remain long. Accessibility would be good, given high speeds of travel and low terminal times (convenient parking, rapid starting); at the very least it would be evenly distributed. Thus communication in the sense of purposeful trips ('I am going out to buy a fur coat') might not be hindered, but spontaneous or accidental communication ('Oh, look at that fur coat in the window!'), which is one of the advantages of present city life, might be impaired by the lack of concentration.

Although such a pattern would require massive movements of the population and the extensive abandonment of equipment at the beginning, in the end it might promote population stability and the conservation of resources, since all areas would be favored alike. It gives no promise, however, of heightening the sense of political identity in the metropolitan community nor of producing a visually vivid and well-knit image of environment. Moreover, the choice of the type of residence would be restricted, although the choice of facility to be patronized (churches, stores, etc.) might be sufficiently wide.

## The Galaxy of Settlements

We might follow a slightly different tack while at the same time encouraging dispersion. Instead of guiding growth into an even distribution, let development be bunched into relatively small units, each with an internal peak of density and each separated from the next by a zone of low or zero structural density. Depending on the transport system, this separation might be as great as several miles. The ground occupied by the whole metropolis would increase proportionately; even if the interspaces were of minimum size, the linear dimensions of the metropolis would increase from thirty to fifty percent.

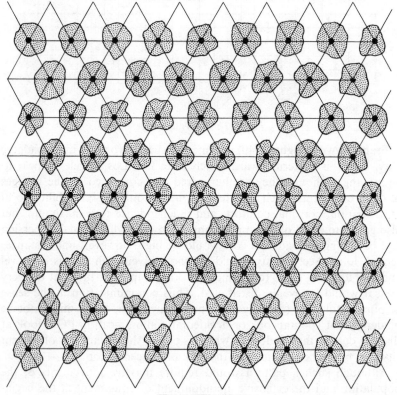

*Fig. 5. The galaxy*

City-wide activities could also be concentrated at the density peak within each urban cluster, thus forming an over-all system of centers, each of which would be relatively equal in importance to any of the others. Such a metropolitan pattern may be called an 'urban galaxy.' The centers might be balanced in composition or they might vary by specializing in a type of activity, so that one might be a cultural center, another a financial center.

The system of flow would also be dispersed but would converge locally at the center of each cluster. It might be organized in a triangular grid, which provides such a series of foci while maintaining an easy flow in all directions over the total area. Since median densities remain low, while the centers of activity are divided into relatively small units, the individual vehicle must be the major mode of transportation, but some supplementary public transportation such as buses or aircraft running from center to center would now be feasible.

While it retains many of the advantages of the dispersed sheet, such as comfort, independence, and stability, this scheme probably enhances general communication, and certainly spontaneous communication, through creating centers of activity. It would presumably encourage participation in local affairs by favoring the organization of small communities, though this might equally work against participation and coordination on the metropolitan scale. In the same sense, the visual image at the local level would be sharpened, though the metropolitan image might be only slightly improved. Flexibility might be lost, since local clusters would of necessity have relatively fixed boundaries, if interstitial spaces were preserved, and the city-wide activities would be confined to one kind of location.

The factor of time-distance might remain rather high, unless people could be persuaded to work and shop within their own cluster, which would then become relatively independent with regard to commutation. Such independent communities, of course, would largely negate many metropolitan advantages: choice of work for the employee, choice of social contacts, of services, and so on. If the transportation system were very good, then 'independence' would be difficult to enforce.

This pattern, however, can be considered without assuming such local independence. It is essentially the proposal advocated by the proponents of satellite towns, pushed to a more radical conclusion, as in Clarence Stein's (1942) diagram. Some of its features would appear to have been incorporated into the contemporary development of Stockholm.

The pattern of an urban galaxy provides a wider range of choice than does pure dispersion, and a greater accessibility to open country, of the kind that can be maintained between clusters. This pattern has a somewhat parochial complexion and lacks the opportunities for in-

195

tensive, spontaneous communication and for the very specialized activities that might exist in larger centers. Local centers, too, might develop a monotonous similarity, unless they were given some specific individuality. That might not be easy, however, since central activities tend to support and depend on one another (wholesaling and entertainment, government and business services, headquarters offices and shopping). A compromise would be the satellite proposal proper: a swarm of such unit clusters around an older metropolitan mass.

## The Core City

There are those who, enamored with the advantages of concentration, favor a completely opposite policy that would set median structural densities fairly high, perhaps at 1.0 instead of 0.1; in other words, let there be as much interior floor space in buildings as there is total ground area in the city, instead of only one-tenth as much. If we consider the open land that must be set aside for streets, parks, and other such uses, this means in practice the construction of elevator apartments instead of one-family houses. The metropolis would then be packed into one continuous body, with a very intensive peak of density and activity at its center. A metropolis of twenty million could be put within a circle ten miles in radius, under the building practice normal today.

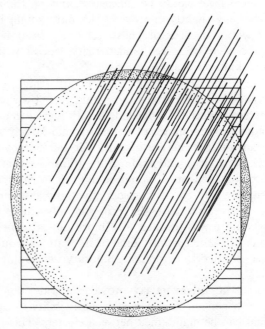

*Fig. 6. The Core*

Parts of the city might even become 'solid,' with a continuous occupation of space in three dimensions and a cubical grid of transportation lines. (The full application of this plan could cram a metropolis within a surprisingly small compass: twenty million people, with generous spacing, could be accommodated within a cube less than three miles on a side.) Most probably there would be a fine grain of specialized activities, all at high intensity, so that apartments would occur over factories, or there might also be stores on upper levels. The system of flow would necessarily be highly specialized, sorting each kind of traffic into its own channel. Such a city would depend almost entirely on public transport, rather than individual vehicles, or on devices that facilitated pedestrian movement, such as moving sidewalks or flying belts. Accessibility would be very high, both to special activities and to the open country at the edges of the city. Each family might have a second house for weekends; these would be widely dispersed throughout the countryside and used regularly three or four days during the week, or even longer, by mothers and their young children. The city itself, then, would evolve into a place for periodic gathering. Some of the great European cities, such as Paris or Moscow, which are currently building large numbers of high-density housing as compact extensions to their peripheries, are approximating this pattern without its more radical features.

Such a pattern would have an effect on living quite different from that of the previous solutions. Spontaneous communication would be high, so high that it might become necessary to impede it so as to preserve privacy. Accessibility would be excellent and time-distance low, although the channels might be crowded. The high density might increase discomfort because of noise or poor climate, although these problems could perhaps be met by the invention of new technical devices. As with the previous patterns, the choice of habitat would be restricted to a single general type within the city proper, although the population could enjoy a strong contrast on weekends or holidays. The nearness of open country and the many kinds of special services should on the whole extend individual choice. Once established, the pattern should be stable, since each point would be a highly favored location. However, a very great dislocation of people and equipment, in this country, at least, would be required to achieve this pattern.

Such a metropolis would indeed produce a vivid image and would contribute to a strong sense of the community as a whole. Individual participation, on the other hand, might be very difficult. It is not clear how running costs would be affected; perhaps they would be lower because of the more efficient use of services and transportation, but initial costs would undoubtedly be very high. The segregation of social groups, as far as physical disposition can influence it, might be discouraged, although there is a level of density above which intercom-

197

munication among people begins to decline again. Certainly this solution is a highly rigid and unadaptable one in which change of function could be brought about only by a costly rearrangement.

## The Urban Star

A fourth proposal would retain the dominant core without so drastic a reversion to the compact city. Present densities would be kept, or perhaps revised upward a little, while low-density development at the outer fringe would no longer be allowed. Tongues of open land would be incorporated into the metropolitan area to produce a density pattern that is star-shaped in the central region and linear at the fringes. These lines of dense development along the radials might in time extend to other metropolitan centers, thus becoming linear cities between the main centers. The dominant core, however, would remain, surrounded by a series of secondary centers distributed along the main radials. At moderate densities (less than the core pattern, and more than the sheet), the radial arms of a metropolis of comparable size might extend for fifty miles from its own center.

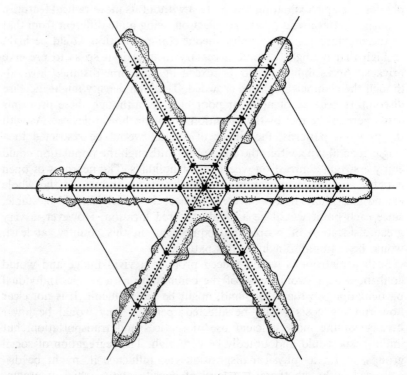

*Fig. 7. The star*

The metropolitan center of the star pattern would again contain the most intensive types of city-wide activity. Elsewhere, either in the sub-centers or in linear formations along the main radials—whichever proved the more suitable—these activities would be carried on at a less intense level. The system of flow would logically be organized on the same radial pattern, with supplementary concentric rings. An efficient public transportation system of high capacity could operate along the main radials, whereas the ring roads could accommodate public transit of lower intensity. To some degree, travel by individual vehicles, although discouraged for centrally bound flows, would be practicable in other directions.

This pattern is a rationalization of the manner in which metropolitan areas were developing till the individual vehicle became the usual means of travel. It is the form the city of Copenhagen has adopted as its pattern for future growth; Blumenfeld (1949) has discussed it at length. This form retains the central core with its advantages of rapid communication and specialized services yet permits the location of other kinds of major activities. Lower residential densities are also possible. Individual choice should be fairly wide, both in regard to living habitat, access to services, and access to open land—this land lies directly behind each tongue of development, even at the core, and leads continuously outward to rural land.

Movement along a sector would be fairly fast and efficient, although terminals at the core might continue to be congested and, with continued growth, the main radials might become overloaded. Movement between sectors, however, would be less favored, especially in the outer regions; there distances are great, transit hard to maintain, and channels costly, since they would span long distances over land they do not directly serve. Accessibility to services would be unequal as between inner and outer locations.

The visual image is potentially a strong one and should be conducive to a sense of the metropolis as a whole, or at least to the sense of one unified sector leading up to a common center. Growth could occur radially outward, and future change could be accomplished with less difficulty than in the compact pattern, since densities would be lower and open land would back up each strip of development. The principal problems with this form are probably those of circumferential movement, of potential congestion at the core and along the main radials, and of the wide dispersion of the pattern as it recedes from the original center.

## The Ring

In the foregoing, the most discussed alternatives for metropolitan growth have been given in a highly simplified form. Other possibilities certainly exist—e.g., the compact high-density core pattern might be turned inside out, producing a doughnut-like form. In this case the center would be kept open, or at very low density, while high densities and special activities surround it, like the rim of a wheel. The principal channels of the flow system would then be a series of annular rings serving the high-intensity rim, supplemented by a set of feeder radials that would converge at the empty center. In fact, this is essentially a linear system, but one that circles back on itself and is bypassed by the

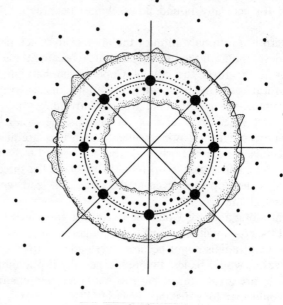

*Fig. 8. The ring*

'spokes' crossing the 'hub.' This system is well-adapted to public transportation, both on the ring roads and the cross radials, while individual vehicles might be used for circulation outside the rim.

Densities within the rim would have to be rather high, while those beyond the rim could be low. A system of weekend houses might also be effectively employed here. The central area could either be kept quite open or devoted to special uses at low densities. City-wide activities could be spotted round the rim in a series of intense centers, supplemented by linear patterns along the annular roadways. There would be no single dominant center but rather a limited number of strong centers (an aristocracy rather than a monarchy). These centers might also be specialized in regard to activity—finance, government, culture, etc.

This pseudo-linear form, like the radial tongues of the star plan, has the linear advantages: a high accessibility, both to services and to open

200

land; a wide choice of habitat and location of activities; and a good foundation for efficient public transit. Congestion at any single center is avoided, yet there is a high concentration. In contrast to the galaxy or satellite form, the variety and strong character inherent in the specialized centers would have some hope of survival because of the relatively close proximity of these centers.

The visual image would be strong (though perhaps a little confusing because of its circularity), producing a particularly clear impression of the centers around the rim, in contrast to the central openness, and of their successive interconnections. The whole metropolis would seem more nearly like one community. One of the most difficult problems would be that of growth, since much development beyond the rim would soon blur the contour and require a new transportation system. A second concentric ring might be developed beyond the first, but it would negate some of the advantages of the first ring and would demand massive initiative by the central government to undertake its development. Another difficulty would be that of control. How can the belts of open land or the accessible center be kept free of building? Even if this problem were solved satisfactorily, a dilemma is also likely to arise in regard to the size of the ring: should it be small enough for the major centers to be in close proximity to one another or big enough to allow all the residences and other local activities to be related to it?

One classic example of this form exists, although on a very large scale—the ring of specialized Dutch cities that surround a central area of agricultural land, Haarlem, Amsterdam, Utrecht, Rotterdam, The Hague, and Leiden. This general pattern is now being rationalized and preserved as a matter of national policy in the Netherlands. In our own country, the San Francisco Bay region appears to be developing in this same direction.

The ring tends to be rather rigid and unadaptable as a form. It would require an extreme reshaping of the present metropolis, particularly with regard to transportation and the central business district; but it might dovetail with an observable trend toward emptying and abandoning the central areas. The plan could be modified by retaining a single major center, separated by a wide belt of open space from all other city-wide activities to be disposed along the rim. It may be noted that this use of open land in concentric belts ('green belts') is exactly opposite to its use as radial tongues in the star form.

## The Objectives of Metropolitan Arrangement

Many other metropolitan forms are hypothetically possible, but the five patterns described (the sheet, the galaxy, the core, the star, and the ring) indicate the variation possible. One of the interesting results of the discussion is to see the appearance of a particular set of values as criteria for evaluating these forms. It begins to be clear that some human objectives are intimately connected with the physical pattern of a city, while others are very little affected by it. For example, there has been little discussion of the healthfulness of the environment or of its safety. Although these factors are influenced by the detailed design of the environment, such as the spacing of buildings or the provision for utilities, it is not obvious that the specific metropolitan pattern has any significant effect on them so long as we keep well ahead of the problems of pollution and supply. Psychological well-being, on the other hand, may be affected by the shape of the urban environment. But again, we are too ignorant of this aspect at present to discuss it further.

We have not referred to the efficiency of the environment in regard to production and distribution. This represents another basic criterion that probably is substantially affected by metropolitan pattern, but unfortunately no one seems to know what the effect is. 'Pleasure' and 'beauty' have not been mentioned, but these terms are nebulous and hard to apply accurately. A number of criteria have appeared, however, and it may well be worth while to summarize them. They might be considered the goals of metropolitan form, its fundamental objectives, either facilitated or frustrated in some significant way by the physical pattern of the metropolis.

The criterion of choice heads the list. As far as possible, the individual should have the greatest variety of goods, services, and facilities readily accessible to him. He should be able to choose the kind of habitat he prefers; he should be able to enter many kinds of environment at will, including the open country; he should have the maximum of personal control over his world. These advantages appear in an environment of great variety and of fine grain, one in which transportation and communication are as quick and effortless as possible. There may very likely be some eventual limit to the desirable increase of choice, since people can be overloaded by too many alternatives, but we do not as yet operate near that limit for most people. In practice, of course, to maximize one choice may entail minimizing another, and compromises will have to be made.

The ideal of personal interaction ranks as high as choice, although it is not quite so clear how the optimum should be defined. We often say that we want the greatest number of social contacts, so as to promote neighborliness and community organization, minimize segregation and social isolation, increase the velocity and decrease the effort of social exchange. And yet, while the evils of isolation are known, we are nevertheless beginning to see problems at the other end of the scale as well. Too much personal communication may cause breakdown, just as surely as too little. Even in moderate quantities, constant 'neighborliness' can interfere with other valuable activities such as reflection, independent thought, or creative work. A high level of local community organization may mean civic indifference or intergovernmental rivalry when the large community is involved.

In this dilemma, a compromise could be found in saying that potential interaction between people should be as high as possible, as long as the individual can control it and shield himself whenever desired. His front door, figuratively speaking, should open on a bustling square, and his back door on a secluded park. Thus this ideal is seen as related to the ideal of choice.

Put differently, individuals require a rhythmical alternation of stimulus and rest—periods when personal interchange is high and to some degree is forced upon them, to be followed by other periods when stimulus is low and individually controlled. A potentially high level of interaction, individually controlled, is not the whole story; we also need some degree of spontaneous or unpremeditated exchange, of the kind that is so often useful in making new associations.

The goal of interaction, therefore, is forwarded by many of the same physical features as the goal of choice: variety, fine grain, efficient communication; but it puts special emphasis on the oscillation between stimulus and repose (centers of high activity versus quiet parks), and requires that communication be controllable. In addition, it calls for situations conducive to spontaneous exchange. Storehouses of communication, such as libraries or museums, should be highly accessible and inviting, their exterior forms clearly articulated and expressive of their function.

These two objectives of choice and interaction may be the most important goals of metropolitan form, but there are others of major importance, such as minimum first cost and minimum operating cost. These seem to depend particularly on continuous occupation along the major transportation channels, on a balanced use of the flow system, both in regard to time and direction of flow, a moderately high structural density, and a maximum reliance on collective transport.

Objectives of comfort, on the other hand, related principally to a good climate, the absence of distracting noise, and adequate indoor and outdoor space, may point either toward generally lower densities or toward expensive ameliorative works, such as sound barriers, air conditioning, and roof-top play areas. The important goal of individual participation may also indicate lower densities and an environment that promotes an active relation between an individual and his social and physical milieu, thus giving him a world that to some extent he can manage and modify by his own initiative.

We must also consider that the urban pattern will necessarily shift and expand, and therefore it is important to ask whether the adjustment to new functions will be relatively easy, and whether growth, as well as the initial state, is achievable with a minimum of control and central initiative and intervention. Adaptability to change seems to be greater at lower densities, since scattered small structures are readily demolished or converted. Both an efficient transport system and some form of separation of one kind of activity from another are also conducive to flexibility. Discontinuous forms like the galaxy or the ring require special efforts to control growth, for these patterns raise problems such as the appearance of squatters and the preservation and use of intervening open land.

Stability is a somewhat contradictory goal; it takes into account the critical social and economic costs of obsolescence, movement of population, and change of function. It is very possible that stability in the modern world will be impossible to maintain, and it runs counter to many of the values cited above. Yet stability may be qualified in this light: if change is inevitable, then it should be moderated and controlled so as to prevent violent dislocations and preserve a maximum of continuity with the past. This criterion would have important implications as to how the metropolis should grow and change.

Finally, there are many esthetic goals the metropolis can satisfy. The most clear-cut is that the metropolis should be 'imageable,' that is, it should be visually vivid and well structured; its component parts should be easily recognized and easily interrelated. This objective would encourage the use of intensive centers, variety, sharp grain (clear outlines between parts), and a differentiated but well-patterned flow system.

## The Relation of Forms to Goals

We have now treated a number of objectives that are crucial, that are on the whole rather generally accepted, and that seem to be significantly affected by the pattern of the metropolis: the goals of choice, interaction, cost, comfort, participation, growth and adaptability, continuity, and imageability. Other goals may develop as we increase our knowledge of city form. What even these few imply for city form is not yet obvious; moreover, they often conflict, as when interaction and cost appear to call for higher densities, while comfort, participation, and adaptability achieve optimal realization at lower levels. Nevertheless, we have immediate decisions to make regarding the growth of urban areas, and if we marshall our goals and our alternatives as best we can, we can the better make these decisions.

The clarifying of alternatives and objectives has an obvious value, for this will permit public debate and the speculative analysis of the probable results of policy as related to any given form. Yet this kind of approach will soon reach a limit of usefulness unless it is supported by experimental data. Such experimentation is peculiarly difficult in regard to so large and complex an organism as a metropolis. To some degree we can form judgments drawn from such different urban regions as Los Angeles, Stockholm, and Paris, but these judgments are necessarily distorted by various cultural and environmental disparities. Possibly we can study certain partial aspects of city form, such as the effects of varying density or the varying composition of centers, but the key questions pertain to the metropolitan pattern as an operating whole. Since we cannot build a metropolis purely for experimental purposes, we can only build and test models, with some simplified code to designate pattern. By simulating basic urban functions in these models, tests might be run for such criteria as cost, accessibility, imageability, or adaptability. Such tests will be hard to relate to the real situation, and it is difficult to see how certain objectives (such as interaction or participation) can be tested, yet this technique is our best current hope for experimental data on the implications of the total metropolitan pattern.

## Dynamic and Complex Forms

Until we have such experimental data, what can we conclude from our imaginary juxtaposition of metropolitan form and human goals? Each of the alternatives proposed has its drawbacks, its failures in meeting some basic objectives. A radical, consistent dispersion of the metropolis appears to restrict choice, impair spontaneous interaction, entail high cost, and inhibit a vivid metropolitan image. A galaxy of small communities promises better, but would still be substandard as regards choice, interaction, and cost, besides being harder to realize. A re-centralization of the metropolis in an intensive core appears to entail almost fatal disadvantages in cost, comfort, individual participation, and adaptability. The rationalization of the old metropolis in a star would work better if central congestion could be avoided and free accessibility maintained, but this form is less and less usable as size increases. The ring has many special advantages but raises great difficulties in cost, adaptability, and continuity with present form.

Of course, these are all 'pure' types that make no concessions to the complications of reality and they have been described as though they were states of perfection to be maintained forever. In actuality, a plan for a metropolis is more likely to be a complex and mixed one, to be realized as an episode in some continuous process, whose form involves rate and direction of change as well as a momentary pattern.

## References

BLUMENFELD, Hans (1949) 'A Theory of City Form', *Society of Architectural Historians Journal*, July reprinted in *The Modern Metropolis*, (editor Paul D. Spreiregen), The M.I.T. Press, Cambridge, Mass.

WRIGHT, Frank Lloyd (1940) 'Broadacre City', in *Taliesin*, **1**.

STEIN, Clarence (1942) 'City Patterns, Past and Future', Pencil Points, June.

# 4. Planning the Future City

## Introduction *by Philip Sarre*

The selection of items for this section is related to its central theme, which is that the most vital feature of future planning will be its relationship to the political process rather than the detailed techniques it uses. This implies that the goals of planning should receive more explicit attention than has often been the case and that we should ask not only *what* goals are to be pursued but *whose* goals. These arguments are expanded in the paper by Davidoff.

The establishment of a planning process which is oriented to future goals involves a change from *ad hoc* attempts to solve current problems to a more coordinated effort to produce programmes to develop from the present toward a desired future. The paper by Webber interprets the history of planning as an attempt to use engineering design methods to solve social problems. This was relatively successful with problems like public health but has been less successful with more complex social problems. He then details an ideal planning process including a future-orientation and recommends its adoption. He also strengthens the argument for political planning by giving numerous examples of situations where private enterprise is ineffectual. Finally, he insists that where possible the output of the planning process should be evaluated and suggests that pricing might be an appropriate mechanism—but only after social justice had been assured by redistribution of income.

These three essays establish the main theme of the section. The extract taken from the *Milton Keynes Plan*, traces this theme in planning practice, in the sense that these goals represent the intentions of an established planning body rather than the pious hopes of planning theorists. Of course they are very generally phrased and not easily evaluated in advance but they do provide a datum against which the next three papers, representing variations on the basic theme, can be measured.

The first of these variations looks at first sight like the negation of our theme. Banham *et al.* strongly criticise current planning and call for some experiments in 'non-planning'. However their argument cannot be sustained at this level because withdrawal of planning would have two results which they do not consider. First, those areas pinpointed by

207

Webber as beyond the reach of private enterprise would be neglected, second, the natural tendency of private enterprise to supply the most lucrative market would lead to increased provision for the affluent and decreased provision for the poor. As Webber pointed out, market mechanisms lead to social injustice unless income disparities are reduced. Banham *et al.* make two valid points, however. First, one cannot disagree with their judgement that many planning projects are visually dull. Indeed, one could extend it to point out that many private developments are just as dull. Second, there is probably a case for some reduction of detailed planning control in the UK—but this should benefit individual members of the public and not business interests. These two points are entirely in harmony with the main theme.

A second variation is provided by the extract from *Blueprint for Survival*. These authors extrapolate current trends and make predictions about the future which are not merely disagreeable but disastrous. They thus suggest policies to change the direction in which society is developing to reach a goal they see as not just desirable but essential, that is the achievement of a steady state relationship between society and environment. While one may disagree with the details of their case, it seems incontrovertible that such an equilibrium must be achieved in the long term. However, some aspects of the programme they suggest seem arguable in the extreme. Perhaps the most debatable section is that concerned with population distribution, which we have reproduced. This would appear to be prohibitively costly since it involves writing off the whole of our investment in urban centres. It also seems socially undesirable since it aims to promote social control and status striving. In spite of these defects the piece contributes to our theme both by showing that some effort is needed to ensure the survival of society and that goal-oriented planning is likely to be more radical than is planning of the ad hoc type.

This radical flavour is more pronounced in the article by Alexander. He rejects both the tendency of futurist architects to produce novel structures for their own sake and that of planners to deal conservatively with the measurable features of environment and behaviour. He insists that the built environment must be designed with human needs and behaviour in mind and sketches one way of doing this. He conceives environmental units as settings which permit and encourage certain kinds of behaviour. Some of the units he describes are appropriate for present-day behaviour patterns, others assume changes in behaviour. His sketch of the way these might be combined into a city shows that this design method can reach very radical proposals from fairly modest assumptions. Alexander recognizes throughout that the relationship between urban form and human needs is still a matter for conjecture and suggests hypotheses which might be tested to clarify the situation. His main contribution to the development of the theme of this section is to provide detailed environmental forms which might be produced by a client-centred planning process. Although the built form he sketches is a radical change, it seems that he sees more initiative remaining with planners than do Davidoff and Webber in their pluralist and permissive proposals.

The final piece, by Mumford, stresses that urban life has always been associated with both the best and the worst aspects of human existence. The city has encouraged both tyranny and individual development. Most people's goals for their own future would presumably favour freedom and self development rather than subjection. If the future city is to have a form and life conducive to these goals it will be necessary to ensure that political power over the planning process remains widely spread rather than concentrated in a few hands, whether they be those of a class elite, business managers or professional planners. However, designers and academics have two important roles to play even in a situation where power is devolved: first to demonstrate that there are future possibilities which are likely to be more satisfactory than the existing environments which the public use as their standards and, second, to point out the likely future consequences of present trends— especially where those lead to disastrous situations. At present these activities occur outside the formal planning process and influence only some of the public. In future they could be a vital part of a planning process in which there is meaningful public participation through the exercise of power.

# 4.1 Normative Planning *Paul Davidoff*

As we speak of inventing the future, it is revealing that we do not address ourselves to 'preventing the future.' The idea that the future is inventable suggests a bias toward both optimism and technological determinism. I question these biases.

As a planner, I am pleased that there is growing concern with thinking about the future. But I am afraid that much of this thinking may be devoid of knowledge and concern with the tremendous problems of poverty, discrimination, and war that beset our society at this time and will remain with us for some time in the future. I think that the futurists

*Source:* S. Anderson, Editor (1968), *Planning for Diversity and choice*, MIT Press Cambridge, Mass., pages 173–179.

of today must be warned not to attempt to practice nonnormative planning.

Today's planning, both conventional agency work and the new concern with the year 2000 or beyond, tends to examine problems in essentially technical terms. But in masking the values underlying their proposals, the planners have weakened their plans. Contemporary comprehensive city plans are often quite unrealistic and appear so to the public precisely because their authors fail to come to grips with the basic issues that confront their society and split the members of the society into different political groups.

In city planning we have had a practice of a single planning body proposing a course of action. The community has then had a yes-or-no referendum: either they accept the plan, or they have no plan.

There has been strong reaction to this form of planning within our field in the past five or six years, and there seems to be a growing practice for planning agencies to make a point of considering alternative policies rather than a single 'technically correct' plan. One who adheres to the recipe for good rational behavior would examine alternative policy choices rather than simply propose one rationally perfect plan.

A single agency, however, continues to be responsible for the discussion of alternative plans or alternative means for achieving a given end. The presentation of alternatives by a single agency still does not recognize the essential political element underlying a planning proposal, that the 'general welfare' or the 'public interest' is not a fact that can be discovered upon deep research. The identification of the public interest is always a contentious point. There are different views about how the public will best be served. Our practice in physical planning often has not accepted that debate; instead, there has been a concept that the technicians, the planners, might be able to develop a good plan or series of alternatives for the community. (The planning staff and planning commission may, of course, develop a good plan, but there is no objective measure of its goodness. Its evaluation in terms of serving the public is necessarily a political judgment. It is a choice of policy and a choice of what ought to be done for the community; as such it is subject to debate, or in a democracy it should be subject to debate, so as to permit different interests to react to the solution offered.)

The alternative to this monolithic agency proposal of plans is 'plural planning,' in which the determination of how the society ought to develop would not be the sole responsibility of a single public agency. Instead, many different groups within the society might participate in determining policy. 'Determining' here means proposing, debating, deciding.

Plans for community development should be included in the platforms of political parties. For many reasons, however, the political parties want to remain as general as possible in their commitment so as not to lose popularity. They do not want to support specific ideologies. Since the political parties are incapable of developing plans themselves, other interest groups may be capable of proposing plans. The development of what has been called 'advocate planning' recognizes this need for interest groups to express their demands in the form of plans.

Planners have begun to operate as professional advocates for neighborhood groups, developing alternative plans to the plans proposed by some public agency. This is a very healthy development, and one that we should take note of at this conference. As we find ourselves more and more concerned with the year 2000 and with specific commission plans for the year 2000 or some later time in the future, we should not expect that a plan for that year can come alone from the 'best minds' in the country. One of these plans, that of the Commission on the Year 2000, prepared by a group of 'experts,' seems to represent a group of characters in search of a future. Here is a group of intellectuals, who, aside from the fact that they have some common background and training in being concerned with intellectual matters, have no real reason for coming together. They do not represent any interest at all, and it is not surprising that, at least so far, they do not seem capable of yielding a plan. There is no common interest that ties them together. They do not have a common political base.

The concept of pluralism in planning has both positive and negative features. In establishing a plural planning system, we have to guard against the abnegation of leadership. In proposing plural planning, we should not say that there is no role for the central planning agency. It will still have a vital role to play. The agency that produces the government plan will be better informed if it produces plans in the context of a societal process of considering what ought to be. The agency does have an important job in recommending what courses of action should be followed. It would be a mistake to minimize that central planning function or to recommend that it be transferred to the many different interests in the society. That would be an unwarranted dissipation of responsibility.

The central agency's role is to give direction; but it must recognize that its views are only one possible set of views. If the central planning agency is sophisticated, it will know how to take advantage of the alternatives proposed by outside groups. It will educate itself, both technically and politically, toward improving its own recommendations.

I should like to highlight my remarks regarding the need for pluralizing planning by suggesting in their definitions of major problems central planning agencies have tended to accept value orientations favoring the present distribution of opportunities in society.

First, let us look at the present concern with urban life. We know that

211

there are problems in the city because *Life* and *Look* have told us so. If we feel insecure with those magazines, the *Saturday Review* has also told us so. Recently, *U.S. News & World Report* told us that there was a crisis in our cities and indicated that we have to spend perhaps a trillion dollars in ten years to combat this problem.

The concern with urbanism is misplaced. The real crisis of our times is not an urban crisis. Instead, the crucial problem is a national problem, an international problem, a social problem. It is the fact of great social injustice. It is the fact that there is vast discrimination, poverty, and hunger. It is the fact that there is great hate, that the world is ready to blow itself up and is very close to doing so, and that very few people are trying to prevent us from destroying ourselves.

Many of these social problems are presently located in urban areas. The poor live increasingly in urban areas, both in our nation and in others. The problems may thus seem more apparent in urban areas, so we call them urban problems. We discover, though, that in 'dealing' with urban problems, we are not often dealing with the problems of injustice, discrimination, and poverty. In fact, we are dealing with *other* problems peculiar to urban areas: the problems of congestion, problems of 'uglification,' to use Lewis Carroll's term, problems of high density and of pollution. But the basic problem that must be confronted is the unjust distribution of opportunities in our society. We cannot hope to solve this problem at the urban level. By focusing on the urban aspect of social problems, we avoid dealing with national distributional questions.

In all our discussions of the future so far at this conference there has hardly been any mention of distribution, whether of the present distribution of opportunities, of education, of health, of leisure time, of wealth and income, or of knowledge.

We live in a society that has accepted the conventional wisdom of modern economists, whose main concern is with growth. The quality of our economy must be determined in terms not only of growth but of how the economy distributes its resources.

In our discussion earlier no one said that the present distribution is wrong or that we should do something to see that the poor get a greater share of what our society and other societies have to offer. Our assumption is that of John Kenneth Galbraith, who wrote in *The Affluent Society* (1958, pages 82, 96–7).

... Few things are more evident in modern social history than the decline of interest in inequality as an economic issue ... While it continues to have a large ritualistic role in the conventional wisdom of conservatives and liberals, inequality has ceased to preoccupy men's minds. ... In the advanced country, ... increased production is an alternative to redistribution. And, as indicated, it has been the great solvent of the tensions associated with inequality ... Yet in this case the facts are inescapable. It is the increase in output in recent decades, not the redistribution of income, which has brought the great material increase, the well-being of the average man. And, however suspiciously, the liberal has come to accept the fact.

The inescapable fact to which Galbraith alludes does not lead to any inescapable conclusions concerning proper public policy. Galbraith comes to grips with the basic value problems by describing what has happened in economic thought, but his implied conclusion is that it is no longer necessary to consider the propriety of present distribution patterns. This is wrong. At a minimum a responsible evaluation of the quality of the national economy would always have to account for the distributional pattern as well as for the absolute quantity of wealth.

Our society is concerned with full employment and with economic growth. We argue whether we ought to have 4 per cent or 2 per cent unemployment, but the amount of employment or unemployment is itself not so significant as the question of who gets what from the society. In a society in which the unemployed were given a decent income, the problems of unemployment would have a different meaning than they do for us today.

I ask for a greater sharing of the goods of the society: of knowledge, health, and wealth. I do not think it is necessary to argue, however, that everybody must have the same. We do not have to consider whether the society that we create will be too bland or whether we shall eliminate incentive.

What we should discuss is the question of whether it is or is not appropriate to maintain the present distribution of social goods. That issue, however, is never discussed. We assume that the present distribution is correct. It is probably a familiar fact that in our society the top 5 per cent of income earners earn three times as much as the bottom 20 per cent. The top 5 per cent earn 15 per cent, the bottom 20 per cent earn about 5 per cent, and the top 20 per cent earn almost ten times as much as the bottom 20 per cent. During the course of the period from the New Deal to the present, whatever redistribution has taken place took some money from the wealthiest group and gave it to the upper-middle-income group. Some resources went to the second quintile and some to the third quintile, but hardly anything has come down to the bottom 40 per cent. The figures since 1948 or 1950 show almost no change in the proportion the bottom 40 per cent received.

In the distribution of knowledge, of the opportunity to enjoy leisure time, we can find patterns quite similar. We know very well that the poor have very little opportunity to get out of the city to enjoy the great resort areas our country possesses. Dean Seifert has mentioned the great increase in airplane traffic. Only about a third of the American people have ever taken even one flight. We have a vast industry serving those of us who fly fairly often. We are only a small percentage of the population, yet a great deal of money from federal funds goes into support of the air travel industry. It is a fine industry, but the question is: Who has the opportunity to share its benefits?

Many may say that economic growth is enough. Some of us may disagree with that point of view; but the crucial point is that we should be debating the distribution issue. It shouldn't be hidden from view.

It is quite irresponsible on the part of any technician to come before the public to make a recommendation about how things ought to be, unless he states very explicitly that the distribution pattern he proposes is the best one. He should say explicitly that in the society he proposes it is right that the poor shall get only their pittance and that this is the best solution for everyone.

It is quite apparent that many people who make solutions today would rather not be so explicit. It is difficult, even if you do believe that ours is the best distribution pattern, to have to admit it.

In our discussions of the future of a particular society or of world society I hope that the underlying social issues, of resource distribution for rich and poor, for warlike and peaceful purposes, for benefit to persons and institutions, will provide the focal point of discussion. This exploration of underlying issues will help us to avoid the myth of the planner as technical specialist, privy to vast secret information banks, who can set out futures for whole societies in a political vacuum. We are all politicians and ideologues, and I hope our conferences and our planning documents will admit and face this fact.

## Reference

GALBRAITH, J. K. (1958) *The Affluent Society*, Boston, Houghton Mifflin.

# 4.2 Permissive Planning *Melvin M. Webber*

An earlier paper (Webber, 1968) suggested that the rapid onset of the post-industrial stage of development is likely to force two major changes in urban planning. One anticipated change is substantive: the increasing pace of history is revealing a new set of problems, different in kind from those that have been occupying city planners. During the industrial age, the profession's work was aimed at improving the cities' efficiency. In

*Source:* M. M. Webber, 'Planning in an environment of change', *Town Planning Review*, **39**, number 4, 1969.

the imminent post-industrial age, unprecedented wealth will turn the equity issues into imperatives. Growing disparities in levels of wealth and welfare among increasingly diverse publics are likely to engender severe conflicts both within the highly developed nations and between the wealthy and the poor nations.

The other major change is largely procedural. New developments in the social and behavioural sciences are increasing our understanding of societal systems—of their component economies, polities, communities, families, and geographies. A consequence of the new theory is a growing capacity to predict future changes in these systems. We are now quickly accumulating the skills for *planning* and then for *engineering* social change.

This could be a highly felicitous development. But it could also be the basis for a new tyranny of technocrats. Already the specialists operating the simulation systems are finding it difficult, sometimes impossible, even to talk to politicians. The concepts they work with are unfamiliar, and the techniques they use seem mysterious. Decision makers are increasingly forced to accept the conclusions of technical specialists, thus putting the specialists in the role of governors. As the planning technologies grow more complex and as the distribution of information and analytical skills shifts from politicians to technicians, there is likely also to be a redistribution of political power. It now looks as though the post-industrial period will be marked by a new style of government. Dominated by the idea and methods of planning, the coming decades will bring new possibilities for creative confrontation with the future.

This paper focuses upon some questions surrounding the relations between technics and politics as they might affect city planning. As before, my observations and comments are limited to the American scene. What happens there has implications for what happens elsewhere, but these interpretations I must leave to the reader. With that disclaimer, let me simply state my thesis with the aim of making it explicit ahead of time.

City planning has not yet adopted either the planning idea or the planning method. It has instead internalized the concepts and methods of design from civil engineering and architecture. In the post-industrial period, when planning will be the characteristic mode of deciding and acting, city planning is likely to adopt a rationalistic posture with respect to valuation and to future change, displacing its traditional ideological posture. It will thus increase its power, including the power to help some groups and to hurt others. If city planning also carries over some of its traditional roles and self-images, the exercise of its new-found power will unwittingly hurt just those groups that are least able to help themselves. To counter that implicit danger, we shall need built-in procedures for *valuating* the wants of increasingly diverse publics and for *evaluating* the planned actions to test whether these actually do serve the valued ends.

## THE IDEA OF PLANNING

I shall be using the term 'planning' to refer to a special way of deciding and acting. The minimum necessary conditions of the planning method are these:

1. The explication of goals, objectives and targets for each subsystem under consideration including, in the public sphere, each of the publics that will be touched by the planned actions.

2. The continuous forecasting of both qualitative and quantitative changes that lie outside the planners' control.

3. The continuous forecasting of likely chains of consequences, within and especially among subsystems, resulting from each set of alternatively hypothesized planned actions.

4. The appraisal of investment costs and welfare pay-offs attached to each alternatively projected history. If a reasonable fit is found between an hypothesized course of action and the value sets, a time-sequenced action strategy is synthesized, comprising shorter-run action tactics, each with its timed targets. Each shorter-run tactic is carefully appraised for its likely net return, and is then expressed in the language of fiscal budgets.

5. The continuous monitoring of the systems being planned. A constant flow of information on actual outcomes is fed back into the planning system to signal forecasting errors and to actuate corrective steps. In addition, early warning of imminent danger or opportunity can alert deciders and, most important, the effectiveness of goal-directed actions can be empirically evaluated for each subsystem and each public.

The distinguishing marks of the planning approach to decision and action are, then, its explicit goals basis, its evaluation of alternative futures and alternative future courses of action, and its reliance upon feedback of outcomes and pay-offs. Planning is *inherently* oriented to outputs; it views inputs, such as public services and facilities, as *investments* which have ascertainable pay-offs to client publics. As such, planning is essentially an *economizing* approach to the future, constantly appraising trade-offs among alternative investment strategies in search of the desired welfare returns.

This is certainly a highly idealized conception of a planning process. As an ideal, it is unattainable. But it is an ideal worth pursuing, for we profit as we approach it. At the present stage in its history, city planning has made but small headway toward this idea.

## Two competing traditions

Two sources have stimulated the city planning movement and have shaped its development. The one, an offspring of the German Rationalization and the scientific management movements, cast city planning in the role of the city engineer who sought to improve efficiency in the city's physical plant. The other, an offspring of the earlier social reform movements, cast it in the role of the social reformer who sought to improve the lot of people living in the cities. The parent of both sources was, of course, the industrial revolution that emptied the farms, crowded the cities, and generated a new society plagued by the problems of adapting to rapid change. Both sources have exerted continuing, albeit competing, influence during this century, but the engineering approach has been dominant.

With the rise of the factory system, populations became concentrated in the cities that housed the new industries; the cities themselves, however, grew in pre-industrial patterns. City engineering and city planning developed as attempts to exploit available city-building technologies and, later, to invent new ones. As a result men soon learned how to dispose of wastes, to supply sanitary water, to build intra-city transportation systems, to provide schools and hospitals, and even to build tolerable housing of some quality for everyone. These were no modest successes. We have only to look to the Calcuttas of the contemporary world to appreciate how far we have come. Despite the many inadequacies of present-day western cities, we must surely agree that their record is impressive. To be sure, we have yet to solve air-, water-, and noise-pollution problems; housing quality does not begin to match our technological capabilities; and no city has yet disposed of traffic congestion. But the early objectives have been won. Epidemics of the dread diseases are gone. Obnoxious spill-overs from factories to adjacent houses have been largely eliminated. Producers are accessible to their suppliers and customers, and retail outlets are accessible to residents. The majority of the cities' residents *can* live with a sense of decency and some even with dignity. Our cities *do* work. If we knew how to measure their overall efficiency, they would probably score pretty high.

Much of that success reflects the comparative simplicity of the problems inherent in the early industrial city. The early city planners could properly consider that solutions to problems stood in direct, one-to-one relation to demonstrated causes—typhoid to a water-carried salmonella, traffic breakdowns to unpaved muddy streets, rodent infestations to accumulated garbage, and so on. The science of the time supplied the explanations that, in turn, led to direct technical solutions. So long as there was consensus on objectives, there was little doubt about the actions to be taken.

The critical step in that process is the epistemological one—the concept that cause and effect are directly related—such that causes of problems can be identified and that correct and direct solutions can be found. This was a reasonable presumption for the kinds of problems being treated in those early days. Because the systems being dealt with could be conceived as being effectively independent, unilateral intervention was initially sufficient. Recourse to the planning method was, therefore, unnecessary.

Later, when the massive problems had been alleviated, when the cities' structures had grown more complex, when ever more refined solutions were sought, and when demands for amenities replaced the easier demands for removal of obstacles—it was then recognized that the workings of the city's physical parts really did affect each other. Engineers and planners began to design sets of systems, searching for overall city plans that would simultaneously attack a number of problems. The step was an important one, for it laid the foundations of the systems-analysis and systems-design efforts that permit positive invention of desired future states while also alleviating undesired present conditons.

Taming of the massive problems came just when incomes were rising rapidly and when cultural urbanization was making for cultural diversity among the cities' residents. Those who wanted and could afford better environmental qualities were able to lay claim to them. The overall city plans reflected this growing search for amenity.

At this juncture the technical problem-solving concepts of the engineer merged with the aspiration-raising efforts of the social reformer. It may have been at this juncture also that city planning split off from city engineering, for the engineers typically remained subsystem specialists while the city planners sought to become system-wide generalists. However wide the split, though, the thoughtways of the engineer continued to dominate the work of the system-wide planners. Although city planning has by now developed a professional subculture and although its practitioners profess social purposes far beyond the resolution of current and discrete problems, the city planning movement, I believe, has never outgrown its intellectual origins in city engineering and architecture. The original premises underpinning civic-works design became overlaid with a social ideology that introduced different purposes, but the premises remained in an epistemological eclecticism that continues to mark the trade today. Engineering contributed an operational style and social ideology contributed the purposive rationale for applying that style as a substitute for market processes. But still the idea of planning never got built into the profession's work.

## Social ideology's influence on early city planning

The ideology arose in response to the horrid living conditions and physical squalor of the early industrial city, but it was more than a reflection of moral indignation. Aimed at effecting fundamental social change, it was a positive credo that was inextricably caught up in the main current of American thought and thus shared in a complex network of beliefs. Despite the danger of over-simplification, we can identify a few of the major precepts that have been shaping the city planning movement.*

1. The city was thought to be unnatural and inherently unhealthy and immoral. In order to counteract its intrinsically evil character, it had to be remoulded to resemble the country town that had preceded it.

2. Especially in America, where immigrants from other parts of the world were considered 'strange' and were seen as a threat to the social order, an effort had to be made to acculturate them. At this time, when the idea of physical environmental determinism was at its peak, the central strategy for turning immigrants into middle-class, stable citizens was to provide them with a middle-class physical environment.

3. In parallel, the middle- and upper-class supporters and leaders of the movement were confident that they knew what was best, both for the migrants to the city and for society at large. They, therefore, selflessly inaugurated a variety of governmental and philanthropic enterprises, designed to improve the conditions of city life. Anticipating similar contemporary efforts by many decades, they substituted a collective rationality for traditional individual rationality, placing decision-making in the hands of those elite groups who were both informed and oriented to the public interest.

4. At the time these efforts were being made, many city governments in America were controlled by political machines, and they had indeed become corrupt. The reformers were, therefore, determined to keep their programmes out of politics. Their tactic was at first also to keep them out of government. But that soon became unnecessary, for it was found that technical professionalism in government was a more effective way of keeping politics out of government.

5. In the spirit of successful captains of industry, the programmes for betterment were launched with the bold optimism that wilful action could control future outcomes: the city, like the factory, could be designed to accord with deliberate purpose. It was at this point that the teleologic and utopian outlook was implanted within city planning, nearly a century ahead of the recent futurists and planners.

*Herbert Gans (1968) has summarised with insight the ideology of the American city planning movement.

## Permissive planning

In brief, then, we can typify the early ideology of the American city planning movement as anti-city, elitist, apolitical, rationalistic, sometimes technocratic, but always oriented to an image of the larger public welfare. As direct descendants of the Enlightenment, the early city planners were out to perfect history.

Surely, these were responses to the failure of market processes that controlled construction and use of buildings and space. The general reaction of urban social reformers was to bring the markets to account.

Two major strategies were pursued. The first was to replace market processes by administered governmental programmes. The second was to constrain market behaviour in an effort to prevent the more outrageous outcomes, by setting limits on the builders and landowners who were profiteering from the city-building bonanza, typically at the expense of the poor. The tactic applied to both strategies was essentially the same. It was, as already noted, to substitute for individual rationality the collective rationality of public-spirited and knowledgeable professionals working inside city government.

These efforts to regulate market processes were in part impelled by an ideological opposition to markets and, in some sectors of the movement, by a distrust of private businessmen. At the time the movement was being organized, though, I suspect it was largely motivated by a recognition that the market was failing to perform as classical economics had promised it would. Pursuing the belief that governments could simply force greedy businessmen to act in the public interest, social reformers adopted the tactics of regulation and direct public enterprise.

## Rationales for governmental intervention

The early planners' actions were taken intuitively and without the theoretic supports their successors can draw upon. By now a considerable body of theory has been accumulated in welfare economics and elsewhere that supplies partial credence to the earlier strategies, while simultaneously raising some doubts. We can here simply catalogue several classes of conditions that have been identified as warrants for governmental intervention; later we can examine their relevance to city planning activities.

It is now understood that, in their very nature, markets are incapable of dealing with certain kinds of economic transactions.

*First*, they are incapable of supplying those goods and services for which it is either impossible or too difficult for a private seller to charge a price and for which he cannot exclude non-paying customers. These, the so-called 'pure public-goods', have the peculiarities that (a) if they are supplied to one, they are thereby supplied to all, and (b) it costs no more to supply an additional person. Since it is costless to serve more customers, social product would be reduced by constraining con-

220

sumption, and governments have thus been wont to offer these goods and services. The classic example is the lighthouse, but there are a great many more—radio broadcasting, mosquito elimination, streets and highways, and national defence are also pure public goods. If governments or philanthropists did not supply them, they would probably not be supplied at all.

A *second* class of public goods is also impossible to price properly in the market because the consumer does not receive *all* the benefits that arise from his having consumed it. 'External' (social) benefits are realized by others who do not themselves use the service, so the seller cannot charge the buyer at a price that reflects the total social value received. For example, a person treated for a communicable disease gets relief, but others in the neighbourhood also benefit by having their risks reduced. It would be virtually impossible for the physician to collect from the neighbours, and so public-health departments have typically had to take over this function, charging the whole neighbourhood through taxes. (Dorfman, 1965, page 8.)

A *third* situation, involving rather the opposite sort of transaction, has been a major cause of governmental regulation in the urban field. These are dealings that result in negative external effects, that is, social costs, such that neighbours have to bear the costs of someone else's valued activity. For example, a factory dumps waste into a river that a town downstream uses for municipal purposes. The town must now treat its water supply, but there is no market mechanism by which it can charge the factory for the purification costs. If the factory is to be made to pay those bills, or, alternatively, if it is to be prevented from generating the social costs, the terms must be set outside the market system. Again, government is the only effective agency for dealing with the situation.

*Fourth*, governments are encouraged to enter business directly when wanted goods are not forthcoming from private enterprise. Some lines of business are just not feasible in the private sector, either because the scale of investment required exceeds available private funding or because the risks involved are too great to entice private capital. Launching vehicles for communications satellites certainly illustrate the first, and probably the second as well. Governments can afford to undertake large and risky investments that private corporations cannot. Modern governments in the western world do not go bankrupt—they only change management.

A *fifth* rationale for public intervention into markets involves the condition, increasingly common in highly integrated societies, in which all persons may profit more if *each* agrees to yield certain of his rights. In this situation a government agency serving as referee facilitates the exchange of information so that all concerned can avoid the hazards attendant upon mutual ignorance of plans. The willingness of the banking community to accept the edicts issued by the central banks is one clear instance; the traffic signal is another; urban renewal programmes are notable ones. Governmental economic stabilization programmes are by far the most dramatic and successful ones. (These are all in the nature of non-zero-sum games in which the total winnings are greater if free market play is constrained.)

A *sixth* situation, closely related, is the circumstance in which private investors acting in accordance with their own relatively short-run calculus of profitability would deprive the public of certain long-run benefits. If, for example, the public values the *future* benefits of a forest more highly than the timber industry (technically, the public applies a lower future-discounting rate), it has the choice of buying the forest and preserving it as a park. Again, when governments' time-horizons have been longer and their discount rates lower than private owners', they have sometimes simply passed laws prohibiting owners from using their resources freely.

*Seventh*, governmental powers are commonly invoked to prohibit individuals from behaving in self-destructive ways when government judges it can command better information about what is harmful to individuals than can the individuals themselves. Thus, thalidomide and other drugs have been banned. Drawing on the same rationale, government has justified less clear-cut prohibitions, making the use of marijuana a criminal offence and imposing censorship on films and books. (In the United States many local governments go much further, having thick statute books aimed at protecting people from their own immorality and from their inherited propensities to sin.)

The *eighth* case is the obverse of the seventh. Governmental regulations are designed to force or encourage individuals to engage in *healthful* behaviour. Children must attend school for a mandatory number of years; in communities which have fluoridated water supplies, all residents must partake of this benefit (unless, of course, they purchase bottled water). Almost all government programmes aimed at positive self-improvement are permissive and encouraging, however, rather than mandatory. The parks, recreation, theatre, and arts programmes are notable examples.

*Ninth*, government has sometimes required individuals either to refrain from self-injurious, or to engage in healthful, behaviour because the *short-run* general public welfare would thereby be improved. This rationale, resembling both the second (the social-benefit case) and the sixth (long-range public benefit), is currently popular in city-planning circles. It is exemplified by architectural control—the imposition of aesthetic standards on new buildings, with the aim of improving the city's visual qualities. The increased costs are borne solely by the builders; external benefits (social benefits) are received by the passing publics at no cost.

These nine circumstances suggest that there are indeed conditions in which markets cannot work at all, others in which the social product is increased if government engages in certain enterprises, and still others where regulatory procedures might assure higher returns to all individual consumers. We could catalogue a longer list, of course, but this inventory will serve our present purposes. I shall later want to mention circumstances in which market-type systems attached to governmental enterprises might better regulate the production and distribution of community services.

## The civil engineering style

In seeking to confront market insufficiencies, city planners early adopted the techniques of civil engineers rather than those of economists. In so doing, they were remarkably inventive. Their major social inventions were the *technical standard*, which set minimum permissible levels of quality; the *master plan*, which set forth overall system design; and the *land-use regulation*, which constrained the locational decisions of individual establishments. These techniques were derived directly from civil engineering; the innovation lay in translating the language of engineering manuals and contracts-and-specifications into governmental laws and regulations. The aim was basically to accomplish in the market place the sorts of deliberate outcomes that are readily accomplished in the centralized decision-setting of an engineer-client relationship or a centrally controlled government enterprise.

This was a quixotic aim, for the city planners paid scant attention to the realities of three major differences between a public market place and a centralized-decision milieu. First, market outcomes are shaped by the actions of thousands of decision-makers, whereas individual buildings are typically designed by only a few. Secondly, market outcomes represent the vector of innumerable valuations by individuals, each behaving in accordance with his own peculiar value bases, in contrast to the usual consensus that marks an engineering work. And thirdly, the cumulated actions of many deciders work *non*-teleologically, shaping the development patterns of a multiplicity of subsystems, often in subtle and imperfectly understood ways. In contrast, decisions on specific civil projects are typically rationalistic, aimed at accomplishing limited ends for single subsystems.

Three concepts underlying the standards-regulations approach thus need to be re-examined: (1) that there is a meaningful community, comprising all residents of a city or conurbation, who hold to and are bound together by a coherent value system; (2) that technical requirements and standards can be discovered that conform to and further those value systems; and (3) that we can conceive a system-wide, city-development policy that is technically valid and that will promote the overall community's interest.

I suggest that the first two are untenable and that the third is unattainable. But the third can stand as an ideal objective, worth pursuing if, but only if, the first two propositions are rejected. However, to reject the current conceptions of community and of standards is also to reject the foundations of the present operational style in city planning, and that will call for a reconstruction of the field.

## Community values

Insofar as there is a city-wide community—that is, a community of persons who share common interests about the city system—it occupies at most but a small part of their attention. It is true enough that everyone living within a single watershed, for example, shares an interest in water supply and flood hazards. But, except during crises, such shared interests are relegated to the far corners of one's concerns, partly because we learned long ago to manage most of these systems.

Most of the place-defined communities to which people belong are small, typically comprising residents living within a few blocks. We have recently been learning something about these local, place-defined communities, and we are beginning to understand how elastic they are, how dramatically their size varies with social class, and how relatively unimportant they are among the many communities to which people belong. As suggested in Part I, the communities most valued by city residents are the thousands of different social groups that are bound together by voluntary association based on common interests attached to occupation, family, religion, hobby, or shared belief. These social communities are non-territorial in character, bringing people together from various localities.

Each social community is held together by a body of values peculiar to itself, and its value-set may put it in direct competition with other communities. Those persons who value open park-space, wherever it or they may be located, are ready to unite in defence of parks at the first sign of a highway-alignment plan; the social communities of people who like redwood trees are the nemesis of the highway engineer and housebuilder. The organized and informal communities of motorists are partial to highways, almost irrespective of alignment; a proposed route would pit them against the park-loving community. And so on. There has been so much written about the so-called 'metropolitan problem' and the 'metropolitan community' in America that we have accepted these catchphrases as though they referred to something real. The location-defined community, I suggest, claims at most but a small segment of the loyalties, interests, and concerns of city dwellers. If true, then the second concept—that technical standards conforming to community-wide goals can be found—is also doubtful.

## Efficiency versus distribution

Every public action generates both efficiency effects and redistribution effects. Engineers have traditionally been alert to the former—the influence of highway alignment on travel costs, the effect of building materials on construction costs, the effects of separating sanitary from storm sewers on the costs of operating a sewage treatment plant. These efficiency effects are internal to the functioning of the subsystems being designed.

There are also *external* efficiency effects, such as the consequences of a flood-control project or a highway project on subsequent settlement patterns. Modern planning technologies are now making it possible to use such public works' subsystems deliberately in shaping land-development subsystems within the larger, city-wide system. If we could determine what arrangement of transportation facilities would fit well with what spatial arrangement of economic activities and residence-based activities, we could then test alternative transportation plans for their internal and external efficiencies. This important task is now occupying transportation planners, land planners, education planners, and economic planners; all are seeking to improve investment efficiencies in their respective fields by tracing the external effects on the economic development of nations. Although we can be optimistic about our growing capabilities thus to improve both internal and external efficiencies of the systems we operate upon, it will not be enough.

In addition to improving the workability of the city's components, every public action also shifts the distribution of benefits and costs among the various segments of the population. These redistributive consequences, commonly external to the sub-system being planned, affect various non-client groups, each in different ways and to different degrees.

The current attention to 'community values' in the western world is being largely generated by the external distributional effects. It is not a debate over whether a new motorway box or a new airport conflicts with some holistic objective of the 'metropolitan community'. That community is largely mythical. Rather, it is a debate over which publics are to pay and which are to profit from the government's action.

It is fruitless—and certainly misleading—to compute overall community values. In a complex urban society there is no viable single community. And, because each of a multiplicity of competing communities values things against different value scales, there can be no set of generalized values or criteria against which to appraise a project. There can be only a plurality of competing values held by a plurality of affected groups. If this assertion be valid, it follows that any grand social accounting for a 'whole community' is meaningless, for it hides the distribution of costs and benefits among the affected groups. I suggest that, until we can make group-specific evaluations about the distribution of goods and services among the various communities, we are bound to neglect just those community-value consequences that matter most.

In recent years a number of sophisticated efforts have been made to trace the magnitudes of costs and benefits that would be generated by proposed governmental actions. These aggregative studies (still the prototype in this field) are inherently oblivious to community pluralism. They are used to justify projects whose overall benefits may well exceed

225

their overall costs all right, but which nonetheless may impose considerable hardships upon some persons. Such studies, therefore, may prove to be more harmful than useful. A few studies, seeking to trace the incidences of costs and benefits, are more promising for they seek to anticipate which persons will be helped and which hurt.

But, even if we could accurately forecast the likely distributions of external costs and benefits to specific groups or communities and compare the consequences of alternative courses of action, how are public decisions then to be made? How are we to know what distribution of benefits and costs would be best? Here our technical analytical heritage fails us; it provides no basis for determining how benefits *should* be distributed. As Princeton economist William Baumol has put it,

'There is nothing in economic analysis which permits us to say that individual A should optimally receive [a fixed amount of income or other benefit more than] B. The value judgments involved in recommending a distribution of income must somehow be grafted onto the economic information . . . (Baumol, 1965, page 356).

Because economic theory has nothing to say about the comparative advantages of alternative distributions, we have always dealt with these questions politically. By now there are many overt governmental practices that are explicitly intended to redistribute incidences of benefits and costs. Unashamedly, they are politically determined. Elderly persons who could not possibly benefit from public education of the young are nonetheless required to pay the taxes that support state schools. Welfare payments to the poor are distributed from general tax revenues. Housing is supplied with governmental funds at low rents that are commensurate with low incomes. In the United States, federal grants for public transit service are now having to pass a new kind of test, a political test, after they have passed their technical tests. The new question is: what will the proposed transit project do for the poor?

However novel the redistributional criteria may be for transportation engineers, they are old ones to city planners. And yet, by having adopted the engineer's idea of *standards*, the distributional objectives are inevitably short-circuited.

## Standards*

These standards establish minimum permissible qualities for goods and services. These are distinct from those other kinds of standards that set units of measurement (for example, the gramme, centimetre, second), or that are used in industry to permit interchangeability of parts (the configuration of screw threads, for example), or that refer to current

*The section on standards owes much to John W. Dyckman.

experiential norms (as with 'standards of living' or 'academic standards').

Behind the conception of administered or legislated quality standards is the more fundamental idea of *requirements*. The source is clear, for the idea has been developed to its most refined stage in the various fields of engineering. If a given span is to be bridged, a beam of specifiable dimensions is required. If a given amount of water is to be transported at a specified pressure, a pipe of determinate dimensions is required. Behind these determinations lies a body of theory in physics and an accumulated body of empirical tests and experimental findings. Each of these statements is also explicit about the *goals* to be served: if your goal is to span that river, do this; if your goal is to carry water, do that. Having a firm scientific and empirical base and an explicit statement of objectives, engineers have been able to write standards that conform to these *conditional* requirements. Their approach was adopted at an early stage by practitioners in public health. In turn, it became standard-operating-procedure in city planning.

But when the requirements-and-standards approach was transplanted into the city planning field, neither the scientific basis nor the explicit goals was attached. Lacking an accumulated body of scientific inquiry in the urban field, we have had little hard evidence on which we could rely. Faced with a multiplicity of communities, each with its own goal systems, how was one to know which standards were appropriate?

The problem was solved by dropping the engineer's *conditional* qualification. The 'if' clause was eliminated, and requirements became the expression of what are called 'needs'. As best I understand the idea, needs are seen as absolute necessities, not as conditional preferences. Of course, no prices are attached because no *comparison* of values is possible, nor are trade-offs among competing 'requirements' and 'needs' possible. As *absolute* necessities, they are all equally, and infinitely, valued ends.

In this manner the economizing basis for selecting standards and for selecting courses of action was rejected in favour of ideologically derived assertions of imperatives. In this fashion, too, markets were cut out as indicators of value. Consumers' own market statements about their mix of preferences were replaced by externally adjudged assertions about their needs. Lacking causal theory that might have permitted one to say 'if a given group wants A, they need to do B,' professional judgments were substituted for both A and B. Lacking knowledge of separate groups' wants, professionals decreed the conditions of a universal public welfare. The effect was inevitably thereby to neglect the wants of some publics. The tactic has been so successful that it is by now wide-spread among the social professions.

Thus, educators proclaim what is good for children. Because they usually do know more than others about education, they have been

227

able to make the operational decisions. Medical people are surely among the most powerful of the professionals; each of us confidently puts his life in his physician's hands, on the presumption that he knows what is best. And so, too, with a growing array of professionals from television repairmen to solicitors.

As the professions have been able to claim expertise and, thus, popular deference, they have taken over control of the various agencies in which they work. Medical people effectively control the governmental medical services, recreationists the park departments, engineers the public-works agencies, and so on. Each field is guided by its own ideology—by profession-specific notions of individuals' 'needs'. Each also has its own altruistic perceptions of the 'public welfare', which typically relies, of course, upon the very sorts of services that the given profession offers.

With his characteristic perceptive acuity, George Bernard Shaw put it most sharply in reporting that 'each profession is a conspiracy against the laity'. His judgment has since been supported by the findings of investigators more systematic than he, who have recently been studying the bureaucratic processes and delivery systems of the social services. Their research is revealing that the lay groups least served are those who enjoy less-than-middle-class status and who have the least developed skills for dealing with professional suppliers. Among the sharpest of these examinations that I have seen are those by Martin Meyerson (1967) and by Martin Rein (1964). Meyerson notes that American social policy has been directed toward servicing the 'center-based majorities', perhaps a necessary consequence of supplying standardized services that conform to the preferences of the greatest number of consumers. But the further consequence is that the multifarious minority groups are not well served. In a field he has studied intensely over the years, Meyerson is led to a discouraging conclusion:

'... Urban housing policy of the federal government had as a major aim the improvement of the position of the low-income consumer of housing. Instead, if it strengthened the position of the consumer of housing at all, it was the middle-income household which benefited. Furthermore, most of the gains accrued to the builders and the mortgage lenders. As for urban renewal, it has often replaced the poor in favor of the rich'. (1967, page 74.)

Similar patterns have emerged in other social services—in law, education, transportation, police protection—even (where one might least expect it) in the 'war on poverty'. The accumulating evidence supports the most cynical view: that the social professions have been in the business of servicing themselves rather than their clients. The professions' orientation to efficiency on the supply side, to the neglect of equity on the demand side of the system, have surely fostered that sort of producer bias. But no conspiratorial motivations nor racial or class prejudice need be read into it. I believe the cause is simply that professionals have been wearing cultural blinders that narrow their peripheral vision. The middle-class professionals have been unable to understand that some people just do not want what middle-class people may want. They find it difficult to communicate with lower-class clients. They have had no empirical output measures of consumer satisfaction, and so they have sought to improve the lot of the relatively deprived by supplying the mix of services and facilities preferred by middle-class consumers. These, at least, have the authoritative majority stamp of adequacy.

Cultural barriers to communication are difficult to cross. That is why psychiatrists, for instance, have found it so hard to treat lower-class patients. The valuational, behavioural, and social organizational differences between their cultures are so wide that they cannot be fully understood by psychiatrists. Teachers are faced with the same problem. So are physicians, nurses, social workers, city planners, and policemen. And so, in turn, are the agencies these professions control. The professional shares the behavioural and value norms of middle-class culture, and middle-class culture is simply different from the non-middle-class cultures of other groups. As Oscar Lewis has been at pains to explain, what he calls 'the culture of poverty' is indeed a different social system. The working-class and lower-class publics, who have inadequate social skills for dealing with the majority culture, thus have difficulty in breaking through the cultural barriers that surround hospitals, schools, housing administrations, and the like. When income deficiencies further reduce their capacities for breaking into the markets, their handicap in accomplishing their own purposes is compounded.

In casting this account in the simplistic language of two or three social classes, I recognize that it cartoons an extraordinarily complicated network of publics. The rapidly increasing pluralism of publics, reflecting the rising affluence of the late-industrial and the early post-industrial periods, may spell the demise of whatever beginnings of a 'mass' society we might once have had. Indeed, it is this growing pluralism that impels me to question the contemporary precepts of professional practice. If the social professions, including city planning, are to hold to their concepts of 'needs', 'requirements' and 'standards'; if they are to continue to seek standardized solutions to problems and standardized objectives for change; if the coming rise of planning should mean further centralization of authority and power in the hands of professional governmental officials—then our style of practice might not permit us to serve the very aims we professionals profess.

## SOME PROSPECTS FOR REDIRECTION

At the outset I described planning as a rational approach to accomplishing explicit purposes, and governmental planning as fundamentally oriented to the welfare pay-offs redounding to the various publics' separate purposes. I suggested that the only acceptable test of a governmental programme is an appraisal of how well-off the various client-groups become as a result. The meaningful test of effectiveness can be applied only on the output side, never on the input side.

If there is a single rule of systems analysis and of economics, if there is a single relevant canon of science, this is it: the only acceptable test of an hypothesis—including a policy or an action hypothesis—is whether it works when you try it out. The measure we must meet is demonstrated-effectiveness of outcomes—effectiveness as measured against explicitly enunciated goals. One of the longstanding habits of the traditional social professions has been to measure worth on the input side. Standards are input criteria. So are land-use and building regulations. So are teacher-student ratios and doctor-patient ratios. So are numbers of hospital beds, school buildings, highways, and the rest of the facilities governments build. And so, too, are monetary and fiscal policies and virtually all governmental programmes.

To be sure, all these constraints and facilities are intended to accomplish certain purposes. They have seldom been overtly considered to be ends in themselves. And yet, because these purposes are so seldom made explicit, and because these means have become the stocks of the trades, it is difficult to avoid the inference that the aim of the professions has been to apply the professional instruments.

The give-away comes when one tries to find out whether they *do* serve intended purposes. The evidence is typically nowhere to be found. Despite the gigantic investments in new towns in Britain, for example, no one has yet attempted to find out whether new town residents are any better off than anyone else. Despite the elaborate epidemiological apparatus, we still do not know whether public health and medical services are making people healthier; we know only about rates of illness. No one has yet attempted to find out whether American land-use zoning has accomplished its purposes—whatever those purposes might be.

There is no evidence because we have not been explicit or specific about our aims for specific publics and because we rarely go back to evaluate what happened. I know of no studies by city planning agencies to appraise the welfare returns to their client groups. Were it not that a few sociologists have been curious, we would have little notion of what it means to live in the Bethnal Greens, the Belfasts, the Levittowns, or the Harlems of this world. City planning measures its success on the input side. We test our productivity by asking how large our staffs and our budgets are, how many cases were processed, how many houses were built, how many miles of highway, how many acres of parks. We do not ask how well-off are the people who live in the houses, use the highways, or play, in the parks. We do not ask about the various consumers' schedules of preferences—about the mix of public commodities and services of various quality they desire as they weigh their wants against the spectra of attached prices.

Charles Lindblom contends that, whenever we do enunciate ends, we select them to conform to the available means' (1962, pages 215–216). Further, it looks as though our ends have become, per se, the sheer application of the available means. Despite the high purposes we proclaim, we seem to live for the professional game. Our pay-offs come from playing the game well, as judged by our professional peers who distribute the rewards that matter most to us. We have no other tangible evidence of success, for we have no external measures of the welfare returns to our client publics.

I expect this picture will be changing swiftly, however. Current work in benefit-cost analysis and cost-effectiveness analysis, the newly emerging social indicators, and the move toward programme-budgeting are now all converging and may soon trigger an output- and client-orientation in the city planning field. The change is already underway in America. But even if we abandon the engineer's thoughtways and internalize the economist's valuational thoughtways, we shall still face the distributional questions that growing pluralism, rising affluence, and persisting poverty will force upon us.

Baumol and his colleagues tell us that economic theory can be of little help in resolving the equity questions. We are, therefore, left with a cluster of political questions that no technical methods can mask. It does not matter that politicians, publics and planners prefer to believe otherwise and commonly mask these questions and their decisions as being 'merely technical' ones. The equity side of every planning coin is political on its face. Planning is unavoidably and inherently a political activity. I mean that the decisions taken on such important matters as sewerage systems, housing, transport, schools and airports are *political decisions*. No matter how competent the supporting scientific analyses, or how sophisticated the simulation models, these techniques can test only efficiency and, at best, only identify distributional consequences. Insofar as the outcomes of planned actions effect a reallocation of benefits and costs (and they almost always do), the problems they address can have no technical solutions—only political ones.

In a democratic society the interplay of partisan groups effectively determines not only what is *wanted*, but, therefore, what is *right*. After the technical criteria have been met, the residual (and often determining) evidence is the preferential statements by consumers and by externally affected groups. Open political debate has always been a way of finding equitable outcomes—in part because competing wants can thus be weighed in the political balance, in part because competing wants can then be adjudicated. But public debate is an operational mode also because political expression of preferences is the only way we have to assess appropriate distributions of benefits and costs.

Market places are the counterpart of political forums—the media through which individual purchasers express their preferences as well as the relative weightings they assign to their competing preferences. There are indeed conditions that markets cannot deal with. But there are also many public enterprises, which at present make no direct charge for their services to consumers, whose services could be priced. We do charge for some governmentally provided services (for example, postal, public housing) and we could use the pricing system for other services as well. As yet we have no better way to find out what consumers want than by observing their behaviour under conditions of wide choice. Whether we are considering art museums or automobiles, the political forum and the market place together provide the sensitive testing instruments (on the output side of the systems) for determining the amounts, types, and qualities of public goods or private goods that *should* be supplied.

This is all very well for the wealthy, of course, but persons with but little money have little effective choice in the market place; persons with but little power have little effective voice in the political arena. This is generally true. But, the issue of income distribution among social groups is a separable question from the issue of appropriate mix of public goods and services, and it must be attacked frontally. Yet, given the current facts about income distribution and about costs attached to the available goods and services, our first question must ask how each person chooses to allocate his income among his various wants. However imperfect, such expressions are likely to be more accurate indicators of goodness than are professional divinations. The professions' problem of determining how much of what kinds of public goods and services to supply could be solved in part by adopting quasi-market processes that will supply feedback about wants from consumer to supplier.

I am suggesting that we attach prices to many governmental services that are now distributed without charge. The aim is not, of course, to return to the laissez-faire traditions of the past. Rather, it is to build into our decision-and-action processes those feedback loops which are essential to accomplishing the welfare objectives we seek. Only if each group has a tap into those loops so that it can express its special wants will we be able to serve the growing numbers of minorities and help those who most need help. The requirements-and-standards approach we have institutionalized is intrinsically insensitive to cultural pluralism. Inherently orientated to the middle of the middle-class, it has worked to the inevitable disadvantage of already disadvantaged groups.

In effect, I am suggesting that the social professions made a mistake somewhere along their historical paths. By substituting profession-specific criteria for markets and political forums, they thought they were removing the problems posed by market imperfections. Instead they created an additional devilish hurdle for consumers. It is not even clear whether American lower-class consumers and other minority groups are any better off for these efforts.

## The validity and variety of planned interventions

As I have already indicated, there are indeed varieties of goods and services that private markets cannot deal with. They cannot handle externalities; private suppliers cannot provide purely public goods; private investors cannot undertake large, high-risk investments; and so on. Certainly all regulations cannot be eliminated. Certainly governmental enterprise will become increasingly necessary.

But even with clear instances of market incapacities (such as the blatant social costs of the river-pollution variety) harmful behaviour might best be constrained by applying incentives rather than direct prohibitions. The voluntary association of Ruhr Valley manufacturers has turned a polluted river into a fresh water supply; the income-tax incentives in America and elsewhere have induced builders to supply needed types of housing; and examples of other successful inducements are now becoming numerous. External social benefits probably cannot be dealt with except through taxation. I, for one, am quite prepared to accept the superiority of governmental information regarding harmful products; the restrictions on drugs, for example, are clear instances in which constraints on individual choice are warranted. But it is equally evident that such constraints must themselves be imposed with severe constraint, lest individuals' prerogatives be usurped by well-meaning moral policemen.

The most difficult questions attach to prohibitions on individual free choice in the name of short-run public benefits (the ninth rationale). Controls of this sort are popular among city planners such as those applying to the use of automobiles and the holding of private land in undeveloped state; among other professionals are various controls on behaviour intended to protect the moral order. I can find no justification for elitist constraints of these kinds; I can see only the erosion of personal freedom at the end of that path. Again, if we could indeed predict confidently that shifts in behaviour would lead to improvements in well-being, it would be far better to devise incentive schemes that encourage individuals rather than to apply the crude administrative regulations to which we have become addicted.

But then, suppose we were clever enough to invent ways of supplying differentiated public goods and services and to price them as a test of consumer wants; suppose we were innovative enough to invent incentive systems which could supplant standards and regulation. These measures alone would not result in satisfied consumers if their purchasing power were low. We would also have to effect a redistribution of incomes so that those who are now poor could acquire the operational capacity for choice and, most important, so that their children could break away from the generational cycle that now turns working-class children into working-class adults.

At an earlier period of history, direct payments to low-income earners and selective distribution of services carried the very sorts of personal degradation that Richard Titmuss has been cautioning us about. In America the welfare system has been so overlaid by social workers' policing activities that 'welfare' has come to mean its antonym. To avoid the symbolic meanings attached to the dole, designers of social service programmes sought to distribute services directly and universally, in the manner of the British National Health Service. But that route carries all the overburden of problems I have been outlining.

Perhaps we are now prepared to accept a minimum level of income as a right, as the British public has come to accept health services. Several methods for redistributing income are now being explored. The negative-income-tax is especially promising, for it would meet many of the problems mentioned above. By creating conditions of effective consumer choice, it might thereby reduce the roles of professionals in making decisions for consumers. Once it gained favour across the entire political spectrum, the negative-income-tax (or some equally automatic way of establishing an income floor) could soon become a new basis for distributing services. If sufficiently high minimum-income levels can be maintained, we could employ market-type distribution systems to expand the range of choice open to minority consumer groups. Even were all families suddenly to become wealthy, the problems of governmental planning would not disappear, of course, but many problems associated with supplying governmental services and facilities would be removed.


SUMMARY

The post-industrial age will be marked by increasingly diverse publics having increasingly diverse wants and being increasingly involved in political affairs. The combination of diversity with political participation will engender vocal demands for widening arrays of services and facilities.

Compound interest rates working on small minorities will inevitably turn them into large minorities, increasingly able, politically, to claim those services. Standards and standardized regulations are not the media that match diversity of wants. Instead, where effective markets do not exist to monitor shifting wants and to feed information back into the planning system, we shall need to invent surrogate market systems to guide public planning.

The burden of my argument is that city planning failed to adopt the planning method, choosing instead to impose input bundles, including regulatory constraints, on the basis of ideologically defined images of goodness. I am urging, as an alternative, that city planning tries out the planning idea and the planning method. During the next decades, planning is likely to become the normal mode of deciding and acting in a wide array of societal affairs. At the same time, we shall be living with increasing affluence, increasing relative poverty, and increasing power in the hands of the few technically proficient planners. It will then be all the more necessary that decisions be guided by the *outputs* of government actions, outputs measured by their welfare benefits to the plurality of publics who will inhabit the post-industrial society. The concepts and methods that emerged during the early days of the industrial age are not likely to suit us in the post-industrial age. Now, and increasingly in the future, the hard decisions will have to rely upon explicit statements of the wants of the publics.

Who, then, is to pay and who is to profit? Only the political process can give us these answers. If we do not agree with the outcomes, we still hold the option of using our growing professional influence to effect the political balance. As I have been contending, planning is inside the political system, and, hence a growing political force in itself. I would wish it to use its growing power toward assuring that the goods, services, and facilities supplied are sufficiently diverse to satisfy even the smallest minority's wants. That is to say, a central principle for public planning is that we use the instruments of government in promoting a diversity of goods and services that the market processes have been failing to deliver.

Who is to decide? Clearly, a wide array of competing groups in and out of government. But if the planning idea can be made to work, an increasing proportion of decisions must be made by individual con-sumers. After all, they are the ones who know what they want. Far more frequently than we permit ourselves to think, they are also the only ones who know what is best for them. The post-industrial age will bring unprecedented affluence to western societies. It will also make possible, for the first time in history, a range of choice sufficient to satisfy the prefer-ences of all groups in those societies. The planning idea would accelerate that development. As the counterpart of the idea of democracy, and as an instrument for promoting freedom, I suggest it is worth our giving it a try.

*References*

BAUMOL, W. J. (1965) *Economic Theory and operations analysis*, Second edition, Englewood Cliffs, N.J.: Prentice Hall.

DORFMAN, R. (1965) *Measuring benefits of government investments*. Washington: the Brookings Institution.

GANS, H. J. (1968) 'City planning in America, a sociological analysis', pages 129–37 in *International Encyclopedia of the Social Sciences*, New York, Macmillan, and Chapter 5 of H. J. GANS, *People and Plans*, Penguin, London.

HIRSCHMANN, A. O. and LINDBLOM, C. E. (1962) 'Economic development, research and development, policy making: some converging views', *Behavioral Science*, 7, Number 2, pages 215–16.

MEYERSON, M. (1967) *National urban policy appropriate to the American Pattern* in Goals for Urban America, B. J. L. BERRY and J. MELTZER (ed) Englewood Cliffs, N. J.: Prentice Hall (Spectrum Books).

REIN, M. (1964) 'The social crisis', *Transactions*, May, pages 3–6, 31–2.

WEBBER,, M. (1968) 'Planning in an environment of change: beyond the industrial age', *Town Planning Review*, 39, Number 3, pages 179–195.

# 4.3 The nature of the plan
## *Milton Keynes Development Corporation*

The Plan for Milton Keynes provides a starting point. It does not attempt to lay down in detail the ultimate structure of the new city. Many of the proposals contained in the Plan are for social and institutional initiative. But it also contains proposals for meeting the physical needs of a large city—for transport, drainage, water supply and the other basic services. They inevitably form a framework within which the social and economic development will to some degree be constrained, and within which detailed decisions must be made.

The central aim of the Plan is to arrange these necessarily fixed elements in the new city so as to allow the greatest possible scope for freedom and change as it is built. They have also been planned as far as possible to allow wide variety in patterns of life and the greatest possible choice for the future inhabitants. This approach to planning, because it leaves the future relatively open, means that the task of developing the city during the next 20 years is changed in character. Had the Plan been much more determinate, it would have provided a clear blue-print

*Source:* The plan for Milton Keynes, 1, pages 12–18, Wavendon: Milton Keynes Development Corporation, 1970

for those engaged in its execution. It might even have legislated for the size and shape of buildings and for the detailed visual appearance of the city. Then the task of building the new city would simply have been to fill in section by section on a pre-determined plan. But at Milton Keynes it will be necessary for the thinking and planning process to be continued throughout the period of building.

GOALS IN PLANNING MILTON KEYNES

Many goals and objectives for Milton Keynes have been discussed and debated during the preparation of the Plan and out of these discussions the Corporation has identified six broad goals which the proposals in the Plan are intended to achieve. These goals are:

i   Opportunity and freedom of choice
ii  Easy movement and access, and good communications
iii Balance and variety
iv  An attractive city
v   Public awareness and participation
vi  Efficient and imaginative use of resources

These goals and examples of the proposals intended to achieve them are discussed below.

## Opportunity and Freedom of Choice

The city should offer to its newcomers and its inhabitants the greatest possible range of opportunities in education, work, housing, recreation, health care and all other activities and services.

Technological and social change and increasing incomes enable and indeed require greatly expanded opportunities for education. Nursery education. Nursery education, for example, will increase opportunities for children and parents, and, while recognising the current constraints on national resources, the Plan allows for a greatly increased programme of nursery education and proposes a number of ways by which it might be achieved.

Variety in the opportunities for work depends on variety in the type of employment to be found in the new city and nearby. The favourable location of Milton Keynes means that little difficulty is expected in attracting industry to the new city. The Corporation's policy is to aim at the greatest possible variety in the types of employment within Milton Keynes. The Corporation will seek to attract all kinds of manufacturing industry as energetically as it will seek offices and commercial development, in order to give diversity in the types of job available. Employment

237

in major institutions will also be important. The Open University is already established in the new city and has built and occupied its first buildings. A major health complex including a hospital is proposed and a wide range of employment opportunities will be available in education and the social services.

Employment opportunities in new towns have hitherto not attracted many unskilled workers. The Corporation will encourage the provision of opportunities for these workers including special arrangements for training for the new industries. In this way it is hoped that the new city can help the problems of London and the national problem of redeploying workers from declining industries into new ones.

The very rapid growth rate and the new city's size will in themselves present a constantly expanding range of opportunities. The creation at the new city centre of a rich and diverse set of activities is also intended as a means of enlarging the range of opportunities open to those in Milton Keynes.

The proposed housing policies have been framed to provide the greatest possible freedom of choice. The Corporation suggests that dwellings should be provided across a wide range of sizes, types and character, and that densities of housing areas should also allow for considerable variation. It is proposed that this variety be available in rented housing and in housing for sale. It is also proposed that there should be the greatest possible variety in the financial arrangements whereby families own or rent their homes. This freedom of choice will not be easy to achieve for the Corporation recognises that under present conditions there is a discrepancy between the quality of houses which should be built and the resources available to pay for such quality, whether the houses are for purchase or rent.

To provide for genuine freedom of choice it is vital that journeys should be equally convenient in all directions across the city from every home and the public transport and road systems are intended to achieve this.

The proposals for residential areas have been influenced by the aim to provide freedom of choice. Bus stops, schools, shops, pubs and sometimes local employment will be grouped at the edges of the areas bounded by the main roads where pedestrian bridges or underpasses connect adjoining residential areas. Each family within a residential area will have a choice of several of these activity centres within easy walking distance.

The plan will enable parents to choose between a number of first schools, all available within walking distance of the home. Again, the grouping of secondary schools and the arrangement of the public transport service will enable parents to choose the school which they feel best suited to the needs of a particular child. This freedom of choice in education will make possible diversity as between one school and another, a diversity which could be undesirable were freedom of choice not available to all families and children.

A corollary to the provision of freedom of choice will be people's need for much better information about the various services and how they differ one from another. It is therefore proposed that the Corporation see that extensive information services are established so that people in the city are fully informed of the choices open to them.

## Easy Movement and Access, and Good Communications

An important advantage which a new town should offer to its inhabitants is ease of movement and freedom of access. Existing towns and cities always have much to offer which a new town cannot provide, but generally they cannot offer full freedom of movement. Their pattern of roads, building and public transport cannot meet the needs of the present day without unacceptable destruction of the old fabric. But in a new city easy access can and must be available to all.

Examining in more detail the implications of this goal the Corporation considered that there should be a high degree of accessibility between all activities and places making up the city: homes, jobs, education, health, shopping and recreation. There should also be freedom of choice between public and private methods of transport and a high quality public transport system from the beginning not only for those who need it but for those who might choose to use it instead of private transport. Provision should be made for the use of the car unrestrained by congestion. There must be flexibility in the transport system to allow for expansion and change and it must be safe and environmentally attractive, and minimise nuisance from noise and pollution. There should be provision for free and safe movement as a pedestrian or as a cyclist.

These objectives are fundamental to increase choice and opportunity but present new problems in planning. It has been possible in the past to plan on the one hand for full use of the motor car with minimal public transport, or, on the other, for public transport systems which depend for their economic viability on restrictions and impediments to the use of private cars. The goals established for Milton Keynes ruled out either of these approaches and required both public and private transport to be provided to high standards.

The proposed public transport system, using buses running at frequent intervals with stops within easy walking distance, is designed to connect all residential areas conveniently to all the points to which people will wish to go—jobs, health centres, schools, colleges, shops, and recreational areas. It also interconnects all the residential areas so that social contact between all parts of the city will be easy.

239

This is a most significant proposal which will differentiate public transport in Milton Keynes from many systems which do not offer this uniform and generalised standard of service. They often impose restraints on the way people can move around, compelling individual families to use particular facilities, to which the journey is very much easier than to others. Children, students, old people and those who for one reason or another are unable or disinclined to use private cars, should have as much freedom to enjoy diverse opportunities in the city as have people who drive.

The Plan provides for easy movement by private cars and their penetration to every point in the city. The individual car offers its users a freedom of choice and opportunity which more and more people will want—and be able—to take advantage of. The proposals accept the fact that if easy movement is possible a high proportion of all journeys are likely to be by private car, as cars become available to most households. But they also take account of the fact that even when car ownership reaches much higher levels in 20 to 30 years' time, some 20% of all journeys to work will still be by public transport, and that given comfortable, fast and convenient public transport, some people may choose it in preference to using cars. The problem posed by accepting these facts is that towards the end of the century in a city of the size of Milton Keynes, where the average journey to work by car will take 15 minutes, demand for public transport will be limited.

The origins and destinations of journeys by public transport, given the goal of freedom of choice, will be diffused over the whole of the city. Children will need public transport for all kinds of activities whatever the income level of their family or the location of their home. The old and sick, and those who cannot or prefer not to drive cars, will be found in all sections of the community and in all parts of the city. Thus public transport has to provide for a relatively small number of journeys which are highly diffused over the whole area in which people live, work and study.

The proposals for transport therefore stem directly from the Corporation's goals. The Corporation attaches great importance to having good communications within and outside the city, whether by road or rail, or use of telecommunications and postal services.

## Balance and Variety

Many proposals in the Plan derive from the Corporation's firm intention to make Milton Keynes a city with rich variety. The Corporation is determined to achieve a wider spread of social, age and racial groups, than has hitherto been achieved and also to attract to live and work in Milton Keynes people with a wide range of incomes. Some of the employment policies that this will require have already been described. Housing policies are also related to this goal and call for an appropriate mix of housing types to attract households of different sizes and ages. It is the Corporation's aim to build a balanced stock of housing capable of meeting the requirements of a representative range of families of every size, age group and level of income. How this can be done is discussed later.

The Plan also proposes that there should be no large scale separation of different kinds of people; for instance, a west-end for the rich and an east-end for the poor, but rather that there should be a general distribution of different kinds of housing over the entire city. It also recognises, however, that the mix of housing types both for social and practical reasons cannot be taken beyond a reasonable point.

There must be some degree of grouping, but it is proposed that a range of housing types and tenure should be maintained within each of the areas bounded by the main roads and within the area served by any school. This will have the important result that every first school will be likely to draw its pupils from a variety of homes.

The existing communities in Milton Keynes present both opportunities and problems in achieving variety and balance. Their integration into the new city is crucial for its success and many of the proposals for social action in the Plan are directed to this end. In particular, the proposal for the first stage of development is based on a determination to connect together the presently separate communities to the north and south of the new city and to give them a common meeting point in the new city centre.

The success of Milton Keynes in achieving a varied community will depend in great measure on the Corporation's policies for social development and on the early provision of community services. Experience has shown the long term detrimental effect of delaying provision of these services and the Corporation is determined that they should be available in step with the population growth.

## *An Attractive City*

There are certain historic cities or parts of cities to which almost everybody responds with pleasure. The qualities that evoke this response are generated by the relationship of man-made buildings to each other and to natural features in such a way as to produce an attractive and comprehensible whole. Milton Keynes is fortunate to have an attractive setting with undulating countryside, crossed by streams and a canal and old villages threaded by lanes. With care and imagination in planning these can give colour and character to the new city.

The city is designed to encourage variety by the mixing of land uses

241

and densities, housing types and tenure, building forms and development over time. If in education, housing or shopping, the city is able to offer a wide range of choice and opportunity then this will be reflected in the variety of character of the buildings. The Corporation intends to give opportunities to many different architects to contribute to the quality of the new city.

The main road system provides a number of alternative routes between any two parts of the city and thus affords a choice of experience on even routine trips. Main roads will be designed to afford a sequence of views changing from buildings to landscape, swinging from distant vistas across open space to urban views and curving along the edges of lakes and past busy industrial complexes and shopping centres. The fact that they are planned to run at ground level, and have no elaborate multi-level interchanges means that travellers will feel in close touch with the city, and a part of it. Main roads in the form of motorways would have had the opposite effect, cutting off and disorienting the traveller.

Off the main roads strong local character will be apparent; some areas will have new housing blending with an older village, others will be crossed by canal or river, others still will have houses clustered round a school, shops and a community hall. Here the visual impact of the city will be from slow moving vehicles or on foot, and there will be variety of scene within walking distance of every home. It is the Corporation's intention that the many interesting buildings within the designated area be preserved and incorporated into the new landscape to provide the continuity and variety which a new city should offer.

Many people identify their city by the character of its central area. In Milton Keynes the new city centre is planned to give the richness and variety offered by existing cities but without their all too common traffic congestion, noise, pollution and general inconvenience. The attractiveness of the centre also depends on the chance of surprise, the random happening, unplanned meetings and exciting discoveries. There will be a mixture of uses to create the vitality of existing centres and there will be quiet squares and water, bright lights and lively places.

The attraction of Milton Keynes must stem from the quality of life enjoyed by individuals in the new city as well as from its physical appearance; the two interact on one another. The aim of the Corporation is to offer an open, mobile, accessible city, with good services that people want to come to, live in, work and retire in.

## Public Awareness and Participation

It would not be sufficient, of course, for Milton Keynes to provide the freedoms and opportunities so far described if the city's residents were not fully aware of them.

The Corporation will provide information through a wide variety of channels: the local press and the authorities providing the education, health and social services; a housing advisory service; also a local radio station, should this become a possibility.

The city should also speak for itself, through its plan and its architecture. People should be able to acquire a clear working knowledge of the city and its form through direct experience. The activity centres, the linear park, the new city centre and all other public places will be designed to make their function apparent. Thus newcomers will be helped in learning to use the city and residents will learn of changes and new developments.

A city planned to accommodate change must encourage the citizen to understand the processes of change so that he is able, if he wishes, to contribute his opinion to help direct change. Demands for public participation in planning are becoming more articulate and the Corporation will encourage this increased public interest as it believes it to be to the benefit and satisfaction of the community as a whole.

The means whereby this is achieved are part of the Corporation's wider social development responsibilities. Exhibitions, public meetings and debate, questionnaires and informative literature will all play a part in the process. The Corporation's monitoring and research services will also be geared to encourage the public to take part in the development of the city. Every effort will be made to ensure that newcomers have the opportunity to become involved in the development of the city as they arrive. In the meantime the active interest of present residents must be stimulated and their participation encouraged.

## Efficient and Imaginative Use of Resources

The Corporation is responsible for ensuring that all the resources available to it are used effectively and efficiently. By means of the Plan it must also enable investment by all other public bodies and from private sources to contribute towards the growth of the new city in the most economic way.

A comprehensive view of the resources being invested in the city is essential to meet this goal and to this end a financial appraisal has been prepared. For its part central government has assured the Corporation that all investment in Milton Keynes, controlled by the various government departments, will be co-ordinated.

The proposals in the Plan have been subjected to stringent tests to satisfy the Corporation that the Plan does represent the most efficient use of resources. For example, the costs and performance of alternative main road systems were investigated and the consultants' evidence demonstrates that the preferred concept of main roads spaced about

1 kilometre (1100 yards) apart provides the best value for money. A detailed analysis of the convenience and financial effect of alternative plans for the first ten years' growth of the new city was also carried out to enable the best plan to be chosen. Joint provision of recreation facilities by the education authority and other local authorities is another proposal intended to make efficient and imaginative use of resources.

Through its programme of monitoring and evaluation, the Corporation will assess whether or not the proposals, when implemented, are still proving to be the most effective and economic way of meeting the needs of the new city.

## 4.4 Non-plan: an experiment in freedom
*Reyner Banham, Paul Barker, Peter Hall and Cedric Price*

'A dispute has arisen about a booklet, *Dorset Building in Rural Areas*, just issued by Dorset County Council, and aspiring to be a guide to good design for people building houses in the countryside—our Architectural Correspondent writes. Most of the examples that it illustrates and recommends as models are utterly commonplace, the sort of house to be found in almost any speculative builder's suburban estate. This view is shared by the Wilts and Dorset Society of Architects, which, through its president, Mr Peter Wakefield, has asked for the publication to be withdrawn'—*The Times*, December 1968.

This news item illustrates the kind of tangle we have got ourselves into. Somehow everything must be watched; nothing must be allowed simply to 'happen.' No house can be allowed to be commonplace in the way that things just *are* commonplace: each project must be weighed, and planned, and approved, and only then built, and only after that discovered to be commonplace after all. Somehow, somewhere, someone was using the wrong year's model.

Once, Rasmussen, in *London: the Unique City* (first published 1934), thought it worth printing a picture of the entirely commonplace domestic architecture built along Parkway, Camden Town, in the early 19th century. It was architecture that worked; it provided what the inhabitants wanted from it. Now there'd be trouble if you tried to knock it down (though the London motorway box will skirt it close). But at least the preservationists didn't get in at ground level, as they do today, in order to

*Source:* New Society, 20 March, 1969, pages 435-443.

try and make sure—*before* the event—that something that will eventually be worth preserving is built.

The whole concept of planning (the town-and-country kind at least) has gone cockeyed. What we have today represents a whole cumulation of good intentions. And what those good intentions are worth, we have almost no way of knowing. To say it has been with us for so long, physical planning has been remarkably unmonitored; ditto architecture itself. As Melvin Webber has pointed out: planning is the only branch of knowledge purporting to be some kind of science which regards a plan as being *fulfilled* when it is merely *completed*; there's seldom any sort of check on whether the plan actually does what it was meant to do, and whether, if it does something different, this is for the better or for the worse.

The result is that planning tends to lurch from one fashion to another, with sudden revulsions setting in after equally sudden acceptances. One good recent example, of course, was the fashion for high flats—which had been dying for some time before Ronan Point gave it a tombstone. This fashion had been inaugurated with bizarre talk of creating 'vertical streets' which would somehow, it was implied, recreate the togetherness of Bethnal Green Road on Saturday morning in (presumably) the lift shaft—this being the only equivalent communication channel in the structure.

Not that one can be too swiftly mocking. We may yet find that for some future twist of social or technological development, tall flats are just the thing. This happened with another fashion—that for the garden city, as promulgated by Patrick Geddes, Ebenezer Howard and Raymond Unwin. It's worth remembering that the garden in this theory was there specifically to grow food in: the acreage was carefully measured out with this fodder ratio in mind. The houses in (say) Welwyn Garden City or Hampstead Garden Suburb were also scattered thinly because of the width of space allotted (for reasons of health) to the loop and sweep of roads.

Welwyn Garden City and Hampstead Garden Suburb were therefore built—and then duly mocked for dull doctrinairism. The layout made public transport almost impossible; the tin and the frozen pack rapidly outdated the vegetable patch. But then the spread of car ownership outdated the mockery: those roads lived to find a justification; the space around the house could absorb a garage without too much trouble; and the garden (as, even, in many inner-London conversions of Georgian houses) became an unexceptionable outdoor room, and meeting space for children, away from the lethal pressed steel and rubber hurtling around the streets.

Now it's nice that a plan should turn out to have reasons for succeeding which the planner himself did not foresee. At every stage in the history of planning, we have cause to be grateful for these quirks of time. It's doubtful if John Nash saw how well his Regent's Park would serve as an arty but fairly democratic pause on the north edge of inner London—just right for football and swings and non-copulating pandas and Sunday-promenading Central Europeans; inhabited not by Regency aristos but by film people, lumps of London University and HM government, the American ambassador and high-class tarts. And did Scott foresee how his St Pancras Hotel, superbly planned to fit in with departing trains and arriving horse-carriages, would survive being a much-mocked office block so successfully that it can now be argued for as a natural home for a sports centre or a transport museum or Birkbeck College?

Nor is it just the cities and towns that have benefited. How many further-education departments can be duly grateful for minor Georgian country houses, or their Victorian imitators—so apt for giving courses in? How many angling clubs can thank the canal-builders for where they spend their peaceful Sundays? How many Highlands-addicted tourists, even, depend for the solitude they love on those harsh men who preferred the glens clear of people and who planned them out of the Highlands and into Canada or Australia?

Yet it's hard to see where, in this, the credit can go to the planner. That last example—which pushes the concept of planning altogether too far—is justified as rubbing in the coerciveness of it. Most planning is aristocratic or oligarchic in method even today—revealing in this its historical origins. The most rigorously planned cities—like Haussman's and Napoleon III's Paris have nearly always been the least democratic.

The way that Haussman rebuilt Paris gladdens the tourist; it was not such a help, though, for the poor through whose homes the demolition gangs went to create those avenues and squares. Similarly, the urban renewal programmes of the American cities gladdened the real estate men; they did not help the Negroes and poor whites who were uprooted with little to compensate them. In Britain, public housing programmes gladden the housing committees and the respectable working class; they don't help the poorest, the most fissile or the most drifting families.

The point is to realise how little planning and the accompanying architecture have changed. The whole ethos is doctrinaire; and if something good emerges, it remains a bit of a bonus. Not to be expected but nice if you can get it—like totalling enough Green Shield stamps to get a Mini. At the moment, most planners in Britain are on a tautness jag: Camden's neatly interlocked squares, or Southwark's high-density juggernauts, or Cumbernauld's and the Elephant's sculptural shopping centres.

Some of these look pleasant enough now—and some don't. But the fact is that, so far as one can judge, taut arrangements last much better when plenty of money can be spent on their upkeep (Oxbridge colleges, Chelsea squares) than when it isn't (remember all those Improved Industrial Dwellings put up in the late 19th century by Mr Peabody and others?).

So it's at least plausible that some other doctrine than the current one would be right for everyday housing and building. It would be pleasant if 'doctrine' were precisely what it wasn't. But how are we to know? Planning is being subjected to increasing scepticism. The Town and Country Planning Act, 1968, tidies up some of the abuses (especially some of those which caused delay in granting permissions); and the Skeffington committee is currently trying to decide how people might be given more say ('participation,' in the jargon) in planning. The New City plan for Milton Keynes tries to shy away completely from planning. At universities, research is being done. The one thing that is not being done is the harshest test, the most valuable experiment of all. What would happen if there were no plan? What would people prefer to do, if their choice were untrammelled? Would matters be any better, or any worse, or much the same? (Might planning turn out to be rather like Eysenck's view of psychoanalysis: an activity which, insofar as it gets credit, gets it for benefits that would happen anyway—minds can cure themselves; maybe people can plan themselves?) But even if matters ended up much the same, in terms of durable successes or disastrous failures, the overall pattern would be sure to be different: the *look* of the experiment would be sure to differ from what we have now.

This is what we're now proposing: a precise and carefully observed experiment in non-planning. It's hardly an experiment one could carry out over the entire country. Some knots—like London—are, by now, far too Gordian for that. Nor are we suggesting (here) that other than physical planning should be shelved.

The right approach is to take the plunge into heterogeneity: to seize on a few appropriate zones of the country, which are subject to a characteristic range of pressures, and use them as launchpads for Non-Plan. At the least, one would find out what people want; at the most, one might discover the hidden style of mid-20th century Britain.

It's 'hidden' for the same reason that caused any good social democrat to shudder at the anarchic suggestion of the previous paragraph. Town planning is always in thrall to some outmoded rule-of-thumb; as a profession, in fact, planners tend to read the *Telegraph* and the *Express*, rather than the *Guardian* or *The Times*. Take a specific example: the filling station.

'Watch the little filling-station,' Frank Lloyd Wright said. 'It is the agent of decentralisation.' Like all focuses of transport, the filling-station could be a notable cause of change. Self-service automats, dispensing food and other goods, could spring up around the forecourt; maybe

247

small post offices, too; telephone kiosks; holiday-gear shops; eateries (*not* restaurants): all this quite apart from the standard BP Viscostatic/ ice cream/map and guidebook shop. (Thus, at Cumbernauld New Town, it's already clear that only the most repressive controls can stop the two conveniently sited filling stations from replacing the inconveniently centred town centre as shopping focus.)

Well, you can watch as long as you like in Britain, but you will see small sign of this happening. It's hard enough to get planning permission to put up a filling station in the first place. (There's still a feeling— dating probably from the hoo-ha which broke out when the Set Britain Free Tories decided to replace pool petrol in the 1950s by commercial brands—that it's very easy to have 'too many' filling stations.) To have anything else on the forecourt is almost impossible. Only in the motor- way service areas (themselves damply overplanned) is there anything like this; and here the unfortunately not unique combination of in- competence and non-spontaneity kills the whole thing.

And yet there's no doubt that the popular arts of our time (i.e. those that everyone thinks he has a valid opinion on) are car design and advertising; and these are doubly symbolised by such characteristic forecourt figures as the Esso tiger or the BP little man. The great recent soap-opera films have been Jacques Demy's *Les Parapluies de Cherbourg* (hero: a filling-station owner) and Claude Lelouch's *Un Homme et Une Femme* (hero: a racing car driver). If you drive down the French Rhone valley motorway—not so planned as ours—one of the most memorable sights is a Total petrol station, writing the letters T-O-T-A-L huge across the valley, with a flutter of flags underneath. Stay in Moscow, and you end up yearning to see a Esso sign.

Ask yourself why it is that almost the only time you ever see flags on any *unofficial* occasion—i.e. not at an ordained festival or other jam- boree, and not on a public building—is on filling-stations or else on the rear windows of cars.

Now the purpose of this is not to write a kind of Elegy in a Country Filling-Station. The purpose is to ask: why don't we dare trust the choices that would evolve if we let them? It's permissible to ask—after the dreariness of much public rebuilding, and after the Ronan Point disaster—what exactly should we sacrifice to fashion?

## SPONTANEITY AND SPACE

Any advocate of Non-Plan is sure to be misrepresented; we had better repeat what we mean. Simply to demand an end to planning, all planning, would be sentimentalism; it would deny the very basis of economic life in the second half of the 20th century.

As Galbraith has reminded us, the economies of all advanced industrial countries are planned, whether they call themselves capitalist or communist. In the United States or Japan or Germany or Britain, the need to make elaborate and long-term plans is as pressing for the individual firm, as it is for the central government. But we are arguing that the word planning itself is misused; that it has also been used for the imposition of certain physical arrangements, based on value judgments or prejudices; and that it should be scrapped.

Three developments in particular makes this argument compelling. They are developments of the last 15 years; their main force has been felt in this country in the last ten. They are: the cybernetic revolution; the mass affluence revolution; and the pop/youth culture revolution.

Cybernetics is commonly described as a technological revolution; but it is much more. It has its technological basis in the computer, as the 18th century industrial revolution had in the steam engine. But just as that revolution arose out of the intellectual ferment of the age of Newton and the Royal Society, so this has gone along with a major revolution in our ways of thought.

The essence of the new situation is that we can master vastly greater amounts of information than was hitherto thought possible—information essentially about the effect of certain defined actions upon the operation of a system. The practical implications are everywhere very large, but nowhere are they greater than in the area we loosely call planning. It is true that the science of decision-making, or management, was being developed in the United States from the 1920s, a quarter century before the cybernetic revolution; and it is almost true that it was this science of management, applied to military ends in World War Two, which made the cybernetic revolution possible.

Now, the two fields—that of scientific management, and that which embraces operations research and systems analysis—are so closely related as to be in practice inseparable. But physical planning flourished in this country when the science of management was almost unknown. Thus, simple, rule-of-thumb value judgments could be made, and were held to have perpetual validity, like tablets of the law. Since the cybernetic revolution, it has become clear that such decisions are meaningless and valueless—as indeed, ought to have become clear before. Instead, physical planning, like anything else, should consist *at most* of setting up frameworks for decision, within which as much objective information as possible can be fitted. Non-Plan would certainly provide such information. But it might do more. Even to talk of a 'general framework' is difficult. Our information about future states of the system is very poor.

If the cybernetic revolution makes our traditional planning technologically and intellectually obsolete, social change reinforces this conclusion. The revolution of rising affluence (despite the current economic

249

problems) means that a growing proportion of personal incomes will be funnelled off into ever more diverse and unpredictable outlets. Non-Plan would let them be funnelled. Galbraith (again) has shown how the modern industrial state depends on the ability to multiply wants for goods and services: certainly a large amount of prediction is involved in this. Car manufacturers have a fair idea of how many cars will be sold in 1984. Similarly with refrigerator manufacturers, colour TV set makers and purveyors of Mediterranean or Caribbean holidays.

But in detail and in combination, the effects are not easy to relate to programmes of public investment. One change, however, Non-plan would inevitably underline: as people become richer they demand more space; and because they become at the same time more mobile, they will be more able to command it. They will want this extra space in and around their houses, around their shops, around their offices and factories, and in the places where they go for recreation. To impose rigid controls, in order to frustrate people in achieving the space standards they require, represents simply the received personal or class judgments of the people who are making the decision.

Worst of all: they are judgments about how they think *other* people— not of their acquaintance or class—should live. A remarkable number of the architects and planners who advocate togetherness, themselves live among space and green fields.

This assertion may be most clearly demonstrated where different value judgments are involved. The most remarkable manifestation so far of mass affluence—above all in Britain—has been the revolution in pop culture. This is a product of newly emergent social groups and, above all, of age groups. Among the young, it has had a remarkable effect in breaking down class barriers, and replacing these by age barriers. Though pop culture is eminently capable of commercial exploitation, it is essentially a real culture, provided by people drawn from the same groups as the customers.

Most importantly for Non-Plan, it is frenetic and immediate culture, based on the rapid obsolescence cycle. Radio One's 'revived 45' is probably three months old, and on the New York art scene fashions change almost as quickly as on the King's Road. Pop culture is anti high bourgeois culture. Though it makes many statements it does not like the big statements.

All these characteristics could not be more opposed to the traditional judgments of the physical planner—which, in essence, are the values of the old bourgeois culture. Pop culture in Britain has produced the biggest visual explosion for decades—or even, in the case of fashion, for centuries. Yet its effect on the British landscape has been nil, for the simple reason that the planners have suppressed it.

Three particularly ripe examples: one, the row over the psychedelic painting on the Beatles' former 'Apple' boutique in Baker Street (objected to, and duly erased, because on a building of architectural merit—though the shop is next door but one to a fairly unreticent cinema); two, the rebuilt Jack Straw's Castle on Hampstead Heath, one of the few bits of pop fantasy to get past the taste censors, but only after a major row among the planners; three, the Prince of Wales pub in Fortune Green Road, north London, internally perhaps the most remarkable piece of pop design in Europe, externally a tedious piece of planner's Old Englishe Good Taste.

The planning system, as now constituted in Britain, is not merely negative; it has positively pernicious results. The irony is that the planners themselves constantly talk—since the appearance of Jane Jacob's *Death and Life of Great American Cities*—about the need to restore spontaneity and vitality to urban life. They never seem to draw the obvious conclusion—that the monuments of our century that have spontaneity and vitality are found not in the old cities, but in the American west.

There, in the desert and the Pacific states, creations like Fremont Street in Las Vegas or Sunset Strip in Beverly Hills represent the living architecture of our age. As Tom Wolfe points out in his brilliant essay on Las Vegas, they achieve their quality by replacing buildings by signs. In Britain you only get occasional hints of how well this could work. The prime example—Piccadilly Circus at night—is apparently so successful it needs to be *preserved*. God help us. Why preserve it? Why not simply allow other efflorescences of fluorescence in other places? Write it in neon: NON-PLAN IS GOOD FOR YOU; I DREAMT I FOUND FREEDOM IN MY NON-PLAN BRA.

To say that Las Vegas is exciting and memorable and fine is also a value judgment. It cannot be supported by facts. But except for a few conservation areas which we wish to preserve as living museums, physical planners have no right to set their value judgment up against yours, or indeed anyone else's. If the Non-Plan experiment works really well, people should be allowed to build what they like. (Oh, and a word for the preservationists: much easier to relieve pressure on medieval town centres by letting the edges of the city sprawl, and give people chance to shop there in drive-in suburban superstores, than by brooding on inner-relief roads or whatever.)

At the very least, Non-Plan would provide accurate information to fit into a 'community investment plan.' The balance of costs and benefits to the individual is not the same as to the community. If there are social costs, the people who are responsible pay them. If low-density development is expensive to the community, the reaction should be to make it proportionately expensive to those who live in it; not to stop it. The notion that the planner has the right to say what is 'right' is really an extraordinary hangover from the days of collectivism in left-wing thought, which has long ago been abandoned elsewhere.

We seem so afraid of freedom. But Britain shouldn't be a Peter Pan Edwardian nursery. Let it at least move into the play school era: why should only the under-sevens be allowed their bright materials, their gay constructions, their wind-up Daleks. In that world, Marx is best known as the maker of plastic, battery-driven dump trucks. Let's become that sort of marxist.

Let's save our breath for genuine problems—like the poor who are increasingly with us. And let's Non-Plan at least some problems of planning into oblivion.

# 4.5 Creating a new social system *The Ecologist*

Possibly the most radical change we propose in the creation of a new social system is decentralization. We do so not because we are sunk in nostalgia for a mythical little England of fêtes, olde worlde pubs, and perpetual conversations over garden fences, but for four much more fundamental reasons.

1. While there is good evidence that human societies can happily remain stable for long periods, there is no doubt that the long transitional stage that we and our children must go through will impose a heavy burden on our moral courage and will require great restraint. Legislation and the operations of police forces and the courts will be necessary to reinforce this restraint, but we believe that such external controls can never be so subtle or so effective as internal controls. It would therefore be sensible to promote the social conditions in which public opinion and full public participation in decision-making become as far as possible the means whereby communities are ordered. The larger a community the less likely this can be: in a heterogeneous, centralized society such as ours, the restraints of the stable society if they were to be effective would appear as so much outside coercion; but in communities small enough for the general will to be worked out and expressed by individuals confident of themselves and their fellows as individuals, 'us and them' situations are less likely to occur—people having learned the limits of a stable society would be free to order their own lives within them as they wished, and would therefore accept the restraints of the stable society

*Source:* 'A blueprint for survival,' *The Ecologist*, **2**, number 1, January 1972, pages 14–17

as necessary and desirable and not as some arbitrary restriction imposed by a remote and unsympathetic government.

2. As agriculture depends more and more on integrated control and becomes more diversified, there will no longer be any scope for prairie-type crop-growing or factory-type livestock-rearing. Small farms run by teams with specialized knowledge of ecology, entomology, botany, etc. will then be the rule, and indeed individual small-holdings could become extremely productive suppliers of eggs, fruit and vegetables to neighbour-hoods. Thus a much more diversified urban-rural mix will be not only possible but, because of the need to reduce the transportation costs of returning domestic sewage to the land, desirable. In industry, as with agriculture, it will be important to maintain a vigorous feedback between supply and demand in order to avoid waste, overproduction, or pro-duction of goods which the community does not really want, thereby eliminating the needless expense of time, energy and money in attempts to persuade it that it does. If an industry is an integral part of a com-munity, it is much more likely to encourage product innovation because people clearly want qualitative improvements in a given field, rather than because expansion is necessary for that industry's survival or because there is otherwise insufficient work for its research and develop-ment section. Today, men, women and children are merely consumer markets, and industries as they centralize become national rather than local and supranational rather than national, so that while entire communities may come to depend on them for the jobs they supply, they are in no sense integral parts of those communities. To a consider-able extent the 'jobs or beauty' dichotomy has been made possible because of this deficiency. Yet plainly people want jobs *and* beauty, they should not in a just and humane society be forced to choose between the two, and in a decentralized society of small communities where industries are small enough to be responsive to each community's needs there will be no reason for them to do so.

3. The small community not only is the organizational structure in which internal or systemic controls are most likely to operate effectively, but its dynamic is an essential source of stimulation and pleasure for the individual. Indeed it is probable that only in the small community can a man or woman be an individual. In today's large agglomerations he is merely an isolate—and it is significant that the decreasing autonomy of communities and local regions and the increasing centralization of decision-making and authority in the cumbersome bureaucracies of the state, have been accompanied by the rise of self-conscious individualism, and individualism which feels threatened unless it is harped upon. Perhaps the two are mutually dependent. It is no less significant that this self-conscious individualism tends to be expressed in ways which cut off one individual from another—for example the accumulation of

material goods like the motor-car, the television set, and so on, all of which tend to insulate one from another, rather than bring them together. In the small, self-regulating communities observed by anthropologists, there is by contrast no assertion of individualism, and certain individual aspirations may have to be repressed or modified for the benefit of the community—yet no man controls another and each has very great freedom of action, much greater than we have today. At the same time they enjoy the rewards of the small community, of knowing and being known, of an intensity of relationships with a few, rather than urban man's variety of innumerable, superficial relationships. Such rewards should provide ample compensation for the decreasing emphasis on consumption, which will be the inevitable result of the premium on durability which we have suggested should be established so that resources may be conserved and pollution minimized. This premium, while not diminishing our real standard of living, will greatly reduce the turnover of material goods. They will thus be more expensive, although once paid for they should not need replacing except after long periods. Their rapid accumulation will no longer be a realizable or indeed socially acceptable goal, and alternative satisfactions will have to be sought. We believe a major potential source of these satisfactions to be the rich and variegated interchanges and responsibilities of community life, and that these are possible only when such communities are on a human scale.

4. The fourth reason for decentralization is that to deploy a population in small towns and villages is to reduce to the minimum its impact on the environment. This is because the actual urban superstructure required per inhabitant goes up radically as the size of the town increases beyond a certain point. For example, the *per capita* cost of high rise flats is much greater than that of ordinary houses; and the cost of roads and other transportation routes increases with the number of commuters carried. Similarly, the *per capita* expenditure on other facilities such as those for distributing food and removing wastes is much higher in cities than in small towns and villages. Thus, if everybody lived in villages the need for sewage treatment plants would be somewhat reduced, while in an entirely urban society they are essential, and the cost of treatment is high. Broadly speaking, it is only by decentralization that we can increase self-sufficiency—and self-sufficiency is vital if we are to minimize the burden of social systems on the ecosystems that support them.

Although we believe that the small community should be the basic unit of society and that each community should be as self-sufficient and self-regulating as possible, we would like to stress that we are not proposing that they be inward-looking, self-obsessed or in any way closed to the rest of the world. Basic precepts of ecology, such as the interrelatedness of all things and the far-reaching effects of ecological processes and their disruption, should influence community decision-making, and therefore there must be an efficient and sensitive communications network between all communities. There must be procedures whereby community actions that affect regions can be discussed at regional level and regional actions with extra-regional effects can be discussed at global level. We have no hard and fast views on the size of the proposed communities, but for the moment we suggest neighbourhoods of 500, represented in communities of 5000, in regions of 500 000, represented nationally, which in turn as today should be represented globally. We emphasize that our goal should be to create *community feeling* and *global awareness*, rather than that dangerous and sterile compromise which is nationalism.

In many of the developed countries where community feeling has been greatly eroded and has given way to heterogeneous congeries of strangers, the task of re-creating communities will be immensely difficult. In many of the undeveloped countries, however, although it will not be easy, because the process of community collapse and flight to the city has begun only recently there is a real chance that it can be halted by such means as the abandonment of large-scale industrial projects for the development of intermediate technologies at village level; and the provision of agro-ecological training teams so that communities can be taught to manage the land together, rather than encourage farmers to turn to expensive and dangerous procedures like the heavy use of pesticides and fertilizers, which tend to reduce the number of people needed on the land.

At home, industry will play a leading role in the programme to decentralize our economy and society. The discussion of taxes, anti-disamenity legislation, and enforceable targets for air, land and water quality in the section on stock economics might lead some to believe that we are willing to bring about the collapse of industry, widespread unemployment, and the loss of our export markets. It is therefore worth emphasizing that we wish strongly to avoid all three, and we do not see that they are necessary or inevitable consequences of our proposals. It is obvious that for as long as we depend on imports for a significant proportion of our food, so we must export. And since we are likely to require food-imports for the next 150 years, we are left with the question of whether it is possible to develop community industries, dedicated to the principles of maximal use/recycling of materials and durability of goods, and at the same time to earn an adequate revenue from exports.

We believe that the answer is yes, if the change-over is conducted in two stages. The first stage is to alter the direction of growth so that it becomes more compatible with the aims of a stable society. We have already mentioned that the recycling industry must be encouraged to

255

expand, and it is obvious that willy-nilly it will do so as over the years taxes and quality targets become more stringent. To give a clearer idea of how the direction can be altered we will consider briefly the question of transport.

There are more than 12 million cars in Britain today, and according to the Automobile Association this figure will rise to 21 million by 1981. About half the households in Britain own a car today, and presumably the car population is expected to rise in response to a rise in this proportion, though presumably, too, more households will own more than one car. At all events we have sufficient experience of traffic congestion in our towns and cities and the rape of countryside and community by ring-roads and motorways to realize that the motor-car is by no means the best way of democratizing mobility. Indeed, if every household had a car, we would be faced with the choice of leaving towns and country worth driving to and thereby imposing immobility on the motorist, or of providing him with the vast expanses of concrete which are becoming increasingly necessary to avoid congestion at the expense of the areas they sterilize and blight.

No one can contemplate with equanimity the doubling of roads within this decade necessary to maintain the *status quo*, and we must therefore seek sensible transportation alternatives. It is clear that broadly speaking the only alternative is public transport—a mix of rapid mass-transit by road and rail. Rail especially should never have been allowed to run down to the extent that it has. The power requirements for transporting freight by road are five to six times greater than by rail and the pollution is correspondingly higher. The energy outlay for the cement and steel required to build a motorway is three to four times greater than that required to build a railway, and the land area necessary for the former is estimated to be four times more than for the latter. Public transport whether by road or rail is much more efficient in terms of *per capita* use of materials and energy than any private alternative. It can also be as flexible, provided it is encouraged at the expense of private transport.

This is the key to the provision of a sound transportation system. First the vicious spiral of congestion slowing buses, losing passengers, raising fares, losing more passengers, using more cars, creating more congestion, etc. must be broken. A commitment to build no more roads and to use the capital released to subsidize public transport would be an excellent way of doing this. The men who would normally live by road-building could be diverted to clearing derelict land and restoring railways and canals as part of a general programme of renewal. From there, the progressive imposition of restrictions on private transport and the stimulation of public transport so that it could provide a fast, efficient and flexible alternative would be a matter of course. Within the motor industry, the decline in production of conventional private vehicles would be compensated for by the increased production of alternative mass-transit systems. There would also be a switch of capital and manpower to the redevelopment of railway systems. In the long term, however, decentralization will bring a diminished demand for mobility itself. As Stephen Boyden (1971) has pointed out, people use their cars for four main reasons: to go to work, to go to the countryside, to visit friends and relations, and to show off. In the stable society, however, each community will provide its own jobs, there will be countryside around it, most friends and relations will be within it, and there will be much more reliable and satisfying ways of showing off.

This brings us to the second stage of the change-over, in which industry turns to the invention, production, and installation of technologies that are materials and energy conservative, that are flexible, non-polluting and durable, employment-intensive and favouring craftsmanship. Progress as we conceive of it today consists in increasing an already arbitrarily high ratio of capital to job availability; but if instead this ratio were to be reduced, then our manpower requirement would go up, while at the same time the pollution which is the inevitable by-product of capital growth would be cut down. The switch in emphasis from quantity to quality will not only stimulate demand for manpower, it will also stabilize it *and* give much greater satisfaction to the men themselves. Instead of men being used as insensate units to produce increasing quantities of components, they should be trained and given the opportunity to improve the quality of their work. The keynotes of the manufacturing sector should come to be durability and craftsmanship—and such a premium on quality should assure us an export revenue large enough for us to continue buying food from abroad, while providing our manpower with more enjoyable occupations. In the case of industries like the aircraft industry, which would naturally have a greatly reduced role in the stable society, their engineering expertise could be turned to the development of such things as total energy systems—designed to provide the requirements of a decentralized society with the minimum of environmental disruption.

Industry can completely fulfil its new role only in close harmony with particular communities, so that the unreal distinction between men as employees and men as neighbours can be abandoned, and jobs then given on the basis that work must be provided by the community for the sake of that community's stability and not because one group wishes to profit from another group's labour or capital as the case may be. As industry decentralizes so will the rest of society. The creation of communities will come from the combination of industrial change and a conscious drive to restructure society.

The principal components of this drive are likely to be the redistribution of government and the gradual inculcation of a sense of community and the other values of a stable society. Over a stated period of time, local government should be strengthened and as many functions as possible of central government should be transferred to it. The redistribution of government should proceed on the principle that issues which affect only neighbourhoods should be decided by the neighbourhood alone, those which affect only communities by the community alone, those which affect only regions by the region alone, and so on. As regions, communities and neighbourhoods come increasingly to run their own affairs, so the development of a sense of community will proceed more easily, though we do not pretend that it will be without its problems.

Those regions which still have or are close to having a good urban-rural mix will be able to effect a relatively smooth transfer, but highly urbanized areas like London, the Lancashire conurbation, and South Wales will find it much more difficult to re-create communities. Nevertheless, even in London the structural remains of past communities (like the villages of Putney, Highgate, Hackney, Islington, etc.) will provide the physical nuclei of future communities—the means of orienting themselves so that they can cut themselves away from those deserts of commerce and packaged pleasure (of which the most prominent example is the Oxford Street, Regent Street, Piccadilly complex) on which so much of London's life is currently focused.

It is self-evident that no amount of legislative, administrative or industrial change will create stable communities if the individuals who are meant to comprise them are not fitted for them. As soon as the best means of inculcating the values of the stable society have been agreed upon, they should be incorporated into our educational systems. Indeed, it may not be until the generation of 40–50 year olds have been educated in these values (so that as far as possible everybody up to the age of 50 understands them) that stable communities will achieve sufficient acceptance for them to be permanently useful.

## Reference

BOYDEN, S. (1971) Environmental change: perspectives and responsibilities. *Journal of the Soil Association* (October).

# 4.6 Major changes in environmental form required by social and psychological demands
## Christopher Alexander

| community scale | I | II | III | I | II | III | IV | V | VI | VII | VIII | IX | X | XI | XII |
|---|---|---|---|---|---|---|---|---|---|---|---|---|---|---|---|
| eristic units | 1 | 2 | 3 | 4 | 5 | 6 | 7 | 8 | 9 | 10 | 11 | 12 | 13 | 14 | 15 |
| | man | room | dwelling | dwelling group | small neigh-bourhood | neighbour-hood | small town | town | large city | metropolis | conurbation | megalopolis | urban region | urbanized continent | ecumeno polis |
| nature | | | | | | | | | | | | | | | |
| man | | | | | | | | | | | | ● | | | |
| society | | | | | | | | | | | | ● | | | |
| shells | | | | | | | | | | | | ● | | | |
| networks | | | | | | | | | | | | | | | |
| synthesis | | | | | | | | | | | | ▒ | | | |

*I*

There is a strange dichotomy between the present architecture and planning professions. On the one hand, the architects are in the habit of creating completely mad idealistic utopias. These utopias often have little meaning, they are unlikely to be implemented; often no one in his right mind would want to implement them. They are personal dreams, not anchored in reality. Archigram's city on legs is an extreme example.

On the other hand, the current generation of city and regional planners —and the regional scientists are included—have established a tradition of boring attention to detailed facts, and extrapolation from these facts. The future, as seen by planners, is merely a tidier version of the present. While architects dream of utterly unimaginable futures, the planners talk about piece-meal incremental planning. The visionary architecture is imaginative, daring, but completely mad. The planners' plans are utterly and boringly sane; though based on facts, they offer no comprehensive vision of a better future.

*Source: Ekistics*, **48**, 1969, pages 78–85.

We may strengthen these statements. It is no exaggeration to say that many of the most imaginative utopian architects actually dislike facts, and have a kind of supercilious disregard for them. And it is no exaggeration either to say that the kind of data gathering which planners most often do, since it is based on data about the status quo, tends to reinforce the status quo; and that planners—perhaps because of their concern with this kind of data—tend to have a rather conservative attitude.

This split is more serious than it seems. It is more than a mere difference of philosophy between the two professions. What it amounts to is this. We have not found a way of making a coherent, criticisable and empirically founded statement about the kind of future we want for the living of life in cities. So long as the split between utopians and data gatherers persists, it will not be possible to make such a statement. The reason is obvious. A statement of this kind will require vital imagination about man's future, based on empirical insights about the really deep forces in a man's life.

The possibility of constructing serious utopias in this sense is being set back, at present, by two beliefs—widely held by planners in the United States.

1. The first of these beliefs says that the physical form of the environment has very little effect on behavior—hence, that the physical form of the environment is not very important socially. According to this view we can tolerate architecture as a kind of amusement which has to do with beauty—the sugar on the cake—but we are supposed to recognise that it really has very little to do with the problem of making cities better to live in. Since most of the 'comprehensive' urban utopians have been physical ones, designed by architects, this belief functions as a kind of backhand attack on utopian thinking.

2. The second belief—not so explicitly stated as the first—says that psychological insights, while no doubt interesting, are as yet too vaguely formulated to have any serious bearing on urban form. According to this view concern with the nature of life cannot have any serious bearing on the day to day work of the urban and regional planner.

As we shall see, both of these beliefs, though clothed in scientific reasonableness, are in fact merely offshoots of the more general refusal of city planners today to make a concrete statement of what life is all about. Let me say a few more words about each of these beliefs.

What about the first belief, that the physical environment has little effect on behavior. This belief has only come into play during the last few years when planners and architects have been claiming that they can influence people's wellbeing by manipulating the physical environment. A typical statement was Neutra's: 'Let me design a house for a happily married couple, and I can have them divorced within six months.' This sort of arrogance naturally invited suspicion. People have begun to quote the famous Hawthorne experiment—where it was shown that the crucial variable, responsible for increased production and worker well-being in an electric plant, was the attitude of management, not the pleasantness of the physical environment. Another famous study of workers in northern California, examined their life style while living in a high density slum in Richmond, and then three years later, their life style living in a low density suburban area of single family houses; their life styles had not changed in any significant respect.

The recent statements by Webber and others, which show that social groupings are not based on spatial proximity, but rather on communality of interest, have been widely received. The planners who take this idea to its most extreme form, say: let the urban sprawl go on any way it wants to—what really matters are the economic and social organizations, not the spatial. This general attitude has gone so far now in the United States that many intelligent students and young professionals have become convinced that the spatial organization of cities does not really matter much—and have gone into other, more obviously social, fields.

What about the second belief; that psychological problems are too subtle to be taken seriously. I have never actually seen this belief expressed in print. But it is reasonable to infer it, from the subjects which planners most often deal with. In urban planning and regional science, two closely associated disciplines predominate: Economics of location, and transportation theory. It is not unfair to say that 90% of the literature on regional science deals with one of these two topics. Even in the architectural literature, where there are occasional references to psychological questions, they are almost never seriously studied.

It is perhaps helpful to ask *why* the regional science literature is so heavily weighted towards the problems of economics and transportation. The answer is very simple. Since these are two disciplines where reasonable models can be made with the help of arithmetic and elementary mathematics, and since the people who started out to develop regional science were enthusiastic 'model builders', wanted to be scientific and precise, and loved playing with numbers, the field of urban planning got slanted in this direction. If you press a regional scientist, and ask him why he does not take social and psychological problems more seriously, he will say that he would like to, but unfortunately these subjects are not yet sufficiently precise, and nothing sensible can be done with them.

## II

I shall now give a series of examples, to show that these two beliefs are mistaken; and to show that, in a modest way, careful consideration of psychological problems will lead to major revisions of environmental form.

261

To begin with, we must face squarely, just what the task of city planning is: it is, in short, the design of culture. A culture is a system of standard situations. Each of these situations specifies certain roles, certain allowed limits of behavior for the persons in these roles, and the requisite spatial setting for this behavior. Each situation thus specifies a certain physical pattern—and each pattern recurs many thousands of times in a given city. The form of the city is generated by the combination of these patterns. In this sense, the city, viewed as a purely physical system, is a direct concrete manifestation of the culture. Any attempt to change the physical organization is an indirect attempt to change the culture. That is why I say that city planning is the design of culture.

Now, each person in a culture lives his life by moving from situation to situation—he builds his life up as a kind of necklace—by stringing together those situations which are available to him in his culture. In a successful culture, the set of situations which is available to him is sufficient to allow all the inner forces which develop in him, free play. In order to criticise a culture, we must find in the lives of its members recurrent situations which expose the members to conflicts which they cannot resolve within the framework of the cultural institutions and situations that the culture normally makes available to them. We may then try to invent new institutions, or institutionalized situations, compatible with the rest of the culture, but capable of letting people resolve this conflict for themselves.

In order to make such a criticism, we need to know something rather concrete about the inner forces which a person is typically exposed to during the course of his life: otherwise, we cannot say what kinds of conflict he will experience. Recent work in psychology and social psychology has done much to help us here. It will perhaps help to make this clear, if I first mention a very early view of human needs, presented by Bronislaw Malinowski. Malinowski said that a culture is a system of institutions designed to satisfy seven basic needs: metabolism, reproduction, bodily comfort, safety, movement, growth and health.

This view does not help us to criticise the culture of a metropolitan United States at all. At this level of analysis, we have every right to be satisfied with our culture. We do have food supply, housing, transportation, schools, parks and hospitals. All we need is more of them, perhaps. But these seven basic needs give an extremely mechanistic view of man's nature. More recent study of needs has shown us a rather more complex picture. Consider, for example, the work of Alexander Leighton, Abraham Maslow, and Erik Erikson.

Leighton indentifies ten basic strivings in man: physical security; sexual satisfaction; the expression of hostility; the securing of love; the securing of recognition; the expression of spontaneity; orientation in terms of one's place in society; the securing and maintenance of membership in a definite human group; and the sense of belonging to a moral order and being right in what one does.

If we assume that these ten strivings are at work in adults, then it already becomes rather clearer that our present culture does not always provide an adequate system of institutions for the expression of these strivings. And, as Leighton says, frustration of these strivings leads not to physical death, but to psychiatric disorder and to spiritual death.

Maslow has described a hierarchical system of evolutionary needs. According to his view, once the basic system of food and drink needs has been met, the system of security and safety needs comes into play. Once these safety needs are being met, a system of need for affection comes into play; and once this system of affection needs is being met, the individual experiences a need for self actualisation—development of the self. In advanced economies the earlier systems are usually met, and the later systems are the most important. The last of all, the effort towards self actualisation is a system which is very inadequately met by people in modern western culture, and the culture does little to support it.

Erikson takes a developmental view. According to this view, each person goes through eight major stages during the course of his life. At each stage the person is fighting a particular spiritual battle: Erikson calls them crises. A healthy person must win each of these battles in order to be able to go on to the next; if any one of the crises is met unsuccessfully, development cannot go on to the next stage: the person gets stuck. The eight stages are:

| | |
|---|---|
| Basic trust—mistrust . . . . . | Infant |
| Autonomy—shame/doubt . | Infant |
| Initiative—guilt . . . . . . . . | Child |
| Industry—inferiority . . . . . | Child |
| Identity—role confusion . . . | Teenager |
| Intimacy—isolation . . . . . . | Young adult |
| Generativity—stagnation . . | Adult . |
| Ego integrity—despair . . . . | Old age |

Again, there is abundant clinical evidence to show that the system of institutions which our culture provides does not give each person a reasonable chance of meeting each of these crises successfully.

With the help of these notions, I shall now state a number of typical recurrent problems, which cannot be solved within the framework of our existing culture. In each case I shall propose a pattern which may help to solve the problem. (Many of these patterns were developed at the Center for Environmental Structure, Berkeley.) I define a pattern as a new cultural institution, together with the physical and spatial changes needed to provide a setting for this new institution. These patterns are intended for the present culture of the metropolitan United States.

In each case, I have tried to put each of these proposals on an empirical basis. I do not claim that any one of these patterns is correct as stated. I am merely trying to show the order of magnitude of the changes which careful consideration of psychological issues will lead to. However, to make this point, it is important to show that these patterns are not merely products of idle dreaming, and are not merely 'utopian' in the bad old architectural sense. I shall therefore propose one or more experiments which could be carried out in connection with each of these patterns, to test its validity.

Each pattern is stated in three parts:

a. A brief summary of the pattern itself.
b. A brief summary of the problem which the pattern solves (with notes showing the relevant concepts in Leighton, Erikson and Maslow).
c. A collection of short refutable hypotheses which, when made more precise, could be used to test the validity of the pattern.

The statements are very sketchy—no more than shorthand. After the statements of the individual patterns, I describe a city where these* and other patterns are present together.

## III

1. Cells. Many small residential areas (diameter 200'–2000'), each one a different subculture—the total variety of subcultures far greater than today, and also the variety of subcultures per square mile greater than today. (Hendricks, Alexander)

People seek their own kind. Character formation. Self-actualization. Require support of 'Same kind of people'. This requires great variety of people. Also requires exposure to many types of people. Requires safety affection all OK. (Maslow, self actualization. Leighton, Orientation.)

Hypotheses.

a. Physical barrier helps formation of more distinct subculture. Homogeneous continuous development prevents formation of subcultures.
b. Support of differentiated subculture helps character formation.
c. Exposure to variety of different subcultures allows fuller choice, and therefore leads to self actualization.
d. Subcultures latent in modern city are very numerous.
e. Provision of appropriate facilities will induce formation of subculture.

---

*Pressure for space has caused us to reduce the number of patterns described in detail from 20 to 9 [Editors].

2. Roads. Cellular network of one-way thigh-speed arteries (parallel, cellular, hexagonal doesn't matter). (Walkey, Hershdorfer, Alexander.) People seek greater average speeds, and will stick to private vehicles as far as possible. Contact. Spontaneity. (Leighton, Expression of love, Securing of love, Spontaneity.)

Hypotheses.

a. For a given arrangement of origin destinations a network of largely one-way arteries optimizes flow (*i.e.* average speed). (Hershdorfer)
b. Capacity of such arterial loops is very large—can clear as many as 8000 cars per hour. (Walkey)
c. Friendship satisfaction varies with the number of acquaintances who can be reached in five minutes.
d. Average number of planned versus unplanned encounters correlates with disorders of spontaneity. (Clinical)

3. Small group work. Scattered semi-autonomous employment—each large organization consisting of many smaller units—loosely connected by phone, etc. Each one largely autonomous.

Efficiency of work. Understanding of the purpose of work. Autonomy, self determination. Self respect. Split work/play. (Erikson, Generativity. Maslow, Self actualization. Leighton, Membership in definite human group.)

Hypotheses.

a. Work efficiency improves under small work conditions.
b. Small work groups report better satisfaction on the part of workers.
c. Work quality, quantity, and worker satisfaction decrease as number of levels of administrative hierarchy increases.
d. Number of cases of mental illness in individual or his family correlated with number of levels of hierarchy above him.
e. Spatial centralization of work effort not correlated with overall efficiency of output.
f. Split in work/play has an effect on mental picture of the world. Test by Osgoods method.
g. Test resentment of wives, children, on not knowing the purpose or details of husbands' work.
h. Under present circumstances few real friends at work. Depth of friendships at work correlated with size of autonomous group.
i. Work efficiency and involvement go up when work/play cycle is freed to each individual's own rhythm. (Schnelle)

4. Old age islands. Each one holds about 75 people (50–100). Scattered as widely as possible, so that they occur in every type of neighbourhood —*i.e.* every type of cell. (Falor)

265

On the one hand, economies of scale—shared facilities, etc. On the other hand, need for interaction with rest of society—both for old and for young. At present old people forced into large relatively isolated aggregations by cost, and by old age cities. (Erikson, Ego integrity—despair. Leighton, Human group.)

Hypotheses.

a. Disease incidence higher among adults who are separated from the young. (Liverpool)
b. Fear of death higher among young people with little contact with old people.
c. Old age trauma (retirement) worse for people who have not had contact with the old.
d. Old people want to live where other old people are: how large must colony be before this want dies out.
e. Retirement trauma improved if people can go on living in the same general type of neighbourhood. (Falor)

5. Schools open to the city, connected with other functions, not closed. Integrated with work-study in commercial institutions. (Hoare and Silverstein)

Adolescent feels disconnected from society. Compare with village culture. Hence no possibility of identity formation; and disenchantment. (Leighton, Recognition. Erikson, Identity.)

Hypotheses.

a. Feeling of teenage alienation inversely correlated with degree of work-study.
b. Gradual mastery of real tasks correlated with strong identity formation (cf. East African example). (Clinical)
c. Correlation of learning speed with relevance of material. (Bruner)
d. Negative correlation between teenage alienation and effective participation in social institutions during childhood.

6. University. Loose aggregation of small centers. Mainly small group work. Use of all members of society in this process. Especially women, old people. No closed campus.

All people involved in the process of education. Adult education. Learning-teaching. Handing on insights to next generation (anthropology). Women's university in Los Angeles. Chinese commune. Life a process, going in and out of university continuously. Budget will not permit seminar type s/f ratio under present circumstances. Giving courses as common as taking them. (Leighton, Orientation. Erikson, Generativity.)

Hypotheses.

a. Research shifting more and more to small centers and institutes.
b. Increase in adult education.
c. More learned by teacher than by student.
d. Greatest influence on education had in small group study. (Midwest)
e. Satisfaction of adults (note specially women and old) related to the extent to which they see themselves as handing on information, culture, etc., to next generation.


7. Group houses. Dwellings where group of people, married and/or single, live in commune.

Family too small. Tensions. Huxley Island. Need for more mixed, less intense, contact-balancing out tensions; close contact with more people. (Erikson, Intimacy. Leighton, Hostility.)

Hypotheses.

a. Increasing tendency for people to seek such arrangements today: (music groups, spread of Kibbutzim, *Telluride*, summer houses.)
b. Correlation of mental health with average size of household. (Indirect evidence of this in high mental health of Italian and Hong Kong areas.)


8. Child care. In areas where families with small children live, each house opens off a common area which is entirely enclosed—connected to nursery supervision.

Small children need each other in play.

Danger to them on streets.

Parents want to go out.

Hypotheses.

a. Greater incidence of mental illness among children who have no playmates in first five years.
b. Correlation between mental trouble for child, and non-activity of mother. (When mother is educated.) (Mead)
c. Even where there are efficient nurseries, away from home, amount of use is considerably reduced. (Denmark)
d. Incidence of child trouble caused by conflict by keeping child in, against wishes, cf. reports of how wonderfully manageable children are, when they can play together, in unlimited amounts.


9. City hall small (max. population, 40 000), and highly accessible place for discussion, complaint, political action. *cf.* Multi-service centers. (Alexander, Ishikawa, Silverstein)

Political effectiveness. Small units. Culture of poverty. (Erikson, Generativity. Leighton, Moral order, Spontaneity, Orientation.) Hypotheses.

a. Need for political action exists; compare well being of those with involvement with those without it. (Check across cultures.)
b. Hopelessness is correlated with non-effectiveness.
c. Effectiveness of citizens a function of the size of community.
d. Involvement correlated with ease of access to city hall, and possibility of starting programs there.
e. Maximum size of institution still capable retaining informal atmosphere, freedom from red-tape, is about 20 persons.

## IV

These patterns are only a few of hundreds of similar large scale patterns which must be combined to create the full form of an urban environment. Nor have I mentioned the literally thousands of patterns at smaller scales, which will combine to give the detailed form of buildings. And I have not described the combinatory rules which allow us to put these few patterns together. However, few as they are, they already begin to define a radically different city from the cities we live in today.

There is no CPD. The city consists of hundreds of small residential islands, each with a different subculture. Density is high at the edge of these islands, and falls off towards the center of each one. The islands are widely separated, and surrounded, by a sea of employment and communal facilities. Also winding around the islands there are nets of high speed one way arteries. All employment is radically decentralised— even when a corporation is large, it consists of many small autonomous group-run workshops. The university and schools are woven in and out of the entire fabric of the city. They do not exist as distinct entities. The process of education is going on all the time, and involves all members of the culture. Houses and households have a much greater variety of size and type than they do today. Some are group houses, in which many individuals live together. At the other extreme there are individual cottages for teenagers and old people. Some houses, for families with small children, surround inaccessible shared gardens which touch all the houses but cannot be reached directly from outside. In some cases, as for teenagers, the one room cottages are attached to larger houses. Thus we shall find many dwelling units grouped hierarchically around slightly larger ones, and these larger ones in turn again grouped hierarchically in larger groups. None of these dwellings will be high-rise in the modern sense—all houses will have at least some part where they come into open, visible contact with the outside. All the dwellings are owned. The city is dotted with many tiny knots of trees, undisturbed by demolition or construction. Many of the cells contain colonies of old people—these colonies smaller than the basic cells themselves—where life runs a little more slowly. There are many kinds of highly specialised places devoted to public meeting—the teenage cruising strip, and covered discussion seats, and the new kind of highly accessible city hall which I described are merely examples. The detailed structure of all these buildings, especially the dwellings, is such that the final details are personal. The walls and materials are capable of remembering the touch of the inhabitants who live there—they are rich with detailed individual adaptations. The sterile thin panels of today will be unknown.

Even without making drawings, or models, or filling in the details, I think it is clear that this is a kind of city utterly different from the one in which we live today.

I do not expect you to agree with the particular patterns which I have presented—on the basis of the scant evidence I have given. That was not my purpose in this paper. What is clear is that physical conceptions as radical as the one which I have sketched out, can be reached on the basis of common sense discussion of the issues concerning human nature, as they are known to anthropologists and psychologists today. Everyone of the patterns which I have described can be discussed, tested, and improved, on the basis of simple, feasible experiments. Yet the overall picture thus presented is as radical, as utopian as the visions of classical artist-architects.

Let us review the two detailed questions which I began with: Are psychological matters too subtle to handle; does the physical form of the environment have an effect on behavior.

First of all, these examples will hardly allow us to accept the view of regional scientists and planners who claim that economic location and transportation—because they can be quantified—are the only problems which can be competently handled. Even the material which I have presented is enough, I think, to discredit the idea that social psychology is too vague to play a useful part in city planning, or too subtle to take seriously. The issues which I have mentioned are, indeed, so unsubtle, so massive, that we tend to pass them by in our everyday lives, as being hopelessly unamenable to change. They are not subtle. We are all aware of them. In order to take these issues seriously, we need only have the courage to take them seriously. Although the scientific evidence which shows that these demands are critical is admittedly weak, this is only, I believe, because we have not so far tried to find evidence of this kind. The idea that we should consciously try to design our own culture, seems crazy at the first sight—and so much so that people simply haven't been trying to gather the right kind of evidence.

Secondly, we come to the question: 'Does the environment influence behavior?' This is a curiously mechanistic and behavioristic question. Of course the physical environment, *alone*, has little effect on human behavior or welfare. Can we seriously expect that the position of a wall is going to make us happy, rather than unhappy. We are not rats in a conditioning experiment. But the conclusion which planners have been drawing from this obvious point—namely, that therefore the organization of the physical environment does not matter much—is false. I have given a number of examples of psychological demands which occur in metropolitan United States. The examples show that if we take these demands seriously, and try to invent cultural institutions which deal with these demands, we shall then have to make major physical changes in the environment. In every case, the argument which connects the psychological demands with the change in spatial pattern is simple and common sense. What does this prove? It does not prove that the environment has an effect upon behavior. I have not claimed, in any one of the examples, that the form of buildings *alone* will have an influence on people's lives, on their behavior, or their needs. In every case, the pattern of walls or doors or buildings that I have specified, is specified along with some kind of social change. The environmental change, without the social, would accomplish nothing. But the reverse is also true. These social changes cannot be made unless the physical changes are made with them. There is no more point in trying to make the social change without the physical, than vice versa.

Let me finally stress, once again, the extremely tentative nature of the patterns which I have proposed, and the empirical results which I have based them on. Experiments in social psychology are notoriously difficult, and always subject to interpretation. However, even the scant evidence which I have presented has clear implications. And, I believe, once it is made clear that new patterns may be derived from these empirical insights, this will greatly sharpen our ability to find evidence. The evidence which I have cited so far has accumulated more or less randomly. If patterns of the type I have described are defined first, and empirical studies made second, with the process of empirical observation specifically designed to refute, or support, hypotheses connected with individual patterns, the whole process will be greatly sharpened.

But I do not apologise for the tentative nature of the patterns. Indeed, in a way it expresses rather clearly their most important feature: the fact that they are set up to be criticised. They are deliberately open to criticism. They invite it.

Each one is stated in such a way that it can be criticized by experiment and observation. This gives each person the chance to disagree with the patterns on the basis of public, empirical findings—there is therefore every prospect that we shall one day be able to define patterns which we agree on. These patterns therefore have an·enormous advantage over the private visions of an architect. However vulnerable they may seem today, they raise the prospect of finding form for the environment that is so firmly based on the demands of human nature, that planners and architects will all be able to agree on it. This is a prospect which current methods of architecture and planning cannot look forward to.

# 4.7 Retrospect and Prospect *Lewis Mumford*

In taking form, the ancient city brought together many scattered organs of the common life, and within its walls promoted their interaction and fusion. The common functions that the city served were important; but the common purposes that emerged through quickened methods of communication and cooperation were even more significant. The city mediated between the cosmic order, revealed by the astronomer priests, and the unifying enterprises of kingship. The first took form within the temple and its sacred compound, the second within the citadel and the bounding city wall. By polarizing hitherto untapped human aspirations and drawing them together in a central political and religious nucleus, the city was able to cope with the immense generative abundance of neolithic culture.

By means of the order so established, large bodies of men were for the first time brought into effective cooperation. Organized in disciplined work groups, deployed by central command, the original urban populations in Mesopotamia, Egypt, and the Indus Valley controlled flood, repaired storm damage, stored water, remodelled the landscape, built up a great water network for communication and transportation, and filled the urban reservoirs with human energy available for other collective enterprises. In time, the rulers of the city created an internal fabric of order and justice that gave to the mixed populations of cities, by conscious effort, some of the moral stability and mutual aid of the village. Within the theatre of the city new dramas of life were enacted.

But against these improvements we must set the darker contributions of urban civilization: war, slavery, vocational over-specialization, and in many places, a persistent orientation towards death. These institutions and activities, forming a 'negative symbiosis', have accompanied the city through most of its history, and remain today in markedly brutal form, without their original religious sanctions, as the greatest

*Source: The City in History*, Lewis Mumford, Secker and Warburg, 1961; Penguin, 1966

threat to further human development. Both the positive and the negative aspects of the ancient city have been handed on, in some degree, to every later urban structure.

Through its concentration of physical and cultural power, the city heightened the tempo of human intercourse and translated its products into forms that could be stored and reproduced. Through its monuments, written records, and orderly habits of association, the city enlarged the scope of all human activities, extending them backwards and forwards in time. By means of its storage facilities (buildings, vaults, archives, monuments, tablets, books), the city became capable of transmitting a complex culture from generation to generation, for it marshalled together not only the physical means but the human agents needed to pass on and enlarge this heritage. That remains the greatest of the city's gifts. As compared with the complex human order of the city, our present ingenious electronic mechanisms for storing and transmitting information are crude and limited.

From the original urban integration of shrine, citadel, village, workshop, and market, all later forms of the city have, in some measure, taken their physical structure and their institutional patterns. Many parts of this fabric are still essential to effective human association, not least those that sprang originally from the shrine and the village. Without the active participation of the primary group, in family and neighbourhood, it is doubtful if the elementary moral loyalties—respect for the neighbour and reverence for life—can be handed on, without savage lapses, from the old to the young.

At the other extreme, it is doubtful, too, whether those multifarious cooperations that do not lend themselves to abstraction and symbolization can continue to flourish without the city, for only a small part of the contents of life can be put on the record. Without the superposition of many different human activities, many levels of experience, within a limited urban area, where they are constantly on tap, too large a portion of life would be restricted to record-keeping. The wider the area of communication and the greater the number of participants, the more need there is for providing numerous accessible permanent centres for face-to-face intercourse and frequent meetings at every human level.

The recovery of the essential activities and values that first were incorporated in the ancient cities, above all those of Greece, is accordingly a primary condition for the further development of the city in our time. Our elaborate rituals of mechanization cannot take the place of the human dialogue, the drama, the living circle of mates and associates, the society of friends. These sustain the growth and reproduction of human culture, and without them the whole elaborate structure becomes meaningless—indeed actively hostile to the purposes of life.

Today the physical dimensions and the human scope of the city have changed; and most of the city's internal functions and structures must be recast to promote effectively the larger purposes that shall be served: the unification of man's inner and outer life, and the progressive unification of mankind itself. The city's active role in future is to bring to the highest pitch of development the variety and individuality of regions, cultures, personalities. These are complementary purposes: their alternative is the current mechanical grinding down of both the landscape and the human personality. Without the city modern man would have no effective defences against those mechanical collectives that, even now, are ready to make all veritably human life superfluous, except to perform a few subservient functions that the machine has not yet mastered.

Ours is an age in which the increasingly automatic processes of production and urban expansion have displaced the human goals they are supposed to serve. Quantitative production has become, for our mass-minded contemporaries, the only imperative goal: they value quantification without qualification. In physical energy, in industrial productivity, in invention, in knowledge, in population the same vacuous expansions and explosions prevail. As these activities increase in volume and in tempo, they move further and further away from any humanly desirable objectives. As a result, mankind is threatened with far more formidable inundations than ancient man learned to cope with. To save himself he must turn his attention to the means of controlling, directing, organizing, and subordinating to his own biological functions and cultural purposes the insensate forces that would, by their very superabundance, undermine his life. He must curb them and even eliminate them completely when, as in the case of nuclear and bacterial weapons, they threaten his very existence.

Now it is not a river valley, but the whole planet, that must be brought under human control: not an unmanageable flood of water, but even more alarming and malign explosions of energy that might disrupt the entire ecological system on which man's own life and welfare depends. The prime need of our age is to contrive channels for excessive energies and impetuous vitalities that have departed from organic norms and limits: cultural flood control in every field calls for the erection of embankments, dams, reservoirs, to even out the flow and spread it into the final receptacles, the cities and regions, the groups, families, and personalities, who will be able to utilize this energy for their own growth and development. If we were prepared to restore the habitability of the earth and cultivate the empty spaces in the human soul, we should not be so preoccupied with sterile escapist projects for exploring interplanetary space, or with policies based on the strategy of wholesale collective extermination. It is time to come back to earth and confront life in all its organic fecundity, diversity, and creativity, instead of taking refuge in the under-dimensioned world of Post-historic Man.

Modern man, unfortunately, has still to conquer the dangerous aberrations that took institutional form in the cities of the Bronze Age and gave a destructive destination to our highest achievements. Like the rulers of the Bronze Age, we still regard power as the chief manifestation of divinity, or if not that, the main agent of human development. But 'absolute power', like 'absolute weapons', belongs to the same magico-religious scheme as ritual human sacrifice. Such power destroys the symbiotic cooperation of man with all other aspects of nature, and of men with other men. Living organisms can use only limited amounts of energy. 'Too much' or 'too little' is equally fatal to organic existence. Organisms, societies, human persons, not least, cities, are delicate devices for regulating energy and putting it to the service of life.

The chief function of the city is to convert power into form, energy into culture, dead matter into the living symbols of art, biological reproduction into social creativity. The positive functions of the city cannot be performed without creating new institutional arrangements, capable of coping with the vast energies modern man now commands: arrangements just as bold as those that originally transformed the overgrown village and its stronghold into the nucleated, highly organized city.

These necessary changes could hardly be envisaged, were it not for the fact that the negative institutions that accompanied the rise of the city have for the last four centuries been falling into decay, and seemed until recently to be ready to drop into limbo. Kingship by divine right has all but disappeared, even as a moribund idea; and the political functions that were once exercised solely by the palace and the temple, with the coercive aid of the bureaucracy and the army, were during the nineteenth century assumed by a multitude of organizations, corporations, parties, associations, and committees. So, too, the conditions laid down by Aristotle for the abolition of slave labour have now been largely met, through the harnessing of inorganic sources of energy and the invention of automatic machines and utilities. Thus slavery, forced labour, legalized expropriation, class monopoly of knowledge, have been giving way to free labour, social security, universal literacy, free education, open access to knowledge, and the beginnings of universal leisure, such as is necessary for wide participation in political duties. If vast masses of people in Asia, Africa, and South America still live under primitive conditions and depressing poverty, even the ruthless colonialism of the nineteenth century brought to these peoples the ideas that would release them. 'The heart of darkness', from Livingstone on to Schweitzer, was pierced by a shaft of light.

In short, the oppressive conditions that limited the development of cities throughout history have begun to disappear. Property, caste, even vocational specialization have—through the graded income tax and the 'managerial revolution'—lost more of their hereditary fixations, What Alexis de Tocqueville observed a century ago is now more true than ever: the history of the last eight hundred years is the history of the progressive equalization of classes. This change holds equally of capitalist and communist systems, in a fashion that might have shocked Karl Marx, but would not have surprised John Stuart Mill. For the latter foresaw the conditions of dynamic equilibrium under which the advances of the machine economy might at last be turned to positive human advantage. Until but yesterday, then, it seemed that the negative symbiosis that accompanied the rise of the city was doomed. The task of the emerging city was to give an ideal form to these radically superior conditions of life.

Unfortunately, the evil institutions that accompanied the rise of the ancient city have been resurrected and magnified in our own time: so the ultimate issue is in doubt. Totalitarian rulers have reappeared, sometimes elevated, like Hitler, into deities, or mummified in Pharaoh-fashion after death, for worship, like Lenin and Stalin. Their methods of coercion and terrorism surpass the vilest records of ancient rulers, and the hoary practice of exterminating whole urban populations has even been exercised by the elected leaders of democratic states, wielding powers of instantaneous destruction once reserved to the gods. Everywhere secret knowledge has put an end to effective criticism and democratic control; and the emancipation from manual labour has brought about a new kind of enslavement: abject dependence upon the machine. The monstrous gods of the ancient world have all reappeared, hugely magnified, demanding total human sacrifice. To appease their super-Moloch in the Nuclear Temples, whole nations stand ready, supinely, to throw their children into his fiery furnace.

If these demoralizing tendencies continue, the forces that are now at work will prove uncontrollable and deadly; for the powers man now commands must, unless they are detached from their ancient ties to the citadel, and devoted to human ends, lead from their present state of paranoid suspicion and hatred to a final frenzy of destruction. On the other hand, if the main negative institutions of civilization continue to crumble—that is, if the passing convulsions of totalitarianism mark in fact the death-throes of the old order—is it likely that war will escape the same fate? War was one of the 'lethal genes' transmitted by the city from century to century, always doing damage but never yet widely enough to bring civilization itself to an end. That period of tolerance is now over. If civilization does not eliminate war as an open possibility, our nuclear agents will destroy civilization—and possibly exterminate mankind. The vast village populations that were once reservoirs of life will eventually perish with those of the cities.

Should the forces of life, on the other hand, rally together, we shall stand on the verge of a new urban implosion. When cities were first founded, an old Egyptian scribe tells us, the mission of the founder was to 'put the gods in their shrines'. The task of the coming city is not essentially different: its mission is to put the highest concerns of man at the centre of all his activities: to unite the scattered fragments of the human personality, turning artificially dismembered men—bureaucrats, specialists, 'experts', depersonalized agents—into complete human beings, repairing the damage that has been done by vocational separation, by social segregation, by the over-cultivation of a favoured function, by tribalisms and nationalisms, by the absence of organic partnerships and ideal purposes.

Before modern man can gain control over the forces that now threaten his very existence, he must resume possession of himself. This sets the chief mission for the city of the future: that of creating a visible regional and civic structure, designed to make man at home with his deeper self and his larger world, attached to images of human nurture and love.

We must now conceive the city, accordingly, not primarily as a place of business or government, but as an essential organ for expressing and actualizing the new human personality—that of 'One World Man'. The old separation of man and nature, of townsman and countryman, of Greek and barbarian, of citizen and foreigner, can no longer be maintained: for communication, the entire planet is becoming a village; and as a result, the smallest neighbourhood or precinct must be planned as a working model of the larger world. Now it is not the will of a single deified ruler, but the individual and corporate will of its citizens, aiming at self-knowledge, self-government, and self-actualization, that must be embodied in the city. Not industry but education will be the centre of their activities; and every process and function will be evaluated and approved just to the extent that it furthers human development, whilst the city itself provides a vivid theatre for the spontaneous encounters and challenges and embraces of daily life.

Apparently, the inertia of current civilization still moves towards a world-wide nuclear catastrophe; and even if that fatal event is postponed, it may be a century or more before the possibility can be written off. But happily life has one predictable attribute: it is full of surprises. At the last moment—and our generation may in fact be close to the last moment—the purposes and projects that will redeem our present aimless dynamism may gain the upper hand. When that happens, obstacles that now seem insuperable will melt away; and the vast sums of money and energy, the massive efforts of science and technics, which now go into the building of nuclear bombs, space rockets, and a hundred other cunning devices directly or indirectly attached to dehumanized and demoralized goals, will be released for the recultivation of the earth and the rebuilding of cities: above all, for the replenishment of the human personality. If once the sterile dreams and sadistic nightmares that obsess the ruling élite are banished, there will be such a release of human vitality as will make the Renaissance seem almost a stillbirth.

It would be foolish to predict when or how such a change may come about; and yet it would be even more unrealistic to dismiss it as a possibility, perhaps even an imminent possibility, despite the grip that the myth of the machine still holds on the Western World. Fortunately, the preparations for the change from a power economy to a life economy have been long in the making; and once the reorientation of basic ideas and purposes takes place, the necessary political and physical transformations may swiftly follow. Many of the same forces that are now oriented towards death will then be polarized towards life.

In discussing the apparent stabilization of the birth-rate, as manifested throughout Western civilization before 1940, the writer of *The Culture of Cities* then observed:

One can easily imagine a new cult of family life, growing up in the face of some decimating catastrophe, which would necessitate a swift revision in plans for housing and city development: a generous urge toward procreation might clash in policy with the views of the prudent, bent on preserving a barely achieved equilibrium.

To many professional sociologists, captivated by the smooth curves of their population graphs, that seemed a far-fetched, indeed quite unimaginable possibility before the Second World War. But such a spontaneous reaction actually took place shortly after the war broke out, and has continued, despite various 'expert' predictions to the contrary, for the last twenty years. Many people who should be vigilantly concerned over the annihilation of mankind through nuclear explosions have concealed that dire possibility from themselves by excessive anxiety over the 'population explosion'—without the faintest suspicion, apparently, that the threat of de-population and that of over-population might in fact be connected.

As of today, this resurgence of reproductive activity might be partly explained as a deep instinctual answer to the premature death of scores of millions of people throughout the planet. But even more possibly, it may be the unconscious reaction to the likelihood of an annihilating outburst of nuclear genocide on a planetary scale. As such, every new baby is a blind desperate vote for survival: people who find themselves unable to register an effective political protest against extermination do so by a biological act. In countries where state aid is lacking, young parents often accept a severe privation of goods and an absence of leisure, rather than accept privation of life by forgoing children. The automatic response of every species threatened with extirpation takes the form of excessive reproduction. This is a fundamental observation of ecology.

No profit-oriented, pleasure-dominated economy can cope with such demands: no power-dominated economy can permanently suppress them. Should the same attitude spread towards the organs of education, art, and culture, man's super-biological means of reproduction, it would alter the entire human prospect: for public service would take precedence over private profit, and public funds would be available for the building and rebuilding of villages, neighbourhoods, cities, and regions, on more generous lines than the aristocracies of the past were ever able to afford for themselves. Such a change would restore the discipline and the delight of the garden to every aspect of life; and it might do more to balance the birth-rate, by its concern with the quality of life, than any other collective measure.

As we have seen, the city has undergone many changes during the last five thousand years; and further changes are doubtless in store. But the innovations that beckon urgently are not in the extension and perfection of physical equipment: still less in multiplying automatic electronic devices for dispersing into formless suburban dust the remaining organs of culture. Just the contrary: significant improvements will come only through applying art and thought to the city's central human concerns, with a fresh dedication to the cosmic and ecological processes that enfold all being. We must restore to the city the maternal, life-nurturing functions, the autonomous activities, the symbiotic associations that have long been neglected or suppressed. For the city should be an organ of love; and the best economy of cities is the care and culture of men.

The city first took form as the home of a god: a place where eternal values were represented and divine possibilities revealed. Though the symbols have changed the realities behind them remain. We know now, as never before, that the undisclosed potentialities of life reach far beyond the proud algebraics of contemporary science; and their promises for the further transformations of man are as enchanting as they are inexhaustible. Without the religious perspectives fostered by the city, it is doubtful if more than a small part of man's capacities for living and learning could have developed. Man grows in the image of his gods, and up to the measure they have set. The mixture of divinity, power, and personality that brought the ancient city into existence must be weighed out anew in terms of the ideology and the culture of our own time, and poured into fresh civic, regional, and planetary moulds. In order to defeat the insensate forces that now threaten civilization from within, we must transcend the original frustrations and negations that have dogged the city throughout its history. Otherwise the sterile gods of power, unrestrained by organic limits or human goals, will remake man in their own faceless image and bring human history to an end.

The final mission of the city is to further man's conscious participation

278

in the cosmic and the historic process. Through its own complex and enduring structure, the city vastly augments man's ability to interpret these processes and take an active, formative part in them, so that every phase of the drama it stages shall have, to the highest degree possible, the illumination of consciousness, the stamp of purpose, the colour of love. That magnification of all the dimensions of life, through emotional communion, rational communication, technological mastery, and above all, dramatic representation, has been the supreme office of the city in history. And it remains the chief reason for the city's continued existence.

# 5. Life in the city of the future

## Introduction *by Andrew Blowers*

Perhaps the most immediate way of anticipating what the future city will be like is to imagine living in it. This approach, which tends to be a mixture of projection and speculation, has been favoured by many writers. In this section we have reproduced a variety of viewpoints, all of which share a concern with what might happen if certain trends are encouraged or suppressed. They are arranged in a sequence that begins with two descriptions of the life style in some American cities at the present time which, arguably, could be the pattern of life experienced elsewhere in the future. The next group of readings prefigure urban life in the year 2000 and beyond but concentrates on the material and physical aspects of living. The final group focuses on the position of the individual in the society of the future. By this stage city and society have become synonymous and the individual has become impotent to control his destiny.

Toffler and Davie describe the rapid change and mobility which has already transformed American society. The accelerating pace of change and the transient relationship of the individual to things, places, people and organisations is the theme of Toffler's *Future Shock*. Relationship to places has changed at least for affluent 'superindustrial' man who is highly mobile. By contrast with the 'immobiles' he is able to adjust to new situations. He is presented as the harbinger of a society in which commitment to place has become outmoded and irrelevant.

This theme of the emerging mobile society is taken up by Davie who perceives it already in being in western U.S.A. Here the affluent have freedom of choice as to where they live and, by and large, they have rejected the city in its conventional form. Instead, they seek a suburban idyll, 'a safe and beautiful rest-home, cut out from the pain of the world, for healthy people'. Consequently Los Angeles, which developed with the car, is a sprawling collection of affluent suburbs linked by freeways. The poorer ghettos of the city remind us of another aspect of present day reality which may also persist in the future.

The next three extracts (Hall, Leicester, and Simak) are essentially forecasts of life in the future assuming certain trends continue. Hall's Dumill family live in London in the year 2000 which, in terms of mobility, has much in common with present day Los Angeles. The Dumills who live in the Kentish new town of 'Hamstreet' have not surrendered their loyalty to it despite the mobility they enjoy. They think of themselves quite commonly not only as Londoners, but also as Hamstreeters. London 2000 differs from Los Angeles in that it has been consciously planned. There is efficient coordination of public and private transport; a balance of public and private housing; a successful compromise between development and conservation and so on. But it is essentially a middle class perspective and a relatively conservative one at that offering no clues as to how pervasive the trends described will become.

Similarly, *Everybrit* is a representative of the educated middle classes of the year 2000. But his life is vastly different from that of the Dumills. Technology has not merely transformed the pyhsical environment but the individual life-style as well. He is no longer constrained by place or family commitments. Work is undemanding, routines are automated, and every conceivable material want is catered for. In such a society we may perceive certain undesirable trends emerging. For example there is more information but less privacy; more personal freedom but increasing conformity; more democracy but less control over decision-making.

Simak's extract describes the abandonment of the city and the dispersal of its inhabitants to the countryside in search of peace and space. The extract is taken from the first two of a series of eight myths from which the Dogs derive their knowledge of the human race which they have succeeded. In the early myths Simak is interested in the effect of dispersal on the individual. He foresees a commitment to place that has become so total that some individuals are afraid to move from their familiar surroundings and become victims of chronic agoraphobia.

The final pieces by Huxley and Forster consider the broader implications of technological change for the individual in society. They foresee the possibility of a dystopia in which the individual may become subservient to technology. In future cities every want is satisfied, and poverty and pain have largely been eliminated. There is a lack of conflict but also of personal freedom or spiritual satisfaction. Huxley's Brave New World is a rigidly stratified society in which technology has made man the master of his environment. The cost has been heavy for complete social control is exercised by a dictatorship which, using a combination of indoctrination and hedonistic diversions, encourages people to 'love their servitude'.

In Forster's short story we witness the apotheosis of technology. People have become excessively dependent on the Machine which someone once created but they can no longer comprehend. Movement has virtually ceased and each individual is incarcerated in his cell in the vast underground city engaging in continuous but trivial communication with others through the Machine. 'Men seldom moved their bodies; all unrest was concentrated in the soul'. Kuno attempts to rediscover his lost humanity and succeeds before the final holocaust as the Machine stops. Even then hope is not finally lost as a new civilization on the surface of the earth is foreshadowed.

The extracts in this section present an urban future some aspects of which we may aspire to, others we may wish to avoid. Technological progress promises a more abundant life. It also gives a premonition of potential social disaster. Such a consequence can only be averted by greater awareness of the future implications of our present actions. The final extracts sound a warning note that we would do well to heed.

# 5.1 Places: the new nomads *Alvin Toffler*

Every Friday afternoon at 4:30, a tall, greying Wall Street executive named Bruce Robe stuffs a mass of papers into his black leather brief-case, takes his coat off the rack outside his office, and departs. The routine has been the same for more than three years. First, he rides the elevator twenty-nine floors down to street level. Next he strides for ten minutes through crowded streets to the Wall Street Heliport. There he boards a helicopter which deposits him, eight minutes later, at John F. Kennedy Airport. Transferring to a Trans-World Airlines jet, he settles down for supper, as the giant craft swings out over the Atlantic, then banks and heads west. One hour and ten minutes later, barring delay, he steps briskly out of the terminal building at the airport in Columbus, Ohio, and enters a waiting automobile. In thirty more minutes he reaches his destination: he is home.

Four nights a week Robe lives at a hotel in Manhattan. The other three he spends with his wife and children in Columbus, 500 miles away. Claiming the best of two worlds, a job in the frenetic financial center of America and a family life in the comparatively tranquil Midwest countryside, he shuttles back and forth some 50 000 miles a year.

The Robe case is unusual—but not that unusual. In California, ranch owners fly as much as 120 miles every morning from their homes on the Pacific Coast or in the San Bernardino Valley to visit their ranches in the Imperial Valley, and then fly back home again at night. One Pennsylvania teen-ager, son of a peripatetic engineer, jets regularly to an

*Source:* Alvin Toffler (1970), *Future Shock*, The Bodley Head, London, Chapter 5

orthodontist in Frankfurt, Germany. A University of Chicago philosopher, Dr. Richard McKeon, commuted 1000 miles each way once a week for an entire semester in order to teach a series of classes at the New School for Social Research in New York. A young San Franciscoan and his girlfriend in Honolulu see each other every weekend, taking turns at crossing 2000 miles of Pacific Ocean. And at least one New England matron regularly swoops down on New York to visit her hairdresser.

Never in history has distance meant less. Never have man's relationships with place been more numerous, fragile and temporary. Throughout the advanced technological societies, and particularly among those I have characterized as 'the people of the future,' commuting, traveling, and regularly relocating one's family have become second nature. Figuratively, we 'use up' places and dispose of them in much the same way that we dispose of Kleenex or beer cans. We are witnessing a historic decline in the significance of place to human life. We are breeding a new race of nomads, and few suspect quite how massive, widespread and significant their migrations are [. . .].

## Migration in the present

In 1914, according to Buckminster Fuller, the typical American averaged about 1640 miles per year of total travel, counting some 1300 miles of just plain everyday walking to and fro. This meant that he traveled only about 340 miles per year with the aid of horse or mechanical means. Using this 1640 figure as a base, it is possible to estimate that the average American of that period moved a total of 88 560 miles in his lifetime.* Today, by contrast, the average American car owner drives 10,000 miles per year—and he lives longer than his father or grandfather. 'At sixty-nine years of age,' wrote Fuller a few years ago, '. . . I am one of a class of several million human beings who, in their lifetimes, have each covered 3 000 000 miles or more'—more than thirty times the total lifetime travel of the 1914 American.

The aggregate figures are staggering. In 1967, for instance, 108 000 000 Americans took 360 000 000 trips involving an overnight stay more than 100 miles from home. These trips alone accounted for 312 000 000 000 passenger miles.

Even if we ignore the introduction of fleets of jumbo jets, trucks, cars, trains, subways and the like, our social investment in mobility is astonishing. Paved roads and streets have been added to the American landscape at the incredible rate of more than 200 miles per day, every single day for at least the last twenty years. This adds up to 75 000 miles of new streets and roads every year, enough to girdle the globe three

*This is based on a life expectancy of 54 years. Actual life expectancy for white males in the United States in 1920 was 54·1 years.

times. While United States population increased during this period by 38·5 percent, street and road mileage shot up 100 percent. Viewed another way, the figures are even more dramatic: passenger miles traveled within the United States have been increasing at a rate six times faster than population for at least twenty-five years [. . .].

This busy movement of men back and forth over the landscape (and sometimes under it) is one of the identifying characteristics of super-industrial society. By contrast, pre-industrial nations seem congealed, frozen, their populations profoundly attached to a single place. Trans-portation expert Wilfred Owen talks about the 'gap between the im-mobile and the mobile nations.' He points out that for Latin America, Africa and Asia to reach the same ratio of road mileage to area that now prevails in the European Economic Community, they would have to pave some 40 000 000 miles of road. This contrast has profound eco-nomic consequences, but it also has subtle, largely overlooked cultural and psychological consequences. For migrants, travelers and nomads are not the same kind of people as those who stay put in one place.

Perhaps the most psychologically significant kind of movement that an individual can make is geographical relocation of his home. This dramatic form of geographical mobility is also strikingly evident in the United States and the other advanced nations. Speaking of the United States, Peter Drucker has said: 'The largest migration in our history began during World War II; and it has continued ever since with undiminished momentum.' And political scientist Daniel Elazar describes the great masses of Americans who 'have begun to move from place to place within each [urban] belt . . . preserving a nomadic way of life that is urban without being permanently attached to any particular city . . .'.

Between March 1967 and March 1968—in a single year—36 600 000 Americans (not counting children less than one year old) changed their place of residence. This is more than the total population of Cambodia, Ghana, Guatemala, Honduras, Iraq, Israel, Mongolia, Nicaragua and Tunisia combined. It is as if the entire population of these countries had suddenly been relocated. And movement on this massive scale occurs every year in the United States. In each year since 1948 one out of five Americans changed his address, picking up his children, some household effects, and starting life anew at a fresh place. Even the great migrations of history, the Mongol hordes, the westward movement of Europeans in the nineteenth century, seem puny by statistical comparison [. . .].

## *Migration to the future*

There are, however, important differences between the kind of people who are on the move in the United States and those caught up in the European migrations. In Europe most of the new mobility can be attributed to the continuing transition from agriculture to industry; from the past to the present, as it were. Only a small part is as yet associated with the transition from industrialism to super-industrialism. In the United States, by contrast, the continuing redistribution of population is no longer primarily caused by the decline of agricultural employment. It grows, instead, out of the spread of automation and the new way of life associated with super-industrial society, the way of life of the future.

This becomes plain if we look at who is doing the moving in the United States. It is true that some technologically backward and disadvantaged groups, such as urban Negroes, are characterized by high rates of geographical mobility, usually within the same neighborhood or county. But these groups form only a relatively small slice of the total population, and it would be a serious mistake to assume that high rates of geographical mobility correlate only with poverty, unemployment or ignorance. In fact, we find that men with at least one year of college education (an ever increasing group) move more, and further, than those without. Thus we find that the professional and technical populations are among the most mobile of all Americans. And we find an increasing number of affluent executives who move far and frequently. (It is a house joke among executives of the International Business Machine Corporation that IBM stands for 'I've Been Moved.') In the emerging super-industrialism it is precisely these groups—professional, technical and managerial—who increase in both absolute number and as a proportion of the total work force. They also give the society its characteristic flavor, as the denim-clad factory worker did in the past [. . .].

A decade ago William Whyte (1956), in *The Organization Man*, declared that 'The man who leaves home is not the exception in American society but the key to it. Almost by definition, the organization man is a man who left home and . . . kept on going.' His characterization, correct then, is even truer today. The *Wall Street Journal* refers to 'corporate gypsies' in an article headlined 'How Executive Family Adapts to Incessant Moving About Country.' It describes the life of M. E. Jacobson, an executive with the Montgomery Ward retail chain. He and his wife, both forty-six at the time the story appeared, had moved twenty-eight times in twenty-six years of married life. 'I almost feel like we're just camping,' his wife tells her visitors. While their case is atypical, thousands like them move on the average of once every two years, and their numbers multiply. This is true not merely because corporate needs are constantly shifting, but also because top management regards frequent relocation of its potential successors as a necessary step in their training.

This moving of executives from house to house as if they were life-size chessmen on a continent-sized board has led one psychologist to propose facetiously a money-saving system called 'The Modular Family.' Under this scheme, the executive not only leaves his house behind, but his family as well. The company then finds him a matching family (personality characteristics carefully selected to duplicate those of the wife and children left behind) at the new site. Some other itinerant executive then 'plugs into' the family left behind. No one appears to have taken the idea seriously—yet.

In addition to the large groups of professionals, technicians and executives who engage in a constant round of 'musical homes,' there are many other peculiarly mobile groupings in the society. A large military establishment includes tens of thousands of families who, peacetime and wartime, move again and again. 'I'm not decorating any more houses,' snaps the wife of an army colonel with irony in her voice: 'The curtains never fit from one house to the next and the rug is always the wrong size or color. From now on I'm decorating my car.' Tens of thousands of skilled construction workers add to the flow. On another level are the more than 750,000 students attending colleges away from their home state, plus the hundreds of thousands more who are away from home but still within their home state. For millions, and particularly for the 'people of the future,' home is where you find it [. . .].

## *The social implications of mobility*

Dramatically different attitudes, however, are evinced by the 'immobiles.' It is not only the agricultural villager in India or Iran who remains fixed in one place for most or all of his life. The same is true of millions of blue-collar workers, particularly those in backward industries. As technological change roars through the advanced economies, outmoding whole industries and creating new ones almost overnight, millions of unskilled and semiskilled workers find themselves compelled to relocate. The economy demands mobility, and most Western governments— notably Sweden, Norway, Denmark, and the United States—spend large sums to encourage workers to retrain for new jobs and leave their homes in pursuit of them. For coalminers in Appalachia or textile workers in the French provinces, however, this proves to be excruciatingly painful. Even for big-city workers uprooted by urban renewal and relocated quite near to their former homes, the disruption is often agonizing [. . .].

287

*Places: the new nomads*

Even some educated and affluent movers show signs of distress when they are called upon to relocate. The author Clifton Fadiman, telling of his move from a restful Connecticut town to Los Angeles, reports that he was shortly 'felled by a shotgun burst of odd physical and mental ailments . . . In the course of six months my illness got straightened out. The neurologist . . . diagnosed my trouble as "culture shock" . . .' For relocation of one's home, even under the most favorable circumstances, entails a series of difficult psychological readjustments.

In a famous study of a Canadian suburb they call Crestwood Heights, sociologists J. R. Seeley, R. A. Sim, and E. W. Loosley (1956), state: 'The rapidity with which the transition has to be accomplished, and the depth to which change must penetrate the personality are such as to call for the greatest flexibility of behavior and stability of personality. Ideology, speech sometimes, food habits, and preferences in décor must be made over with relative suddenness and in the absence of unmistakable clues as to the behavior to be adopted.'

The steps by which people make such adjustments have been mapped out by psychiatrist James S. Tyhurst of the University of British Columbia. 'In field studies of individuals following immigration,' he says, 'a fairly consistent pattern can . . . be defined. Initially, the person is concerned with the immediate present, with an attempt to find work, make money, and find shelter. These features are often accompanied by restlessness and increased psychomotor activity . . .'

As the person's sense of strangeness or incongruity in the new surroundings grows, a second phase, 'psychological arrival,' takes place. 'Characteristic of this are increasing anxiety and depression; increasing self-preoccupation, often with somatic preoccupations and somatic symptoms; general withdrawal from the society in contrast to previous activity; and some degree of hostility and suspicion. The sense of difference and helplessness becomes increasingly intense and the period is characterized by marked discomfort and turmoil. This period of more or less disturbance may last for . . . one to several months.'

Only then does the third phase begin. This takes the form of relative adjustment to the new surroundings, a settling in, or else, in extreme cases, 'the development of more severe disturbances manifested by more intense disorders of mood, the development of abnormal mental content and breaks with reality.' Some people, in short, never do adjust adequately.

Even when they do, however, they are no longer the same as before, for any relocation, of necessity, destroys a complex webwork of old relationships and establishes a set of new ones. It is this disruption that, especially if repeated more than once, breeds the 'loss of commitment' that many writers have noted among the high mobiles. The man on the move is

288

ordinarily in too much of a hurry to put down roots in any one place. Thus an airline executive is quoted as saying he avoids involvement in the political life of his community because 'in a few years I won't even be living here. You plant a tree and you never see it grow.'

This non-involvement or, at best, limited participation, has been sharply criticized by those who see in it a menace to the traditional ideal of grass-roots democracy. They overlook, however, an important reality: the possibility that those who refuse to involve themselves deeply in community affairs may be showing greater moral responsibility than those who do—and then move away [. . .].

Does it not make more sense, is it not more responsible, to disqualify oneself in advance? Yet if one does withdraw from participation, refusing to join organizations, refusing to establish close ties with neighbors, refusing, in short, to commit oneself, what happens to the community and the self? Can individuals or society survive without commitment?

Commitment takes many forms. One of these is attachment to place. We can understand the significance of mobility only if we first recognize the centrality of fixed place in the psychological architecture of traditional man. This centrality is reflected in our culture in innumerable ways. Indeed, civilization, itself, began with agriculture—which meant settlement, an end, at last, to the dreary treks and migrations of the paleolithic nomad. The very word 'rootedness' to which we pay so much attention today is agricultural in origin. The precivilized nomad listening to a discussion of 'roots' would scarcely have understood the concept [. . .].

## The demise of geography

The nomad of the past moved through blizzards and parching heat, always pursued by hunger, but he carried with him his buffalo-hide tent, his family *and* the rest of his tribe. He carried his social setting with him, and, as often as not, the physical structure that he called home. In contrast, the new nomads of today leave the physical structure behind. (It becomes an entry in the tables showing the turnover rate for things in their lives.) And they leave all but their family, the most immediate social setting, behind [. . .].

Mobility has stirred the pot so thoroughly that the important differences between people are no longer strongly place-related. So far has the decline in commitment to place gone, according to Prof. John Dyckman of the University of Pennsylvania, that 'Allegiance to a city or state is even now weaker for many than allegiance to a corporation, a profession, or a voluntary association.' Thus it might be said that commitments are shifting from place-related social structures (city, state, nation or neighborhood) to those (corporation, profession, friendship network) that are themselves mobile, fluid, and, for all practical purposes, place-less.

Commitment, however, appears to correlate with duration of relationship. Armed with a culturally conditioned set of durational expectancies, we have all learned to invest with emotional content those relationships that appear to us to be 'permanent' or relatively long-lasting, while withholding emotion, as much as possible, from short-term relationships. There are, of course, exceptions; the swift summer romance is one. But, in general, across a broad variety of relationships, the correlation holds. The declining commitment to place is thus related not to mobility per se, but to a concomitant of mobility—the shorter duration of place relationships.

In seventy major United States cities, for example, including New York, average residence in one place is less than four years. Contrast this with the lifelong residence in one place characteristic of the rural villager. Moreover, residential relocation is critical in determining the duration of many other place relationships, so that when an individual terminates his relationship with a home, he usually also terminates his relationship with all kinds of 'satellite' places in the neighborhood. He changes his supermarket, gas station, bus stop and barbershop, thus cutting short a series of other place relationships along with the home relationship. Across the board, therefore, we not only experience more places in the course of a lifetime, but, on average, maintain our link with each place for a shorter and shorter interval.

Thus we begin to see more clearly how the accelerative thrust in society affects the individual. For this telescoping of man's relationships with place precisely parallels the truncation of his relationship with things. In both cases, the individual is forced to make and break his ties more rapidly. In both cases, the level of transience rises. In both cases, he experiences a quickening of the pace of life.

## References

SEELEY, J. R., SIM, R. A., and LOOSLEY, E. W. (1956), *Crestwood Heights*, Basic Books, New York.
WHYTE, W. H. (1956), *The Organization Man*, Jonathan Cape.

# 5.2 The end of the city *Michael Davie*

Southern California is the one place in the world where it is possible
to see how the mass of people, given the chance to decide for themselves,
really want to live. Largely because of modern technology, the majority
of them seem to have come to the conclusion that they do not want to
live in cities. They are, so to speak, voting with their wheels. Elsewhere,
and especially elsewhere in the United States, town planners are struggling to adapt traditional cities to modern pressures: trying to work out
how to fit everyone in, whether to build high or low, how to fend off the
private cars and improve public transport, how to pump new life into
decaying city cores. In southern California, the plans and the planners
scarcely exist; nor, of course, do traditional cities. Jane Jacobs, the
diagnostician of urban diseases, has said that either the car will destroy
the city, or the city will have to fight back and defeat the car. In southern
California, the car was declared the victor before the city climbed into
the ring. Los Angeles is the first giant city to have grown up since the
invention of the car; and the car has turned it into a city of an entirely
new kind. Other cities have ways of warning a visitor that he is approaching: railway lines, wider roads, bigger road signs, more traffic, fingers of
housing pushing out into the surrounding country, a factory in a field.
But you can drive into Los Angeles without being sure whether you have
arrived or not: travelling south on the main freeway from San Francisco,
the Los Angeles city limits sign appears, without warning, when the
road slices between two ragged brown hills. Even in the central city,
there are few landmarks by which even residents can get their bearings,
apart from the hump of Beverly Hills and what is known as 'downtown
Los Angeles', a forlorn huddle of larger buildings that includes City Hall,
the *Los Angeles Times*, the new Music Centre, some apartment blocks
and a big store. The heart of Los Angeles is simply a vast expanse of low
buildings, petrol stations and parking lots, strewn across a huge saucer
edged by what the poet Karl Shapiro called 'dry purple mountains'.
There is no concentrated business district, no special residential centre;
even Hollywood does not exist. The famous gibe about Los Angeles

*Source:* Davie, Michael (1972), *'In the Future Now: a report from California'*, London,
Hamilton, Chapter 4, pages 72–83

being a series of suburbs in search of a city has ceased to be accurate; the search, half-hearted even twenty years ago, has been abandoned. The suburbs do not press inwards to the city centre, wherever that may be, but outwards into the empty spaces, up into the mountains, down the coast to San Diego, further and further into the San Fernando Valley. Without the freeway signs, few people would be able to find their way round Los Angeles at all. Seen from the air, the freeways clamp down over the houses, as a British conservationist has written, 'like a Crown-of-Thorns Starfish devouring the thin living layer of coral on a tropical reef.' When Los Angelenos are not on the move—unless they are very rich, resident in Brentwood or Bel Air, or very poor, for instance in Watts—they mostly live hemmed into the interstices between the rivers of concrete, as dependent on cars as Venetians upon *vaporettos*.

Few Los Angelenos object to the dominance of the automobile. One way to reduce its power would be to build a public transport system; but only the old, the poor and the crippled do not own cars, and, of the rest, only a minority think that a public transport system would make Los Angeles more civilised.* A particularly detailed proposal for such a system was decisively defeated in a referendum in November 1968—despite a propaganda campaign with pamphlets showing drawings of happy newspaper-reading Los Angelenos being whisked about the smogless city in relaxing stainless-steel tubes. In other cities of the Western world it is sometimes hoped that the day will come when the ordinary motorist will revolt against the automobile, and sacrifice some of the freedom it gives him in order to launch a counter-attack on its effects—on the noise, the pollution, and the relentless voracity with which it consumes space for parking lots and petrol stations. Some Europeans, watching what is happening to, say, Rome, where the cars jamming the Via del Corso drown even Italian kerbside conversation, say hopefully that Europeans are still in the adolescent stage of car-worship, which will gradually give way to the age of automobile maturity, when they realise that the car is merely a means of transport. Judging from Los Angeles, where the car has been a commonplace much longer than it has been in Europe, that day is a long way off. Californians may *drive* with a relaxed lack of competitiveness that is nowadays unusual in Europe—as much the result of taking the car for granted as of the strict and efficient highway patrols. But the car in California remains an important social asset: as one rich young Los Angeleno said, 'you can spend an extra two hundred thousand dollars on a house, and where does it show? But spend fifteen thousand dollars on a B.M.W. and

*Even by 1980, it is expected that fifteen per cent of all households in Los Angeles County will still not own a car, meaning that 450 000 households will be dependent on other forms of transport. Today, more than a million people depend on the virtually non-existent public transport system at one time or another. Bank of America booklet on *California* (1970).

every head turns to look!' Still more important, the car in Los Angeles is the essential passport to a mode of living in which the city, as traditionally conceived, has little if any place: the car is the main technological item that is making the city out of date and prefiguring the end of the city altogether. Who wants cities? The answer is, in the one place where people are free to choose: practically nobody. [. . .].

For the need for a city in California is, quite simply, disappearing. Historically, cities have grown up to supply the need for protection, for a power-centre, for social life and entertainment, and for trade. Most American cities, if they do not supply all these needs, still at least supply some. Los Angeles does not. A selling point often stressed by the salesmen of new housing estates is that these provide better protection against vandals and rioters than the city itself. So they do. Nor does living in Los Angeles have any relevance to the exercise of political power. Governor Reagan's kitchen cabinet of Los Angeles businessmen can be in touch with him as effectively from Palm Springs—by telephone, or if necessary by private plane—as from Wilshire Boulevard. Anyone who seeks a private word with Mayor Yorty would be wiser to take him off for a weekend cruise than hang about his outer office. The power-circles in California are as dispersed as every other circle. As for social life and entertainment, Los Angeles is one of the few cities in the world where, because of the automobile, social life no longer centres on the neighbourhood.

People move to Southern California—the surveys invariably show— partly for the climate, partly to take part in the prosperity of the state, and partly to be successful. When they get there, they find that Southern California does not have a recognised hierarchy of success; there is no social ladder to climb. In San Francisco, you can still make a name in the neighbourhood by being on the school board, or by running for office, or by being a success in your trade [. . .]. For most new arrivals the only means of demonstrating—both to the folks back home and to themselves—that the move to California was a wise decision is by buying as expensive a house as they can afford, a visible proof of success, and by taking advantage of the great outdoors. For all these purposes— personal safety, good housing, fresh air, and often a well-paid job— residence in the city is no advantage. Indeed, the closer you live to the geographical centre of Los Angeles, the harder these aims may be to achieve.

What is true of individuals is becoming true of firms: the city is losing its point for them, too.* After the Watts riots, the whites learned

*'Industry is looking now to Orange County and beyond for new sites—away from the heavily urbanised and costly regions of Los Angeles County.' Bank of America pamphlet on *California* (1970). A survey of business firms by L. A. County showed that the cost of providing parking for their employees was a powerful stimulus towards making them think of moving out of the county.

with surprise that part of their city was visibly decaying, breeding un-employment and violence; so they decided that Watts must be renewed, above all by introducing some enlivening industry. But businessmen now seem inclined to think that there may not be much point in the idea after all. Thomas Paine, who was a general manager for General Electric in the peaceful town of Santa Barbara before he became deputy administrator of NASA, said recently: 'We should make reasonable efforts to improve things in the ghetto, but fundamentally we are dealing with an obsolete urban area, the streets, sewers, transportation, etc. To bring a modern factory into that and expect it to compete with a factory out on the crossroads of a couple of superhighways is pretty unrealistic. The alternative would be to move people out to the suburban part of the city, where there are some clean houses near some factories that offer job opportunities after we give them some training. I don't expect this to happen overnight, but it *is* happening. It *is* going to happen, and in our long-range planning it seems to me that speeding it up is a sound direction to go. Let's make the exits bigger and the aisles wider. We should look at the city, and state, as a geographic social system which will encourage people to do what they want to do. There are institutions that have become, and institutions that are becoming. Cities are in-herently the second. They never should be finished. Americans are criticised by Europeans as being in a throwaway society. We should be criticised; but only because we build too permanently. We should make things with fairly short useful lives so we can rearrange our structures to meet the needs of living people. Our big office buildings are an artefact of the paper-and-typewriter society, and already we see the writing on the wall in the magnetic blips of microwave communication that will put these buildings out of date.'

## WHAT DO PEOPLE REALLY WANT?

Given the chance, people want to live in houses with plenty of space, and are ready to abandon the city to get them. This is a point especially noticed by Americans from Eastern cities who move to the West coast. One reporter from an Eastern paper, was amazed to discover, on moving to the *Los Angeles Times*, that whereas her colleagues on the New York paper almost all lived in apartments in Brooklyn, in Los Angeles they all lived in houses, many of them a long way from the *Times* office. 'Space is very, very important to everyone, I find,' the girl told me. 'They are not interested in urban living. It is hard for them to conceive of someone who likes there to be people on the streets at eight o'clock at night. I unconsciously sought out an area where that happens, but for the same money I pay for an apartment, my colleagues rent a house out in Hacienda Heights. Even the apartments here are not apartments at all in the Eastern sense. In west Los Angeles there are these streets, like Barrington Avenue, of garden apartments, two storeys at the most, very shrubby, with balconies and lawns and a pool, so that even life in an apartment isn't urban living as I understand it. Eventually Los Angeles may have to become a city like the others, but I don't know anyone who wants it. One reason many people seek space is for their children. Parents think it is almost immoral to live in a place where the kids can't play the stereo as loud as they want or where they don't have a private pool.'

So the citizens move further and further out, seeking space, and business encourages the centrifugal migration. Aerospace plants are moving into San Bernadino, seventy miles east of central Los Angeles, and the employees are perfectly content to move with the plant and to have their place of living determined by their place of work, because they know that the suburban environment in which they have lived hitherto will be reproduced wherever the plants are built. They will not object to having to move further away from the city, because they rarely use the city. The *Times*, at least, is certain that the spread will continue: they have an Orange County edition, and a huge plant in Costa Mesa. In other cities, one characteristic of urban life that might counter this spread, drawing people to the centre, is entertainment; but the satellite suburbs of Los Angeles are rich enough to construct their own entertainment centres, so that life can be just as metropolitan in one part of the 'urban area' is in any other.

THE NEW CITIES

Whole new communities in California are being planned, built and sold by private entrepreneurs on the proposition that escape from the anxieties of the times is not only desirable but possible. The American dream may have gone sour in the old style of city, but it can be re-captured in the new, where people with enough cash for the down payment on a house can shelter from the changes that have spoiled life elsewhere. The trend of the times seems to be that people have tried out cities, don't like them, and now want to retreat to a new kind of one-class super-village. Two advertisements, typical of many, illustrate the trend:

*Being created now: Orange County's only town with water and woods*

Lake Forest will be different. A place where your children will grow up remembering happy hours sailing, swimming, hiking. Here, life will be easy. You'll know your neighbours by first names. You'll walk down to the Village Centre, with its quaint shops, a restaurant, bank, supermarket and offices. Your home in the Village will be close to your own private recreation center ... the Lake Forest Swim and Racquet Club ... where you'll swim, play tennis, meet friends, or set sail on a sparkling lake from the docks of your own private marina. You'll enjoy an afternoon stroll through a tall, green forest. And your children will walk to their own new school. Lake Forest ... 'the little town with water and woods' ... the only town of its kind in Orange County. Come today, and be counted among the first families of Lake Forest.

## The city that never lets the country out of its sight: Westlake

Twenty years ago, if you had wandered about this big and gentle valley, you'd have seen it dotted with great, gnarled live oaks, patriarchs of their kind. Whispering streamlets meandering their bright and aimless way through wide-stretched meadows. Grazing horses. Softly rolling hillocks and grassy landswells. All of it held in a protective ring of giant hills, under a sky so fresh and clear you could almost see the other side of the universe.

You can still see it, exactly the same, today. None of it has changed. Only now, Westlake is here. A new kind of city. A different kind of city. What makes it different is that this city didn't push the country out of the picture. This city moved in carefully, so it wouldn't disturb the centuries-old beauty of the area.

The country round Westlake is as fine as the advertisement says it is: wide-screen California at her best. The 'city' occupies eighteen square miles, with winding roads, neat groups of spruce and comfortable houses, and in the middle a home-made lake of a hundred and fifty acres—the crucial part of the plan. Unlike a real town, each neighbourhood is sharply distinguished from the next: the Island Homes (which have a bridge to the mainland and a twenty-four-hour security guard) selling at from fifty-three to seventy-three thousand dollars; the Foxmoor Homes, already equipped with carpets and lawn sprinklers; the Westlake Trails Estates, grouped near riding stables ('for people who don't want to kick the riding habit'). There is a golf course, lit at night, a motel, a neighbourhood shopping centre, putting greens, the most discreet petrol station in California, and, on the fringes, carefully landscaped light-industry factories and a burial ground (Memorial Park), which sold off lots at specially reduced rates to early buyers. The developers of Westlake have taken great care with details, and the place possesses a manicured look far removed from the bleak and raw appearance of most new housing estates: old oak trees have been transplanted to strategic sites, a landscape architect has constructed small artificial islands in the lake, and all wires and television aerials are kept out of sight. The houses are close together, but so placed that they do not overlook one another. Inside, each home seems like a *House and Garden* magazine feature come true: gleaming kitchens with views to the mountains, picture windows, double garages, marble coffee tables, and manly rumpus rooms with dart boards and prints of The Gun that Won the West. So successfully has the place been geared to what people want that on selling days queues of eager buyers lined up outside the sales-office long before it opened and were fed, while waiting, on coffee and sandwiches by the sales staff [. . .].

Westlake has no old people, no modern architecture, and no Negroes. Besides, it has no poor, no advertisement hoardings, no overhead wires, no television aerials, no works of art, no bars, no poolrooms, no weeds, no city centre, no annoyances (no power boats on the lake, for instance), no vulgarity, no visible sex (unless one counted the waitresses showing their pants in the Westlake Inn beside the golf course), no flashy night-time scene. Both the developers and the inhabitants are evidently striving to create a form of community life—nearer to a daydream of village life in Europe than to city life in the United States—from which any source of unpleasantness has been as far as possible removed. The white lifesize statue of Christ in the Memorial Park, imported from Italy, looks as unfamiliar with suffering as if he too were a satisfied Westlake home-owner. Undoubtedly, as the sales prove, Westlake is what people want. It is a gathering of like-minded people of similar incomes who are all seeking the same 'way of life' revolving round the family, the home, and (what everyone mentioned) 'the water'. The pressure to conform, at Westlake, must be very strong. The developers have provided everything: they have even decided the layout inside the houses (the master-bedroom, the children's bedroom, the television table). Any deviation from the norm, indoors or out, would show. It struck me that the people of Westlake did not want, any longer, their ambience to be interesting or stimulating: they wanted it perfect: a safe and beautiful rest-home, cut out from the pain of the world, for healthy people.

# 5.3 The Dumills: Londoners 2000 *Peter Hall*

The Dumills are four representative Londoners, though they are not the average Londoners; an average, in a city of sixteen million people, would be a meaningless statistical abstraction.

> Edward Dumill. 54. University Administrative Officer.
> Mary Dumill. 51. Public Opinion Consultant.
> Sebastian Dumill. 24. Trainee Works Manager, Electronics.
> Chloe Dumill. 20. Student in Catering Technology.

By even the most generous standards of the early nineteen-sixties, the Dumills would not have been called Londoners. They live sixty-one miles from Charing Cross, at Hamstreet in Kent, only eight miles from the English Channel. Hamstreet is the farthest from London of all the New Towns built under the ten-year programme announced in 1968.* It received its first family in 1973; by 1980 it had 20 000 people—including the Dumills, who had moved there in 1976, three years after their marriage; by 2000 it had nearly reached its target population of 95 000; and plans were in hand to raise the target to 120 000 to house a first generation of Hamstreet sons and daughters, who were beginning to marry.

From the Dumills' window, you have the immediate impression that Hamstreet is a tight, enclosed, compact town. So it is: 70 000 of its 95 000 people can walk to the central shopping district within a quarter of an hour: as quick as driving and parking a car there. At the front, the Dumills' house is grouped with four others round a small, irregular cul-de-sac court, which gives off a pedestrian alley; at the back it looks at neighbours' kitchens just across the deep, narrow vehicle road which runs down at basement level, where the garages are.

Three of the four Dumills spend every working day outside Hamstreet. Chloe alone stays, though even she sometimes goes to courses in Canter-

*Source:* Hall, P. (1963), *London 2000*, pages 204–209

---

*Although a number of new houses were designated during the late 1960s, none of them was in Kent. Hamstreet is, therefore, a representative rather than a specific location [Editors]

bury. She is numbered among the 20 000 Hamstreet people working, or enjoying education, in the town centre. Next term, when she goes to get practical experience in a local biscuit factory, she will join the stream of 20 000 Hamstreeters who every morning make their way to the factory zones at the edge of the town, there joining 10 000 who have come in from outside by train, bus, car and scooter. Mrs. Dumill leaves every morning to travel to Canterbury. She is numbered among the 8000 daily Hamstreet commuters to other Kentish towns. Sebastian, who works at Headcorn, twenty miles nearer London, is one of Hamstreet's weekly commuters; from Monday till Friday he lives in a hostel built by the Headcorn College of Technology. In the summer he will marry and get a job in Hamstreet; then he will take one of the Corporation's rented flats until he saves for the deposit on one of the new houses being built for purchase. And Mr. Dumill (who bought this house from the Corporation when he moved here) is one of the 2000 remaining Hamstreet workers, who daily make the long trek up to London.

When movements like these first attracted attention in the seventies, they caused alarm and despondency among the older generation of planners. These people were violating the New Town ideal of the closed community where the problem of journey to work had been practically abolished. But as the tendency increased, the concern largely evaporated. People, the planners came to accept, were becoming more mobile. They thought as little of going twenty-five miles to work as of driving fifty miles in the evening to see friends, or going over to Brittany for a week-end. The fact was that the range of modern jobs was so wide, people's special skills so varied, their ambition and appetite for higher pay so great, their propensity to travel so high and their ownership of vehicles so great, that you could never hope to employ them all satisfactorily in a community of one hundred thousand people. And finally, the sociologists reassured the planners even about the London commuters; many of them actually rather enjoyed the two oases in their working day.

Two of the Dumills leave their house this Friday morning by the front door: Chloe walks to the College of Technology and Mr. Dumill to the station. And two habitually leave by vehicle at the back: Sebastian, each Monday, on his scooter, for a week in Headcorn; Mrs. Dumill, daily, in her car, for Canterbury. Their paths will never cross on the same level; the road system of Hamstreet, planned in a series of gigantic one-way loops, passes under and over the pedestrian alleys and paths, and finally converges on a main spine road under the quarter-square-mile of pedestrian deck which carries the town centre.

The railway station is eighteen minutes' walk from the Dumills' front door across one corner of this great deck. The train Mr. Dumill catches there is the 8.28 semi-fast from Paris via the Channel Tunnel.

It has already picked up a few London-bound commuters in Boulogne—labour mobility was already establishing that habit by the seventies—and quite a lot more in Folkestone. It will collect yet more at Headcorn, twenty miles along the line; at Bromley it will lose one-fifth of its passengers, to join the 175 000 people who work in this great shopping and office centre; and at Brixton it will lose another fifth, including Mr. Dumill.

Brixton cannot, as Bromley perhaps could, be described as a 'suburban' shopping and office centre; it is part of the central complex itself. That is not to say that Brixton was swallowed up in a mighty sea of offices, that washed down from the South Bank via the Elephant and Castle. It remains a separate entity, and the Brixton of 2000, apart from the new tall buildings near the station, looks curiously like the Brixton of 1960, or the Brixton of 1910. There are the same rows of Early Victorian porridge-grey terrace houses; the same bright, brash, gay, vulgar shopping centre, huddled under the elevated railway arches. But on a closer look the whole has been subtly remodelled. All that was good is there still; but the problems of the sixties have been mitigated, or cured. The terrace houses have been rehabilitated and modernized; their road pattern has been broken up and sealed off from the main traffic streams. The shopping centre, likewise, is no longer bisected by a stream of through traffic; some has been diverted to a new through motorway, the rest to an inner loop. On a pedestrian deck above part of the inner loop, and carrying the motorway at high level, are the new shops and offices and campus of higher education, which bring 200 000 people into the middle of Brixton every working day. But they do not destroy the character of the old Brixton; they have made it even livelier and more bustling.

All this is the result of sympathetic replanning under the Town Planning Act of 1970.* Through taxes on obsolescence and pooling schemes, this at last gave the possibility of comprehensive renewal in areas like Brixton. When Brixton's turn came, in the seventies and early eighties, a school of planners trained up in the decades 1960–80 were conscious of the terrible truth, that failures of urban renewal in North America had taught: in rebuilding, you must not destroy the qualities that make cities live. You must keep the old buildings people like: you must mix up land uses; you must not let the place go dead at night. In these aims the planners succeeded.

Edward Dumill is an administrative officer with the University of South London. 'SL' is the result of the crash programme for higher education introduced in the early sixties. The planners then had just realized that one of the fastest-growing 'industries' in the central area

---

*Such legislation is advocated elsewhere in *London 2000* by the author but has not been enacted [Editors].

was education; and under the crash programme it would grow yet faster. So the programme diverted the growth of the University of London into separate institutions, of which SL was only one result. In 2000, students are a much commoner sight than in 1960, not only on the streets of Brixton, but in any British town; twenty-seven per cent of our young people between eighteen and twenty-one are receiving whole-time education, and another forty-four per cent are attending courses for part of the day or week. And educational buildings are a much more important feature of the urban landscape. SL spreads out beyond Brixton; some departments are in Battersea, Clapham, and Tooting; halls of residence are in Streatham and Wandsworth. There are separate University centres in Rochester, Dartford, Woolwich, Croydon, Kingston and Guildford.

Edward Dumill's job takes him to one of these other centres of SL and often he has to get there quickly. So he takes a pool car. SL's underground garage always has some; others are in open public parks. All London's cars, whether they are public pool cars or privately owned, are metered and their driver has to pay for his use of the road, according to the amount of congestion on it. But the pool car driver puts shillings in the slot; the owner has to rent his meter, and in addition pays a quarterly bill. Most people find it cheaper, and less trouble, to pick up a pool car; few private cars are seen on London streets till meter time ends, at half-past six every working evening.

So Mary Dumill, who is bringing the second family car up to London, has to wait till that time to cross the border into inner London on her way to Brixton. Tonight the Dumills are celebrating their twenty-seventh wedding anniversary with dinner by the river in Hammersmith. Since the sixties, London's restaurant belt has spread wide afield: after 1945 it had reached Knightsbridge, Chelsea and Kensington, but it was not till the seventies that it got to Hammersmith and only in the eighties that it affected Strand-on-the-Green and Kew. The process was part and parcel of the explosion of London's West End, which the planners had guided. By 2000 the West End spreads along the arterial roads to London Airport. But the centres of shops and offices are highly concentrated. 200 000 people work in Hammersmith, 150 000 in Ealing, 100 000 at Shepherd's Bush and Wood Lane. Hammersmith was the earliest of these major 'sub-centres', as planning jargon described them. Superficially, it looks like Brixton; there are the same tall office blocks and shops gathered around the station, though here the rebuilders swept away most of the old Victorian Hammersmith. But functionally it is different. Its bigger shops are West End shops, drawing customers from all over the country. Its offices house prestige headquarters for national companies, and two big advertising agencies. Education is less important there. And in character Hammersmith is smarter, more brittle, less

301

earthy and uninhibited than Brixton. But it shares with Brixton some of the same advantages. It is not just a place that attracts commuters by day, and goes dead at night; it brings in each evening a new flow of people to eat and drink and visit its specialized theatres and cinemas. And besides, people still live there; by night, they throng the shop-fronts and arcades and riverside walks too.

At 11.30, as the Dumills drive out of London by the New Kent Motorway, the expressways of London are a brilliant sight. When the first ones were built, back in the late sixties, the pessimists confidently predicted that they would wreck London. By 2000 most people admit that they gave it a new dimension, now trenching by the sides of railways, now flying over rooftops, now burrowing through the heart of the re-constructed shopping and office centres. In these centres, on average three to four miles across London, are the sharp concentrations of very tall buildings, grouped around railway stations and reachable direct from the motorways through special car parks. Each of these concentra-tions houses between fifty thousand and three hundred thousand workers; Brixton and Hammersmith are only two out of a score.

Between these new concentrations, the London of 2000 is still the recognizable old London. No cataclysm has swept away the rows of terrace houses or the corner pubs, the busy shopping centres, the miles of suburban semi-detached. Even in the dynamic economy which Britain has become, change does not occur in a day. Nor would we welcome it if it did.

There is heavy traffic on the New Kent Way, though it is now past midnight. It is Friday night, and apart from a few special lorryloads moving to the continent, the private car dominates the road. Most of these cars are moving out, from theatres and cinemas and restaurants and parties in central London. But not a few are coming in, from country eating places or visiting friends or going to parties in places up to sixty miles from Central London. For the Londoners of 2000, distance is no longer an object. They learned to do without cars for much of their working day, but for living their own lives the car has become part of themselves. Just as they no longer can work in isolated communities, so they can no longer form their friendships and their social lives within bounds of space. For them Hammersmith to Dover has no more signifi-cance than would Hammersmith to Hampstead in 1960.

Most of the towns you see from New Kent Way, towns like Maidstone and Ashford, are big old-established towns, important centres for the areas around them. Maidstone has 150 000 people and Ashford 100 000. All these towns have complex functions. They have their contingents of London commuters; their local factory, shop and office staffs; and their quotas of workers who emigrate to factories in other towns. The lights over there belong to a new town: Headcorn, built in the same ten-year plan which produced Hamstreet. Twenty miles up the line to London from Hamstreet, Headcorn rapidly became a big commuter town, and most of its houses are owner-occupied. Its architects, finding they had to build a town on ill-drained Weald Clay, made a virtue of water. They built the town along canals and designed its houses in the neo-formal style which had become popular in American architecture by the sixties.* The canals turn Headcorn into a series of islands, and effectively channel the motor-car into its proper place, as in any old Dutch town. The rival school of architects—the uncompromising functionalists who had designed Hamstreet—condemned Headcorn's formalism as 'escape architecture'; but it proved popular with the commuters, and soon had plenty of imitators. Now, it is only the very old-fashioned people—Mr. Dumill counts himself one—who faintly disapprove of it.

And so back to Hamstreet. It seems strange for people who move so easily across the face of southern England and northern France, but the Dumills think of themselves quite unconsciously not only as Londoners, but also as Hamstreeters. Hamstreet is their town, and when they stroll next morning along its pedestrian alleys and paths, pushing their big wire trolleys, to do their weekly shopping in the big central supermarkets, they will feel as much at home in it, and part of it, as they felt themselves Londoners on the banks of the Thames last night.

The Dumills are us—or our children—forty years on. We must ask whether the picture I have drawn of their lives is valid. Our answer will depend on whether we accept the hypothesis on which this sketch of the future London is based.

First: do we accept that the present course of economic and social evolution will make many features of their lives inevitable, whether we like them or not? I mean the facts that by 2000 London has grown so big, and that many Londoners live so far from the centre of it; that they commute in different directions so far each day to work, and that some of them still travel very long distances to the centre each day; that they depend so completely, for an important part of their lives, on the motor vehicle; that though they have loyalties, these are complex ones, and that they cannot live their lives within the social and economic bounds of a small enclosed community.

Second: accepting these things, is the London which I have described the best we can devise, for them to live the lives they want to live? This London is the result of a set of positive planning actions by the community, which it need not have taken. It need not have built these New Towns; these motorways; these new shopping and office sub-centres. Indeed, it would have been easier to turn the blind eye; to prepare

---

*Cf. William H. Jordy (1960).

wholly specious and impracticable alternatives on paper, and to fail to make plans where plans would be effective. In that case we should have a different London 2000. It also would be recognizable; but chiefly through the ugliness and frustrations which have been maintained, and intensified, from the London we know now. We could have formless, inadequately planned sprawl of offices out from central London, as suburbs sprawled between the wars; traffic gradually congealing to a stop in the centre and along the main arteries; ugly, dispiriting, demoralizing suburbs sprouting like fungi from every old town within sixty miles of St Paul's. These things are not possibilities; if my argument is correct, they also are certainties, unless the community acts soon, to recognize the practicable limits of planning, and within those limits to devise a new concept of planning, more total and effective than that which it produced in those intense wartime and early postwar years.

Which?

## Reference

JORDY, William H. (1960), 'The Formal Image: U.S.A.', *Architectural Review*, 127, pages 157–65.

# 5.4 Life in the year AD 2000 *Colin Leicester*

## Date-line: 1 May 2000 AD

7.00 a.m. Somewhere in the megalopolis of Manbirlon, which cuts a built-up swathe across Britain from merseyside to thameside, Everybrit (the average Briton), awakes from a controlled sleep. Over his underwear made from paper, he pulls a synthetic outer garment, temperature-regulated and powered by a tiny fuel cell. As he begins a breakfast of synthetic proteins, one complete wall of the living room flickers into coloured, three-dimensional, televisual life. The newscast that morning contained another report from the second manned expedition to Mars, a film of the United Nations patrol taking fresh stock from coastal hatcheries to the Dogger Bank fish-farms, and an urgent statement from the International Weather Bureau's network of communication satellites and deep ocean buoys: fast ATOL and VTOL aircraft were speeding

*Source:* MacArthur, Brian (Editor) (1970), *New Horizons for Education*, pages 14–18

with loads of an organic salt of magnesium into the Western Pacific to quell an incipient hurricane.

8.00 a.m. Breakfast over, Everybrit attends to some private matters. At the electronic console in the living room, he dials for all the sporting sections of the local newspapers; and while they are being printed, he does a week's shopping. The catalogues of retail warehouses flash onto the visual display screen. Every item is a mass-produced, standardised good, well-packaged for convenience, hygiene and for transportation by underground conveyor to his cellar; but each category of goods is a variety of brands and styles from all over the globe. He quantifies his demands, adding Japanese oysters as an afterthought. His order, like countless others, has two repercussions: his bank account is automatically debited, and the information of the sale has passed back from retailer to manufacturer to supplier of raw materials via an automatic system of inventory control and production scheduling. Musing over the high-efficiency, integrated economy in which he works, Everybrit dials the central library and checks his memory of a quotation from an old, venerated economic philosopher; and the display screen then reads—

'. . . *thus for the first time since his creation man will be faced with his real, his permanent problem—how to use his freedom from pressing economic cares, how to occupy his leisure, which science and compound interest will have won for him, to live wisely and agreeably and well . . .*'
(Keynes, 1931)

Keynes, thinks Everybrit to himself, was partly right after all. This being his last 30-hour working week of his 10-month working year, Everybrit checks his reservation for a month's holiday in the underwater oceanic resort of Atlantis: it is in order, and his custom-built submersible is promised for delivery at the same time. Finally, he calls for a list of the day's political issues and votes on them, sometimes making reference to the aggregate economic and social statistics of the population of Britain. Somewhere in the central computerised databank of what was still nostalgically called Whitehall, there is a dossier containing all the legal, medical and social details of himself; it had formed a minute part of the information he had just used. Exercising his civil right, Everybrit demanded via the console to know if this personal dossier had been opened by anybody during the last seven days. The answer was reassuring: no one.

9.00 a.m. Walking into his office next door, Everybrit notices that letters have already arrived by light-pipe. Printing them out, he reads his correspondence; dictates replies into a phonetic typewriter; makes one or two minor revisions which the machine immediately duplicates; and despatches the finished copy by light-pipe. Letters received and sent are mechanically recorded and filed.

10.00 a.m. A conference of the technical directors from all subsidiaries of the firm has been arranged. The on-light of the visual telephone winks; five screens light up; and Everybrit pushes the encoding button to ensure that, at least, his part of the six-man conversation will remain a business secret. The South-American opens the discussion, describing the simulation results of marketing the new multi-purpose synthetic material under different assumptions, his lips out of synchronism with the voice of the automatic translator. The Frenchman interjects a series of questions; the American makes a blunt remark; Everybrit concurs. At a later stage, the matter is decided.

11.00 a.m. Everybrit leaves home. The weather forecast was spot on again, he notes. No sooner is he out of the door, than a domestic robot trundles out of the cupboard under the stairs and performs its chores, beginning by clearing up the breakfast table. Everybrit makes a mental note to change the structure and configuration of the living-room at the end of the week. He hops nimbly into the vehicle outside, his cyborg legs appearing to any bystander no different from the real legs he lost in an accident 30 years ago in an ill-famed motorway pile-up. Once inside the hovercar, he presses a button and the machine rises on its cushion of air. He presses another, and the control system engages with the cybernated traffic control network. He dials his destination (the air-city of Foulness) and already, he knows, the least congested route is being selected for him by the control network. The electric motor moves the hovercar onto the highway, scanning devices altering speed persistently to keep the vehicle a safe distance from all other vehicles. And Everybrit leans back in his seat, reads the sports news, thinks ahead to his 30-minute transoceanic flight by rocket jet to visit a new factory installation at Boswash on the eastern seaboard of the U.S. Taking hovercar, rather than hovertrain, to Foulness would allow him time to read the documents he had brought. Time, also, to think ahead to this evening, when on return he would play tennis with a blind friend, sight-provided by radar spectacles. Perhaps, after that, he would visit the fun laboratory. The last thoughts Everybrit had, before he turned to his technical documents, were non-sequiturs. They were: 'shall I decide to have a girl as my next child?' . . . 'what paintings would I be painting in the last part of my two-month holiday?' . . . and 'what shall I choose to study in the sabbatical year following?' [. . .]

In presenting the sketch above, as a possible slice of the British way of life at the turn of the century, I am aware of the same difficulties I met on a previous occasion.

The first is a limitation of expertise: no one person can put himself forward as a trustworthy seer of the world in the year 2000. The second is a limitation of space: if tomorrow's world is to enter adequately into present-day decision-making, it should be painted in far richer detail than in the present chapter. The third is a limitation of style: the narrative may be my form of poetic licence, but it only accentuates the apparent similarity between forecasts of the future and science fiction.

The following is accordingly worth saying. Almost every detail of the above sketch is taken, somewhere, from the published work of a large number of different experts: organised in panels (Helmer, 1966) working in research institutes (Kahn and Wiener, 1967) gathered collectively in symposia (Bell 1967, Calder 1965, Jungk 1967) or simply writing independently with the courage of their convictions and the clarity of their imaginations (Abrams 1968, Clarke 1962, Gaber 1968). I have chosen to highlight some of the details forecast by them; and for the use of such a subjective criterion as plausibility, I accept full responsibility. Those wishing to follow the same trail, and to find a richer picture, are advised to expose themselves to the same works.

Such forecasts of the future are, however, not to be confused with science-fiction—though both describe events that have not happened. Yet such forecasts are necessary. Educational decisions taken currently will need a long time to work themselves out. And make no mistake about it: the world of 2000 will be as different from the world of 1970, as the latter is from 1920. To help us anticipate it, the futurists have assembled a systematic methodology, have extrapolated trends, have worked out the implications for the future of scientific break-throughs and inventions already with us *now*. And they have gone about such a task honestly.

The prime factor dictating events during the next 30 years is the pace of technological change: it is accelerating; it is becoming increasingly institutionalised [. . .].

[. . .] By the year 2000, the average Briton will have a standard of living in the region of four times that of 1970, measured in real terms. His income will by then have put him into the mass-consumption bracket; and he will be working in industries with some radical differences from today's economic scene.

The farming of the oceans will have begun, the hunting of sea-life having given way to what may appropriately be called piscaculture. This will provide an extra source of natural nutrients; synthetic nutrients will be factory-made. New, more versatile artificial materials will be developed, e.g. hybridised metals; and new uses found for old ones, e.g. disposable paper clothes. The further miniaturisation of electronic components will have continued.

Power generation, storage and transmission will almost certainly have changed. Nuclear energy, from both the fission and fusion process, will make available cheap and abundant electricity, coal and oil being relegated more to the role of raw materials. The development of super-conductors would put power lines underground; micro-wave transmission of electricity could abolish them altogether. Portable fuel cells would make power sources independent.

The quiet and clean electric motor for transport might be economically viable. And forms of transport would be faster, safer, more varied: from moving pavements, through hovercars, to inter-city monorail trains moving on air. The invention of the wheel might have been a turning point in the history of Man; the widespread use of ground effect machines (hovercraft) might make the use of the wheel for transport obsolete. Short-distance flying would be by extensions of present VTOL aircraft and helicopters; trans-global rocket planes would fly at speeds of Mach 9, nine times faster than the speed of sound.

Manufacturing production, distribution and banking will be highly automated. Telecommunications will have expanded enormously, providing rapid data transmission in visual, aural and digital forms. This will be facilitated not only by finely engineered receptors and transmitters, but also by new types of conductors that handle vast quantities of information, e.g. lasers arranged in light-pipes.

Above all, the future increase, by a factor of 10 every few years, in the reliability, capacity and speed of electronic computers will usher in an age of cybernation. Management decision-making will increasingly use computer models; data files and centralised libraries will be stored on holographic micro-film; medical diagnosis and legal search will be computerised. It is in this area of information technology—the automatic storage, retrieval and processing of data—that we can expect the greatest changes in the industrial scene.

Firms will become increasingly international in character; and countries will be organised for economic co-operation in more numerous economic blocs. Trade between them will form a much higher proportion of Gross Domestic Product, and will be supported by an international currency, and a fully operational World Bank. A global agreement to equalise the distribution of incomes between countries will imply a poverty floor for less-developed nations and internationally organised subsidies.

By the year 2000, there may be 20 per cent more Britons than there are now. Less easy to forecast are their personal and physical groupings, the size of family and even whether the family will survive as the basic unit of social life. The 'immediate family', united by blood between only two generations may be supplemented by the clan or the tribe, united by intellectual interests. The average durability of houses may continue to decline, and structures will be light, pressurised and transformable (in the design sense) at the owners' will. Manchester, Birmingham and London may have joined to form a megalopolis (Manbirlon).

The health of the individual, however, will be considerably improved by relative immunity against most viral and bacterial diseases. Artificial cyborg limbs and sensory organs will be freely available; and natural transplants and synthetic implants will be commonplace. More effective contraception will be practised; and extra-uterine gestation may be chosen by some. Genetic engineering will have begun to eliminate known hereditary defects. The sex of an unborn child may be chosen; personality drugs will be used; many mental illnesses will be curable. The debilitating effects of senility will be avoidable. Some of the possible developments listed above may cause us to question the basic notion of individual personality; some raise the matter of medical ethics; some would require a definite revision of social attitudes for their implementation. All we know is that they are probably going to become technologically possible. And socially, too?

## References

ABRAMS, Mark (1968) 'Consumption in the year 2000' in Michael Young (Editor): *Forecasting and the Social Sciences*, Heinemann, London.

BELL, Daniel and others (1967), 'Towards the Year 2000', Special Issue of *Daedalus*, Summer.

CALDER, Nigel (Editor) (1965) 'The World in 1984, **1** and **2**, Penguin, London.

CLARKE, Arthur C. (1965) 'Profiles of the Future', Pan, London.

GABOR, Dennis (1968) 'Technological forecasting in a social frame', Paper for the Science of Science Foundation, London, February.

HELMER, Olaf (1966) 'Social Technology', Basic Books, New York.

JUNGK, Robert and others (1967) 'Forecasting the Future'. Special Issue of *Science Journal*, October.

KAHN, Herman and WIENER, Anthony J. (1967) *The Year 2000*, Collier-Macmillan, London.

KEYNES, John Maynard (1931) 'Economic possibilities for our grandchildren', in *Essays in Persuasion*, Macmillan, London.

LEICESTER, Colin (1968) 'Tomorrow's World' in *Careers of the Future*, Supplement 17 of *Where*, Advisory Centre for Education, Cambridge, December.

# 5.5 City *Clifford Simak*

*The extract begins with a speech by John J. Webster to the City Council which presides over a near deserted city* [Editors].

'The city is an anachronism. It has outlived its usefulness. Hydroponics and the helicopter spelled its downfall. In the first instance the city was a tribal place, an area where the tribe banded together for mutual protection. In later years a wall was thrown around it for additional protection. Then the wall finally disappeared but the city lived on because of the conveniences which it offered trade and commerce. It continued into modern times because people were compelled to live close to their jobs and the jobs were in the city.

'But to-day that is no longer true. With the family plane, one hundred miles to-day is a shorter distance than five miles back in 1930. Men can fly several hundred miles to work and fly home when the day is done. There is no longer any need for them to live cooped up in a city.

'The automobile started the trend and the family plane finished it. Even in the first part of the century the trend was noticeable—a movement away from the city with its taxes and its stuffiness, a move towards the suburb and close-in acreages. Lack of adequate transportation, lack of finances held many to the city. But now, with tank farming destroying the value of land, a man can buy a huge acreage in the country for less than he could a city lot forty years ago. With planes powered by atomic there is no longer any transportation problem.'

## Huddling place

*Jerome A. Webster living in the year 2117, occupies the family home founded by his great-great-grandfather John J. Webster* [Editors]

This was home. It had been home for the Websters since that day when the first John J. had come here and built the first unit of the sprawling house. John J. had chosen it because it had a trout stream, or so he

*Source:* Clifford Simak (1952), *City*, Weidenfeld and Nicolson (Science Fiction Book Club, 1961)

always said. But it was something more than that. It must have been, Webster told himself, something more than that.

Or perhaps, at first, it had only been the trout stream. The trout stream and the trees and meadows, the rocky ridge where the mist drifted in each morning from the river. Maybe the rest of it had grown, grown gradually through the years, through years of family association until the very soil was soaked with something that approached, but wasn't quite, tradition. Something that made each tree, each rock, each foot of soil a Webster tree or rock or clod of soil. It all belonged.

John J., the first John J., had come after the break-up of the cities, after men had forsaken, once and for all, the twentieth century huddling places, had broken free of the tribal instinct to stick together in one cave or in one clearing against a common foe or a common fear. An instinct that had become outmoded, for there were no fears or foes. Man revolting against the herd instinct economic and social conditions had impressed upon him in ages past. A new security and a new sufficiency had made it possible to break away.

The trend had started back in the twentieth century, more than two hundred years before, when men moved to country homes to get fresh air and elbow room and a graciousness in life that communal existence, in its strictest sense, never had given them.

And here was the end result. A quiet living. A peace that could only come with good things. The sort of life that men had yearned for years to have. A manorial existence, based on old family homes and leisurely acres, with atomics supplying power and robots in place of serfs.

Webster smiled at the fireplace with its blazing wood. That was an anachronism, but a good one—something that Man had brought forward from the caves. Useless, because atomic heating was better—but more pleasant. One couldn't sit and watch atomics and dream and build castles in the flames.

Even the crypt out there, where they had put his father that afternoon. That was family, too. All of a piece with the rest of it. The sombre pride and leisured life and peace. In the old days the dead were buried in vast plots all together, stranger cheek by jowl with stranger—

*He never goes anywhere.*

That is what Jenkins had told the minister.*

And that was right. For what need was there to go anywhere? It all was here. By simply twirling a dial one could talk face to face with any-one one wished, could go, by sense, if not in body, anywhere one wished. Could attend the theatre or hear a concert or browse in a library half-way around the world. Could transact any business one might need to transact without rising from one's chair.

*Jenkins is Webster's robot servant.

'City'

Webster drank the whisky, then swung to the dialled machine beside his desk.

He spun dials from memory without resorting to the log. He knew where he was going.

His finger flipped a toggle and the room melted away—or seemed to melt. There was left the chair within which he sat, part of the desk, part of the machine itself and that was all.

The chair was on a hillside swept with golden grass and dotted with scraggly, wind-twisted trees, a hillside that straggled down to a lake nestling in the grip of purple mountain spurs. The spurs, darkened in long streaks with the bluish-green of distant pine, climbed in staggering stairs, melting into the blue-tinged snow-capped peaks that reared beyond and above them in jagged saw-toothed outline.

The wind talked harshly in the crouching trees and ripped the long grass in sudden gusts. The last rays of the sun struck fire from the distant peaks.

Solitude and grandeur, the long sweep of tumbled land, the cuddled lake, the knife-like shadows on the far-off ranges.

[...] The first breath of spring came through the window, filling the study with the promise of melting snows, of coming leaves and flowers, of north-bound wedges of waterfowl streaming through the blue, of trout that lurked in pools waiting for the fly.

Webster lifted his eyes from the sheaf of papers on his desk, sniffed the breeze, felt the cool whisper of it on his cheek. His hand reached out for the brandy glass, found it empty, and put it back.

He bent back above the papers once again, picked up a pencil and crossed out a word.

Critically, he read the final paragraphs:

'The fact that of the two hundred and fifty men who were invited to visit me, presumably on missions of more than ordinary importance, only three were able to come, does not necessarily prove that all but those three are victims of agoraphobia. Some may have had legitimate reasons for being unable to accept my invitation. But it does indicate a growing unwillingness of men living under the mode of Earth existence set up following the break-up of the cities to move from familiar places, a deepening instinct to stay among the scenes and possessions which in their mind have become associated with contentment and graciousness of life.

What the result of such a trend will be, no one can clearly indicate since it applies to only a small portion of Earth's population. Among the larger families economic pressure forces some of the sons to seek their fortunes either in other parts of the Earth or on one of the other planets. Many others deliberately seek adventure and opportunity in

312

space while still others become associated with professions or trades which made a sedentary existence impossible.'

He flipped the page over, went on to the last one.

It was a good paper, he knew, but it could not be published, not just yet. Perhaps after he had died. No one, so far as he could determine, had ever so much as realized the trend, had taken as matter of course the fact that men seldom left their homes. Why, after all, should they leave their homes?

[*Webster, a surgeon, is summoned to Mars to save the life of a great Martian philosopher. He cannot bring himself to go. Editors*]

Webster sat at the desk and held his hands in front of him, staring at them. Hands that had skill, held knowledge. Hands that could save a life if he could get them to Mars. Hands that could save for the solar system, for mankind, for the Martians an idea—a new idea—that would advance them a hundred thousand years in the next two generations.

But hands chained by a phobia that grew out of this quiet life. Decadence—a strangely beautiful—and deadly—decadence.

Man had forsaken the teeming cities, the huddling places, two hundred years ago. He had done with the old foes and the ancient fears that kept him around the common campfire, had left behind the hobgoblins that had walked with him from the caves.

And yet—and yet—

Here was another huddling place. Not a huddling place for one's body, but one's mind. A psychological campfire that still held a man within the circle of its light.

Still, Webster knew, he must leave that fire. As the men had done with the cities two centuries before, he must walk off and leave it. And he must not look back.

He had to go to Mars—or at least start for Mars. There was no question there, at all. He had to go.

Whether he would survive the trip, whether he could perform the operation once he had arrived, he did not know. He wondered vaguely, whether agoraphobia could be fatal. In its most exaggerated form, he supposed it could.

He reached out a hand to ring, then hesitated. No use having Jenkins pack. He would do it himself—something to keep him busy until the ship arrived.

From the top shelf of the wardrobe in the bedroom, he took down a bag and saw that it was dusty. He blew on it, but the dust still clung. It had been there for too many years.

As he packed, the room argued with him, talked in that mute tongue with which inanimate but familiar things may converse with a man.

'You can't go,' said the room. 'You can't go off and leave me.'

313

And Webster argued back, half pleading, half explanatory. 'I have to go. Can't you understand? It's a friend, an old friend. I will be coming back.'

Packing done, Webster returned to the study, slumped into his chair.

He must go and yet he couldn't go. But when the ship arrived, when the time had come, he knew that he would walk out of the house and towards the waiting ship.

He steeled his mind to that, tried to set it in a rigid pattern, tried to blank out everything but the thought that he was leaving.

Things in the room intruded on his brain, as if they were part of a conspiracy to keep them there. Things that he saw as if he were seeing them for the first time. Old, remembered things that suddenly were new. The chronometer that showed both Earthian and Martian time, the days of the month, the phases of the moon. The picture of his dead wife on the desk. The trophy he had won at prep school. The framed short snorter bill that had cost him ten bucks on his trip to Mars.

He stared at them, half unwilling at first, then eagerly, storing up the memory of them in his brain. Seeing them as separate components of a room he had accepted all these years as a finished whole, never realizing what a multitude of things went to make it up.

Dusk was falling, the dusk of early spring, a dusk that smelled of early pussy willows.

The ship should have arrived long ago. He caught himself listening for it, even as he realized that he would not hear it. A ship, driven by atomic motors, was silent except when it gathered speed. Landing and taking off, it floated like thistledown, with not a murmur in it.

It would be here soon. It would have to be here soon or he could never go. Much longer to wait, he knew, and his high-keyed resolution would crumble like a mound of dust in beating rain. Not much longer could he hold his purpose against the pleading of the room, against the flicker of the fire, against the murmur of the land where five generations of Websters had lived their lives and died.

He shut his eyes and fought down the chill that crept across his body. He couldn't let it get him now, he told himself. He had to stick it out. When the ship arrived he still must be able to get up and walk out of the door to the waiting port.

A tap came on the door.

'Come in,' Webster called.

It was Jenkins, the light from the fireplace flickering on his shining metal hide.

'Had you called earlier, sir?' he asked.

Webster shook his head.

'I was afraid you might have,' Jenkins explained, 'and wondered why I didn't come. There was a most extraordinary occurrence, sir. Two

314

men came with a ship and said they wanted you to go to Mars.'

'They are here,' said Webster. 'Why didn't you call me?'

He struggled to his feet.

'I didn't think, sir,' said Jenkins, 'that you would want to be bothered. It was so preposterous. I finally made them understand you could not possibly want to go to Mars.'

Webster stiffened, felt chill fear gripping at his heart. Hands groping for the edge of the desk, he sat down in the chair, sensed the walls of the room closing in about him, a trap that would never let him go.


## 5.6 Brave New World *Aldous Huxley*


By eight o'clock the light was failing. The loud-speakers in the tower of the Stoke Poges Club House began, in a more than human tenor, to announce the closing of the courses. Lenina and Henry abandoned their game and walked back towards the Club. From the grounds of the Internal and External Secretion Trust came the lowing of those thousands of cattle which provided, with their hormones and their milk, the raw materials for the great factory at Farnham Royal.

An incessant buzzing of helicopters filled the twilight. Every two and a half minutes a bell and the screech of whistles announced the departure of one of the light monorail trains which carried the lower-caste golfers back from their separate course to the metropolis.

Lenina and Henry climbed into their machine and started off. At eight hundred feet Henry slowed down the helicopter screws, and they hung for a minute or two poised above the fading landscape. The forest of Burnham Beeches stretched like a great pool of darkness towards the bright shore of the western sky. Crimson at the horizon, the last of the sunset faded, through orange, upwards into yellow and a pale watery green. Northwards, beyond and above the trees, the Internal and External Secretions factory glared with a fierce electric brilliance from every window of its twenty storeys. Beneath them lay the buildings of the Golf Club—the huge lower-caste barracks and, on the other side of a dividing wall, the smaller houses reserved for Alpha and Beta members.* The approaches to the monorail station were black with the ant-like pullulation of lower-caste activity. From under the glass vault a lighted

*Source:* Aldous Huxley (1932), *Brave New World*, Chatto and Windus and Penguin, Chapter 5, pages 60–64

*Brave New World is a rigidly stratified society divided into five castes: Alphas and Betas constituting the intelligentsia and the semi-moronic Gammas, Deltas, and Epsilons, the lower castes. Class prejudice (Elementary Class Consciousness) is instilled at birth in the State Conditioning Centres. Thereafter castes live and work separately [Editors].

train shot out into the open. Following its south-easterly course across the dark plain their eyes were drawn to the majestic buildings of the Slough Crematorium. For the safety of night-flying planes, its four tall chimneys were flood-lighted and tipped with crimson danger signals. It was a landmark.

'Why do the smoke-stacks have those things like balconies round them?' inquired Lenina.

'Phosphorus recovery,' exclaimed Henry telegraphically. 'On their way up the chimney the gases go through four separate treatments. $P_2O_5$ used to go right out of circulation every time they cremated someone. Now they recover over ninety-eight per cent of it. More than a kilo and a half per adult corpse. Which makes the best part of four hundred tons of phosphorus every year from England alone.' Henry spoke with a happy pride, rejoicing wholeheartedly in the achievement, as though it had been his own. 'Fine to think we can go on being socially useful even after we're dead. Making plants grow.'

Lenina, meanwhile, had turned her eyes away and was looking perpendicularly downwards at the monorail station. 'Fine,' she agreed. 'But queer that Alphas and Betas won't make any more plants grow than those nasty little Gammas and Deltas and Epsilons down there.'

'All men are physico-chemically equal,' said Henry sententiously. 'Besides, even Epsilons perform indispensable services.'

'Even an Epsilon . . .' Lenina suddenly remembered an occasion when, as a little girl at school, she had woken up in the middle of the night and become aware, for the first time, of the whispering that had haunted all her sleeps. She saw again the beam of moonlight, the row of small white beds; heard once more the soft, soft voice that said (the words were there, unforgotten, unforgettable after so many night-long repetitions): 'Everyone works for everyone else. We can't do without anyone. Even Epsilons are useful. We couldn't do without Epsilons. Everyone works for everyone else. We can't do without anyone . . .' Lenina remembered her first shock of fear and surprise; her speculations through half a wakeful hour; and then, under the influence of those endless repetitions, the gradual soothing of her mind, the soothing, the smoothing, the stealthy creeping of sleep. . . .

'I suppose Epsilons don't really mind being Epsilons,' she said aloud.

'Of course they don't. How can they? They don't know what it's like being anything else. We'd mind, of course. But then we've been differently conditioned. Besides, we start with a different heredity.'

'I'm glad I'm not an Epsilon,' said Lenina, with conviction.

'And if you were an Epsilon,' said Henry, 'your conditioning would have made you no less thankful that you weren't a Beta or an Alpha.' He put his forward propeller into gear and headed the machine towards London. Behind them, in the west, the crimson and orange were almost faded; a dark bank of cloud had crept into the zenith. As they flew over the Crematorium, the plane shot upwards on the column of hot air rising from the chimneys, only to fall as suddenly when it passed into the descending chill beyond.

'What a marvellous switchback!' Lenina laughed delightedly.

But Henry's tone was almost, for a moment, melancholy. 'Do you know what that switchback was?' he said. 'It was some human being finally and definitely disappearing. Going up in a squirt of hot gas. It would be curious to know who it was—a man or a woman, an Alpha or an Epsilon. . . .' He sighed. Then, in a resolutely cheerful voice, 'Anyhow,' he concluded, 'there's one thing we can be certain of; whoever he may have been, he was happy when he was alive. Everybody's happy now.'

'Yes, everybody's happy now,' echoed Lenina. They had heard the words repeated a hundred and fifty times every night for twelve years.

Landing on the roof of Henry's forty-storey apartment house in Westminster, they went straight down to the dining-hall. There, in a loud and cheerful company, they ate an excellent meal. *Soma* was served with the coffee. Lenina took two half-gramme tablets and Henry three. At twenty past nine they walked across the street to the newly opened Westminster Abbey Cabaret. It was a night almost without clouds, moonless and starry; but of this on the whole depressing fact Lenina and Henry were fortunately unaware. The electric sky-signs effectively shut off the outer darkness. 'CALVIN STOPES AND HIS SIXTEEN SEXOPHONISTS.' From the façade of the new Abbey the giant letters invitingly glared. 'LONDON'S FINEST SCENT AND COLOUR ORGAN. ALL THE LATEST SYNTHETIC MUSIC.'

They entered. The air seemed hot and somehow breathless with the scent of ambergris and sandalwood. On the domed ceiling of the hall, the colour organ had momentarily painted a tropical sunset. The Sixteen Sexophonists were playing an old favourite: 'There ain't no Bottle in all the world like that dear little Bottle of mine.' Four hundred couples were five-stepping round the polished floor. Lenina and Henry were soon the four hundred and first. The sexophones wailed like melodious cats under the moon, moaned in the alto and tenor registers as though the little death were upon them. Rich with a wealth of harmonics, their tremulous chorus mounted towards a climax, louder and ever louder— until at last, with a wave of his hand, the conductor let loose the final shattering note of ether music and blew the sixteen merely human blowers clean out of existence. Thunder in A flat major. And then, in all but silence, in all but darkness, there followed a gradual deturgescence, a *diminuendo* sliding gradually, through quarter tones, down, down to a faintly whispered dominant chord that lingered on (while the five-four rhythms still pulsed below) charging the darkened seconds with an intense expectancy. And at last expectancy was fulfilled. There was a sudden explosive sunrise, and simultaneously, the Sixteen burst into song:

> Bottle of mine, it's you I've always wanted!
> Bottle of mine, why was I ever decanted?
>   Skies are blue inside of you,
>   The weather's always fine;
> For
> There ain't no Bottle in all the world
> Like that dear little Bottle of mine.

Five-stepping with the other four hundred round and round Westminster Abbey, Lenina and Henry were yet dancing in another world—the warm, the richly coloured, the infinitely friendly world of *soma*-holiday. How kind, how good-looking, how delightfully amusing everyone was! 'Bottle of mine, it's you I've always wanted . . .' But Lenina and Henry had what they wanted . . . They were inside, here and now—safely inside with the fine weather, the perennially blue sky. And when, exhausted, the Sixteen had laid by their sexophones and the Synthetic Music apparatus was producing the very latest in slow Malthusian Blues, they might have been twin embryos gently rocking together on the waves of a bottled ocean of blood-surrogate.

'Good night, dear friends. Good night, dear friends.' The loudspeakers veiled their commands in a genial and musical politeness. 'Good night, dear friends . . .'

Obediently, with all the others, Lenina and Henry left the building. The depressing stars had travelled quite some way across the heavens. But though the separating screen of the sky-signs had now to a great extent dissolved, the two young people still retained their happy ignorance of the night.

Swallowed half an hour before closing time, that second dose of *soma* had raised a quite impenetrable wall between the actual universe and their minds. Bottled, they crossed the street; bottled, they took the lift up to Henry's room on the twenty-eighth floor. And yet, bottled as she was, and in spite of that second gramme of *soma*, Lenina did not forget to take all the contraceptive precautions prescribed by the regulations. Years of intensive hypnopaedia* and, from twelve to seventeen, Malthusian drill three times a week had made the taking of these precautions almost as automatic and inevitable as blinking.

---

*Hypnopaedia: the principle of conditioning the individual while asleep [Editors].

# 5.7 The Machine Stops E. M. Forster

I: *The airship* Imagine, if you can, a small room, hexagonal in shape, like the cell of a bee. It is lighted neither by window nor by lamp, yet it is filled with a soft radiance. There are no apertures for ventilation, yet the air is fresh. There are no musical instruments, and yet, at the moment that my meditation opens, this room is throbbing with melodious sounds. An armchair is in the centre, by its side a reading desk—that is all the furniture. And in the armchair there sits a swaddled lump of flesh—a woman, about five feet high, with a face as white as a fungus. It is to her that the little room belongs.

An electric bell rang.

The woman touched a switch and the music was silent.

'I suppose I must see who it is,' she thought, and set her chair in motion. The chair, like the music, was worked by machinery, and it rolled her to the other side of the room, where the bell still rang importunately.

'Who is it?' she called. Her voice was irritable, for she had been interrupted often since the music began. She knew several thousand people; in certain directions human intercourse had advanced enormously.

But when she listened in to the receiver, her white face wrinkled into smiles, and she said, 'Very well, Let us talk, I will isolate myself. I do not expect anything important will happen for the next five minutes—for I can give you fully five minutes, Kuno. Then I must deliver my lecture on "Music during the Australian Period."'

She touched the isolation knob, so that no one else could speak to her. Then she touched the lighting apparatus, and the little room was plunged into darkness.

'Be quick!' she called, her irritation returning. 'Be quick, Kuno; here I am in the dark wasting my time.'

But it was fully fifteen seconds before the round plate that she held in her hands began to glow. A faint blue light shot across it, darkening to

*Source:* E. M. Forster (1928), *The Machine Stops*, from *The Eternal Moment and Other Stories*, Sidgwick and Jackson, London [Reprinted in Damon Knight, Editor (1966), *Cities of Wonder* (Sphere Books Edition, 1970)].

purple, and presently she could see the image of her son, who lived on the other side of the earth, and he could see her.

'Kuno, how slow you are.'

He smiled gravely.

'I really believe you enjoy dawdling.'

'I have called you before, Mother, but you were always busy or isolated. I have something particular to say.'

'What is it, dearest boy? Be quick. Why could you not send it by pneumatic post?'

'Because I prefer saying such a thing. I want—'

'Well?'

'I want you to come and see me.'

Vashti watched his face in the blue plate.

'But I can see you!' she exclaimed. 'What more do you want?'

'I want to see you not through the Machine,' said Kuno. 'I want to speak to you not through the wearisome Machine.'

'Oh, hush!' said his mother, vaguely shocked. 'You mustn't say anything against the Machine.'

'Why not?'

'One mustn't.'

'You talk as if a god had made the Machine,' cried the other. 'I believe that you pray to it when you are unhappy. Men made it, do not forget that. Great men, but men. The Machine is much, but it is not everything. I see something like you in this plate, but I do not see you. I hear something like you through this telephone, but I do not hear you. That is why I want you to come. Come and stop with me. Pay me a visit, so that we can meet face to face, and talk about the hopes that are in my mind.'

She replied that she could scarcely spare the time for a visit.

'The airship barely takes two days to fly between me and you.'

'I dislike airships.'

'Why?'

'I dislike seeing the horrible brown earth, and the sea, and the stars when it is dark. I get no ideas in an airship.'

'I do not get them anywhere else.'

'What kind of ideas can the air give you?'

He paused for an instant.

'Do you not know four big stars that form an oblong, and three stars close together in the middle of the oblong, and hanging from these stars, three other stars?'

'No, I do not. I dislike the stars. But did they give you an idea? How interesting; tell me.'

'I had an idea that they were like a man.'

'I do not understand.'

'The four big stars are the man's shoulders and his knees. The three stars in the middle are like the belts that men wore once, and the three stars hanging are like a sword.'

'A sword?'

'Men carried swords about with them, to kill animals and other men.'

'It does not strike me as a very good idea, but it is certainly original. When did it come to you first?'

'In the airship—' He broke off and she fancied that he looked sad. She could not be sure, for the Machine did not transmit nuances of expression. It only gave a general idea of people—an idea that was good enough for all practical purposes, Vashti thought. The imponderable bloom, declared by a discredited philosophy to be the actual essence of intercourse, was rightly ignored by the manufacturers of artificial fruit. Something 'good enough' had long since been accepted by our race.

'The truth is,' he continued, 'that I want to see these stars again. They are curious stars. I want to see them not from the airship, but from the surface of the earth, as our ancestors did, thousands of years ago. I want to visit the surface of the earth.'

She was shocked again.

'Mother, you must come, if only to explain to me what is the harm of visiting the surface of the earth.'

'No harm,' she replied, controlling herself. 'But no advantage. The surface of the earth is only dust and mud, no life remains on it, and you would need a respirator, or the cold of the outer air would kill you. One dies immediately in the outer air.'

'I know; of course I shall take all precautions.'

'And besides—'

'Well?'

She considered and chose her words with care. Her son had a queer temper, and she wished to dissuade him from the expedition.

'It is contrary to the spirit of the age,' she asserted.

'Do you mean by that, contrary to the Machine?'

'In a sense, but—'

His image in the blue plate faded.

'Kuno!'

'Kuno!'

He had isolated himself.

For a moment Vashti felt lonely.

Then she generated the light, and the sight of her room, flooded with radiance and studded with electric buttons, revived her. There were buttons and switches everywhere—buttons to call for food, for music, for clothing. There was the hot-bath button, by pressure of which a basin of (imitation) marble rose out of the floor, filled to the brim with a warm deodorized liquid. There was the cold-bath button. There was the button that produced literature. And there were of course the buttons by which she communicated with her friends. The room, though it contained nothing, was in touch with all that she cared for in the world.

Vashti's next move was to turn off the isolation switch, and all the accumulations of the last three minutes burst upon her. The room was filled with the noise of bells and speaking tubes. What was the new food like? Could she recommend it? Had she had any ideas lately? Might one tell her one's own ideas? Would she make an engagement to visit the public nurseries at an early date—say this day month?

To most of these questions she replied with irritation—a growing quality in that accelerated age. She said that the new food was horrible. That she could not visit the public nurseries through press of engagements. That she had no ideas of her own but had just been told one— that four stars and three in the middle were like a man: she doubted there was much in it. Then she switched off her correspondents, for it was time to deliver her lecture on Australian music.

The clumsy system of public gatherings had long since been abandoned; neither Vashti nor her audience stirred from their rooms. Seated in her armchair she spoke, while they in their armchairs heard her, fairly well, and saw, her fairly well. She opened with a humorous account of music in the pre-Mongolian epoch and went on to describe the great outburst of song that followed the Chinese conquest. Remote and primeval as were the methods of I-San-So and the Brisbane school she yet felt (she said) that study of them might repay the musician of today: they had freshness; they had, above all, ideas.

Her lecture, which lasted ten minutes, was well received, and at its conclusion she and many of her audience listened to a lecture on the sea; there were ideas to be got from the sea; the speaker had donned a respirator and visited it lately. Then she fed, talked to many friends, had a bath, talked again, and summoned her bed.

The bed was not to her liking. It was too large, and she had a feeling for a small bed. Complaint was useless, for beds were of the same dimension all over the world, and to have had an alternative size would have involved vast alterations in the Machine. Vashti isolated herself—it was necessary, for neither day nor night existed under the ground—and reviewed all that had happened since she had summoned the bed last. Ideas? Scarcely any. Events—was Kuno's invitation an event?

By her side, on the little reading desk, was a survival from the ages of litter—one book. This was the Book of the Machine. In it were instructions against every possible contingency. If she was hot or cold or dyspeptic or at loss for a word, she went to the book, and it told her which button to press. The Central Committee published it. In accordance with a growing habit, it was richly bound.

Sitting up in the bed, she took it reverently in her hands. She glanced round the glowing room as if someone might be watching her. Then, half ashamed, half joyful, she murmured, 'O Machine! O Machine!' and raised the volume to her lips. Thrice she kissed it, thrice inclined her head, thrice she felt the delirium of acquiescence. Her ritual performed, she turned to page 1367, which gave the times of the departure of the airships from the island in the southern hemisphere, under whose soil she lived, to the island in the northern hemisphere, whereunder lived her son.

She thought, 'I have not the time.'

She made the room dark and slept; she awoke and made the room light; she ate and exchanged ideas with her friends, and listened to music and attended lectures; she made the room dark and slept. Above her, beneath her, and around her, the Machine hummed eternally; she did not notice the noise, for she had been born with it in her ears. The earth, carrying her, hummed as it sped through silence, turning her now to the invisible sun, now to the invisible stars. She awoke and made the room light.

'Kuno!'

'I will not talk to you,' he answered, 'until you come.'

'Have you been on the surface of the earth since we spoke last?'

His image faded.

Again she consulted the Book. She became very nervous and lay back in her chair palpitating. Think of her as without teeth or hair. Presently she directed the chair to the wall and pressed an unfamiliar button. The wall swung apart slowly. Through the opening she saw a tunnel that curved slightly, so that its goal was not visible. Should she go to see her son, here was the beginning of the journey.

Of course she knew all about the communication system. There was nothing mysterious in it. She would summon a car and it would fly with her down the tunnel until it reached the lift that communicated with the airship station: the system had been in use for many, many years, long before the universal establishment of the Machine. And of course she had studied the civilization that had immediately preceded her own—the civilization that had mistaken the functions of the system and had used it for bringing people to things, instead of bringing things to people. Those funny old days, when men went for change of air instead of changing the air in their rooms! And yet—she was frightened of the tunnel: she had not seen it since her last child was born. It curved—but not quite as she remembered; it was brilliant—but not quite as brilliant as a lecturer had suggested. Vashti was seized with the terrors of direct experience. She shrank back into the room, and the wall closed up again.

'Kuno,' she said, 'I cannot come to see you. I am not well.'

Immediately an enormous apparatus fell onto her out of the ceiling, a thermometer was automatically inserted between her lips, a stethoscope was automatically laid upon her heart. She lay powerless. Cool pads soothed her forehead. Kuno had telegraphed to her doctor.

So the human passions still blundered up and down in the Machine. Vashti drank the medicine that the doctor projected into her mouth, and the machinery retired into the ceiling. The voice of Kuno was heard asking how she felt.

'Better.' Then with irritation: 'But why do you not come to me instead?'

'Because I cannot leave this place.'

'Why?'

'Because, any moment, something tremendous may happen.'

'Have you been on the surface of the earth yet?'

'Not yet.'

'Then what is it?'

'I will not tell you through the Machine.'

She resumed her life.

But she thought of Kuno as a baby, his birth, his removal to the public nurseries, her one visit to him there, his visits to her—visits which stopped when the Machine had assigned him a room on the other side of the earth. 'Parents, duties of,' said the Book of the Machine, 'cease at the moment of birth P. 422327483.' True, but there was something special about Kuno—indeed there had been something special about all her children—and, after all, she must brave the journey if he desired it. And 'something tremendous might happen.' What did that mean? The nonsense of a youthful man, no doubt, but she must go. Again she pressed the unfamiliar button, again the wall swung back and she saw the tunnel that curved out of sight. Clasping the Book, she rose, tottered onto the platform, and summoned the car. Her room closed behind her: the journey to the northern hemisphere had begun.

Of course it was perfectly easy. The car approached and in it she found armchairs exactly like her own. When she signaled, it stopped, and she tottered into the lift. One other passenger was in the lift, the first fellow creature she had seen face to face for months. Few travelled in these days, for, thanks to the advance of science, the earth was exactly alike all over. Rapid intercourse, from which the previous civilization had hoped so much, had ended by defeating itself. What was the good of going to Pekin when it was just like Shrewsbury? Why return to Shrewsbury when it would be just like Pekin? Men seldom moved their bodies; all unrest was concentrated in the soul.

The airship service was a relic from the former age. It was kept up, because it was easier to keep it up than to stop it or to diminish it, but it now far exceeded the wants of the population. Vessel after vessel would rise from the vomitories of Rye or Christchurch (I use the antique names), would sail into the crowded sky, and would draw up at the wharves of the south—empty. So nicely adjusted was the system, so independent of meteorology, that the sky, whether calm or cloudy, resembled a vast kaleidoscope whereon the same patterns periodically recurred. The ship on which Vashti sailed started now at sunset, now at dawn. But always, as it passed above Rheims, it would neighbour the ship that served between Helsinfors and the Brazils, and every third time it surmounted the Alps, the fleet of Palermo would cross its track behind. Night and day, wind and storm, tide and earthquake impeded man no longer. He had harnessed Leviathan. All the old literature, with its praise of Nature, and its fear of Nature, rang false as the prattle of a child.

Yet as Vashti saw the vast flank of the ship, stained with exposure to the outer air, her horror of direct experience returned. It was not quite like the airship in the cinematophote. For one thing it smelt—not strongly or unpleasantly, but it did smell, and with her eyes shut she should have known that a new thing was close to her. Then she had to walk to it from the lift, had to submit to glances from the other passengers. The man in front dropped his Book—no great matter, but it disquieted them all. In the rooms, if the Book was dropped, the floor raised it mechanically, but the gangway to the airship was not so prepared, and the sacred volume lay motionless. They stopped—the thing was unforeseen—and the man, instead of picking up his property, felt the muscles of his arm to see how they had failed him. Then someone actually said with direct utterance: 'We shall be late'—and they trooped on board, Vashti treading on the pages as she did so.

Inside, her anxiety increased. The arrangements were old-fashioned and rough. There was even a female attendant, to whom she would have to announce her wants during the voyage. Of course a revolving platform ran the length of the boat, but she was expected to walk from it to her cabin. Some cabins were better than others, and she did not get the best. She thought the attendant had been unfair, and spasms of rage shook her. The glass valves had closed, she could not go back. She saw at the end of the vestibule, the lift in which she had ascended going quietly up and down, empty. Beneath those corridors of shining tiles were rooms, tier below tier, reaching far into the earth, and in each room there sat a human being, eating, or sleeping, or producing ideas. And buried deep in the hive was her own room. Vashti was afraid.

'O Machine! O Machine!' she murmured, and caressed her Book, and was comforted.

Then the sides of the vestibule seemed to melt together, as do the passages that we see in dreams, the lift vanished, the Book that had been dropped slid to the left and vanished, polished tiles rushed by like a stream of water, there was a slight jar, and the airship, issuing from its tunnel, soared above the waters of a tropical ocean.

It was night. For a moment she saw the coast of Sumatra edged by the phosphorescence of waves, and crowned by lighthouses, still sending forth their disregarded beams. These also vanished, and only the stars distracted her. They were not motionless, but swayed to and fro above her head, thronging out of one skylight into another, as if the universe and not the airship was careening. And, as often happens on clear nights, they seemed now to be in perspective, now on a plane; now piled tier beyond tier into the infinite heavens, now concealing infinity, a roof limiting forever the visions of men. In either case they seemed intolerable. 'Are we to travel in the dark?' called the passengers angrily, and the attendant, who had been careless, generated the light, and pulled down the blinds of pliable metal. When the airships had been built, the desire to look direct at things still lingered in the world. Hence the extraordinary number of skylights and windows, and the proportionate discomfort to those who were civilized and refined. Even in Vashti's cabin one star peeped through a flaw in the blind, and after a few hours' uneasy slumber, she was disturbed by an unfamiliar glow, which was the dawn.

Quick as the ship had sped westwards, the earth had rolled eastwards quicker still and had dragged back Vashti and her companions towards the sun. Science could prolong the night, but only for a little, and those high hopes of neutralizing the earth's diurnal revolution had passed, together with hopes that were possibly higher. To 'keep pace with the sun,' or even to outstrip it, had been the aim of the civilization preceding this. Racing airplanes had been built for the purpose, capable of enormous speed, and steered by the greatest intellects of the epoch. Round the globe they went, round and round, westward, westward, round and round, amidst humanity's applause. In vain. The globe went eastward quicker still, horrible accidents occurred, and the Committee of the Machine, at the time rising into prominence, declared the pursuit illegal, unmechanical, and punishable by Homelessness.

Of Homelessness more will be said later.

Doubtless the Committee was right. Yet the attempt to 'defeat the sun' aroused the last common interest that our race experienced about the heavenly bodies, or indeed about anything. It was the last time that men were compacted by thinking of a power outside the world. The sun had conquered, yet it was the end of his spiritual dominion. Dawn, midday, twilight, the zodiacal path touched neither men's lives nor their hearts, and science retreated into the ground, to concentrate herself upon problems that she was certain of solving.

So when Vashti found her cabin invaded by a rosy finger of light, she was annoyed, and tried to adjust the blind. But the blind flew up altogether, and she saw through the skylight small pink clouds, swaying against a background of blue, and as the sun crept higher, its radiance entered direct, brimming down the wall, like a golden sea. It rose and fell with the airship's motion, just as waves rise and fall, but it advanced steadily, as a tide advances. Unless she was careful, it would strike her face. A spasm of horror shook her and she rang for the attendant. The attendant too was horrified, but she could do nothing; it was not her place to mend the blind. She could only suggest that the lady should change her cabin, which she accordingly prepared to do.

People were almost exactly alike all over the world, but the attendant of the airship, perhaps owing to her exceptional duties, had grown a little out of the common. She had often to address passengers with direct speech, and this had given her a certain roughness and originality of manner. When Vashti swerved away from the sunbeams with a cry, she behaved barbarically—she put out her hand to steady her.

'How dare you!' exclaimed the passenger. 'You forget yourself!'

The woman was confused, and apologized for not having let her fall. People never touched one another. The custom had become obsolete, owing to the Machine.

'Where are we now?' asked Vashti haughtily.

'We are over Asia,' said the attendant, anxious to be polite.

'Asia?'

'You must excuse my common way of speaking. I have got into the habit of calling places over which I pass by their unmechanical names.'

'Oh, I remember Asia. The Mongols came from it.'

'Beneath us, in the open air, stood a city that was once called Simla.'

'Have you ever heard of the Mongols and of the Brisbane school?'

'No'.

'Brisbane also stood in the open air.'

'Those mountains to the right—let me show you them.' She pushed back a metal blind. The main chain of the Himalayas was revealed. 'They were once called the Roof of the World, those mountains.'

'What a foolish name!'

'You must remember that, before the dawn of civilization, they seemed to be an impenetrable wall that touched the stars. It was supposed that no one but the gods could exist above their summits. How we have advanced, thanks to the Machine!'

'How we have advanced, thanks to the Machine!' said Vashti.

'How we have advanced, thanks to the Machine!' echoed the passenger who had dropped his Book the night before, and who was standing in the passage.

'And that white stuff in the cracks—what is it?'

'I have forgotten its name.'

'Cover the window, please. These mountains give me no ideas.'

The northern aspect of the Himalayas was in deep shadow: on the Indian slope the sun had just prevailed. The forests had been destroyed during the literature epoch for the purpose of making newspaper pulp, but the snows were awakening in their morning glory, and clouds still hung on the breasts of Kinchinjunga. In the plain were seen the ruins of cities, with diminished rivers creeping by their walls, and by the sides of these were sometimes the signs of vomitories, marking the cities of today. Over the whole prospect airships rushed, crossing and inter-crossing with incredible aplomb, and rising nonchalantly when they desired to escape the perturbations of the lower atmosphere and to traverse the Roof of the World.

'We have intended advanced, thanks to the Machine,' repeated the attendant, and hid the Himalayas behind a metal blind.

The day dragged wearily forward. The passengers sat each in his cabin, avoiding one another with an almost physical repulsion and longing to be once more under the surface of the earth. There were eight or ten of them, mostly young males, sent out from the public nurseries to inhabit the rooms of those who had died in various parts of the earth. The man who had dropped his Book was on the homeward journey. He had been sent to Sumatra for the purpose of propagating the race. Vashti alone was travelling by her private will.

At midday she took a second glance at the earth. The airship was crossing another range of mountains, but she could see little, owing to clouds. Masses of black rock hovered below her and merged indistinctly into gray. Their shapes were fantastic; one of them resembled a prostrate man.

'No ideas here,' murmured Vashti, and hid the Caucasus behind a metal blind.

In the evening she looked again. They were crossing a golden sea, in which lay many small islands and one peninsula.

She repeated, 'No ideas here,' and hid Greece behind a metal blind.

II: *The mending apparatus* By a vestibule, by a lift, by a tubular rail-way, by a platform, by a sliding door—by reversing all the steps of her departure did Vashti arrive at her son's room, which exactly resembled her own. She might well declare that the visit was superfluous. The buttons, the knobs, the reading desk with the Book, the temperature, the atmosphere, the illumination—all were exactly the same. And if Kuno himself, flesh of her flesh, stood close beside her at last, what profit was there in that? She was too well-bred to shake him by the hand. Averting her eyes, she spoke as follows:

Here I am. I have had the most terrible journey and greatly retarded the development of my soul. It is not worth it, Kuno, it is not worth it. My time is too precious. The sunlight almost touched me, and I have met with the rudest people. I can only stop a few minutes. Say what you want to say, and then I must return.'

'I have been threatened with Homelessness,' said Kuno.

She looked at him now.

'I have been threatened with Homelessness, and I could not tell you such a thing through the Machine.'

Homelessness means death. The victim is exposed to the air, which kills him.

'I have been outside since I spoke to you last. The tremendous thing has happened, and they have discovered me.'

'But why shouldn't you go outside!' she exclaimed. 'It is perfectly legal, perfectly mechanical, to visit the surface of the earth. I have lately been to a lecture on the sea; there is no objection to that; one simply summons a respirator and gets an Egression permit. It is not the kind of thing that spiritually-minded people do, and I begged you not to do it, but there is no legal objection to it.'

'I did not get an Egression permit.'

'Then how did you get out?'

'I found out a way of my own.'

The phrase conveyed no meaning to her, and he had to repeat it.

'A way of your own?' she whispered. 'But that would be wrong.'

'Why?'

The question shocked her beyond measure.

'You are beginning to worship the Machine,' he said coldly. 'You think it irreligious of me to have found out a way of my own. It was just what the Committee thought, when they threatened me with Homelessness.'

At this she grew angry. 'I worship nothing!' she cried. 'I am most advanced. I don't think you irreligious, for there is no such thing as religion left. All the fear and the superstition that existed once have been destroyed by the Machine. I only meant that to find out a way of your own was—Besides, there is no new way out.'

'So it is always supposed.'

'Except through the vomitories, for which one must have an Egression permit, it is impossible to get out. The Book says so.'

'Well, the Book's wrong, for I have been out on my feet.'

For Kuno was possessed of a certain physical strength.

By these days it was a demerit to be muscular. Each infant was examined at birth, and all who promised undue strength were destroyed. Humanitarians may protest, but it would have been no true kindness to let an athlete live; he would never have been happy in that state of life to which the Machine had called him; he would have yearned for trees to climb, rivers to bathe in, meadows and hills against which he might measure his body. Man must be adapted to his surroundings, must he not? In the dawn of the world our weak must be exposed on Mount Taygetus, in its twilight our strong will suffer euthanasia, that the

329

Machine may progress, that the Machine may progress, that the Machine may progress eternally.

'You know that we have lost the sense of space. We say "space is annihilated," but we have annihilated not space, but the sense thereof. We have lost a part of ourselves. I determined to recover it, and I began by walking up and down the platform of the railway outside my room. Up and down, until I was tired, and so did recapture the meaning of "Near" and "Far." "Near" is a place to which I can get quickly *on my feet*, not a place to which the train or the airship will take me quickly. "Far" is a place to which I cannot get quickly on my feet; the vomitory is "far", though I could be there in thirty-eight seconds by summoning the train. Man is the measure. That was my first lesson. Man's feet are the measure for distance, his hands are the measure for ownership, his body is the measure for all that is lovable and desirable and strong. Then I went further: it was then that I called to you for the first time, and you would not come.

'This city, as you know is built deep beneath the surface of the earth, with only the vomitories protruding. Having paced the platform outside my own room, I took the lift to the next platform and paced that also, and so with each in turn, until I came to the topmost, above which begins the earth. All the platforms were exactly alike, and all that I gained by visiting them was to develop my sense of space and my muscles. I think I should have been content with this—it is not a little thing—but as I walked and brooded, it occurred to me that our cities had been built in the days when men still breathed the outer air, and that there had been ventilation shafts for the workmen. I could think of nothing but these ventilation shafts. Had they been destroyed by all the food tubes and medicine tubes and music tubes that the Machine has evolved lately? Or did traces of them remain? One thing was certain. If I came upon them anywhere, it would be in the railway tunnels of the topmost story. Everywhere else, all space was accounted for.

'I am telling my story quickly, but don't think that I was not a coward or that your answers never depressed me. It is not the proper thing, it is not mechanical, it is not decent to walk along a railway tunnel. I did not fear that I might tread upon a live rail and be killed. I feared something far more intangible—doing what was not contemplated by the Machine. Then I said to myself, "Man is the measure," and I went, and after many visits I found an opening.

'The tunnels, of course, were lighted, Everything is light, artificial light; darkness is the exception. So when I saw a black gap in the tiles, I knew that it was an exception and rejoiced. I put in my arm—I could put in no more at first—and waved it round and round in ecstasy. I loosened another tile, and put in my head, and shouted into the darkness:

' "I am coming, I shall do it yet," and my voice reverberated down endless passages. I seemed to hear the spirits of those dead workmen who had returned each evening to the starlight and to their wives, and all the generations who had lived in the open air called back to me, "You will do it yet, you are coming." '

He paused, and, absurd as he was, his last words moved her. For Kuno had lately asked to be a father, and his request had been refused by the Committee. His was not a type that the Machine desired to hand on.

'Then a train passed. It brushed by me, but I thrust my head and arms into the hole. I had done enough for one day, so I crawled back to the platform, went down in the lift, and summoned my bed. Ah, what dreams! And again I called you, and again you refused.'

She shook her head and said:

'Don't. Don't talk of these terrible things. You make me miserable. You are throwing civilization away.'

'But I had got back the sense of space and a man cannot rest then. I determined to get in at the hole and climb the shaft. And so I exercised my arms. Day after day I went through ridiculous movements, until my flesh ached, and I could hang by my hands and hold the pillow of my bed outstretched for many minutes. Then I summoned a respirator, and started.

'It was easy at first. The mortar had somehow rotted, and I soon pushed some more tiles in, and clambered after them into the darkness, and the spirits of the dead comforted me. I don't know what I mean by that. I just say what I felt. I felt, for the first time, that a protest had been lodged against corruption, and that even as the dead were comforting me, so I was comforting the unborn. I felt that humanity existed, and that it existed without clothes. How can I possibly explain this? It was naked, humanity seemed naked, and all these tubes and buttons and machineries neither came into the world with us, nor will they follow us out, nor do they matter supremely while we are here. Had I been strong, I would have torn off every garment I had, and gone out into the outer air unswaddled. But this is not for me, nor perhaps for my generation. I climbed with my respirator and my hygienic clothes and my dietetic tabloids! Better thus than not at all.

'There was a ladder, made of some primeval metal. The light from the railway fell upon its lowest rungs, and I saw that it led straight upwards out of the rubble at the bottom of the shaft. Perhaps our ancestors ran up and down it a dozen times daily, in their buildings. As I climbed, the rough edges cut through my gloves so that my hands bled. The light helped me for a little, and then came darkness and, worse still, silence which pierced my ears like a sword. The Machine hums! Did you know that? Its hum penetrates our blood, and my even guide our thoughts. Who knows! I was getting beyond its power. Then I thought: "This silence means that I am doing wrong." But I heard voices in the silence, and again they strengthened me.' He laughed. 'I had need of them. The next moment I cracked my head against something.'

She sighed.

'I had reached one of those pneumatic stoppers that defend us from the outer air. You may have noticed them on the airship. Pitch dark, my feet on the rungs of an invisible ladder, my hands cut; I cannot explain how I lived through this part, but the voices still comforted me, and I felt for fastenings. The stopper, I suppose, was about eight feet across. I passed my hand over it as far as I could reach. It was perfectly smooth. I felt it almost to the centre. Not quite to the centre, for my arm was too short. Then the voice said: "Jump. It is worth it. There may be a handle in the centre, and you may catch hold of it and so come to us your own way. And if there is no handle, so that you may fall and are dashed to pieces—it is still worth it: you will still come to us your own way." So I jumped. There was a handle, and—'

He paused. Tears gathered in his mother's eyes. She knew that he was fated. If he did not die today he would die tomorrow. There was not room for such a person in the world. And with her pity disgust was mingled. She was ashamed at having borne such a son, she who had always been so respectable and so full of ideas. Was he really the little boy to whom she had taught the use of his stops and buttons, and to whom she had given his first lessons in the Book? The very hair that disfigured his lip showed that he was reverting to some savage type. On atavism the Machine can have no mercy.

'There was a handle, and I did catch it. I hung tranced over the darkness and heard the hum of these workings as the last whisper in a dying dream. All the things I had cared about and all the people I had spoken to through tubes appeared infinitely little. Meanwhile the handle revolved. My weight had set something in motion and I span slowly, and then—

'I cannot describe it. I was lying with my face to the sunshine. Blood poured from my nose and ears and I heard a tremendous roaring. The stopper, with me clinging to it, had simply been blown out of the earth, and the air that we make down here was escaping through the vent into the air above. It burst up like a fountain. I crawled back to it—for the upper air hurts—and, as it were, I took great sips from the edge. My respirator had flown goodness knows where, my clothes were torn. I just lay with my lips close to the hole, and I sipped until the bleeding stopped. You can imagine nothing so curious. This hollow in the grass—I will speak of it in a minute—the sun shining into it, not brilliantly but through marbled clouds—the peace, the nonchalance, the sense of space, and, brushing my cheek, the roaring fountain of our artificial air! Soon I spied my respirator, bobbing up and down in the current high above my head, and higher still were many airships. But no one ever looks out of airships, and in my case they could not have picked me up. There I was, stranded. The sun shone a little way down the shaft, and revealed the topmost rung of the ladder, but it was hopeless trying to reach it. I should either have been tossed up again by the escape, or else have fallen in, and died. I could only lie on the grass, sipping and sipping, and from time to time glancing around me.

'I knew that I was in Wessex, for I had taken care to go to a lecture on the subject before starting. Wessex lies above the room in which we are talking now. It was once an important state. Its kings held all the southern coast from the Andredswald to Cornwall, while the Wansdyke protected them on the north, running over the high ground. The lecturer was only concerned with the rise of Wessex, so I do not know how long it remained an international power, nor would the knowledge have assisted me. To tell the truth I could do nothing but laugh, during this part. There was I, with a pneumatic stopper by my side and a respirator bobbing over my head, imprisoned, all three of us, in a grass-grown hollow that was edged with fern.'

Then he grew grave again.

'Lucky for me that it was a hollow. For the air began to fall back into it and to fill it as water fills a bowl. I could crawl about. Presently I stood. I breathed a mixture, in which the air that hurts predominated whenever I tried to climb the sides. This was not so bad. I had not lost my tabloids and remained ridiculously cheerful, and as for the Machine, I forgot about it altogether. My one aim now was to get to the top, where the ferns were, and to view whatever objects lay beyond.

'I rushed the slope. The new air was still too bitter for me and I came rolling back, after a momentary vision of something gray. The sun grew very feeble, and I remembered that he was in Scorpio—I had been to a lecture on that, too. If the sun is in Scorpio and you are in Wessex, it means that you must be as quick as you can, or it will get too dark. (This is the first bit of useful information I have ever got from a lecture, and I expect it will be the last.) It made me try frantically to breathe the new air, and to advance as far as I dared out of my pond. The hollow filled so slowly. At times I thought that the fountain played with less vigour. My respirator seemed to dance nearer the earth; the roar was decreasing.'

He broke off.

'I don't think this is interesting you. The rest will interest you even less. There are no ideas in it, and I wish that I had not troubled you to come. We are too different, Mother.'

She told him to continue.

'It was evening before I climbed the bank. The sun had very nearly slipped out of the sky by this time, and I could not get a good view. You, who have just crossed the Roof of the World, will not want to hear an account of the little hills that I saw—low colorless hills. But to me they were living and the turf that covered them was a skin, under which their muscles rippled, and I felt that those hills had called with incalculable force to men in the past, and that men had loved them. Now they sleep—perhaps forever. They commune with humanity in dreams. Happy the man, happy the woman, who awakes the hills of Wessex. For though they sleep, they will never die.'

His voice rose passionately.

'Cannot you see, cannot all your lecturers see, that it is we who are dying, and that down here the only thing that really lives is the Machine? We created the Machine, to do our will, but we cannot make it do our will now. It has robbed us of the sense of space and of the sense of touch, it has blurred every human relation and narrowed down love to a carnal act, it has paralyzed our bodies and our wills, and now it compels us to worship it. The Machine develops—but not on our lines. The Machine proceeds—but not to our goal. We only exist as the blood corpuscles that course through its arteries, and if it could work without us, it would let us die. Oh, I have no remedy—or, at least, only one—to tell men again that I have seen the hills of Wessex as Aelfred saw them when he overthrew the Danes.

'So the sun set. I forgot to mention that a belt of mist lay between my hill and other hills, and that it was the colour of pearl.'

He broke off for the second time.

'Go on,' said his mother wearily.

He shook his head.

'Go on. Nothing that you say can distress me now. I am hardened.'

'I had meant to tell you the rest, but I cannot: I know that I cannot: good-bye.'

Vashti stood irresolute. All her nerves were tingling with his blasphemies. But she was also inquisitive.

'This is unfair,' she complained. 'You have called me across the world to hear your story, and hear it I will. Tell me—as briefly as possible, for this is a disastrous waste of time—tell me how you returned to civilization.'

'Oh—that!' he said, starting. 'You would like to hear about civilization. Certainly. Had I got to where my respirator fell down?'

'No—but I understand everything now. You put on your respirator, and managed to walk along the surface of the earth to a vomitory, and there your conduct was reported to the Central Committee.'

'By no means.'

He passed his hand over his forehead, as if dispelling some strong impression. Then, resuming his narrative, he warmed to it again.

'My respirator fell about sunset. I had mentioned that the fountain seemed feebler, had I not?'

'Yes.'

'About sunset, it let the respirator fall. As I said, I had entirely forgotten about the Machine, and I paid no great attention at the time, being occupied with other things. I had my pool of air, into which I could dip when the outer keenness became intolerable, and which would possibly remain for days, provided that no wind sprang up to disperse it. Not until it was too late, did I realize what the stoppage of the escape implied. You see—the gap in the tunnel had been mended; the Mending Apparatus; the Mending Apparatus, was after me.

'One other warning I had, but I neglected it. The sky at night was clearer than it had been in the day, and the moon, which was about half the sky behind the sun, shone into the dell at moments quite brightly. I was in my usual place—on the boundary between the two atmospheres—when I thought I saw something dark move across the bottom of the dell, and vanish into the shaft. In my folly, I ran down. I bent over and listened, and I thought I heard a faint scraping noise in the depths.

'At this—but it was too late—I took alarm. I determined to put on my respirator and to walk right out of the dell. But my respirator had gone. I knew exactly where it had fallen—between the stopper and the aperture —and I could even feel the mark that it had made in the turf. It had gone, and I realized that something evil was at work, and I had better escape to the other air, and, if I must die, die running toward the clouds that had been the colour of a pearl. I never started. Out of the shaft—it is too horrible. A worm, a long white worm, had crawled out of the shaft and was gliding over the moonlit grass.

'I screamed. I did everything that I should not have done. I stamped upon the creature instead of flying from it, and it at once curled round the ankle. Then we fought. The worm let me run all over the dell, but edged up my leg as I ran. "Help!" I cried. (That part is too awful. It belongs to the part that you will never know.) "Help!" I cried. (Why cannot we suffer in silence?) "Help!" I cried. Then my feet were wound together, I fell, I was dragged away from the dear ferns and the living hills, and past the great metal stopper (I can tell you this part), and I thought it might save me again if I caught hold of the handle. It also was enwrapped, it also. Oh, the whole dell was full of the things. They were searching it in all directions, they were denuding it, and the white snouts of others peeped out of the hole, ready if needed. Everything that could be moved they brought—brushwood, bundles of fern, everything, and down we all went intertwined into hell. The last things that I saw, ere the stopper closed after us, were certain stars, and I felt that a man of my sort lived in the sky. For I did fight, I fought till the very end, and it was only my head hitting against the ladder that quieted me. I woke up in this room. The worms had vanished. I was surrounded by artificial air, artificial light, artificial peace, and my friends were calling to me down speaking tubes to know whether I had come across any new ideas lately.'

Here his story ended. Discussion of it was impossible, and Vashti turned to go.

'It will end in Homelessness,' she said quietly.

'I wish it would,' retorted Kuno.

'The Machine has been most merciful.'

'I prefer the mercy of God.'

'By that superstitious phrase, do you mean that you could live in the outer air?'

'Yes.'

'Have you ever seen, round the vomitories, the bones of those who were extruded after the Great Rebellion?'

'Yes.'

'They were left where they perished for our edification. A few crawled away, but they perished, too—who can doubt it? And so with the Homeless of our own day. The surface of the earth supports life no longer.'

'Indeed.'

'Ferns and a little grass may survive, but all higher forms have perished. Has any airship detected them?'

'No.'

'Has any lecturer dealt with them?'

'No.'

'Then why this obstinacy?'

'Because I have seen them,' he exploded.

'Seen *what*?'

'Because I have seen her in the twilight—because she came to my help when I called—because she, too, was entangled by the worms, and, luckier than I, was killed by one of them piercing her throat.'

He was mad. Vashti departed, nor, in the troubles that followed, did she ever see his face again.

III: *The homeless* During the years that followed Kuno's escapade, two important developments took place in the Machine. On the surface they were revolutionary, but in either case men's minds had been prepared before hand, and they did but express tendencies that were latent already.

The first of these was the abolition of respirators.

Advanced thinkers, like Vashti, had always held it foolish to visit the surface of the earth. Airships might be necessary, but what was the good of going out for mere curiosity and crawling along for a mile or two in a terrestrial motor? The habit was vulgar and perhaps faintly improper:

it was unproductive of ideas, and had no connection with the habits that really mattered. So respirators were abolished, and with them, of course, the terrestrial motors, and except for a few lecturers, who complained that they were debarred access to their subject matter, the development was accepted quietly. Those who still wanted to know what the earth was like had after all only to listen to some gramophone, or to look into some cinematophote. And even the lecturers acquiesced when they found that a lecture on the sea was none the less stimulating when compiled out of other lectures that had already been delivered on the same subject. 'Beware of firsthand ideas!' exclaimed one of the most advanced of them. 'Firsthand ideas do not really exist. They are but the physical impressions produced by love and fear, and on this gross foundation who could erect a philosophy? Let your ideas be secondhand, and if possible tenth-hand, for then they will be far removed from the disturbing element—direct observation. Do not learn anything about this subject of mine—the French Revolution. Learn instead what I think that Enicharmon thought Urizen thought Gutch thought Ho-Yung thought Chi-Bo-Sing thought Lafcadio Hearn thought Carlyle thought Mirabeau said about the French Revolution. Through the medium of these eight great minds, the blood that was shed at Paris and the windows that were broken at Versailles will be clarified to an idea which you may employ profitably in your daily lives. But be sure that the intermediates are many and varied, for in history one authority exists to counteract another. Urizen must counteract the scepticism of Ho-Yung and Enicharmon, I must myself counteract the impetuosity of Gutch. You who listen to me are in a better position to judge about the French Revolution than I am. Your descendants will be even in a better position than you, for they will learn what you think I think, and yet another intermediate will be added to the chain. And in time'—his voice rose—'there will come a generation that has got beyond facts, beyond impressions, a generation absolutely colourless, a generation

*seraphically free*
*From taint of personality,*

which will see the French Revolution not as it happened, nor as they would like it to have happened, but as it would have happened, had it taken place in the days of the Machine.'

Tremendous applause greeted this lecture, which did but voice a feeling already latent in the minds of men—a feeling that terrestrial facts must be ignored, and that the abolition of respirators was a positive gain. It was even suggested that airships should be abolished, too. This was not done, because airships had somehow worked themselves into the Machine's system. But year by year they were used less, and mentioned less by thoughtful men.

The second great development was the reestablishment of religion.

This, too, had been voiced in the celebrated lecture. No one could mistake the reverent tone in which the peroration had concluded, and it awakened a responsive echo in the heart of each. Those who had long worshiped silently, now began to talk. They described the strange feeling of peace that came over them when they handled the Book of the Machine, the pleasure that it was to repeat certain numerals out of it, however little meaning those numerals conveyed to the outward ear, the ecstasy of touching a button, however, unimportant, or of ringing an electric bell, however superfluously.

'The Machine,' they exclaimed, 'feeds us and clothes us and houses us; through it we speak to one another, through it we see one another, in it we have our being. The Machine is the friend of ideas and the enemy of superstition: the Machine is omnipotent, eternal; blessed is the Machine.' And before long this allocution was printed on the first page of the Book, and in subsequent editions the ritual swelled into a complicated system of praise and prayer. The word 'religion' was sedulously avoided, and in theory the Machine was still the creation and the implement of man. But in practice all, save a few retrogrades, worshiped it as divine. Nor was it worshiped in unity. One believer would be chiefly impressed by the blue optic plates, through which he saw other believers; another by the mending apparatus, which sinful Kuno had compared to worms; another by the lifts, another by the Book. And each would pray to this or to that, and ask it to intercede for him with the Machine as a whole. Persecution—that also was present. It did not break out, for reasons that will be set forward shortly. But it was latent, and all who did not accept the minimum known as 'undenominational Mechanism' lived in danger of Homelessness, which means death, as we know.

To attribute these two great developments to the Central Committee is to take a very narrow view of civilization. The Central Committee announced the developments, it is true, but they were no more the cause of them than were the kings of the imperialistic period the cause of war. Rather did they yield to some invincible pressure, which came no one knew whence, and which, when gratified, was succeeded by some new pressure equally invincible. To such a state of affairs it is convenient to give the name of progress. No one confessed the Machine was out of hand. Year by year it was served with increased efficiency and decreased intelligence. The better a man knew his own duties upon it, the less he understood the duties of his neighbour, and in all the world there was not one who understood the monster as a whole. Those master brains had perished. They had left full directions, it is true, and their successors had each of them mastered a portion of those directions. But humanity, in its desire for comfort, had overreached itself. It had exploited the riches of nature too far. Quietly and complacently, it was sinking into decadence and progress had come to mean the progress of the Machine.

As for Vashti, her life went peacefully forward until the final disaster. She made her room dark and slept; she awoke and made the room light. She lectured and attended lectures. She exchanged ideas with her innumerable friends and believed she was growing more spiritual. At times a friend was granted Euthanasia, and left his or her room for the Homelessness that is beyond all human conception. Vashti did not much mind. After an unsuccessful lecture, she would sometimes ask for Euthanasia herself. But the death rate was not permitted to exceed the birth rate, and the Machine had hitherto refused it to her.

The troubles began quietly, long before she was conscious of them.

One day she was astonished at receiving a message from her son. They never communicated, having nothing in common, and she had only heard indirectly that he was still alive, and had been transferred from the northern hemisphere, where he had behaved so mischievously, to the southern—indeed, to a room not far from her own.

'Does he want me to visit him?' she thought. 'Never again, never. And I have not the time.'

No, it was madness of another kind.

He refused to visualize his face upon the blue plate, and speaking out of the darkness with solemnity said:

'The Machine stops.'

'What do you say?'

'The Machine is stopping. I know it, I know the signs.'

She burst into a peal of laughter. He heard her and was angry, and they spoke no more.

'Can you imagine anything more absurd?' she cried to a friend. 'A man who was my son believes that the Machine is stopping. It would be impious if it was not mad.'

'The Machine is stopping?' her friend replied. 'What does that mean? The phrase conveys nothing to me.'

'Nor to me.'

'He does not refer, I suppose, to the trouble there has been lately with the music?'

'Oh no, of course not. Let us talk about music.'

'Have you complained to the authorities?'

'Yes, and they say it wants mending, and referred me to the Committee of the Mending Apparatus. I complained of those curious gasping sighs that disfigure the symphonies of the Brisbane school. They sound like someone in pain. The Committee of the Mending Apparatus say that it shall be remedied shortly.'

Obscurely worried, she resumed her life. For one thing, the defect in the music irritated her. For another thing, she could not forget Kuno's speech. If he had known that the music was out of repair—he could not know it, for he detested music—if he had known that it was wrong, 'the Machine stops' was exactly the venomous sort of remark he would have made. Of course he had made it at a venture, but the coincidence annoyed her, and she spoke with some petulance to the Committee of the Mending Apparatus.

They replied, as before, that the defect would be set right shortly.

'Shortly! At once!' she retorted. 'Why should I be worried by imperfect music? Things are always put right at once. If you do not mend it at once, I shall complain to the Central Committee.'

'No personal complaints are received by the Central Committee,' the Committee of the Mending Apparatus replied.

'Through whom am I to make my complaint, then?'

'Through us.'

'I complain then.'

'Your complaint shall be forwarded in its turn.'

'Have others complained?'

This question was unmechanical, and the Committee of the Mending Apparatus refused to answer it.

'It is too bad!' she exclaimed to another of her friends. 'There never was such an unfortunate woman as myself. I can never be sure of my music now. It gets worse and worse each time I summon it.'

'I too have my troubles,' the friend replied. 'Sometimes my ideas are interrupted by a slight jarring noise.'

'What is it?'

'I do not know whether it is inside my head, or inside the wall.'

'Complain, in either case.'

'I have complained, and my complaint will be forwarded in its turn to the Central Committee.'

Time passed, and they resented the defects no longer. The defects had not been remedied, but the human tissues in that latter day had become so subservient, that they readily adapted themselves to every caprice of the Machine. The sigh at the crisis of the Brisbane symphony no longer irritated Vashti; she accepted it as part of the melody. The jarring noise, whether in the head or in the wall, was no longer resented by her friend. And so with the mouldy artificial fruit, so with the bath water that began to stink, so with the defective rhymes that the poetry machine had taken to emit. All were bitterly complained of at first, and then acquiesced in and forgotten. Things went from bad to worse unchallenged.

It was otherwise with the failure of the sleeping apparatus. That was a more serious stoppage. There came a day when over the whole world— in Sumatra, in Wessex, in the innumerable cities of Courland and Brazil —the beds, when summoned by their tired owners, failed to appear. It may seem a ludicrous matter, but from it we may date the collapse of humanity. The Committee responsible for the failure was assailed by complainants, whom it referred, as usual, to the Committee of the Mending Apparatus, who in its turn assured them that their complaints would be forwarded to the Central Committee. But the discontent grew, for mankind was not yet sufficiently adaptable to do without sleeping.

'Someone is meddling with the Machine—' they began.

'Someone is trying to make himself king, to reintroduce the personal element.'

'Punish that man with Homelessness.'

'To the rescue! Avenge the Machine! Avenge the Machine!'

'War! Kill the man!'

But the Committee of the Mending Apparatus now came forward, and allayed the panic with well-chosen words. It confessed that the Mending Apparatus was itself in need of repair.

The effect of this frank confession was admirable.

'Of course,' said a famous lecturer—he of the French Revoultion, who gilded each new decay with splendor—'of course we shall not press our complaints now. The Mending Apparatus has treated us so well in the past that we all sympathize with it, and will wait patiently for its recovery. In its own good time it will resume its duties. Meanwhile let us do without our beds, our tabloids, our other little wants. Such, I feel sure, would be the wish of the Machine.'

Thousands of miles away his audience applauded. The Machine still linked them. Under the seas, beneath the roots of the mountains, ran the wires through which they saw and heard, the enormous eyes and ears that were their heritage, and the hum of many workings clothed their thoughts in one garment of subserviency. Only the old and the sick remained ungrateful, for it was rumoured that Euthanasia, too, was out of order, and that pain had reappeared among men.

It became difficult to read. A blight entered the atmosphere and dulled its luminosity. At times Vashti could scarcely see across her room. The air, too, was foul. Loud were the complaints, impotent the remedies, heroic the tone of the lecturer as he cried: 'Courage, courage! What matter so long as the Machine goes on? To it the darkness and the light are one.' And though things improved again after a time, the old brilliancy was never recaptured, and humanity never recovered from its entrance into twilight. There was an hysterical talk of 'measures', of 'provisional dictatorship', and the inhabitants of Sumatra were asked to familiarize themselves with the workings of the central power station, the said power station being situated in France. But for the most part panic reigned, and men spent their strength praying to their Books, tangible proofs of the Machine's omnipotence. There were gradations of terror—at times came rumours of hope—the Mending Apparatus was almost mended—the enemies of the Machine had been got under—new 'nerve centers' were evolving which would do the work even more magnificently than before. But there came a day when, without the slightest warning, without any previous hint of feebleness, the entire communication system broke down, all over the world, and the world, as they understood it, ended.

Vashti was lecturing at the time and her earlier remarks had been punctuated with applause. As she proceeded the audience became silent, and at the conclusion there was no sound. Somewhat displeased, she called to a friend who was a specialist in sympathy. No sound: doubtless the friend was sleeping. And so with the next friend whom she tried to summon, and so with the next, until she remembered Kuno's cryptic remark, 'The Machine stops.'

The phrase still conveyed nothing. If Eternity was stopping it would of course be set going shortly.

For example, there was still a little light and air—the atmosphere had improved a few hours previously. There was still the Book, and while there was the Book there was security.

Then she broke down, for with the cessation of activity came an unexpected terror—silence.

She had never known silence, and the coming of it nearly killed her—it did kill many thousands of people outright. Ever since her birth she had been surrounded by the steady hum. It was to the ear what artificial air was to the lungs, and agonizing pains shot across her head. And scarcely knowing what she did, she stumbled forward and pressed the unfamiliar button, the one that opened the door of her cell.

Now the door of the cell worked on a simple hinge of its own. It was not connected with the central power station, dying far away in France. It opened, rousing immoderate hopes in Vashti, for she thought that the Machine had been mended. It opened, and she saw the dim tunnel that curved far away towards freedom. One look, and then she shrank back. For the tunnel was full of people—she was almost the last in that city to have taken alarm.

People at any time repelled her, and these were nightmares from her worst dreams. People were crawling about, people were screaming, whimpering, gasping for breath, touching each other, vanishing in the dark, and ever and anon being pushed off the platform onto the live rail. Some were fighting round the electric bells trying to summon trains which could not be summoned. Others were yelling for Euthanasia or for respirators, or blaspheming the Machine. Others stood at the doors of their cells fearing, like herself, either to stop in them or to leave them. And behind all the uproar was silence—the silence which is the voice of the earth and of the generations who have gone.

No—it was worse than solitude. She closed the door again and sat down to wait for the end. The disintegration went on, accompanied by horrible cracks and rumbling. The valves that restrained the Medical Apparatus must have been weakened, for it ruptured and hung hideously from the ceiling. The floor heaved and fell and flung her from her chair. A tube oozed towards her serpent fashion. And at last the final horror approached—light began to ebb, and she knew that civilization's long day was closing.

She whirled round, praying to be saved from this, at any rate, kissing the Book, pressing button after button. The uproar outside was increasing, and even penetrated the wall. Slowly the brilliancy of her cell was dimmed, the reflections faded from her metal switches. Now she could not see the reading stand, now not the Book, though she held it in her hand. Light followed the flight of sound, air was following light, and the original void returned to the cavern from which it had been so long excluded. Vashti continued to whirl, like the devotees of an earlier religion, screaming, praying, striking at the buttons with bleeding hands.

It was thus that she opened her prison and escaped—escaped in the spirit: at least so it seems to me, ere my meditation closes. That she escapes in the body—I cannot perceive that. She struck, by chance, the switch that released the door, and the rush of foul air on her skin, the loud throbbing whispers in her ears, told her that she was facing the tunnel again, and that tremendous platform on which she had seen men fighting. They were not fighting now. Only the whispers remained, and the little whimpering groans. They were dying by hundreds out in the dark.

She burst into tears.

Tears answered her.

They wept for humanity, those two, not for themselves. They could not bear that this should be the end. Ere silence was completed their hearts were opened, and they knew what had been important on the earth. Man, the flower of all flesh, the noblest of all creatures visible, man who had once made god in his image, and had mirrored his strength on the constellations, beautiful naked man was dying, strangled in the garments that he had woven. Century after century had he toiled, and here was his reward. Truly the garment had seemed heavenly at first, shot with the colours of culture, sewn with the threads of self-denial. And heavenly it had been so long as it was a garment and no more, so long as man could shed it at will and live by the essence that is his soul, and the essence, equally divine, that is his body. The sin against the body—it was for that they wept in chief; the centuries of wrong against the muscles and the nerves, and those five portals by which we can alone apprehend— glazing it over with talk of evolution, until the body was white pap, the home of ideas as colourless, last sloshy stirrings of a spirit that had grasped the stars.

'Where are you?' she sobbed.

His voice in the darkness said, 'Here.'

'Is there any hope, Kuno?'

'None for us.'

'Where are you?'

She crawled towards him over the bodies of the dead. His blood spurted over her hands.

'Quicker,' he gasped, 'I am dying—but we touch, we talk, not through the Machine.'

He kissed her.

'We have come back to our own. We die, but we have recaptured life, as it was in Wessex, when Aelfred overthrew the Danes. We know what they know outside, they who dwelt in the cloud that is the colour of pearl.'

'But, Kuno, is it true? Are there still men on the surface of the earth? Is this—this tunnel, this poisoned darkness—really not the end?'

He replied.

'I have seen them, spoken to them, loved them. They are hiding in the mist and the ferns until our civilization stops. Today they are the Homeless—tomorrow—'

'Oh, tomorrow—some fool will start the Machine again, tomorrow.'

'Never,' said Kuno, 'never. Humanity has learned its lesson.'

As he spoke, the whole city was broken like a honeycomb. An airship had sailed in through the vomitory into a ruined wharf. It crashed downwards, exploding as it went, rending gallery after gallery with its wings of steel. For a moment they saw the nations of the dead, and, before they joined them, scraps of the untainted sky.

# Index of Concepts

Accessibility of services, activities
  achievement in various forms of
    development, 205
  in Milton Keynes Plan, 239–40
  relation to adequacy of metropolis,
    190–2, 193, 197, 199, 200
Activities, choice of, a goal in Milton
  Keynes Plan, 238, 240–1; *see also*
  Accessibility
Adelaide, Ebenezer Howard's concept of,
  48, 49
Affluence, implications of increasing,
  248–50; *see also* Standards of Living,
  Wealth
Air-cushion craft, potential of, 76
Air transport, role in future of developing
  countries, 126–7
Amenity, planners', city engineers'
  concern with, 218; *see also* Environ-
  ment
America *see* United States of America
Anti-utopian approach to urban develop-
  ment, 1, 3, 5, 10, 12, 15
Aquaculture, future of, 125, 307
Architecture, architects
  dichotomy between creative work of
    planners and, 259–60
  planners' preoccupation with design
    concepts derived from, 207, 215
  various concepts of role of, in urban
    development, 38–42, 43, 44–6
Automation, effects on occupational
  structure, 56

Birth rates
  forecasting problems, 102–3
  interaction with threat to survival of
    Man, 277–8
  trends in, 66–7
Broadacre City, Frank Lloyd Wright's
  concept of, 7–8, 17, 43–6, 153, 193
Building forms, in grid-based cities,

180–3, 187–8
Building technology, concept of need to
  industrialize, 38–42
Buildings
  different parameters for study of land
    use by, 186–7
  relation of density, condition of, to
    to adequacy of metropolis, 190, 192,
    194–6, 197, 198–9
  *see also* Housing
Business, future of telecommunications
  in, 87–9, 162–3

Caricature, in utopian concepts, 10, 11,
  12
Cells, concept of, as pattern for satisfaction of human needs, 264–5, 268
Child care facilities, concept of, as
  pattern for satisfaction of human
  needs, 267
Choice, freedom, variety of
  a goal in Milton Keynes Plan, 237–9,
    240, 242
  a goal of metropolitan planning, 202,
    205
  arguments for, against prohibitions on,
    in exercises of planning process,
    233–4
Circulation, circulation systems
  freedom of, a goal of metropolitan
    form, 203
  relation to adequacy of metropolis,
    190–2, 193, 195, 197, 199
Cities
  life in future, 281–3
  functions in ancient times, 271–2
  future purposes, 272–9
  *see also* Metropolitan areas, Urban
    development
City Hall, concept of, as pattern for
  satisfaction of human needs, 267–8,
    269

345

Necessities, and adoption of technical standards, 227
New Harmony, Indiana, 13–14
New Towns, concept of, 8, 139, 299
Noise, pollution by, 133
'Non-planning', arguments for, 207–8, 244–52
Nuclear power, threat to civilization from, 275–7
Nuclear urban forms, and linear development, contrasted, 168–9, 171–2

Occupational structure, trends in Britain, 53, 55–7
Old age islands, concept of, as pattern for satisfaction of human needs, 265–6, 268–9
Open spaces, in Le Corbusier's work, 37
Opportunity, a wide range of, a goal in Milton Keynes Plan, 237–9, 240, 242

Participation, individual, public
a goal of metropolitan form, 203, 205
concept of, in utopian tradition, 13, 14, 15
effects on, of increasing personal mobility, 287–90
in Milton Keynes Plan, 242–3
need for, in planning process, 209, 252–3
opportunities for, in various forms of urban development, 194, 195, 196, 197
Planning, planners
and concept of community values, 223–4
and opportunity for public consideration of alternatives, 210
arguments for, against, detailed controls, 207–8
basic conditions of method, 216
concept of function as design of culture, 262
concern with interaction of efficiency effects and cost distribution, 224–6
concern with technical standards, 222–3, 226–9
dichotomy between creative work of architects and, 259–60
historical association with city engineering, social policies, 207, 217–18, 219–20, 222–3
impact of advances in telecommuni-

cations on, 90–2
implications of orientation to future goals, 207
need for continuous review, 4, 8, 51–2, 142, 203–4, 216
need for systematic evaluation, 207, 215–16, 230–3
pluralism in, 210–11, 225–6
radical nature of goal-orientated, 208
rationales for government intervention in, 220–2
relationship with political processes, 1–2, 5, 207, 209, 210–11, 225–6, 231–2, 235
role in development of future cities, 209
role of local, central government in, 1–2, 5
role of professional, 5, 11–12, 19–21
validity and variety of government intervention in, 233–4
*see also* 'Non-planning'
Pluralism in planning, need for, 210–11, 225–6
Political institutions, utopian concepts of, 9
Politics, politicians,
increasing problems of communication between technologists and, 214–15
relationship of planning and, 1–2, 5, 207, 209, 210–11, 225–6, 231–2, 235
relationship of social class and attitudes to, 61
Pollution, planning for amelioration of, 133
Pop culture, implications for planning of rise of, 250–1
Population
and trends in family size, 66–7
concept of stabilization, in utopian tradition, 13
distribution in garden city concept, 47–9
forecast of trends in urban fields, 158–9
in Le Corbusier's work, 7, 17, 30, 34, 36–7
interaction of size, structure, with requirements of built environment, 106–8, 115, 116
ratio between vehicle numbers and, 79
relation of growth in developing countries to availability of resources, 117–19